dBASE IV™ Tips, Tricks, and Traps

2nd Edition

George Tsu-der Chou

Revised by Steve Davis

QUE®
CORPORATION
LEADING COMPUTER KNOWLEDGE

dBASE IV™ Tips, Tricks, and Traps

2nd Edition

Library of Congress Catalog No.: 88-61115
ISBN No.: 0-88022-359-6

92 91 90 89   8 7 6 5 4 3 2 1

Interpretation of the printing code: the rightmost double-digit number is the year of the book's printing; the rightmost single-digit number, the number of the book's printing. For example, a printing code of 89-1 shows that the first printing of the book occurred in 1989.

dBASE IV Tips, Tricks, and Traps, 2nd Edition, is based on dBASE IV.

DEDICATION

My wife, Jane-Wen
and our children
Doris, Tina, and Tom

Publishing Director

David Paul Ewing

Acquisitions Editor

Terrie Lynn Solomon

Developmental Editor

Kathie-Jo Arnoff

Editors

Mary Bednarek
Martin E. Brown
Joseph P. Goodwin

Technical Editor

William McGirr

Indexer

Sherry Massey

Book Design and Production

Dan Armstrong
Brad Chinn
Cheryl English
Lori A. Lyons
Cindy Phipps
Joe Ramon
Dennis Sheehan
Mae Louise Shinault
Carolyn A. Spitler

Composed in Garamond and American Typewriter
by Que Corporation

ABOUT THE AUTHOR

George Tsu-der Chou

George Tsu-der Chou, of Vancouver, Washington, is a consultant in the field of database design and development. He has developed database management systems for many clients, including Gregory Government Securities, Morley Capital Management, Hi-Tech Electronics, West Coast Lumber Inspection Bureau, NERCO, Inc., and others.

The author earned his Ph.D. in Quantitative Methods, with supporting studies in Computer Science, Economics, and Econometrics, from the University of Washington. He is currently a full professor at the University of Portland in Oregon, where he teaches courses in business data processing and data management, quantitative methods, operations research, business forecasting, and other subjects.

Dr. Chou wrote the *dBASE III® Plus Handbook*, *dBASE IV™ Handbook*, and *Using Paradox®*, all published by Que Corporation.

CONTENTS AT A GLANCE

TABLE OF CONTENTS ▼

II   Working with Data

III   Programming and Advanced Topics

9   Using Basic Programming Techniques 335

10   Using Advanced Programming Techniques 379

$\mathbf{A}$ CKNOWLEDGMENTS

$\mathbf{Q}$ ue Corporation thanks the following individuals for their contributions to this book:

Steve Davis, who revised *dBASE IV Tips, Tricks, and Traps* for this 2nd Edition. He has been writing and editing books on computers and technology, as well as general nonfiction and reference works, for more than seven years. His books include *Programs for the TI Home Computer, The Electric Mailbox: A User's Guide to Electronic Mail Systems*, and *The Writer's Yellow Pages*. He is president of Steve Davis Publishing in Dallas, Texas.

Kathie-Jo Arnoff and Mary Bednarek, who provided quality editing and direction and kept this book on schedule during the final editing and production stages.

Joe Goodwin and Marty Brown, who completed the preliminary edit on this book.

Ashton-Tate dBASE IV technical support and development staff, who provided assistance during the early stages of developing *dBASE IV Tips, Tricks, and Traps*, 2nd Edition.

*T*RADEMARK
*A*CKNOWLEDGMENTS

Que Corporation has made every attempt to supply trademark information about company names, products, and services mentioned in this book. Trademarks indicated below were derived from various sources. Que Corporation cannot attest to the accuracy of this information.

1-2-3, DIF, and VisiCalc are registered trademarks of Lotus Development Corporation.

CHART-MASTER is a registered trademark of Ashton-Tate Corporation and is used under license from Chartmasters, Inc.

Clipper is a trademark of Nantucket, Inc.

dBASE IV, FrameWork II, RapidFile, and Step IVWard are trademarks, and dBASE, dBASE II, dBASE III, and dBASE III Plus are registered trademarks of Ashton-Tate Corporation.

Microsoft Word and Multiplan are registered trademarks of Microsoft Corporation.

OKIDATA is a registered trademark of Oki America, Inc.

PC Tools is a trademark of Central Point Software.

PFS:File is a registered trademark of Software Publishing Corporation.

QuickSilver is a trademark of WordTech Systems, Inc.

SideKick is a registered trademark of Borland International, Inc.

WordPerfect is a registered trademark of WordPerfect Corporation.

WordStar is a registered trademark of MicroPro International Corporation.

XTree is a trademark of Executive Systems, Inc.

CONVENTIONS USED IN THIS BOOK

Certain conventions were used to help make *dBASE IV Tips, Tricks, and Traps*, 2nd Edition, easy to use. These conventions include the following:

☐ The names of Control Center menus (such as **Organize** menu and **Append** menu) appear in boldface type.

☐ Options selected from the Control Center menus appear in boldface type (as in "Select the **Print database structure** option from the **Layout** menu.").

☐ dBASE IV commands entered at the dot prompt and all program listings appear in a special typeface (as in "Enter USE EMPLOYEE at the dot prompt.").

☐ In the dBASE IV command lines that are used to show the syntax of the command, the angle brackets and italicized information represent variable information. You should substitute your own information for the variable. For example, note the following command line:

. SAVE TO *<name of memory file>*

After you type the SAVE TO portion of the command, you should enter the name of the memory file to which you want to save the variables. Do not type the angle brackets (<>).

Introduction

A shton-Tate's dBASE IV™ is unquestionably the leading computer program for data management applications. Along with its earlier versions—dBASE II ®, dBASE III ®, and dBASE III ® Plus—dBASE ® has revolutionized the way data is managed and manipulated in a microcomputer system.

Beginning users of dBASE IV appreciate the new dBASE IV Control Center—an easy-to-use interface with a system of pull-down menus that simplifies accessing and using dBASE files. Those with more experience can use dBASE IV's powerful programming language to develop programs for effectively managing complex databases.

The Scope of This Book

To make the best use of the program's power and flexibility, you should be familiar with the dBASE IV commands and programming tools. Used intelligently, some of these commands and tools can give you efficient shortcuts for many data management operations.

A major objective of this book is to share with you some *tips*: ideas, simple techniques, or simply better ways to use the program.

Here also you will find *tricks*—sophisticated techniques you can use to enhance the basic functions of many dBASE IV commands and programming tools. Some of the tricks in this book are the result of extensive experimentation with the program. Others were discovered accidentally while working on database applications.

All the tips and tricks in this book are meant to help you manage data more effectively. Many reduce the number of steps required for certain tasks.

1

You also will find *traps*. A trap is a potential hazard. Some traps cause annoying results but do not present serious problems. Others, however, can result in a loss of valuable information. This book warns you about traps, explains how to avoid them, and tells you what to do when you find one. The descriptions of many of the traps are followed by tricks that offer solutions to the problems.

Who Should Read This Book

This book was written primarily for dBASE IV users, but many of the subjects covered in the book are relevant also to dBASE III Plus. Many of the tips and tricks have to do with the dot prompt commands and procedures. Users of the Control Center can see how to achieve greater power and flexibility with these commands and procedures. If you want to go beyond using the Control Center to manage a complex database, this book will serve as an excellent guide.

Because this book covers the program's intermediate and advanced features, readers must understand the commonly used dBASE IV commands. To understand the proper use of these commands, refer to the *dBASE IV Handbook*, 3rd Edition, published by Que Corporation.

How This Book Is Organized

dBASE IV Tips, Tricks, and Traps, 2nd Edition, is divided into three parts:

    I: Getting Started
    II: Working With Data
    III: Programming and Advanced Topics

Part I, "Getting Started," describes the steps for preparing to use dBASE IV: starting the program, organizing disk files, working with DOS, and configuring both your computer and the dBASE IV program to meet your needs.

Part II, "Working with Data," covers dBASE IV's most important functions: creating and modifying databases, entering and editing data, organizing data, sorting and indexing data, displaying data, and generating reports and mailing lists.

Part III, "Programming and Advanced Topics," explores the advanced features of dBASE IV. Making use of the powerful dBASE IV command language, the compiler, and the use of SQL (Structured Query Language) are explored in this section.

Following is a chapter-by-chapter breakdown of the book's contents:

The first chapter, "Organizing Disk Files and Configuring the System," shows you how to work with the DOS operating system to use directories for effective file management. Knowing how to create and maintain a directory is vital to ensuring the integrity of data stored in your files. This chapter also covers the procedure for using the CONFIG.SYS file to allocate sufficient file buffers to dBASE IV. You also will learn effective ways of issuing commands at the dot prompt and tips for managing files and directories with the Control Center.

Chapter 2, "Configuring dBASE IV," focuses on the powerful commands you can include in the CONFIG.DB configuration file. By using these commands, you can set the environment and parameters for the program. After you have set up the CONFIG.DB file, you can eliminate many tedious steps in the data-manipulation process.

Chapter 3, "Creating and Modifying Databases," covers tips, tricks, and traps related to creating a new database. Shortcuts include borrowing the file structure or records from an existing database to create a new database file. You also will find tips and warnings related to modifying the field attributes in an existing file structure. And, because errors frequently result from poorly organized data, the chapter explains in detail the layout of a database file.

Chapter 4, "Entering and Editing Data," discusses the features and proper use of commands related to data entry and modification of data. You can use this chapter's shortcuts and tricks to take advantage of the dBASE IV form design screen, a powerful tool for designing custom data-entry forms.

Chapter 5, "Organizing Data," shows you how to organize files so that you can access them quickly. This chapter also focuses on the program's powerful catalog feature, which allows you to access only the data files you need for a particular application. You will find many tips for creating and using a catalog file to organize your data, as well as information on linking database files.

Chapter 6, "Sorting and Indexing Data," deals with using the SORT and INDEX commands to rearrange records in a database file. The chapter explores the strengths and weaknesses of sorting and indexing so that you know when and how to choose the correct operation. You will also learn tricks for taking advantage of the strengths and overcoming the weaknesses of the SORT and INDEX commands.

Chapter 7, "Displaying Data," introduces special features that enhance the basic functions of commonly used commands for displaying data. The Query-By-Example design screen is also described, with tips on designing a query to extract selected data.

Chapter 8, "Generating Mailing Lists and Reports," focuses on generating mailing labels and producing custom reports. Reporting is one of the most important functions of database management, and the dBASE IV label and report generator is one of the program's most flexible components. This chapter includes tips on using the report and label design screens.

Chapter 9, "Using Basic Programming Techniques," discusses the power of command-language programming. Although you can perform many database management operations by choosing appropriate options from the Control Center, program and procedure files can help you perform more complex operations. This chapter shows you how to write many different types of program modules. Creating and editing a program, using memory variables, controlling the screen display, and designing menus are discussed. You also learn to use color to enhance your screen displays.

Chapter 10, "Using Advanced Programming Techniques," continues the discussion of how to write programs. Conditional branching, program loops, subprograms and procedures, and debugging are explored. The chapter also shows you how to create graphs.

Chapter 11, "Exploring Advanced Topics," teaches you how to exchange data between dBASE IV and other programs. Converting dBASE IV files, and processing and importing data are covered. This chapter also includes a discussion of SQL (Structured Query Language) and the dBASE IV compiler.

Finally, you will find four useful appendixes and a comprehensive index. Appendix A presents the standard ASCII character codes. Appendix B summarizes the dBASE IV function and control keys. Appendix C contains a summary of dBASE IV commands and functions, and Appendix D lists SQL commands. The thorough index helps you locate the particular information you need among the tips, tricks, and traps.

Part I

Getting Started

Includes

Organizing Disk Files and
Configuring the System

Configuring dBASE IV

Organizing Disk Files and Configuring the System

A microcomputer system's most important permanent storage medium is the disk unit. The floppy disk used to be adequate for most database-applications programs. But with recent advances in database-management programs, storage requirements have changed drastically. The floppy disk is no longer adequate for the power of these new programs.

With more storage space available to you and more files to manage, you need an efficient way to access and manipulate data. Sophisticated organization of your files is the answer. This chapter explores the important use of subdirectories for organizing your disk files.

The Control Center, a feature new with dBASE IV, offers great versatility in file handling and DOS operations. You can manipulate data even more effectively if you supplement dBASE IV with DOS commands. This chapter includes some tips, tricks, and traps for using DOS commands and accessing DOS commands and file-management operations from within dBASE IV.

Configuring your system to make the most efficient use of dBASE IV is also explored in this chapter. Included are tips, tricks, and traps dealing with procedures for allocating memory for disk files and memory buffers.

Finally, this chapter presents shortcuts for executing dBASE IV commands.

Using DOS and Directories
To Organize Your Files

Files organized in directories and subdirectories are easily identified and maintained. If you can't remember the exact name of a particular file, for example, you can display the contents of that file's directory to locate the file.

When you turn on your computer, you start from the root directory, which was created automatically when you formatted your disk. The root directory stores the names of other file directories. In turn, these directories can store any number of subdirectories at any number of levels.

This section includes tips, tricks, and traps to help you use DOS functions and commands to organize your dBASE files efficiently in directories.

Grouping Files in Separate Directories

1.1 Tip: **Save time and trouble by grouping files in separate directories.**

The structure of all the disk files stored on a given disk can be organized in multiple levels of directories (see fig. 1.1).

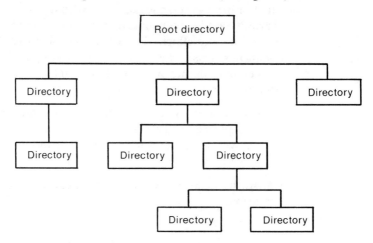

Fig. 1.1. *The structure of disk file directories.*

For example, you can put all the files related to DOS operations in a directory named DOSFILES and all the dBASE IV system files in another directory named DBASE.

You can also create subdirectories in the DBASE directory for storing groups of files. Then, if you need to access a word processing program such as WordStar®, you can save all your WordStar files in another directory (named WORDPROC) directly below the root directory (see fig. 1.2).

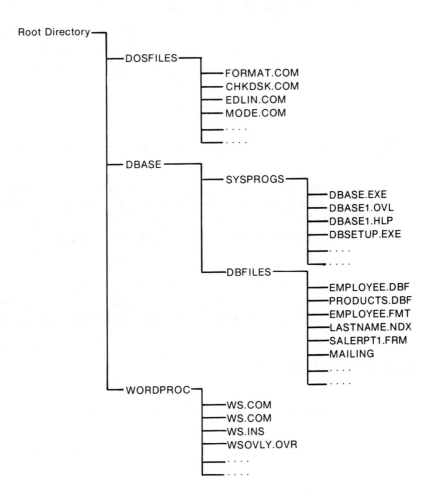

Fig. 1.2. An example of disk file directories.

1.2 Tip: **Use the directory PATH to access your files easily.**

To access your files quickly and easily, you need to know about paths. A directory *path* is a chain of directory names that tells DOS how to move through this chain to find a specific directory or disk file.

In the following examples of paths, the directory names are separated by a backslash (\):

> \DBASE\DBFILES
> DBFILES\EMPLOYEE.DBF

When the backslash is the first character of the path, DOS starts with the root directory. Otherwise, DOS begins from the current directory.

To identify a disk drive other than the current drive, you specify a disk drive name before you type the path:

> D:\LOTUS\DATAFILE

1.3 Tip: **To find the file you need in the root directory, use the DIR \ command.**

Once you've begun grouping files in directories, you may want to display your list of directories to find the file you need. To display the contents of the root directory from any level, use the DIR \ command at the DOS prompt (the root directory is designated by a backslash):

> C>DIR \

When you are at the root directory, you can display the contents by simply typing DIR, omitting the backslash. (Issuing the DIR command without the backslash always displays the current directory.)

Creating a Directory

1.4 Tip: **Create a directory for your dBASE files.**

To create a directory, at the DOS prompt (>), type the DOS command MD or MKDIR (Make Directory) followed by the name of the directory (DBASE, for example):

> C>MD DBASE

In response to the command, a directory with the specified name is created under the current directory. If you issue the MD command when you are in the root directory, the new directory becomes a subdirectory of the root directory.

1.5 Tip:

To create a subdirectory under a particular directory, specify the parent directory in the MD command.

To create a subdirectory in a directory different from the one you are working in, be sure to include the parent directory in the directory path. If you do not specify the parent directory when you use the MD command to create a subdirectory, you will create a subdirectory in the current directory.

For example, to create a subdirectory named DBFILES under the DBASE directory in the current disk drive, issue the following command at the DOS prompt:

```
C>MD \DBASE\DBFILES
```

To create the subdirectory DBFILES from the DBASE directory, use the following command without specifying a parent directory:

```
C>MD DBFILES
```

1.6 Trap:

You can lose track of your files if you create a subdirectory from the wrong directory.

Know where you are in the directory structure before you create a subdirectory. Otherwise, you may create the subdirectory under the wrong directory and have trouble finding it later. Be sure to specify the correct directory path in the MD or MKDIR (Make Directory) command unless you want to create a subdirectory under the current directory.

Identifying the Current Directory

1.7 Trick:

Use the CD command to identify the current directory.

You can identify the current directory in a number of ways, but the simplest is to issue the CD or CHDIR (Change Directory) command at the DOS prompt:

```
C>CD
```

You can use the CD command to change from the current directory to a new directory and to show where you are in the directory structure. For example, if you are working in DBFILES, a subdirectory of the parent DBASE directory, the CD command displays the following.

```
C:\DBASE\DBFILES
```

1.8 Trick: **To always know the current directory path, include the PROMPT pg command in the AUTOEXEC.BAT file.**

An excellent way to always know the current directory path is to include in the AUTOEXEC.BAT file the following command:

```
PROMPT $p$g
```

This command yields a DOS prompt made up of the current directory path, followed by a greater-than symbol (>). The DOS prompt changes as you change directories with the CD command.

For example, if you are in the DBFILES subdirectory of the DBASE directory on drive C:, the DOS prompt appears as the following:

```
C:\DBASE\DBFILES >
```

Moving between Directories

1.9 Tip: **Use the CD command to switch from one directory to another.**

To switch from the current active directory to another directory, issue the DOS command CD or CHDIR (Change Directory) at the DOS prompt, followed by the path and name of the directory you want to switch to, as shown in the following example:

```
C:\DBASE\DBFILES > CD \WORDPROC
C:\WORDPROC >
```

Moving Down in the Directory Structure

1.10 Tip: **To move to the subdirectory immediately below the current directory, specify the name of the subdirectory in the CD command.**

To switch from a directory to one of its subdirectories, specify the name of the subdirectory in the CD command:

```
C>CD
C:\

C>CD DBASE

C>CD
C:\DBASE

C>CD DBFILES

C>CD
C:\DBASE\DBFILES

C>CD SALES

C>CD
C:\DBASE\DBFILES\SALES

C >
```

You use the command CD DBASE to switch from the root directory to the DBASE directory. Similarly, the CD DBFILES command transfers you from the DBASE directory to its DBFILES subdirectory.

1.11 Tip: **To move down more than one level below the current directory, specify the path beginning from one level below the current directory.**

To move to a directory below the current directory's immediate subdirectory, the path you specify in the CD command should begin from one level below the current directory.

For example, if you want to move from the second level in the directory structure (C:\DBASE\DBFILES) to a directory at the fourth level, you begin your path from the third level:

```
C>CD SALES\REGION1
```

With a directory structure of C:\DBASE\DBFILES\SALES\REGION1, you can move from the DBASE directory to REGION1 (which is three levels below the current directory) by specifying a path that begins with DBFILES (the current directory's immediate subdirectory):

```
C>CD
C:\DBASE

C>CD DBFILES\SALES\REGION1

C>CD
C:\DBASE\DBFILES\SALES\REGION1

C>
```

Moving Up in the Directory Structure

1.12 Tip:

To return directly to the root directory from any level of directory, use the CD \ command.

The command CD \ returns you to the root directory from anywhere in the directory structure.

The following sequence illustrates that the CD \ command, issued from the C:\DBASE\DBFILES subdirectory, returns you to the root directory:

```
C>CD
C:\DBASE\DBFILES

C>CD \
C>CD
C:\
```

1.13 Tip:

Use the command CD .. to move to the parent directory.

To move up one level from the current directory to its parent directory, use the CD .. (double dot) command.

For example, you can switch from the DBFILES subdirectory of the DBASE directory to the parent directory by issuing the CD .. command at the DOS prompt:

```
C>CD
C:\DBASE\DBFILES

C>CD ..

C>CD
C:\DBASE

C>
```

After the CD .. command is executed, the current directory changes from C:\DBASE\DBFILES to C:\DBASE.

1.14 Tip: **To move to another directory that is not associated with the current directory, specify the root directory at the beginning of the directory path.**

To move from a given directory to a directory that is higher than its parent directory, specify (in the CD command) a directory path that begins with the root directory.

For example, to move up to the DBASE directory from the SALES directory, which is three levels below the root directory (C:\DBASE\DBFILES\SALES), you must specify a directory path that begins with a backslash (which designates the root directory):

```
C>CD \DBASE
```

The following code illustrates the principle that you can't begin the path from a directory below the root directory.

```
C>CD
C:\DBASE\DBFILES\SALES

C>CD DBASE
Invalid directory

C>CD \DBASE

C>CD
C:\DBASE

C>
```

Issuing the CD DBASE command from the C:\DBASE\DBFILES\SALES directory results in an Invalid directory error message. You must move to a directory one level below the root directory without including the backslash in the CD command. Leaving off the initial backslash in any DOS command makes DOS assume that the file or directory is in the current directory or below it. For all directory commands, leaving off the initial backslash assumes that the desired directory is below the current directory.

Similarly, if you want to move from the fourth-level REGION1 directory (C:\DBASE\DBFILES\SALES\REGION1) to the DBFILES directory, you must begin the path from the root directory:

```
C>CD
C:\DBASE\DBFILES\SALES\REGION1

C>CD \DBASE\DBFILES

C>CD
C:\DBASE\DBFILES

C>
```

As you can see from the preceding code, the path must begin with \DBASE.

If you specify the path in the CD command as \DBFILES or DBFILES, you receive an Invalid directory error message.

```
C>CD
C:\DBASE\DBFILES\SALES\REGION1

C>CD \DBFILES
Invalid directory

C>CD DBFILES
Invalid directory

C>
```

Displaying a Directory

1.15 Tip: **Use the DIR command to display the contents of the current directory.**

From the DOS prompt, use the DIR command to display a listing of the current directory (see fig. 1.3).

```
C:\DBASE
DIR

Volume in drive C is HARD DISK
Directory of   C:\DBASE

DBASE      EXE    146432  12-01-88    3:10p
DBASE1     HLP    247155  10-20-88   11:26p
DBASE1     OVL    349120  10-20-88   11:23p
DBASE1     RES     74594  10-20-88   11:22p
DBASE2     HLP     79971  10-20-88   11:31p
DBASE2     OVL    361616  10-20-88   11:25p
DBASE2     RES    101545  12-21-88   11:17a
DBASE3     OVL     85024  10-21-88   12:25a
DBASE3     RES      7842  10-20-88   11:23p
DBASE4     OVL    349712  10-20-88   11:30p
DBASE5     OVL    321904  10-20-88   11:28p
DBASE6     OVL    114832  10-20-88   11:22p
        12 File(s)    7260160 bytes free
```

Fig. 1.3. *An example of a directory listing.*

1.16 Tip: **To list files that are not in the current directory, specify the directory path in the DIR command.**

You can use either of two methods to list files that are not in the current directory. One method is to move from the current directory to the directory that contains the files and then issue the DIR command. (For instructions on moving from one directory to another, see this chapter's "Moving between Directories" section.)

The other method is to display the contents of a specific directory by specifying the appropriate directory path in the DIR command. Whether you begin the path with the root directory or with a subdirectory depends on which directory structure level you are working in.

1.17 Tip: **To list disk files in the root directory while you are in any other directory, use the DIR \ command.**

Without leaving the current directory, you can list the contents of the root directory by using the command DIR \ from any level in the directory structure:

    C>DIR \

1.18 Tip: **To display the contents of the parent directory, use the DIR ..**
command.

From a subdirectory, you can list files in the parent directory by using
the DIR .. (double dot) command:

    C>DIR ..

Listing Selected Files in a Directory

1.19 Tip: **Use a wild-card character to list files by type.**

From a given directory, you can display a selected group of files by
using the asterisk (*) or the question mark (?) as a *wild-card*
character.

For example, the DIR *.DBF command displays all the database files in
the directory. Similarly, the command DIR *.NDX displays all the index
files in the directory.

To list all the files whose names begin with DB, enter the following
command at the DOS prompt:

    DIR DB??????.*

The following command displays all database files with names that
begin with DB and are followed by up to three other characters:

    DIR DB???.DBF

Deleting an Existing Directory

1.20 Tip: **Before you can delete a directory, you must empty it.**

You must delete all the files in an existing directory before removing
it from the directory structure. Use the ERASE *.* command to delete
all the disk files in the current directory.

If the directory you want to delete contains one or more
subdirectories, you must first delete the subdirectories. Erase all the
files in the subdirectories before deleting them. Also, you cannot
currently be in the directory you want to remove.

To remove an empty directory, use the RD or RMDIR (Remove Directory) command:

C>RD <*name of the empty directory to be deleted*>

1.21 Trap:

The ERASE *.* command is extremely powerful and potentially destructive.

When you issue the ERASE *.* command, DOS returns the following prompt:

Are you sure (Y/N)?

Before you proceed, take a moment to make sure that you are in the correct directory and that you really do want to erase all the files in the current directory. Otherwise, you may have to test your backup procedures or reenter valuable data.

Note: The DEL (Delete) command is the same as the ERASE command.

Renaming a Directory

1.22 Trick:

Because you cannot change the name of an existing directory with any DOS command or program, you must create a new directory to rename an existing directory.

To use DOS commands for renaming a directory, create a new directory with the name you want. Copy the contents of the existing directory to the new directory. Then remove the original directory.

Note: Utility programs that rename directories are available through various bulletin board systems, PC user groups, and software interest groups, as well as in commercial programs such as XTree™ and PC Tools™.

1.23 Trap:

Be careful when renaming directories.

If a directory name appears in your DOS PATH command or your dBASE IV SET PATH TO command, or if it is the default directory used for finding files by any applications program you use, do not rename the directory. Otherwise, your applications may not be able to find the files in that directory. For example, assume that your FORMAT.COM file is in a directory called \DOS, and your PATH command includes the \DOS directory in the path so that the file can be accessed from any directory. If you rename the \DOS directory to \DOSFILES, and \DOSFILES is not in your path, you will receive a File not found error message if you try to format a disk from another directory.

Using dBASE IV Dot-Prompt Commands for File Management

Many file-management operations can be performed using dBASE IV commands issued from the dot prompt. This section includes tips, tricks, and traps that help you use DOS and dBASE IV commands from the dot prompt to perform directory and file operations.

Displaying Directories within dBASE IV

1.24 Tip: **Use the DIR or LIST FILES command to display a list of database files.**

From within dBASE IV, you can display a list of all the database files in the current directory by issuing either the DIR command or LIST FILES command at the dot prompt (see figs. 1.4 and 1.5).

1.25 Tip: **To list the names of all the disk files in the current directory, use asterisks as wild-card characters.**

Issuing the DIR command at the dot prompt from within dBASE IV displays only database files (with the file extension .DBF) in the current directory of the default disk drive.

To list all the files in the current directory, you can use asterisks as wild-card characters in the DIR or LIST FILES command:

```
. DIR*.*
. LIST FILES*.*
```

When asterisks replace a file name and its extension in a DIR or LIST FILES command, the command tells the program to list files of all names and types.

```
. DIR
Database Files      # Records      Last Update       Size
STORES.DBF              224        12/21/88          30626
MAIL.DBF                  6        01/09/89           1490
EXHIBIT.DBF              61        01/05/89           8830
SOFTWR.DBF               10        12/05/88            834

   41780 bytes in       4 files
7256064 bytes remaining on drive
```

Fig. 1.4. *Using the DIR command at the dot prompt.*

```
. LIST FILES
Database Files      # Records      Last Update       Size
STORES.DBF              224        12/21/88          30626
MAIL.DBF                  6        01/09/89           1490
EXHIBIT.DBF              61        01/05/89           8830
SOFTWR.DBF               10        12/05/88            834

   41780 bytes in       4 files
7256064 bytes remaining on drive

.
```

Fig. 1.5. *Using the LIST FILES command at the dot prompt.*

1.26 Tip: **To list disk files of a given type, specify the file extension in the command.**

If you want to display files other than database (.DBF) files, use an asterisk (`*`) as a wild-card character and specify the file extension in the DIR or LIST FILES command:

. DIR *. < *file extension*>
. LIST FILES *. < *file extension*>

For example:

. DIR *.NDX
. LIST FILES*.TXT

1.27 Tip: **To list disk files with certain file names, use question marks (?) as wild-card characters.**

You can list disk files with names that share one or more common characters. To do so, specify the shared characters in the DIR or LIST FILES command and replace the remaining characters in the file name with question marks (?) as wild-card characters.

For example, to display all files with names that begin with ABC, you can issue either of the following DIR commands at the dot prompt:

. DIR ABC?????.*

or

. DIR ABC*.*

You can also use the dBASE IV LIST FILES command at the dot prompt:

. LIST FILES ABC?????.*

or

. LIST FILES ABC*.*

The question marks in the file name match any character in the file name.

1.28 Trick: **Use the correct number of question marks in the file name.**

A file-name prefix can be up to eight characters long; the extension can be up to three characters long. Because each question mark replaces a character in the file name, you must be sure to specify exactly as many question marks as there are characters in the file name.

For example, when . DIR ABC?????.* is executed, all file names that have a prefix of up to eight characters and that begin with ABC are displayed.

If you use two question marks to define a file name that begins with ABC (. DIR ABC??.*), only those files with names that are up to five characters long are displayed.

1.29 Tip: **To display files that are not in the current directory, specify the directory path.**

Unless you specify a directory path when you issue the DIR or LIST FILES command at the dot prompt, only the files in the current active directory of the default drive are displayed.

To remain in the current active directory and display files in another directory, include the directory path in the DIR or LIST FILES command.

Use the . DIR *.* command to display all the files in the root directory.

All the .SYS files in the DBASE directory are displayed by the following command:

. DIR \DBASE*.SYS

The following command displays all the index files (.NDX) in the DBFILES directory, which is a subdirectory of the DBASE directory:

. LIST FILES \DBASE\DBFILES*.NDX

1.30 Tip: **To display files that are not in the default disk drive, specify the disk drive.**

If you do not include the disk drive in the directory path, the default disk drive is assumed. You can, however, specify a different drive in the path.

For example, if drive C: is the default disk drive and you want to display files in drive B: or D:, you must specify a disk drive in the directory path of the DIR or LIST FILES command, as in the following examples:

. DIR B:*.*

or

. LIST FILES D:\LOTUS*.PRN

1.31 Tip:

Use the SET PATH TO command within dBASE IV to access files that are not in the current directory.

From a given directory within dBASE IV, use the SET PATH TO command to gain access to a database file and its associated files in another directory.

To select a database file from the SALEDATA directory, for example, you specify the directory path as in the following command:

. SET PATH TO \SALEDATA

The path specification can be up to 60 characters in length. Entering the SET PATH TO command with no path name specified resets the path to the default path.

1.32 Trap:

If different directories contain files with the same name, only the file in the current directory is used.

If you have more than one database file with the same name (one in the current directory and another in the directory specified in the SET PATH TO command), only the file in the current directory will be selected.

For example, if you are currently working in the DBFILES (C:\DBASE\DBFILES) directory and want to gain access to a database file (SALEITEM.DBF) in the SALEDATA directory (C:\DBASE\SALEDATA), you could issue the following dot commands:

. SET PATH TO \DBASE\SALEDATA
. USE SALEITEM

In most cases, dBASE IV will find the database file SALEITEM.DBF from the directory C:\DBASE\SALEDATA.

If, however, the current directory (C:\DBASE\DBFILES) also contains a database file named SALEITEM.DBF, dBASE IV will select that file. The program always searches the current directory first.

When you use a subdirectory structure, it is possible that two files can have the same name if they reside in different subdirectories. You must be sure to access the correct file when you select files from these subdirectories.

1.33 Trap: **The SET PATH TO command does not change the current directory.**

The directory path specified by the SET PATH TO command simply provides a searching path for file retrieval in dBASE IV. The command does not change the current directory.

1.34 Trap: **You cannot save a new database file to the directory defined by the SET PATH TO command.**

The SET PATH TO command instructs dBASE IV to search the specified directory path for an existing file if it is not in the current directory.

When you create a database file, the new database created at any point in the processing is saved in the current directory, not in the directory specified in the SET PATH TO command's path.

For example, if you create a database file named EMPLOYEE.DBF in the DBFILES directory (C:\DBASE\DBFILES), the new file is saved in that directory, even though you may have set the path to another directory:

```
. SET PATH TO \DBASE SALEDATA
. CREATE EMPLOYEE
```

1.35 Trap: **The path defined by the SET PATH TO command does not affect the DIR command.**

When you issue the DIR command, only those files in the current directory are displayed. The DIR command ignores the path defined in the SET PATH TO command (see fig. 1.6).

```
.DIR
Database Files    # Records    Last Update    Size
EMPLOYEE.DBF           10      01/09/89        835
      835 bytes in      1 files
 768000 bytes remaining on drive
. SET PATH TO D:\SALEDATA
. USE SOFTWARE
. LIST NEXT 4
Record#  STOCK_NO   DSCRIPTION          TYPE
COST    PRICE
     1   ASH-DB400  dBASE IV v 1.0        database
495.00  795.00
     2   ANS-DB110  Paradox v.1.1        database
525.00  695.00
     3   CLP-DB100  Clipper DB Compiler  database compiler
450.00  595.00
     4   WOR-DB100  WordTech DB Compiler database compiler
469.00  595.00
. DIR
Database Files    # Records    Last Update    Size
EMPLOYEE.DBF           10      01/09/89        835
      835 bytes in      1 files
 768000 bytes remaining on drive
```

Fig. 1.6. *Effects of the SET PATH TO action on the DIR command.*

Moving between Directories within dBASE IV

1.36 Tip: **From within dBASE IV, you can move from the current directory to another directory by using the RUN (or !) command to execute the DOS CD or CHDIR (Change Directory) command.**

You use the RUN command to execute a DOS command at the dot prompt as if you were at the DOS prompt. Because the RUN command puts you in DOS mode temporarily, you can process any CD command at the dot prompt.

For example, from DOS you switch directly from the current directory to the root directory by issuing the CD \ command at the DOS prompt:

    C>CD \

Instead of exiting to DOS from dBASE IV, you can issue the DOS command CD \ at the dot prompt by adding the word RUN to the following command:

    . RUN CD \

(For instructions about using the DOS CD command to move between directories, see the section, "Moving between Directories.")

Using the RUN Command
To Execute DOS Commands

The dBASE IV RUN command enables you to execute DOS commands from within dBASE IV. Because the COMMAND.COM file contains instructions that translate DOS commands into actions, that file must be present when you execute a DOS command. This section includes tips, tricks, and traps that demonstrate how to access the DOS command interpreter and to use the RUN command.

Accessing the DOS Command Interpreter

1.37 Tip: **You need the COMMAND.COM file to use the RUN command within dBASE IV.**

To use the RUN command within dBASE IV, you must put the COMMAND.COM file in the root directory and include the root directory in your PATH command in your AUTOEXEC.BAT file. Then, when you issue the RUN command in dBASE IV, the program will be able to locate the file.

Monitoring the Current Directory

1.38 Tip: **Use the RUN CD command to monitor the current directory within dBASE IV.**

From the DOS prompt, you can always determine where you are in the directory structure by using the CD or CHDIR (Change Directory) command without specifying the name of a directory.

You can use the RUN command to execute the DOS CD command from within dBASE IV:

```
. RUN CD
```

Changing the System Date and Time

1.39 Trick: **Use the RUN command to execute the DOS DATE and TIME commands.**

From within dBASE IV, you can display the current system date and time on-screen or in your reports by using the built-in functions DATE() and TIME(). For example, you can monitor the current date and time by using the ? operator to display the value of these built-in functions in a dot-prompt command:

```
. ? DATE(),TIME()
Ø1/Ø3/89 22:13:47
```

If you have a built-in clock and calendar that are set automatically to the correct date and time when you start the computer, you probably will not have to change these values. Otherwise, you may need to set the date and time whenever you start the computer. If you forget to set the date or time or if you want to change their values while you work in dBASE IV, the RUN command is handy.

To process the DOS DATE and TIME commands within dBASE IV, simply issue the RUN command:

```
. ? DATE(),TIME()
Ø1/Ø3/89  22:13:47
. RUN DATE

Current date is Tue 1-Ø3-1989
Enter new date:1-Ø2-1989

. RUN TIME

Current time is 22:23:Ø1.ØØ
Enter new time:Ø8:ØØ

. ? DATE(),TIME()
Ø1/Ø5/89  Ø8:ØØ:11
```

Deleting Disk Files

To conserve disk space when you are processing data within dBASE IV, you sometimes want to delete files you no longer need. For example, whenever you modify the structure of an existing database file, the program includes the changes in a new database (.DBF) file and, at the same time, saves the original data table in a backup (.BAK) file. If you decide to change the data structure back to the original version, you can delete the modified database file and then rename the backup file. Otherwise, it is good practice to clean up your disk space by deleting these backup files.

As you can see from the following examples, you can delete a file by issuing the ERASE command at the dot prompt:

```
. ERASE EMPLOYEE.BAK
. ERASE EMPLOYEE.DBF
. ERASE PRODUCTS.NDX
```

To delete a file in another directory, specify the directory path with the file name.

Note: The DELETE FILE command is the same as the ERASE command in dBASE IV.

1.40 Trick: **Use the command ERASE ? to select a file for deletion.**

If you are not sure of the name of the file to be deleted, enter the ERASE ? command to see a menu of files.

1.41 Trap: **The dBASE IV DELETE command is not the same as the DOS DEL command.**

In dBASE IV, DELETE is used to mark database records for deletion. Use the ERASE or DELETE FILE commands to delete disk files.

1.42 Trap: **Deleting a database file does not automatically delete files associated with it.**

A database (.DBF) file can have several kinds of files associated with it, such as a memo field (.DBT) file or an index (.MDX or .NDX) file. Remember to delete these files separately.

1.43 Trap: **You cannot delete an open file in dBASE IV.**

Do not try to delete a file that is currently open. From the dBASE IV dot prompt, enter the CLOSE ALL command to be sure that all database and related files are closed before you delete files.

1.44 Trap: **You cannot use asterisks (*) and question marks (?) as wild-card characters in the dBASE IV ERASE command to delete a group of files.**

Each of the following dot-prompt commands is invalid:

```
. ERASE *.BAK
. ERASE ABC.*
. ERASE ABC ????.DBF
```

1.45 Trick: **Use the RUN ERASE command to delete selected files from within dBASE IV.**

You can delete a group of files by using asterisks and question marks as wild-card characters in the RUN ERASE command:

```
. RUN ERASE *.BAK
. RUN ERASE ABC.*
. RUN ERASE ABC ????.DBF
```

You can also use the RUN command to delete files in other directories:

```
. RUN ERASE B:*.BAK
. RUN ERASE \DBASE\SALEDATA\*.NDX
. RUN ERASE D:\LOTUS\SALES\REGION?.WK1
```

Note: The RUN DEL command is the same as RUN ERASE.

Copying Disk Files

1.46 Tip: **You can duplicate files by using the COPY FILE command or the RUN COPY command.**

You can use the dBASE IV COPY FILE command to duplicate the contents of a disk file. (A more flexible method of copying files is using the RUN command to issue the powerful DOS COPY command in dBASE IV.)

You can use the COPY FILE command to duplicate a disk file within one directory or from one directory to another. The following examples show how to use the command:

```
. COPY FILE EMPLOYEE.DBF TO B:EMPLOYEE.DBF
. COPY FILE EMPLOYEE.DBF TO D:\BACKUP\EMPLOYEE.DBF
```

1.47 Trap: **You cannot use asterisks (*) and question marks (?) as wild-card characters in the** COPY FILE **command.**

Each of the following dot-prompt commands is invalid:

. COPY FILE *.DBF TO B:*.DBF
. COPY FILE B:ABC ???.DBF TO XYZ ???.DBF

1.48 Trick: **Use the RUN COPY command to copy groups of files within dBASE IV.**

You can use the RUN COPY command at the dot prompt to copy groups of disk files from one directory to another. Each of the following commands works:

. RUN COPY *.DBF B:*.DBF
. RUN COPY *.BAK D:\BACKUP*.BAK
. RUN COPY REGION ?.DBF B:

See the section on the **Operations/Copy** menu in the Control Center's **DOS Utilities** menu for directions on copying groups of files.

1.49 Trap: **The COPY FILE command is not the same as the dBASE IV COPY command.**

Do not confuse the COPY FILE command with the dBASE IV COPY command, which is used to copy records from one database file to another.

Renaming Disk Files

1.50 Trick: **Use the RUN RENAME command to rename files.**

Although you can use the dBASE IV RENAME command for renaming a file at the dot prompt, you must comply with certain restrictions when you use this command. A major restriction is that you cannot use asterisks (*) and question marks (?) in the RENAME command.

You can, however, use the RUN RENAME command to rename one or more files with few restrictions. The following commands illustrate ways to use the RUN RENAME command:

```
. RUN RENAME EMPLOYEE.DBF STAFF.DBF
. RUN RENAME *.BAK *.TMP
. RUN RENAME D:\WORDSTAR\*.DOC *.PRG
```

Note: See the section on using the **Operations** menu in the **DOS Utilities** menu for directions on renaming groups of files.

Formatting a Disk within dBASE IV

1.51 Tip: **Use the RUN FORMAT command to format a blank disk.**

Although it is unlikely that you will need to format a disk in dBASE IV, you may want to save some of your working files to a floppy disk as backup without leaving the program. To do this, you can format a floppy disk with the RUN command:

```
. RUN FORMAT B:
```

1.52 Trap: **The FORMAT.COM file must be accessible through the DOS path while you use the RUN FORMAT command.**

One way to gain access to the FORMAT.COM file is to have the file in the current directory when you execute the RUN FORMAT command at the dot prompt.

1.53 Trick: **Before entering dBASE IV, put the FORMAT.COM file in a separate directory. At the DOS prompt, use a PATH command to tell DOS where to find the file.**

Another way to access the FORMAT.COM file from dBASE IV is to put the file in a separate directory and then tell DOS where to find it by using a PATH command at the DOS prompt. You need to do this before you enter dBASE IV.

For example, if you put all the DOS command files in a directory named DOSFILES, you can use the following PATH command to tell DOS where to find the command files:

```
C>PATH C:\DOSFILES
```

You also can set multiple paths so that DOS will search the directories in these paths for any command or program file that you subsequently request. As you can see from the following example, these paths must be separated by semicolons:

```
C>PATH C:\DOSFILES;C:\DBASE;C:\DBASE\DBFILES
```

Including the directory that contains DOS programs such as FORMAT.COM in the PATH command in your AUTOEXEC.BAT file in the root directory makes these programs accessible from any directory.

Executing an External Applications Program

1.54 Tip: **Use the RUN command to execute an external applications program.**

Executing a non-dBASE IV applications program from within dBASE IV is one of the RUN command's most powerful features.

You can use the command with a commercially developed program such as WordStar or with a program you've written in a programming language such as BASIC, Pascal, FORTRAN, and so on.

For example, if you want to switch to a word processor such as WordStar in the middle of your dBASE IV application, you can issue the following RUN command:

```
. RUN WS
```

1.55 Tip: **To execute an external applications program, be sure that its system files are accessible to dBASE IV.**

Before you use the RUN command to execute an external applications program from within dBASE IV, be sure that the working directory contains the system files you need to execute the application.

For example, before you issue the RUN WS command to execute the external WordStar program, make sure that the current directory contains the WordStar WS.COM program and its associated system files. Otherwise, you receive a Bad command or file name message.

Because most applications programs require more than one file for the different functions provided by the program, be sure that all these disk files are in the current directory. Otherwise, you may have to change your directory.

While you run an applications program at the dot prompt from within dBASE IV, whatever you are doing in dBASE IV is suspended temporarily. Control of the program is transferred to the applications program until you have finished processing in that program. After you exit the external applications program, control is returned to dBASE IV and processing continues where you left off.

You can also execute applications programs written in either an interpretive or a compiled language from the dBASE IV dot prompt. For example, you can run a BASIC program (such as MAIN.BAS) that is written in BASICA by using the following command at the dot prompt:

. RUN BASICA MAIN

Again, before you execute the command, be sure that the current directory contains the BASICA.COM system file and the necessary data files for the BASIC program or that these files can be found in the DOS path.

If the BASIC program has been compiled into an executable file such as MAIN.EXE, you can execute the program by using the following command:

. RUN MAIN

1.56 Trap: **Be sure that you have enough memory to run external programs.**

Because dBASE IV uses most of the memory on a 640K system, there may not be enough memory available to run external programs from within dBASE IV. To determine the amount of available RAM, type RUN CHKDSK at the dot prompt. If your applications program requires more memory than you have available, you must leave dBASE IV and run the program from the DOS prompt.

Configuring the System for dBASE IV

Because dBASE IV uses a substantial amount of memory space for data storage and manipulation, you must allocate sufficient RAM (Random Access Memory) to the program before you use dBASE IV.

The dBASE IV program consists of a set of commands that instruct the computer to perform the tasks required for managing a database. These commands are coded and stored on the dBASE IV system disks.

Before dBASE IV is loaded into the computer's memory, the computer must be informed about the environment in which the program is to be operated. For example, the number of disk files that can be used by the program and the amount of memory to be reserved for data storage must be specified before the program is loaded. You provide this type of information in the CONFIG.SYS file in the root directory during the system configuration procedure. This section covers tips, tricks, and traps that help you configure your system for dBASE IV.

Setting Up the CONFIG.SYS File

1.57 Tip: **Before using dBASE IV for the first time, allocate sufficient files and buffers to the program by configuring the system.**

A typical CONFIG.SYS file contains the following two lines for allocating a certain number of files and buffers to applications programs such as dBASE IV:

```
FILES=20
BUFFERS=15
```

The instructions in the CONFIG.SYS file tell the computer to reserve the disk files and memory buffers for the program. The CONFIG.SYS file can also contain lines that specify other system devices or parameters. You use a line editor (such as the DOS EDLIN.COM) or a text editor to create or modify the contents of the file. (For detailed instructions on using a text editor, refer to its manual, or see Tip 1.84 on the **Edit** option in the **Operations** menu.)

By default, DOS ordinarily sets to 8 the number of disk files that can be open at one time. However, because DOS uses 5 of these files, only 3 are available for your applications. dBASE IV can accommodate a total of 99 files, but for most dBASE applications, 15 files are adequate. You should set the number of files to at least 20 in the CONFIG.SYS file.

If you do not specify the number of files in the CONFIG.SYS file or if the file is missing, the default setting (FILES=8) is assumed.

Before processing the dBASE IV program, DOS reserves a certain amount of RAM as temporary working space for the manipulation of data. This temporary working space is reserved in blocks of RAM called *buffers*. The size of this working space influences processing speed when you manipulate data in dBASE IV.

If the working space is large, the computer easily finds unused spots in which to store information. As the working space fills with information, DOS takes more time to search for and find the remaining memory available for new information. In theory, the more buffer space you set aside, the faster the processing speed for your data manipulation will be.

Because dBASE IV requires a certain minimum amount of RAM and DOS always puts aside memory space for buffers, it is important that you do not use too much memory for buffers. You must be sure that sufficient memory space is available for dBASE IV and other applications programs.

Allocating Memory Buffers

1.58 Tip: **Set more buffers if you have RAM space to spare.**

Because each buffer takes up 528 bytes of RAM, you must balance the memory needs of the buffers against those of the applications programs.

You can experiment with setting the number of buffers to more than 15—perhaps to 20. In determining how many buffers to set, be sure to take into account all the memory requirements for your applications, including a RAM-resident program such as SideKick® or a device driver such as a RAM disk.

1.59 Trap: **By not reserving sufficient memory in buffers, you run the risk of losing valuable data.**

If you do not have enough RAM for reserving a large number of buffers, you can run out of memory space during your dBASE IV operations. On one hand, you want to process your data as quickly as possible by setting a large number of buffers. On the other hand, reserving too much memory space for the buffers and leaving

insufficient memory for the applications program results in an
Insufficient memory error message. Even worse, by exceeding the
available memory space, you run the risk of losing some or all of your
data.

Using Abbreviated Command Words

1.60 Trick: **Use the abbreviated form of keywords in a command.**

To reduce typing time, use the abbreviated forms of the dBASE IV
commands.

When you issue a dBASE IV command at the dot prompt or in a
program file, the first four characters of each keyword identify the
command.

For example, you can display the structure of the active database in
two ways. You can issue the full command, as in the following
example:

DISPLAY STRUCTURE

You can also issue an abbreviated form of the command:

DISP STRU

Using abbreviated keywords reduces the amount of typing. More
important, by using the abbreviated command words when you code a
large set of commands in a program file, you reduce the size of the
program.

Refer to Appendix C for a list of dBASE IV commands.

1.61 Trap: **Use abbreviated command keywords carefully.**

When you use the abbreviated command keywords, a few words of
caution are in order:

❑ You cannot abbreviate the name of a file, a data field, or a
memory variable. You cannot access the file if you use an
abbreviated file name.

❑ Although only the first four characters of a keyword are
sufficient to execute the command, more letters can be used
to identify the keyword.

For example, you can use DISP, DISPL, DISPLA to abbreviate the keyword DISPLAY. However, you cannot add any other character to the abbreviated or the original keyword. DISPIT, DISPLAYS, and DISPLAYIT are not valid substitutes for the DISPLAY command. dBASE IV will not execute these invalid commands. An Unrecognized command verb message is displayed.

Reissuing an Interactive dBASE IV Command

1.62 Trick: **Use the up-arrow (↑) and down-arrow (↓) keys to reissue a dot command line.**

Instead of retyping a dBASE IV command you have just typed, you can use the up-arrow (↑) and down-arrow (↓) keys at the dot prompt to reissue the command.

In many database-management applications, you can manipulate data by executing a series of interactive dBASE IV commands you enter from the keyboard at the dot prompt.

dBASE IV normally saves up to 20 of these commands in a command buffer called a HISTORY buffer. (See Chapter 3 for a detailed discussion of the HISTORY buffer.) When the buffer is full, the new commands you enter replace those entered earlier in a first-in, first-out order.

Redisplaying the contents of the HISTORY buffer is handy when you need to modify a command you've just entered. Instead of retyping the command, you can recall it by pressing the up-arrow (↑) key. Each time you press the up-arrow (↑) key, the most recently entered command is displayed at the dot prompt.

If you issue a command that contains a syntax error, dBASE IV displays an error box giving you three choices: **Cancel**, **Edit**, or **Get Help**. If you select **Edit**, the cursor is placed at the end of the line that contains the error so that you can correct it (see fig. 1.7).

In the example, the .AND clause needs a period after it. You can use the arrow keys to position the cursor at the characters to be changed and make the necessary corrections. After you make the correction, press Enter and execute the command as usual.

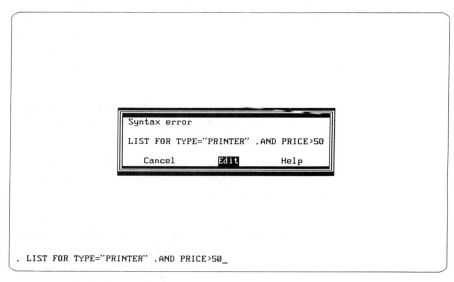

```
 Syntax error

 LIST FOR TYPE="PRINTER" .AND PRICE>50

      Cancel          Edit          Help
```

. LIST FOR TYPE="PRINTER" .AND PRICE>50_

Fig. 1.7. *Editing a command at the dot prompt.*

If the HISTORY buffer contains more than one command, you can use the up-arrow (↑) and down-arrow (↓) keys to scroll up and down the buffer and select the appropriate command. When the command appears at the dot prompt, press Enter to execute it.

Properly Saving dBASE IV Data

1.63 Trap: **If you switch data disks during data manipulation, you can lose valuable data.**

In most cases, you will store dBASE IV database files on your hard disk. However, if you store data on a floppy disk, do not switch data disks while you manipulate data.

Information about the disk files on the default disk drive is saved in a file allocation table that tells the computer where data is stored and how it is arranged on the disk. Whenever you change the contents of the disk files, the file allocation table is updated to reflect the changes, and the contents of the file are saved correctly to the disk.

To preserve these updated files, avoid switching data disks during data manipulation. If you change the disks, information in the file allocation table may not agree with your disk files in the current drive. As a result, information in both the original and the new disk files can be damaged. Changes made to the original file are saved incorrectly to the new disk.

1.64 Trick: **To change data disks during your dBASE IV session, first issue the CLEAR ALL command to close all the open files and clear all the memory variables.**

If you must change data disks during your dBASE IV session, conserve memory by issuing the CLEAR ALL command to close all open files and clear all the memory variables.

Then reselect the default disk drive with the SET DEFAULT TO command at the dot prompt, or select **Set default drive** from the **DOS** menu (in the **Tools/DOS Utilities** menu) in the Control Center.

Using the Control Center for DOS, Directory, and File Operations

The dBASE IV Control Center menus provide an easy way to perform various file-management and directory operations, including a few things you cannot do in DOS.

To access the Control Center, type ASSIST at the dot prompt or press F2 (Assist, unless the F2 key has been reprogrammed). If you place the command COMMAND=ASSIST in your CONFIG.DB file, the Control Center appears when you start dBASE. (See Chapter 2 for information on the CONFIG.DB file).

The tips, tricks, and traps in this section cover the use of the **DOS Utilities** menu to perform directory and file operations.

Using the DOS Utilities Menu

1.65 Tip: **Remember three keys to help you navigate through the dBASE IV Control Center menus.**

While you are using most menus in the Control Center, three important keys can help you choose or exit various operations:

F1 (Help)	Use this key to receive information on using the currently selected operation.
F10 (Menus)	Use this key to access menus from the current menu bar.
Esc (Escape)	Use this key to cancel the current operation without saving any changes.

1.66 Tip: **Use the DOS Utilities menu to perform DOS, directory, and file management functions.**

From the Control Center, press F10 (Menus) to access the menu bar; then select **Tools**. From the **Tools** menu, select **DOS Utilities** (see fig. 1.8). Six options are available in the **DOS Utilities** menu: **DOS**, **Files**, **Sort**, **Mark**, **Operations**, and **Exit** (see fig. 1.9).

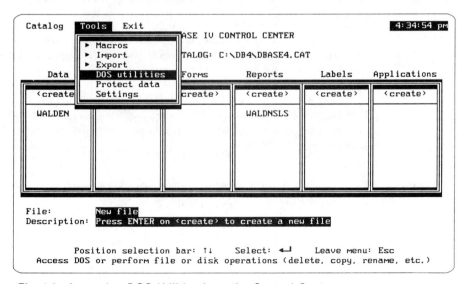

Fig. 1.8. Accessing DOS Utilities from the Control Center.

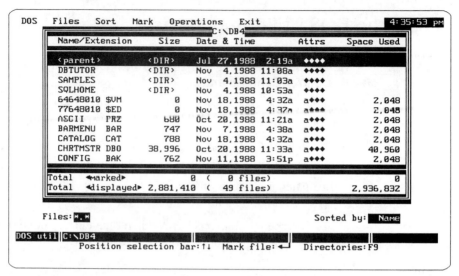

Fig. 1.9. *The DOS Utilities screen.*

Using the DOS Menu

1.67 Tip: **Use the DOS menu to issue DOS commands from within dBASE IV.**

From the **DOS Utilities** menu, choose the **DOS** menu, and then select the **Perform DOS command** option. A prompt box appears. Enter the DOS command (such as DIR or CHKDSK) and press Enter (see fig. 1.10).

This sequence is equivalent to entering the RUN (or !) command at the dot prompt, but you do not have to type RUN, just the name of the DOS command itself.

1.68 Tip: **To run other programs from within dBASE IV, use the Go to DOS option from the DOS menu.**

The **Go to DOS** option from the **DOS** menu enables you to use the entire screen to issue DOS commands or run other programs. After the program or command is completed, type Exit at the DOS prompt to return to dBASE IV.

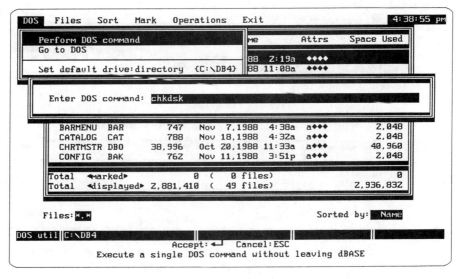

Fig. 1.10. *Using the Perform DOS command option to run CHKDSK.*

1.69 Trap: **Be sure that you have enough memory before you run external programs.**

Because dBASE IV uses most of the memory available on a 640K system, you may not have sufficient memory to run an external program, such as a word processing or spreadsheet program.

You can determine the amount of RAM available by typing CHKDSK at the **Perform DOS command** prompt in the Control Center **DOS** menu, or by entering the RUN CHKDSK command at the dot prompt.

1.70 Tip: **Change the dBASE IV default drive or directory by using the DOS menu.**

Select the **Set default drive:directory** option from the **DOS** menu to change the default drive and directory. When a prompt box appears, type the drive or directory name and press Enter (see fig. 1.11).

To see a directory tree, press Shift-F1 (Pick) and move the cursor to choose the directory you want (see fig. 1.12), or press F9 to return to the **Files** display. New files are saved to the default drive and directory you specify unless a drive or path name is included with the file name.

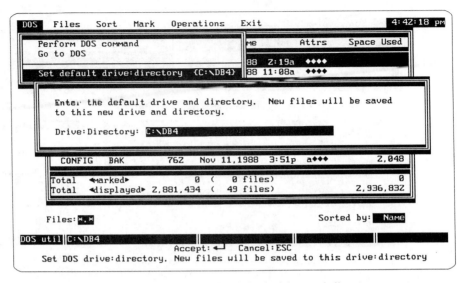

Fig. 1.11. *Using DOS Utilities to set the default drive and directory.*

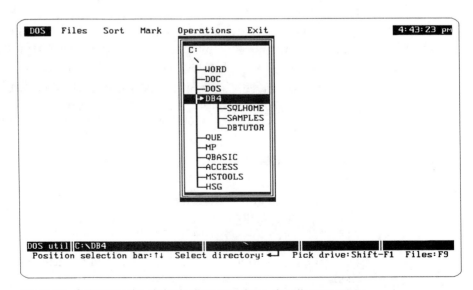

Fig. 1.12. *Selecting the default directory from the directory tree.*

Using the Files Menu

1.71 Tip: **Use the Files menu to display different types of files.**

The **Files** menu under the **DOS Utilities** menu offers two options: **Change drive:directory** and **Display only**. Use the **Change drive:directory** option to specify the location of files to be displayed on the DOS Utilities work surface.

You use the **Display only** option to specify the files to be displayed. For example, you specify F*.DBT to display only file names beginning with F and having an extension of DBT (see fig. 1.13).

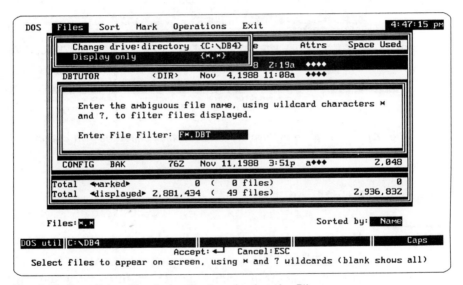

Fig. 1.13. *Specifying files to be displayed using the Files menu.*

Using the Sort Menu

1.72 Tip: **Examine directories in an orderly manner by using the Sort menu.**

You use the **Sort** menu within the **DOS Utilities** menu to choose the order in which file names will appear in the files list. The choices are **Name**, **Extension**, **Date & Time**, and **Size**. For example, to display files in the order of the date and time they were created, select **Date & Time** from the **Sort** menu (see fig. 1.14).

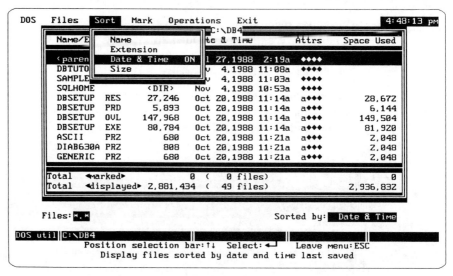

| DOS | Files | Sort | Mark | Operations | Exit | | 4:48:13 PM |

C:\DB4

Name/E	Name		tc & Time		Attrs	Space Used
	Extension					
‹paren	Date & Time	ON	l 27,1988 2:19a	◆◆◆◆		
DBTUTO	Size		v 4,1988 11:08a	◆◆◆◆		
SAMPLE			v 4,1988 11:03a	◆◆◆◆		
SQLHOME		‹DIR›	Nov 4,1988 10:53a	◆◆◆◆		
DBSETUP	RES	27,246	Oct 20,1988 11:14a	a◆◆◆	28,672
DBSETUP	PRD	5,893	Oct 20,1988 11:14a	a◆◆◆	6,144
DBSETUP	OVL	147,968	Oct 20,1988 11:14a	a◆◆◆	149,504
DBSETUP	EXE	80,784	Oct 20,1988 11:14a	a◆◆◆	81,920
ASCII	PRZ	680	Oct 20,1988 11:21a	a◆◆◆	2,048
DIAB630A	PRZ	808	Oct 20,1988 11:21a	a◆◆◆	2,048
GENERIC	PRZ	680	Oct 20,1988 11:21a	a◆◆◆	2,048

| Total | ◄marked► | | 0 | (| 0 files) | | 0 |
| Total | ◄displayed► | 2,881,434 | (| 49 files) | | 2,936,832 |

Files: ▓.▓   Sorted by: ▓Date & Time▓

DOS util C:\DB4

Position selection bar:↑↓   Select:↵   Leave menu:ESC
Display files sorted by date and time last saved

Fig. 1.14. *Specifying the display order for files using the Sort option.*

Using the Mark Menu

1.73 Tip: **Use the Mark menu to mark files before performing operations on groups of files.**

From the **Mark** menu within the **DOS Utilities** menu, you can mark or unmark groups of files. Three options are available: **Mark all**, **Unmark all**, and **Reverse marks**. Only files that appear in the files list can be marked. Once files are marked, operations can be performed on these files from the **Operations** menu.

1.74 Tip: **To mark groups of files by type, use the Display only option with the Mark all option.**

From the **Files** menu, use the **Display only** option to specify file types to be displayed. Then, from the **Mark** menu, choose **Mark all** to mark all files of the type specified. For example, if you want to mark all files to have an extension of .TXT, specify ***.TXT** in the Display only menu; then select **Mark all** from the **Mark** menu.

1.75 Trap: **Marked files are unmarked when you return to the Control Center or go to DOS.**

When a file has been marked, it remains marked only until returned to the Control Center menu or until you select **Go to DOS** from the **DOS** menu. In the latter case, a screen message alerts you that files will no longer be marked, and you are prompted to **Proceed** or **Cancel**.

Using the Operations Menu

1.76 Tip: **Use the Operations menu to copy files from within dBASE IV.**

Choose the **Copy** option from the **Operations** menu within the **DOS Utilities** menu to copy selected files to a different directory. You are offered three options: copy a single file (the current file), all marked files, or all displayed files. To copy a group of files, mark them by using the **Mark** menu or select them with the **Display only** option of the **Files** menu. To copy one file, move the cursor to the file name to be copied, and then choose the **Single File** option from the **Copy** menu and press Enter.

A prompt box enables you to specify the drive and directory to which the file is to be copied (see fig. 1.15). The default drive and directory is the destination specified in the last copy, move, or rename file operation. To carry out the operation, press Ctrl-End.

1.77 Tip: **Use the F8 (Copy) key to copy the current file.**

If you want to copy only the currently selected file, a shortcut is to press the F8 (Copy) key. You are prompted for the path and name for the copy.

1.78 Trap: **When copying marked files, use wild cards in the destination file name.**

When prompted for the destination file name, use wild cards when copying a group of marked files. Otherwise, all the marked files can be

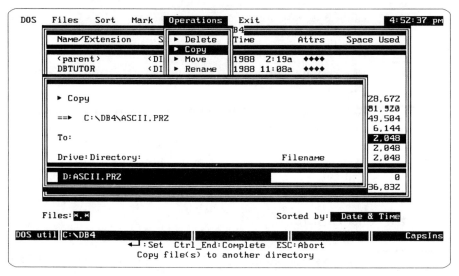

Fig. 1.15. *Copying a single file to another drive or directory.*

copied to the one file name that appears in the prompt box. For example, use *.* as the destination file name to give the copies of the files the same names as the originals.

1.79 Tip: **Use the Move option to move files to another directory quickly.**

In DOS, to move a group of files to another directory, you must first copy the files and then delete them from the original directory. The **Move** option of the **Operations** menu speeds this process; you use the option to select files to be moved and specify the destination directory. The **Move** option works like the **Copy** option, except that the original files are deleted once they have been copied to the new directory. To complete the operation, press Ctrl-End.

1.80 Tip: **Use the F7 (Move) key to move the current file to another directory.**

A shortcut for accessing the **Move** option is to press the F7 (Move) key. You are prompted for the name of the directory to which the current file is to be moved. Press Ctrl-End to complete the move operation.

1.81 Tip:

To rename groups of files from within dBASE IV, use the Rename option from the Operations menu.

After selecting the **Rename** option from the **Operations** menu, you are prompted for the destination file names. You can use wild-card characters (* or ?) as the new file names. For example, if you specify *.DOC as the file name, the files are renamed with their original names plus the .DOC extension.

1.82 Trap:

Be careful when specifying the destination file name in a Rename operation.

File names cannot be changed to the names of files that already exist in the same directory, and a file cannot be renamed as itself. dBASE IV displays a warning message if you try to do this.

1.83 Tip:

To examine the contents of a file quickly, use the View option from the Operations menu.

Suppose that you can't remember the contents of a particular file, or you simply need to read the file without editing it. Instead of invoking the text editor, you can choose **View** from the **Operations** menu. Non-text characters, such as formatting codes in a word processing file or program file, are not displayed. Text is displayed one screen at a time. Press the space bar to view the next screen, or press Esc to exit the display.

1.84 Tip:

To edit a text file, use the Edit option from the Operations menu.

To edit an ASCII text file with the built-in program editor, select the file from the **DOS Utilities** menu; then choose the **Edit** option from the **Operations** menu. The text editor loads the selected file. When finished, choose **Exit**; then choose to save or abandon changes made to the file.

From the dot prompt, you can use the program editor by typing MODIFY COMMAND.

Using the Reverse Marks Option

1.85 Trick: **To perform an operation on a large group of files, use the Reverse marks option.**

If you want to perform an operation on a group of files that do not meet certain criteria, the **Reverse marks** option saves time.

For example, from a list of 30 files, suppose that you want to copy every file that has the extension .DBT except for three files. Instead of marking the 27 other files one at a time, specify *.DBT from the **Display only** menu within the **Files** menu. Then select **Mark all** from the **Mark** menu. Choose **Display only** again from the **Files** menu and enter *.* as the file specification. Then select **Reverse marks** from the **Mark** menu. All files except the three with the .DBT extension are then marked. From the **Operations** menu, you can choose **Copy/Marked Files** to copy the 27 marked files.

Exiting dBASE IV

The dBASE IV QUIT command closes all the open files and saves the contents of all files to disk before terminating the program. This ensures that no data is lost. Any other methods of quitting dBASE IV may endanger your work in progress.

1.86 Trap: **Do not turn off the power to quit dBASE IV.**

Turning off the power to quit dBASE IV can cause the loss of valuable information or damage the contents of your files.

1.87 Trap: **Do not use the Ctrl-Alt-Del key combination to restart the computer before you exit dBASE IV.**

Using a Ctrl-Alt-Del key combination (performing a "warm boot") can cause data to be lost and may damage your disk file.

1.88 Trick: **Always use the QUIT command to exit dBASE IV.**

The safest way to end a dBASE IV session is to exit the program by using the QUIT command. You can execute the command at the dot prompt:

. QUIT

You can also select **Exit/Quit to DOS** from the Control Center menu.

2

Configuring dBASE IV

d BASE IV provides a powerful tool—the CONFIG.DB file—for specifying the commands that define your working environment. By predefining certain function parameters and commands in the CONFIG.DB file, you can use dBASE IV's many features more efficiently. This chapter includes tips, tricks, and traps that help you set up the CONFIG.DB file and make the most of the commands and functions dBASE IV has to offer.

Using the CONFIG.DB File

The CONFIG.DB file can perform many functions for you automatically. At start-up, for example, the default data disk drive may be identified to make sure that all disk files are saved to the correct disk. The type of display monitor (either a monochrome or color monitor) you are using and its setting (background and foreground colors, for example) may also be identified. If you are using several memory variables, you may have to reserve sufficient memory space to store the values of the variables properly.

If you plan to use an independent word processor or text editor, you can save time by setting the function keys on the keyboard to perform predetermined editing operations. And you can set the size of the keyboard buffers so that a certain number of keys can be stored temporarily as you type ahead. You can also specify which printer drivers you will be using.

The CONFIG.DB file is the first disk file dBASE IV processes. All the commands stored in the configuration file are executed when you start dBASE IV. The tips, tricks, and traps in this section help you set up the CONFIG.DB file and customize your system to your specifications.

Setting Up the CONFIG.DB File

Following is a summary of the commands and parameter settings you can use in the CONFIG.DB file:

❑ Commands for identifying the default disk drive and the type of display monitor

❑ Keywords for defining function keys

❑ Keywords for selecting a custom text editor and word processor

❑ Keywords for selecting one or more printer drivers

❑ Keywords for allocating memory space

❑ Keywords for setting the size of the keyboard buffer

❑ Keywords used by the SET commands for specifying parameter settings

❑ Other keywords for specifying parameters to control data-display operations

Database management operations can be completed efficiently when the settings and commands in the configuration file are chosen appropriately.

You can set the options and parameters you need in the CONFIG.DB file by using the following format:

$<$ *option* $>$ = $<$ ON (*or* OFF) $>$

or

$<$ *option* $>$ = $<$ *parameter* $>$

2.1 Tip:

The CONFIG.DB file is especially useful when you design a turnkey system.

When you design a turnkey database management system, the CONFIG.DB file is especially useful because you can run the program automatically. The command is the program name. For example, by including the command for executing the first program module (such as the main menu module) in the CONFIG.DB file, control of the program is transferred to the program module as soon as the configuration file is executed.

If you don't have a CONFIG.DB file, you can set most of these options and parameters at the dot prompt when you enter the program by using the SET command. You can use either of the following formats:

SET < *option*> < ON (*or* OFF)>

or

SET < *option*> TO < *parameter*>

Selecting the Default Disk Drive

2.2 Tip: **Set the default disk in the configuration file.**

In most cases, you will store dBASE IV database files on your hard disk. However, there may be times when your data files may be stored in more than one disk drive. In that case, you need to set the default disk drive to the drive that holds your data files. The default data disk drive, which stores all the disk files during your program operations, usually is displayed in the status line at the bottom of the screen. You can use one of several methods to set it.

Assuming that you will be using drive C: to store data, set the data disk drive before you enter the program, and add the line DEFAULT = C to the CONFIG.DB file.

At the dot prompt, you can set the default data disk drive by issuing the following command:

. SET DEFAULT TO < *default drive*>

You type the following:

. SET DEFAULT TO C:

2.3 Trap: **A directory path specified in the SET DEFAULT TO command has no effect.**

The DEFAULT keyword in the CONFIG.DB file identifies the data disk drive. For example, do not include a directory path in the DEFAULT statement, such as the following:

DEFAULT = C:\DBASE\DBFILES

A directory path specified in the DEFAULT statement will be ignored, and the disk files you create thereafter will not be saved in the specified directory in the default drive. To verify the current directory, use the RUN CD command at the dot prompt after you have entered the program.

2.4 Trick: **Use the DOS Utilities menu to set a default directory.**

The default disk drive and directory can be changed from the Control Center menu. Set the default by using the following option sequence:

Tools/DOS Utilities/DOS/Set default drive:directory

Each slash indicates a choice from the submenu. You first press Alt-T to select the **Tools** menu; you then make subsequent choices by either typing the first letter of a menu selection or by highlighting the selection and pressing Enter.

After following the option sequence, press Shift-F1 (Pick); then place the cursor on the name of the drive and directory you want to set as the default.

Defining Function Keys

With dBASE IV, you can use either the default function key settings, or you can customize the function key settings to fit your operations.

Using the Default Function Key Settings

2.5 Tip: **Save time by using the default settings of the function keys.**

Function keys are set up to perform commonly used program commands. Use these function keys to minimize keystrokes when you issue program commands at the dot prompt.

Each function key can be set to perform a specific function, except for function key F1, which is always set to invoke the Help facility. Table 2.1 lists the normal operations assigned to the function keys:

Table 2.1
Function Key Commands and Operations

Key	Command	Designated Operation
F1	HELP;	Access Help facility
F2	ASSIST;	Invoke Control Center menu
F3	LIST;	List records in active database
F4	DIR;	Display database files in active directory
F5	DISPLAY STRUCTURE;	Display structure of database in use
F6	DISPLAY STATUS;	Display current processing status and function key settings
F7	DISPLAY MEMORY;	Display values of memory variables
F8	DISPLAY;	Display records in active database file
F9	APPEND;	Append data record to active database file
F10	EDIT;	Edit contents of data records in active database file

(Note that the function keys have different uses when you are using the Control Center menus. See Appendix B for a complete list of function key operations.)

Customizing Function Keys

2.6 Trick: **For increased power, reassign the function keys to a set of custom operations.**

You can create program modules for performing database management functions when you design a turnkey database management system.

For example, your database management system can consist of several program modules, such as INVOICE.PRG, MAILLIST.PRG, and REPORTS.PRG (for preparing invoices, mailing lists, and financial reports, respectively). Rather than writing a menu program in which you select an operation from the main menu, you can designate a function key for each operation.

Function keys F2, F3, and F4, for example, could perform the following operations:

Function Key	Designated Operation
F2	Create invoices
F3	Produce mailing lists
F4	Generate financial reports

You can define the operation of a function key by specifying the operation in a SET FUNCTION TO command. dBASE IV enables you to assign to a function key a string of up to 238 characters. To define the function key before you enter the program, specify the operation as a line in the CONFIG.DB file:

< key label > = *< expression>*

For example, you can designate F2 to execute the INVOICE.PRG program module by including the following line in the CONFIG.DB file:

```
F2 = "DO INVOICE;"
```

The semicolon (;) at the end of the operation instructs the computer to issue a carriage return (or press Enter). Without the semicolon, you must press F2, and then press Enter, to execute the designated operation.

2.7 Trick:

Assign multiple operations to a function key.

You can assign more than one operation to a function key. For example, you can instruct the program to clear the screen before it executes the MAILLIST.PRG program by defining F3 as follows:

```
F3 = "CLEAR; DO MAILLIST;"
```

2.8 Trap:

You cannot redefine the operation of the F1 and Shift-F10 function keys.

You can redefine function keys F2 through F10, Shift-F1 through Shift-F9, and Ctrl-F1 through Ctrl-F10 to perform other prespecified operations. F1 is reserved for the HELP facility; Shift-F10 and all Alt-key functions are reserved for macros and cannot be reprogrammed.

Using an External Text Editor

2.9 Tip:

Use an external word processor to edit a text file within dBASE IV.

The built-in text editor provided by dBASE IV lets you create and modify text files, such as program or command (.PRG) files. Any file that contains text in ASCII format can be created and edited using the dBASE IV editor. From the dot prompt, you invoke the editor by entering the following command (see fig. 2.1):

. MODIFY COMMAND *< name of file to be created or edited >*

```
  Layout   Words   Go To   Print   Exit                    12:38:22 pm
[....•...▼1...•..▼..2...•...▼..3..▼.•...4▼..•....▼5...•.▼..6....▼...7.▼.•....
SET BELL ON
SET CARRY OFF
SET CENTURY OFF
SET CONFIRM OFF
SET DELIMITERS TO ""
SET DELIMITER OFF
SET ESCAPE ON
SET INSTRUCT OFF
SET SAFETY ON
SET SCOREBOARD OFF
SET STATUS OFF
SET TALK OFF
SET ESCAPE OFF
@ 4,9 TO 14,69 DOUBLE .
@ 7,10 SAY "         Welcome to the Main Program"
@ 9,10 SAY "   You may Enter Names & Addresses, Print Reports, and"
@ 11,10 SAY "            View your data on the screen."



 Program  C:\db4\MAINPROG          Line:22 Col:1                      Ins
```

Fig. 2.1. *Using the dBASE IV text editor.*

You can also reach the editor from the Control Center. From the **Tools** menu, you can select a file and then choose **Edit** from the **Operations** menu. Remember that the text file being edited by an external text editor or word processor must be saved in ASCII format.

You may prefer to use another text editor with which you are more familiar, such as Microsoft Word®, WordStar, or WordPerfect®. To select an external text editor to use within the program, you must specify the text editor in the CONFIG.DB file. The format of the configuration command in the file is as follows:

TEDIT = < *name of text editor*>

For example, to choose WordStar as your external text editor, you add the following command to the CONFIG.DB file:

TEDIT = WS.COM

After the commands in the CONFIG.DB file are executed and the cursor is at the dot prompt, you can invoke the text editor by entering MODIFY COMMAND (see fig. 2.2).

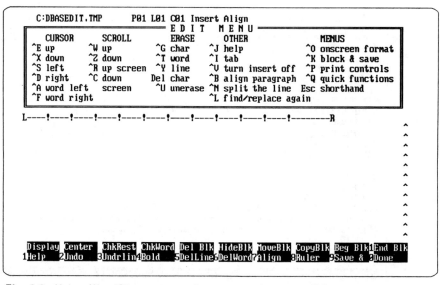

Fig. 2.2. *Using WordStar as a word processor for text editing.*

2.10 Trap: **To use an external text editor, the files must be accessible to DOS.**

When you use an external text editor in dBASE IV, make sure that all the files can be accessed by DOS. The files usually include all the related files that have .COM or .EXE file extensions. If these programs are saved in a separate directory, you must use the PATH command to tell DOS where to find them. Otherwise, when you attempt to invoke the text editor at the dot prompt, the error message Bad command or file name appears on-screen.

2.11 Trick: Use the PATH command to tell DOS where to find the word processing programs.

If you want to use an external word processor (and the external programs are saved in a separate directory), you must specify—before you enter the program—the path that tells DOS where to find the programs. For example, if all the programs associated with your word processor are saved in the WORDPROC directory, you need to issue the PATH = \WORDPROC command at the DOS prompt. Or you can specify the path in the TEDIT command as in TEDIT = C:\WORD\WORD.

2.12 Trap: Have enough memory before you run external programs.

Because dBASE IV uses most of the memory available on a 640K system, you may not have sufficient memory to run an external word processing program.

You can determine the amount of RAM available by typing CHKDSK at the Perform DOS command prompt in the Control Center **DOS** menu or by entering the RUN CHKDSK command at the dot prompt.

2.13 Tip: Use an external word processor to edit the contents of memo fields.

Memo fields in a database table can be used effectively to store large blocks of text. When editing text in the memo field, you can take advantage of some of the powerful editing features offered by external word processors. You first specify the word processor in the CONFIG.DB file. Following is the format of the configuration command:

WP = < *name of word processor*>

For example, to choose WordStar as your external word processor, you add the following line to the CONFIG.DB file:

WP = WS.COM

2.14 Tip: **Use a DOS PATH command when the external text editor programs are not in the current directory.**

When the external text editor programs are not in the current directory, be sure to tell DOS where to find these files by using a DOS PATH command before you enter dBASE IV. Otherwise, the program won't be able to find and execute the word processor you specified. Or you can specify the path in the WP command, as in the following:

```
WP = C:\WORDSTAR\WS.COM
```

After the commands in the CONFIG.DB file are executed and the cursor is at the dot prompt, you call the external word processor that you specified by pressing Ctrl-Home. Figure 2.3 shows an example of editing a memo field with WordStar.

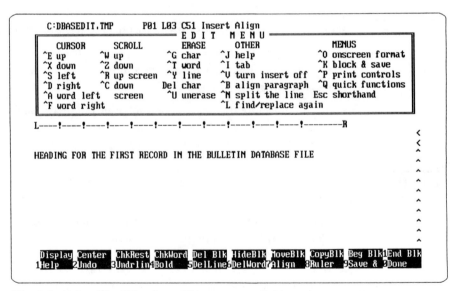

Fig. 2.3. *Using WordStar for editing a memo field.*

2.15 Tip: **The contents of edited memo fields are held in a temporary file.**

When you are using an external word processor such as WordStar to edit text in a memo field, a temporary file is created to hold the contents. The actual contents of the memo field in the database file are saved in a memo text file (such as BULLETIN.DBT). After you edit the memo field, you exit from the word processor by using the appropriate command. (In WordStar, you press Ctrl-KD and then X.) You then can edit the next data field in the database file.

2.16 Tip: **You can edit the contents of memo fields with the built-in text editor.**

To invoke the built-in text editor while the cursor is in a memo field, press Ctrl-Home. For example, to add a new record to a database file named BULLETIN.DBF that contains two memo fields named HEADING and TEXT, you issue the USE BULLETIN and APPEND commands at the dot prompt.

In response to the dot-prompt commands, the record to be appended to the database file is displayed (see fig. 2.4).

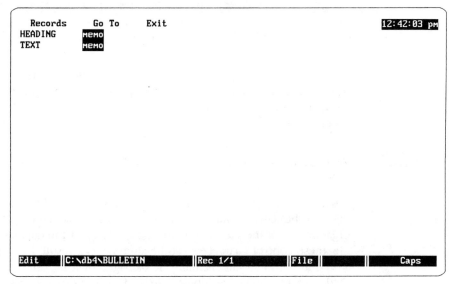

Fig. 2.4. *Editing the contents of a memo field.*

Then, to edit (or enter) the contents for the first memo field (HEADING), press Ctrl-Home. The built-in text editor is invoked, and you can type the text for the memo field (see fig. 2.5).

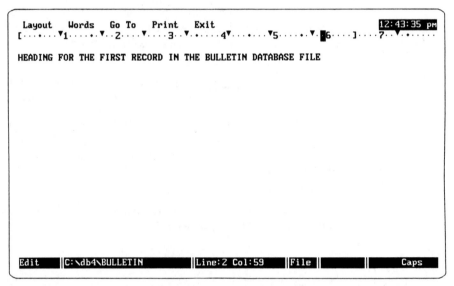

Fig. 2.5. *Using the dBASE IV text editor for editing a memo field.*

The memo field being edited (HEADING) is shown at the top of the screen. After you edit this memo field, press Ctrl-W to save the text in the memo field and continue editing the next data field in the database file.

2.17 Trap: **You can't edit the contents of a .DBT file directly with a text editor or a word processor.**

A database memo file (.DBT) stores the contents of all the memo fields in the database file, including the control characters, for internal organization of the file. If you edit the contents of the database memo file, these control characters can be altered. As a result, information stored in the memo fields might be damaged or lost. You can edit the field contents only by editing the individual fields themselves while you are editing the database file, not by trying to edit the entire .DBT file.

Allocating Memory

2.18 Tip: **Allocate sufficient memory space when you use a large number of memory variables.**

The term *variable* is used in algebra to define a quantity that can assume different values. In dBASE IV, a *variable* is a name assigned to a memory location that can be used to hold a data element. The value stored in a memory variable can be the value in a data field or some other data item. Dates, alphanumeric strings, and numeric values can be stored in memory variables.

The maximum number of memory variables of all types that can be used in the program is determined by the MVMAXBLKS (memory variable maximum blocks) and MVBLKSIZE (memory variable block size) settings in the CONFIG.DB file. The default settings are as follows:

```
MVMAXBLKS = 10
MVBLKSIZE = 50
```

To calculate the number of memory variables you can have, multiply these two figures. In other words, the default in the preceding example is 500 memory variables (50 × 10). Because each memory variable in a block uses 64 bytes of memory, this default setting reserves 32,000 bytes of memory for use by memory variables. This amount is adequate for most applications. If, however, you anticipate using a greater number of variables, you can reserve more memory by increasing one of the values. For example, the setting MVMAXBLKS = 20 reserves 64,000 bytes of memory for use by up to 1,000 memory variables (20 × 50 = 1,000 variables × 64 bytes = 64,000 bytes).

The MVMAXBLKS setting must be between 1 and 25, and the MVBLKSIZE settings must be between 25 and 1,000.

2.19 Tip: **To use a large format file with multiple screens and PICTURE clauses, allocate space in CONFIG.DB.**

You can design a custom data-entry form that includes command lines for defining the data format; you can then save this form in a format file. (See Chapters 3 and 9 for more information.)

Memory space for storing the PICTURE and RANGE clauses is allocated by the BUCKET size, which is measured by the number of kilobytes. As the default, the program allocates two kilobytes (BUCKET = 2 or 2 × 1,024 bytes) for saving all the PICTURE and RANGE options.

This default setting provides sufficient memory space to accommodate formatting operations with PICTURE and RANGE clauses in the GET commands of most applications. However, if your application requires an unusually large amount of memory space for saving the PICTURE and RANGE values, you can increase the BUCKET size by including the following line in the CONFIG.DB file:

BUCKET = < *size of bucket in kilobytes*>

The maximum size of BUCKET is 16 kilobytes.

2.20 Tip: **Use the AUTOSAVE feature to avoid data loss.**

dBASE IV's AUTOSAVE feature saves each record to disk after it has been changed, rather than waiting for the record buffer to fill. If the program is interrupted by a power loss or other problem, records in the buffer won't be lost. The default is AUTOSAVE OFF, which enables you to abort editing of records without saving changes. To use the AUTOSAVE feature, you include the following command in the CONFIG.DB file:

AUTOSAVE = ON

Customizing the Display

2.21 Tip: **To display commands and results on your monitor in color, set the colors in the configuration file.**

When you use a color monitor, you can instruct dBASE IV to display standard text, enhanced text, borders, or backgrounds in colors by including a COLOR command in the CONFIG.DB file in the following format:

COLOR = < *standard*>,< *enhanced*>,< *border*>,< *background*>

From within dBASE IV, you can change the screen colors by issuing the SET COLOR TO command at the dot prompt. (See Chapter 7 for a detailed discussion of setting screen colors for displaying output.)

You can also specify color settings for the following items in the CONFIG.DB file:

```
COLOR OF NORMAL =
COLOR OF TITLES =
COLOR OF BOX =
COLOR OF MESSAGES =
COLOR OF FIELDS =
COLOR OF HIGHLIGHT =
COLOR OF INFORMATION =
```

2.22 Trap: **Using color settings that are inappropriate for your monitor can cause unpredictable results.**

If you set colors while using a monochrome monitor, or if you specify colors that cannot be displayed with your monitor and display adapter, a blank screen may appear or dBASE IV may lock up your system. Specify only colors that can be supported by your system configuration.

2.23 Trap: **Specify the correct monitor and display adapter in your CONFIG.DB file.**

Your CONFIG.DB file should contain a command specifying the type of monitor and display adapter you are using:

DISPLAY = < *monitor type*>

The setting choices for monitor type include the following:

```
    MONO =    Monochrome display
   COLOR =    Color graphics display
   EGA25 =    EGA 25-line color display
   EGA43 =    EGA 43-line color display
  MONO43 =    Monochrome 43-line display
```

If you change monitors or display adapters, be sure to change the DISPLAY setting in your CONFIG.DB file.

If you use both a color and a monochrome monitor, you may switch between them using the SET COLOR ON (or OFF) command at the dot prompt, or by including the following statement in the CONFIG.DB file:

COLOR = ON (*or* OFF)

2.24 Tip: **Define your own prompt symbol in the configuration file.**

If you do not want to use the dot (.) as the command prompt symbol in the program, you can select your own command prompt.

In the interactive mode of processing, you can choose either the Control Center menu or the dot prompt to issue processing commands. Although the Control Center menu provides a user-friendly environment for communicating with the dBASE IV processor, the dot prompt is a powerful and flexible way to issue commands for manipulating data.

Many users have grown accustomed to the dot as a command prompt and find it quite satisfactory. However, new users of the program often complain about the nondescriptive dot. They dislike the dot because it does not provide any information about the action the processor requests. If you agree, you can replace the prompt with your own symbols or messages. To define your own prompt, include a PROMPT configuration line in the CONFIG.DB file in the following format:

    PROMPT = < *character string*>

Character strings used as command prompts can be up to 19 characters in length. Following are several examples:

    PROMPT = - >
    PROMPT = Command >
    PROMPT = Enter a command:

For example, if you define your command prompt as Enter a command: when you are in dot-prompt mode, this string is displayed in place of a normal dot. You then can issue the command at the prompt, which will look like these examples:

    Enter a command:USE EMPLOYEE
    Enter a command:LIST

In this example, you can see that there is no space between the cursor (where you begin typing the command) and the last character of the prompt (:). To separate the prompt and the command, add a blank space at the end of the character string that is used as the prompt. Even though a space may not show on the monitor, the space is considered a valid string character. If you add a space, the command prompt will look like these examples:

    Enter a command: USE EMPLOYEE
    Enter a command: LIST

Using Special Files and Commands within dBASE IV

This section covers special files and commands that you can include in your CONFIG.DB file to make your use of dBASE IV more efficient. The tips, tricks, and traps deal with these special features of dBASE IV.

Executing a Program Automatically

2.25 Tip: **Configure dBASE IV to execute a command automatically after entering the program.**

You can instruct a turnkey database management system to execute a command automatically at start-up.

When you design a database management system, you can create several program modules that perform specific data manipulation operations. Then, if you want to execute one of these dBASE IV programs (a program with a .PRG file extension), you can issue the DO command and include the name of the program to be executed. For example, . DO MAINPROG is the dot prompt command for executing a program named MAINPROG.PRG.

This approach for processing data requires that you know the name of each program module so that you can specify the name in the DO command. If your system is designed for your own use, you shouldn't have a problem because you probably can remember the program modules involved in your database application.

If you create program modules intended for other people to use, you need to design a turnkey system that doesn't require users to remember the names of all the program modules. Users just select menu items by pressing designated keys to perform specified tasks. (A detailed discussion about this procedure appears in Chapter 9.) A program that automatically specifies all the menu choices as soon as you enter dBASE IV is especially useful.

To execute a dot prompt command as soon as you enter the program, include the following command in the CONFIG.DB file:

COMMAND = *< dBASE IV command >*

Following are two examples:

```
COMMAND = DO MAINMENU
COMMAND = DO DBFILES\MAINMENU
```

If you examine the CONFIG.DB file contents originally supplied by the program (by issuing the TYPE CONFIG.DB command at the DOS prompt), you can see COMMAND = ASSIST in the configuration file. When the configuration line is executed, the Control Center menu is displayed automatically. If you delete this line from the configuration file, the cursor moves to the dot prompt when you invoke the program.

On the other hand, when you include another program command in its place (such as DO MAINMENU), that command is executed automatically when the program is invoked. Control of the program then shifts to the program module to be executed. After the program module is executed, unless directed otherwise in the program, the dot prompt regains control. Therefore, do not specify more than one program module in the CONFIG.DB file. If you do, the second DO command will not be executed.

Setting Up the ALTERNATE File

2.26 Tip: **Assign a default ALTERNATE file during configuration.**

When the program is in interactive mode and is processing a program command at the dot prompt, you can save a list of all commands issued to a text file. This convenient method documents your data processing operations. Such a command list is especially useful in the program development stage because it documents all the processing steps in your application.

To save program commands issued at the dot prompt, along with their related output on-screen, use the SET ALTERNATE TO and SET ALTERNATE ON commands. An example of an ALTERNATE file is shown in figure 2.6. (Chapter 3 includes a detailed discussion of the ALTERNATE file and its functions.)

To assign a name to an ALTERNATE file, use the ALTERNATE command in the CONFIG.DB file:

ALTERNATE = < *name of text file*>

```
. SET ALTERNATE TO LISTING.TXT
. SET ALTERNATE ON
. USE EMPLOYEE
. DISPLAY FOR POSITION="Sales Rep"
Record#  ID_NO      FIRST_NAME      LAST_NAME      POSITION    EMPLY_DATE MALE
      4  732-88-4589 Doris Y.        Taylor         Sales Rep   08/14/83    .F.
      7  554-34-7893 Vincent M.      Corso          Sales Rep   07/20/84    .T.

. SET ALTERNATE OFF
. CLOSE ALTERNATE
. TYPE LISTING.TXT

. USE EMPLOYEE
. DISPLAY FOR POSITION="Sales Rep"
Record#  ID_NO      FIRST_NAME      LAST_NAME      POSITION    EMPLY_DATE MALE
      4  732-88-4589 Doris Y.        Taylor         Sales Rep   08/14/83    .F.
      7  554-34-7893 Vincent M.      Corso          Sales Rep   07/20/84    .T.

. SET ALTERNATE OFF

.
```

Fig. 2.6. *Saving screen contents in a text file with the SET ALTERNATE ON command.*

The name of the text file may or may not include the directory path or a file extension. If you do not include a file extension, the .TXT extension is assumed. Unless otherwise specified, the directory from which the program is invoked also is assumed. To save the text file in another directory, be sure to specify it accordingly, as in the following examples:

```
ALTERNATE = LISTING.TXT
ALTERNATE = B:LISTING.DOC
ALTERNATE = C:\DBASE\DBFILES\LISTING.TXT
```

When you include this setting with a file name in your CONFIG.DB file, ALTERNATE is set to ON automatically.

2.27 Tip: **Use the ADDITIVE option to append output to a single file.**

dBASE IV enables you to append output data to an existing file instead of creating a new file each time you use the SET ALTERNATE command. The syntax is as follows:

SET ALTERNATE TO < *file name* > ADDITIVE

2.28 Tip: **If you use a large ALTERNATE file, be sure that you have enough disk space to hold it.**

The text file created by the SET ALTERNATE TO command requires a certain amount of disk space. You need to make sure that you have enough space on your disk drive and in the file directory before you create the text file. Otherwise, the following error message is displayed:

```
ALTERNATE could not be opened
```

Setting the BELL Feature

2.29 Tip: **To turn the beeping sound off during a data-entry operation, set the BELL command in configuration.**

As a warning or a reminder, the program beeps during certain data-entry operations. For example, when you enter data that fills the specified width of a data field, a beeping sound warns you that the cursor has moved to the next data field. You can turn off the beeping sound by including the following command in the CONFIG.DB file:

```
BELL = OFF
```

2.30 Trick: **Use different bell sounds for various types of warnings.**

If you choose to leave the bell on, dBASE IV enables you to specify the default sound frequency and duration of the beep by including the setting in your CONFIG.DB file:

BELL = < *frequency*>, < *duration*>

As an example, to set the bell to 1,000Hz (cycles per second) frequency and 3 ticks duration, the bell setting in the CONFIG.DB file would look like the following:

```
BELL = 1000, 3
```

The normal default is 512Hz frequency, 2 ticks duration. To hear the bell, type the following at the dot prompt:

```
. ? CHR(7)
```

Use the following commands at the dot prompt to experiment with different settings to determine the one you like best:

```
. SET BELL TO <frequency>, <duration>
. ? CHR(7)
```

Settings range from 18Hz to 10,000Hz for frequency, and 2 to 20 ticks for duration.

You may want to use the SET BELL TO command to sound different tones for various purposes in your programs. For example, you may want to issue a short, high-pitched tone to acknowledge user input and a long, low-pitched tone when an error has occurred. To reinstate the dBASE IV default setting, type SET BELL TO with no settings specified.

Setting the CARRY Feature

2.31 Tip: **To carry the contents of an existing data record over to another record, set CARRY to ON during configuration.**

When you add new data records to a database file by using the APPEND and INSERT commands, you can carry the contents of a preceding record to the next record. You then can create new data records by replicating the contents of an existing record.

The data replication operation is useful when most of the field values in the new records are the same as the existing record. Instead of entering all the data field values using the keyboard, you can copy the contents of an existing record to a new record and then make modifications. (The replication of data records is discussed in Chapter 3.)

To invoke the replication operation, issue the SET CARRY ON command at the dot prompt. The SET CARRY OFF command deactivates the replication operation. CARRY = ON and CARRY = OFF are the configuration commands you can include in the CONFIG.DB file for the replicating operation. Normally, the program starts by assuming that CARRY is set to OFF.

Assigning the CATALOG File

2.32 Tip: **When you are designing a turnkey system, assign a catalog file during configuration.**

You can use a .CAT file extension to group all the related disk files in a catalog file. Then you can see and use only the files for that application. The name of the catalog file also can be specified in your CONFIG.DB file by including the following command line:

CATALOG = < *name of catalog file*>

Cataloging files is an efficient method for organizing data. An active catalog file, however, occupies one working area (work area 10). As a result, only nine working areas remain for other data manipulation operations. (The advantages and disadvantages of using catalog files in database management are discussed in Chapter 5.)

Defining the CENTURY

2.33 Tip: **Define the CENTURY command during configuration.**

If you use dates from different centuries, be sure to use the CENTURY command to display the century prefix properly.

When the contents of a date variable or a date field are displayed, the century prefix for a date normally does not appear. For example, if you issue the ?DATE( ) command at the dot prompt, the system date displayed by the command may look like 01/25/89. To show the century prefix, however, you issue the SET CENTURY ON command at the dot prompt:

```
. SET CENTURY ON
. ?DATE( )
01/25/1989
```

The default CENTURY setting is OFF. When you use dates that are not in the 20th century, you set CENTURY to ON. For example, if you use a date variable from the 19th century and another from the 20th century in your application, but you don't set CENTURY to ON, you cannot distinguish one century from another (see fig. 2.7).

```
. SET CENTURY OFF
. ADATE={07/04/1776}
07/04/76
. BDATE={07/04/1976}
07/04/76
. ?ADATE,BDATE
07/04/76 07/04/76
. ?"Number of days in between =",BDATE-ADATE
Number of days in between =                73048
. SET CENTURY ON
. ?ADATE,BDATE
07/04/1776 07/04/1976
.
```

Fig. 2.7. *Displaying the century prefix with SET CENTURY ON.*

As shown in figure 2.7, the variables ADATE and BDATE show the same value when they are displayed with the question mark (?) after SET CENTURY OFF is executed. However, you can see that the two dates are correctly stored internally when you display the number of days between the two dates (73,048 days).

You also can set CENTURY ON and OFF by including CENTURY = ON or CENTURY = OFF in the CONFIG.DB file.

Setting the Clock Display

2.34 Tip: **Turn the CLOCK display ON or OFF.**

dBASE IV always displays the time in full-screen operations such as Browse or when using the Control Center. You may choose to turn off the clock or reposition the time display by using the SET CLOCK command. To turn off the clock, use the SET CLOCK OFF command. To reposition the clock display, use the following command:

SET CLOCK TO < *row*> , < *column*>

The default position is row 1, column 68.

To place the settings in your CONFIG.DB file, use the following statements:

    CLOCK = ON (or OFF)
    CLOCK = <*row*> , <*column*>

2.35 Tip: **Choose a 24-hour or 12-hour time display.**

The default time display is a 12-hour clock. If you prefer to have the clock display time in 24-hour format (as the DOS clock does when you enter the TIME command), include the following command in your CONFIG.DB file:

    HOURS = 24

To restore a 12-hour clock, use the HOURS = 12 setting.

Setting the CONFIRM Feature

2.36 Tip: **Set the CONFIRM operation during configuration.**

To ensure that a data value is correctly entered in a data field, use the CONFIRM command to control the cursor movement.

Normally, when you enter data in a data field with an Append or Edit operation, the cursor moves automatically to the next field as soon as the current field is filled. However, you can force the cursor to stay in the same data field. Then you can press Enter to confirm the entered value and make sure that the data value is correctly entered in the data field.

To keep the cursor in the data field after data entry, issue the SET CONFIRM ON command at the dot prompt before you begin entering data. (The default setting of the CONFIRM operation is OFF.) To invoke the CONFIRM operation before entering the program, include the CONFIRM = ON configuration line in the CONFIG.DB file.

Setting the DEBUG feature

2.37 Tip: **Set DEBUG during configuration.**

When you execute a dBASE IV program, you can locate all the program errors if you invoke the SET DEBUG ON command at the dot prompt. You also can invoke the DEBUG operation by including the DEBUG = ON configuration line in the CONFIG.DB file. To terminate the DEBUG operation, issue the SET DEBUG OFF command at the dot prompt.

Normally, when DEBUG is set to ON, all the error messages in the program you are executing are displayed on-screen. However, to avoid interference between the program's operations (such as requesting data entry) and the error messages, you can route the error messages to the printer by using the SET ECHO ON command in conjunction with SET DEBUG ON.

Specifying Decimals

2.38 Tip: **Specify the number of decimal places for displayed values during configuration.**

The minimum number of decimal places used by dBASE IV for displaying both the results of most numeric functions and arithmetic operations is set by default to two:

```
. ? SQRT(1Ø)
        3.16
. ? LOG(1Ø)
        2.3Ø
. ? EXP(1Ø)
     22Ø26.47
. ? 1Ø/3
        3.33
```

You have two choices for showing more decimal places in the results of these numeric functions and calculations. First, you can specify the value in the function argument with more decimal places. The returning values of the functions will then be displayed with the same number of decimals as the argument:

```
. ? SQRT(10.000000)
        3.162278
. ? LOG(10.00000)
        2.30259
. ? EXP(10.0000)
     22026.4658
. ? 10.0000000000/3
        3.3333333333
```

If the argument of these functions is a numeric memory variable, you can express the value in the desired number of decimal places when you assign it to the variable:

```
. A=10
        10
. ? LOG(A)
        2.30
. A=10.0000
     10.0000
. ? LOG(A)
        2.3026
. B=5.000
        5.000
. ? EXP(B)
     148.413
. ? A/B
        2.0000
```

Second, you can define the number of decimal places for these values by issuing the SET DECIMALS TO command at the dot prompt:

```
. SET DECIMALS TO < number of decimal places to display>
```

For example, when you set the number to 4 by using the SET DECIMALS TO command, the resulting values are displayed in 4 decimal places. A maximum of 15 decimal places can be set, and a minimum of 0.

```
. SET DECIMALS TO 4
. ? SQRT(10)
        3.1623
. ? LOG(10)
        2.3026
. ? EXP(10)
     22026.4658
```

```
. ? 10/3
         3.3333
. A=10
        10
. B=5
         5
. ? LOG(A)
        2.3026
. ? EXP(5)
       148.4132
. ? A/B
        2.0000
```

The number of decimal places also can be set by including the following line in the CONFIG.DB file:

DECIMALS = < *number of decimal places to display*>

Remember that the number of decimals defined by this step and the SET DECIMALS TO command applies to mathematical, trigonometric, and financial calculations.

Setting the DELETED Feature

2.39 Tip: **Set the DELETED feature during configuration.**

You can filter the records marked for deletion from the database file by using the SET DELETED command without the PACK operation.

Normally, to remove data records from the active database file, you first mark these records by issuing the DELETE command and then use the PACK command. However, before packing the data records, remember that the records marked for deletion are treated as unmarked records when you apply the LIST and LOCATE operations (see fig. 2.8).

Figure 2.8 shows that the records marked for deletion (records #4 and #7) still appeared when the LIST operation was executed. The record pointer pointed to the "deleted" record when the LOCATE command was performed. If you do not want to use these "deleted" records in the LIST and LOCATE operations, you can issue the SET DELETED ON command before the operations (see fig. 2.9).

```
. SET DELETE OFF
. USE EMPLOYEE
. DELETE FOR POSITION="Sales Rep"
      2 records deleted
. LIST
Record#  ID_NO        FIRST_NAME     LAST_NAME      POSITION    EMPLY_DATE MALE
      1  123-45-6789 Thomas T.       Smith          President   03/01/1981 .T.
      2  254-63-5691 Tina Y.         Thompson       VP          09/22/1982 .F.
      3  467-34-6789 Peter F.        Watson         Manager     10/12/1982 .T.
      4 *732-08-4589 Doris Y.        Taylor         Sales Rep   08/14/1983 .F.
      5  563-55-8900 Tyrone T.       Thorsen        Engineer    06/20/1982 .T.
      6  823-46-6213 Cathy J.        Faust          Secretary   04/15/1983 .F.
      7 *554-34-7893 Vincent M.      Corso          Sales Rep   07/20/1984 .T.
      8  321-65-9087 Jane W.         Kaiser         Accountant  11/22/1982 .F.
      9  560-56-9321 Tina K.         Davidson       Trainee     05/16/1986 .F.
     10  435-54-9876 James J.        Smith          Trainee     01/23/1986 .T.

. LOCATE FOR POSITION="Sales Rep"
Record =       4
. DISPLAY
Record#  ID_NO        FIRST_NAME     LAST_NAME      POSITION    EMPLY_DATE MALE
      4 *732-08-4589 Doris Y.        Taylor         Sales Rep   08/14/1983 .F.
```

Fig. 2.8. *Listing and locating deleted records.*

```
. SET DELETE ON
. LIST
Record#  ID_NO        FIRST_NAME     LAST_NAME      POSITION    EMPLY_DATE MALE
      1  123-45-6789 Thomas T.       Smith          President   03/01/1981 .T.
      2  254-63-5691 Tina Y.         Thompson       VP          09/22/1982 .F.
      3  467-34-6789 Peter F.        Watson         Manager     10/12/1982 .T.
      5  563-55-8900 Tyrone T.       Thorsen        Engineer    06/20/1982 .T.
      6  823-46-6213 Cathy J.        Faust          Secretary   04/15/1983 .F.
      8  321-65-9087 Jane W.         Kaiser         Accountant  11/22/1982 .F.
      9  560-56-9321 Tina K.         Davidson       Trainee     05/16/1986 .F.
     10  435-54-9876 James J.        Smith          Trainee     01/23/1986 .T.

. LOCATE FOR POSITION="Sales Rep"
End of LOCATE scope
. DISPLAY
Record#  ID_NO        FIRST_NAME     LAST_NAME      POSITION    EMPLY_DATE MALE
```

Fig. 2.9. *Effects of the SET DELETED ON command.*

Figure 2.9 shows that the records marked for deletion were not displayed by the LIST command. Furthermore, you cannot find these records by using the LOCATE operation.

The SET DELETED ON command, however, does not hide the "deleted" record from the GOTO, GO TOP, and GO BOTTOM operations.

2.40 Trap: **When you use SET DELETED ON, the records marked for deletion still are subject to the INDEX and REINDEX operations.**

Contrary to what you might expect, SET DELETED ON does not exclude any records marked for deletion when you apply the INDEX and REINDEX operations (see fig. 2.10).

```
. SET DELETE ON
. LIST
Record#  ID_NO       FIRST_NAME   LAST_NAME    POSITION    EMPLY_DATE MALE
      1  123-45-6789 Thomas T.    Smith        President   03/01/1981 .T.
      2  254-63-5691 Tina Y.      Thompson     VP          09/22/1982 .F.
      3  467-34-6789 Peter F.     Watson       Manager     10/12/1982 .T.
      5  563-55-8900 Tyrone T.    Thorsen      Engineer    06/20/1982 .T.
      6  823-46-6213 Cathy J.     Faust        Secretary   04/15/1983 .F.
      8  321-65-9087 Jane W.      Kaiser       Accountant  11/22/1982 .F.
      9  560-56-9321 Tina K.      Davidson     Trainee     05/16/1986 .F.
     10  435-54-9876 James J.     Smith        Trainee     01/23/1986 .T.

. INDEX ON LAST_NAME TO BYLAST
  100% indexed          10 Records indexed
.
```

Fig. 2.10. *Effects of the SET DELETED ON command on indexing records.*

For example, the EMPLOYEE.DBF database file contains 10 records—two that have been marked for deletion. However, when you index the database file, all the records are indexed.

2.41 Trap: **The records marked for deletion when you use SET DELETED ON will not be sorted by the SORT operation; they will be deleted.**

When you use SET DELETED ON, the records marked for deletion are excluded from the sorting operation. When you issue the SORT command, these records are removed from the database (see fig. 2.11).

```
. SET DELETE OFF
. LIST
Record#  ID_NO       FIRST_NAME    LAST_NAME    POSITION    EMPLY_DATE MALE
     7 *554-34-7893 Vincent M.    Corso        Sales Rep   07/20/1984 .T.
     9  560-56-9321 Tina K.       Davidson     Trainee     05/16/1986 .F.
     6  823-46-6213 Cathy J.      Faust        Secretary   04/15/1983 .F.
     8  321-65-9087 Jane W.       Kaiser       Accountant  11/22/1982 .F.
     1  123-45-6789 Thomas T.     Smith        President   03/01/1981 .T.
    10  435-54-9876 James J.      Smith        Trainee     01/23/1986 .T.
     4 *732-08-4589 Doris Y.      Taylor       Sales Rep   08/14/1983 .F.
     2  254-63-5691 Tina Y.       Thompson     VP          09/22/1982 .F.
     5  563-55-8900 Tyrone T.     Thorsen      Engineer    06/20/1982 .T.
     3  467-34-6789 Peter F.      Watson       Manager     10/12/1982 .T.

. SORT ON LAST_NAME TO SORTLAST
100% Sorted          10 Records sorted
. SET DELETE ON
. SORT ON FIRST_NAME TO SRTFIRST
100% Sorted           8 Records sorted
.
```

Fig. 2.11. Effects of the SET DELETED ON command on sorting records.

In addition to issuing the SET DELETED ON or SET DELETED OFF commands at the dot prompt, you also can include the DELETED = ON command in the CONFIG.DB file. If you do not set the DELETED command to ON, the program automatically sets the command to OFF.

Setting the DEVICE Feature

2.42 Tip: **Define output routing during configuration.**

Normally, output generated by @..SAY.. commands is displayed on-screen. You can, however, instruct the program to route the output to the printer by issuing the SET DEVICE TO PRINT command at the dot prompt or by including the DEVICE = PRINTER command in the CONFIG.DB file. The normal setting for the DEVICE command is SCREEN.

You may also send output to a file by using the following setting in your CONFIG.DB file:

DEVICE = FILE < *file name*>

Setting the ECHO Command

2.43 Tip: **Set the ECHO command during configuration.**

The ECHO operation instructs dBASE IV to display every command being executed so that you can monitor operations as they are completed by the program. This useful tool traces the execution process step-by-step. To invoke the ECHO operation, you insert the SET ECHO ON command at the beginning of your program or issue the command at the dot prompt. You can save a few keystrokes if you set the ECHO operation to ON by including the ECHO = ON command in the CONFIG.DB file.

If both the ECHO and DEBUG commands are on when you debug your program, all the commands are echoed automatically to the printer.

Using the Escape Feature

2.44 Tip: **Define ways to terminate dBASE IV operations during configuration.**

When you press the Esc key, you stop whatever the program is doing at the time. You can prevent the execution of an incorrect command by pressing Esc. If you press Esc in certain operations, however, you may get undesirable results. For example, if you accidentally press Esc when you enter data in a record, all the data you entered is lost. When you rearrange data records with one of the SORT, INDEX, or REINDEX operations, the integrity of the data can be damaged if you press Esc. You therefore need to disable the Esc key for these and other database applications.

To disable the Esc key, issue the SET ESCAPE OFF command at the dot prompt or in the program. Or, you can include the ESCAPE = OFF command in your CONFIG.DB file.

(Note that SET ESCAPE OFF also disables the Ctrl-S key, which is used to suspend scrolling of text on-screen.)

Defining Match Control

2.45 Tip: **Define data match control during configuration.**

When you use the LOCATE, FIND, or SEEK commands to search data records in a database file, the program matches only as many characters as specified in the search key. For example, if you want to find only the employee whose first name is Jo, you normally issue these commands:

```
. USE EMPLOYEE
. LOCATE FOR FIRST_NAME = "Jo"
```

Unless you instruct the program to do otherwise, all the first names that begin with "Jo" (such as Joe, Joseph, John, and Jon) are considered a match. To ensure that the program searches for the employee's exact first name (Jo), you can issue the SET EXACT ON command at the dot prompt. Or, you can specify the EXACT = ON command in the CONFIG.DB file. As a result, the search operation finds only the record that yields an exact match.

2.46 Tip: **Use the NEAR option to locate an approximate record match.**

If you issue the SET NEAR ON command, or if you include the statement NEAR = ON in the CONFIG.DB file, when you search for a record and a match is not found, the record pointer is positioned at the record that most closely resembles the one sought. You can then use Edit or Browse to view the records in the vicinity of the place where the record would have been. Ordinarily, with NEAR set to OFF, the record pointer is set to the end of the file if a match is not found.

Remember that NEAR indicates the position of the record pointer after an unsuccessful search—either at the end-of-file marker or at the next record. EXACT indicates the comparison of two strings. EXACT does not indicate whether the strings were found or not, nor does it indicate the position of the record pointer.

Setting the HEADING Fields

2.47 Tip: **Set the field HEADING ON or OFF during configuration.**

When you use the LIST, DISPLAY, SUM, or AVERAGE commands, the output to be displayed also includes the column headings of field names and their related information. These headings can be suppressed either by issuing the SET HEADING OFF command at the dot prompt or by including the HEADING = OFF command in the CONFIG.DB file.

Setting the HELP Feature

2.48 Tip: **Deactivate the HELP feature during configuration.**

Normally, when you enter an incorrect command, dBASE IV displays a pop-up window offering Help options: Cancel the command, Edit the command syntax, or get more Help. You can suppress this Help window by using the SET HELP OFF command or by including the HELP = OFF command in the CONFIG.DB file. The HELP command does not activate or disable the F1 (Help) function key, however.

Using the INSTRUCT Command

2.49 Tip: **You can disable instruction boxes using the INSTRUCT command.**

The first time you use full-screen operations such as Browse, Append, or Edit at the dBASE IV dot prompt, or when you select certain operations from the Control Center menu, an instruction box is displayed. You can suppress instruction boxes with the SET INSTRUCT OFF command or by including INSTRUCT = OFF in your CONFIG.DB file.

Also, if you press Enter when the cursor is on a file name in the Control Center menu, a special instruction box that offers the selections USE FILE, MODIFY STRUCTURE/ORDER, or DISPLAY DATA is displayed. If INSTRUCT is set to OFF, pressing Enter activates the USE command.

Setting the HISTORY Buffer

2.50 Tip: **Set the size of the HISTORY buffer during configuration.**

One of the powerful features in dBASE IV is the capability to save the commands you have just entered in an area called the HISTORY buffer. Later, the buffer's contents can be replayed like a script. (Chapter 3 discusses how to activate and use the HISTORY buffer in database management operations.)

Before saving a set of commands in a HISTORY buffer, you need to define the size of the buffer in terms of the maximum number of commands you anticipate storing. To establish the size of the HISTORY buffer in the CONFIG.DB file, use the following command:

HISTORY = < *number of commands*>

Although the default limit is 20, the HISTORY buffer can hold up to 16,000 commands. After setting the buffer size, you can start saving commands in the HISTORY file by issuing the SET HISTORY ON command at the dot prompt. Use the SET HISTORY OFF command at the dot prompt to terminate the saving operation.

Setting the MARGIN

2.51 Tip: **Define a report MARGIN during configuration.**

When you print reports and screen output, you can set the left margin by issuing this MARGIN command in the CONFIG.DB file:

MARGIN = < *number of characters*>

Setting the MEMOWIDTH

2.52 Tip: **Set the MEMOWIDTH on the screen display during configuration.**

You can use memo fields to store large blocks of textual data. If you try to display memo fields that are wider than your screen, however, your text will be displayed in a disorganized manner. To display such memo fields, you specify the desired memo width in the CONFIG.DB file by using the following line:

MEMOWIDTH = < *number of characters*>

The width (number of characters) specified in the command determines the width of the text displayed on-screen or the printer. The minimum number of characters specified for the width of a memo field is 5; the maximum is 250. The default width is 50 characters.

Setting the Default Printer Driver

2.53 Tip: **Put your default printer-driver specification in your CONFIG.DB file.**

With dBASE IV, you can use up to four different printers. Each type of printer uses a "driver" file that converts text formatting codes to instructions the printer can use to format your reports properly. (dBASE IV printer-driver files can be identified on your program disks as those with the extension .PR2). The default printer-driver file can be specified in your CONFIG.DB file as follows:

PDRIVER = < *file name*>

For example, to use the GENERIC.PR2 file (which will work with almost any printer), the statement would read as follows:

PDRIVER = GENERIC.PR2

This value is stored in the system variable _PDRIVER. To determine the current default driver from the dBASE IV dot prompt, you can type the following:

. ? _pdriver

2.54 Tip:

Specify printers, fonts, and output ports in your configuration file.

You can have up to four different printers configured in your CONFIG.DB file. Then you can choose a printer from dBASE IV by using the pull-down printer-selection menu.

To specify the printers in your CONFIG.DB file, use the PRINTER statement:

> PRINTER < *number*> = < *driver file*> NAME < *printer name*>
>   DEVICE < *device*>

number must be a number from 1 to 4. The optional *printer name* should be a character string; this name will appear on the pull-down printer-selection menu in dBASE IV. The optional *device* should be a valid printer port, such as LPT1, as in the following examples:

```
PRINTER 1 = OKI2410.PR2 NAME "OKIDATA Pacemark 2410"
    DEVICE LPT1

PRINTER 2 = DIAB630A.PR2 NAME "Diablo (Xerox) 630 API"
    DEVICE COM1

PRINTER 3 = HPLAS100.PR2 NAME "Hewlett-Packard LaserJet"
    DEVICE LPT2

PRINTER 4 = GENERIC.PR2 NAME "Generic Driver"
    DEVICE COM2
```

2.55 Tip:

Install printer fonts in your configuration file.

You can also use the PRINTER command in your CONFIG.DB file to specify type fonts that will be used when printing reports. (See Chapter 8 for more information on printing reports and labels). Use the following format:

> PRINTER < *number*> FONT < *number*> = < *begin code*>,
>   < *end code*> NAME < *name*>

The printer *number* corresponds to the number of the printer installed with the previous PRINTER command. You can designate up to five fonts for each printer, so the font *number* must be 1 through 5. The *begin code* and *end code* values indicate the codes your printer requires to turn the desired font on or off. (See your printer manual for a list of appropriate codes.) The optional NAME clause includes a string specifying the *name* for the font.

For example, to use expanded type with the OKIDATA® 2410 printer, you send the following sequence to the printer:

Esc A Esc C

To cancel expanded type, you send the sequence Esc Z. The following command installs expanded type as font number 2:

PRINTER 1 FONT 2 = {ESC} A {ESC} C , {ESC} Z
    NAME "Expanded type"

Setting the SAFETY Feature

2.56 Tip: **SAFETY is set ON by default.**

The SAFETY = ON default warns you before executing commands that will overwrite an existing file. You are offered the choice of overwriting the file or canceling the operation. If you cancel the operation, you may want to specify a new file name. This safety feature prevents you from accidentally erasing a file by replacing it with new data. If SAFETY is OFF, you do not receive the warning message. In most cases, it is not advisable to set SAFETY OFF.

Setting the Path for SQL (Structured Query Language)

2.57 Tip: **Set the path for the SQL directory in your configuration file.**

So that you can access the SQL (Structured Query Language) database operations from dBASE IV, you should specify the location of your SQL files. Include this information in your CONFIG.DB file by using the following commands:

SQLDATABASE = < *directory*>
SQLHOME = < *directory*>

Following is an example:

SQLDATABASE = C:\DBASE\SQLSAMPL
SQLHOME = C:\DBASE\SQLHOME

See Appendix D for a complete list of SQL commands.

Setting the STATUS line

2.58 Tip: **Set the STATUS line ON or OFF.**

The status line appears at the bottom of the screen during most dBASE IV operations. It shows you the default disk drive, the current record number, whether the Insert key has been engaged, if the current record is marked for deletion, and other information. To turn off this display, use the SET STATUS OFF command or enter the following line in your CONFIG.DB file:

    STATUS = OFF

Setting the TYPEAHEAD Buffer

2.59 Tip: **Set the size of the keyboard buffer during configuration.**

As you enter program commands from the keyboard, your keystrokes are stored temporarily (and in sequence) in a typeahead buffer. If the buffer is filled before you finish typing, you will hear a warning beep.

The typeahead buffer normally holds 20 keystrokes. This small buffer size can be restrictive when you type fast or when you want to enter several commands at one time from the keyboard. If you are concerned about running out of space, you can increase the size of the keyboard buffer by using the TYPEAHEAD command. The size of the typeahead buffer can be increased up to 32,000 keystrokes in the CONFIG.DB file with the following line:

    TYPEAHEAD = < *number of keystrokes*>

Following is an example:

    TYPEAHEAD = 100

If you set the typeahead buffer size to zero, the INKEY and ON KEY commands are disabled.

Part II

Working with Data

Includes

Creating and Modifying Databases

Entering and Editing Data

Organizing Data

Sorting and Indexing Data

Displaying Data

Generating Mailing Lists and Reports

3

Creating and Modifying Databases

Every database management program organizes its data in a unique way; dBASE IV is no exception. This chapter discusses the organization of data in dBASE IV, and the tips, tricks, and traps deal with managing your database material and using dBASE IV techniques and features to modify your database to suit your needs.

Understanding the Layout of a Database File

You can make costly errors if you don't understand the layout of database files and how to rearrange the elements of the database properly. This section discusses the layout of the database file, and the tips, tricks, and traps are intended to help you create and modify your database more efficiently.

Understanding the File Header

The file header contains valuable information: the structure of the file, the record count, and the date of the last update. The data record section contains the actual data records, and the end-of-file (EOF) marker tells dBASE IV where to stop reading records.

3.1 Tip: **Use the information in the file header to find the record you want quickly.**

The record-count and record-length information contained in the header allows the program to find a specified record in the database file without reading every record in the file. For example, when you use the GOTO command (as in GOTO 38), the number of bytes GOTO moves within the file is calculated by multiplying the record number by the record length, plus the length of the header. This calculation yields the byte position of the beginning of the desired record.

If you issue the GO BOTTOM command at the dot prompt and you know the current record number and the total number of records in the file, the program can position its record pointer at the desired record and not have to search the record section sequentially.

3.2 Tip: **To determine the date of your last update of a file, check the information in the file header.**

The LIST STRUCTURE or DISPLAY STRUCTURE command displays all the data fields and their attributes, as well as the number of records in the file and the date of the last update (see fig. 3.1).

```
. USE EMPLOYEE
. DISP STRU
Structure for database: C:\DB4\EMPLOYEE.DBF
Number of data records:        0
Date of last update    : 09/29/88
Field  Field Name  Type       Width    Dec    Index
    1  ID_NO       Character     11              N
    2  FIRST_NAME  Character     15              N
    3  LAST_NAME   Character     15              N
    4  POSITION    Character     10              N
    5  EMPLY_DATE  Date           8              N
    6  MALE        Logical        1              N
** Total **                     61
```

Fig. 3.1. Displaying the file structure of EMPLOYEE.DBF.

Notice the character count in the Field Width column of figure 3.1. If you add all the field widths (11 + 15 + 15 + 10 + 8 + 1), the sum is 60 instead of 61, as shown after ** Total **. The extra character is reserved for the deletion marker after you issue the DELETE command.

Also note the Index column in figure 3.1. If the file structure was created in dBASE IV, you were given the option of including an index tag for any of the fields in a production index file. A Y in the Index column would indicate that an index tag had been created for that field. (See Chapter 6 for more information on indexing.)

Understanding the Record Counter and End-of-File Marker

3.3 Trap: **The record count in your file will not be updated if you exit the file improperly.**

Usually, every time you add new records to the database file (by using one of the APPEND or INSERT commands) or remove records from the database file (by using the ZAP command or the DELETE and PACK commands), the record count is updated accordingly.

If you improperly exit from the data-entry operation, however, the record count will not be updated, even though you may have added new records to the file. The record count will be smaller than the actual number of records in the file. As a result, you will not have access to all the records in the file when the database file is selected.

On the other hand, if you improperly exit from the data deletion process (by resetting the computer during the Pack or Zap operation, for example), the record count is not updated after certain records are permanently removed from the file. In this case, the record count shows more records than are actually in the file. As a result, the cursor reaches the end-of-file marker before the program retrieves the correct number of records.

Note that using the DIR or LIST/DISPLAY FILES commands does not accurately reflect the new record count after a Pack until the file is closed.

3.4 Tip: **Data records are saved sequentially.**

As shown in figure 3.2, the contents of the first data record (123-45-6789 Thomas T, . . .) are stored right after the file header. Information about the other data records is saved sequentially in this section.

```
. USE EMPLOYEE
. LIST
Record#  ID_NO        FIRST_NAME    LAST_NAME     POSITION    EMPLY_DATE MALE
      1  123-45-6789 Thomas T.      Smith         President   03/01/1981 .T.
      2  254-63-5691 Tina Y.        Thompson      VP          09/22/1982 .F.
      3  467-34-6789 Peter F.       Watson        Manager     10/12/1982 .T.
      4  732-88-4589 Doris Y.       Taylor        Sales Rep   08/14/1983 .F.
      5  563-55-8900 Tyrone T.      Thorsen       Engineer    06/20/1982 .T.
      6  823-46-6213 Cathy J.       Faust         Secretary   04/15/1983 .F.
      7  554-34-7893 Vincent M.     Corso         Sales Rep   07/20/1984 .T.
      8  321-65-9087 Jane W.        Kaiser        Accountant  11/22/1982 .F.
      9  560-56-9321 Tina K.        Davidson      Trainee     05/16/1986 .F.
     10  435-54-9876 James J.       Smith         Trainee     01/23/1986 .T.
```

Fig. 3.2. Listing records in the EMPLOYEE.DBF file.

3.5 Tip: **The end-of-file marker tells the program where to stop reading.**

When you issue the LIST command, the program continuously lists the contents of the records until it reaches the end-of-file marker. Similarly, when you search a database for a record with a particular key field (by using the LOCATE, SEEK, or FIND commands, for example) and the end-of-file marker is encountered, you are told that no record matching the key field exists.

Displaying the Layout of a Database File

3.6 Tip: **To examine the information saved in your data records, use the LIST or DISPLAY ALL command.**

You can examine records, such as the employment records in figure 3.2, by using either the LIST or DISPLAY ALL command.

3.7 Trap: **You cannot use the dBASE IV commands to display the layout of a file.**

The information in a database file is saved in an ASCII format, including various control characters. You cannot, however, use commands such as LIST, DISPLAY, or TYPE to display the actual layout of the file components. For example, if you issue the TYPE SOFTWR.DBF command at the dot prompt, the program displays scrambled text and incomprehensible symbols (see fig. 3.3).

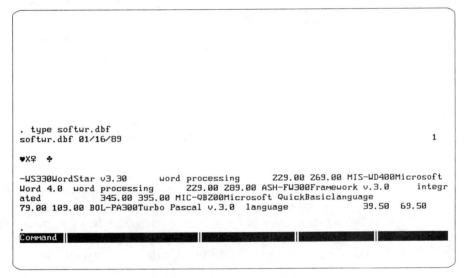

```
. type softwr.dbf
softwr.dbf 01/16/89                                                    1

♥X♀  ♣

-WS330WordStar v3.30      word processing     229.00 269.00 MIS-WD400Microsoft
Word 4.0   word processing      229.00 289.00 ASH-FW300Framework v.3.0      integr
ated           345.00 395.00 MIC-QBZ00Microsoft QuickBasiclanguage
79.00 109.00 BOL-PA300Turbo Pascal v.3.0  language           39.50  69.50
.
┌─────────┐
│Command  │
└─────────┘
```

Fig. 3.3. *Displaying a database file by using the TYPE command.*

3.8 Tip: **Use DEBUG.COM to examine the layout of the database file.**

You can examine the actual layout of the database file by using DEBUG.COM (a file that comes with the DOS system disk). To display the contents of a file, copy the DEBUG.COM file to the directory that contains that file. Then issue the DEBUG command at the DOS prompt.

For the EMPLOYEE.DBF file, you type the following command at the C> prompt:

DEBUG EMPLOYEE.DBF

In response to the command, the DEBUG file displays a dash [-] prompt to ask for the next command (see fig. 3.4).

```
C>DEBUG EMPLOYEE.DBF
-D
3306:0100  03 57 01 1A 0A 00 00 00-E1 00 3D 00 00 00 00 00   .W........a.=.....
3306:0110  00 00 00 00 00 00 00 00-00 00 00 00 00 00 00 00   ................
3306:0120  49 44 5F 4E 4F 00 00 00-00 00 00 43 09 00 A0 40   ID_NO......C..@
3306:0130  0B 00 00 00 01 00 00 00-00 00 00 00 00 00 00 00   ................
3306:0140  46 49 52 53 54 5F 4E 41-4D 45 00 43 14 00 A0 40   FIRST_NAME.C..@
3306:0150  0F 00 00 AA A1 AA AA 00-00 00 00 00 00 00 00 00   ................
3306:0160  4C 41 53 54 5F 4E 41 4D-45 00 00 43 23 00 A0 40   LAST_NAME..C#.@
3306:0170  0F 00 00 00 01 00 00 00-00 00 00 00 00 00 00 00   ................
-D
3306:0180  50 4F 53 49 54 49 4F 4E-00 00 43 32 00 A0 40       POSITION...C2.@
3306:0190  0A 00 00 00 01 00 00 00-00 00 00 00 00 00 00 00   ................
3306:01A0  45 4D 50 4C 59 5F 44 41-54 45 00 44 3C 00 A0 40   EMPLY_DATE.D<.@
3306:01B0  00 00 00 00 01 00 00 00-00 00 00 00 00 00 00 00   ................
3306:01C0  4D 41 4C 45 00 00 00 00-00 00 00 4C 44 00 A0 40   MALE.......LD.@
3306:01D0  01 00 00 00 01 00 00 00-00 00 00 00 00 00 00 00   ................
3306:01E0  0D 20 31 32 33 2D 34 35-2D 36 37 38 39 54 68 6F   . 123-45-6789Tho
3306:01F0  6D 61 73 20 54 2E 20 20-20 20 20 20 53 6D 69 74   mas T.      Smit
-Q

C>
```

Fig. 3.4. *Using the DOS DEBUG command to display the contents of a database file.*

You then can enter the letter D to Display (or Dump) a section of the database file contents. The program displays the first eight lines of the file and then asks you for another command. When you enter D (for Display), another set of eight lines is displayed. To terminate the display and exit from the DEBUG program, enter Q (for Quit).

3.9 Tip: **The display is divided into three major columns.**

The first column (3306:0100, for example, in fig. 3.4) is a set of numbers that represents the memory locations where the file contents are stored. The numbers may appear differently on your screen, depending on your computer system and the RAM-resident programs (SideKick® and a RAM disk, for example) that you loaded into memory before you invoked the DEBUG program.

The middle column is a section of numeric codes (in hexadecimal format) that corresponds to the contents of the file displayed in the third column. If you are not familiar with hexadecimal numbers, you can think of them as machine codes that are relevant only to the computer. They are not significant for examining the file's contents.

The third column contains the actual contents of the database file. In addition to some control characters, you see field names such as ID_NO, FIRST_NAME, and LAST_NAME.

Saving Data to Disk and Closing Files

If you experience system errors that cause you to shut off your computer and restart it before you close the file, you may lose some or all of the new records you have entered. A power failure during your data-entry process also can have a disastrous effect on the integrity of your data records. The tips, tricks, and traps in this section tell you how to save data and close files properly so that you do not lose any important information.

3.10 Trick: **To avoid losing data, close your file frequently when entering new records.**

When you add data records to an existing database file by issuing the APPEND or INSERT command, the information is not saved immediately in the disk file. Instead, the information is held temporarily in the RAM working area. Similarly, at this point, only the record count in RAM is updated; the record count of the database file on the disk is not revised.

The data records and updated record count held in the RAM working area are copied back to the disk file only when you close the file. When you modify the contents of your database, exit to the dot prompt by pressing Ctrl-End—not the Esc key—to close a file.

3.11 Trick: **Use the AUTOSAVE feature to avoid data loss.**

Use the SET AUTOSAVE ON command to tell dBASE IV to save records to disk after each record is changed, rather than waiting for the record buffer to fill. That way, in case the program is interrupted by a power loss or other problem, records in the buffer won't be lost. The default is AUTOSAVE OFF, which permits you to abort editing of records without saving changes.

3.12 Trick: **To close an active file without opening another one, issue the USE command.**

You can close an active database file with the USE command:

. USE XYZ

. . . . .

. USE

You also can close an active file by replacing it with another database file in the current active work area. Issue the USE command and type the name of the file that will replace the active one, as in the following example:

. USE XYZ

. . . . .

. USE ABC

When you issue the USE ABC command while the XYZ database is active in the work area, the active database closes.

3.13 Tip: **You can close multiple files with one command.**

CLOSE ALL closes dBASE IV files that are currently open. These files include all the database (.DBF), format (.FMT), index (.NDX), label (.LBL), memo (.DBT), query (.QRY), text (.TXT), and view (.VUE) files. Work area 1 is selected.

CLOSE DATABASES closes only the database, index, and format files that are open in the work areas. It does not affect work area 10, where catalog files are located, if a catalog is in use.

3.14 Tip: **Only one work area is active.**

Although you can simultaneously open as many as 10 files in 10 separate work areas, only one area can be the active or primary work area. The other areas are inactive or secondary work areas.

3.15 Trick: **You can access data from other work areas in dBASE IV.**

Although you can select only one work area at a time, dBASE IV does allow certain commands and functions to operate on files in unselected work areas. This feature is called *alias support*. As an example, if work area 1 was selected, you can USE a file in work area 2 by executing the following command:

. USE <*file*> IN 2

Creating Database Structures

Before you can begin entering and using data, you must define the structure of your database file. Whether you are creating a new file from scratch or using the structure of an existing file, the tricks and traps in this section will help you create and modify the database structure for greater efficiency.

Using the CREATE Command

The CREATE command calls up the database design screen, which allows you to enter information about the structure of the database you want to create.

The CREATE command, used to create new database files, has the following syntax:

. CREATE <*file name*>

You can also create a file by highlighting the <**create**> option in the Data column from the Control Center and then pressing Enter. (For more information on using the database design screen, refer to the section "Modifying Data Structure.")

3.16 Trick: **Use an indirect reference when creating a database file.**

dBASE IV enables you to use an indirect reference in place of the actual file name when you use the CREATE command. An indirect reference must be a character expression. For example, if the memory variable MNAME contains the string "YOURFILE.DBF", you can substitute the variable in parentheses for the file name:

. MNAME = "YOURFILE.DBF"
. CREATE (MNAME)

You can also use macro substitutions as in the following example:

```
. MNAME = "YOURFILE.DBF"
. CREATE &MNAME
```

See Chapter 9 for more information on memory variables and macros.

Borrowing an Existing Data Structure

3.17 Tip: **Use the COPY STRUCTURE TO command to borrow a data structure from an existing database file.**

Often you need to duplicate part or all of the contents of a file in a new file. For example, you can borrow the structure from one set of data files to create a set of new tables for other applications. Or, if the data related to all your products is stored in a database file, you can split the contents into several files.

To borrow structure from an existing database file, use the following procedure:

1. Select the database file from which you are borrowing the structure.

2. Use the COPY STRUCTURE TO command to copy the structure to a new database file.

You might, for instance, own a small computer store and want to create a new file to store information about the items you have in stock. To borrow the structure from an existing database file (PRODUCTS.DBF) to create a new database file (HARDWARE.DBF), issue the following commands:

```
. USE PRODUCTS
. COPY STRUCTURE TO HARDWARE
```

After these two commands are given, the program sets up a new database file (HARDWARE.DBF) that has the borrowed structure. To examine the data structure, select the database file and issue the DISPLAY STRUCTURE command after the dot prompt (see fig. 3.5).

```
. USE PRODUCTS
. COPY STRUCTURE TO HARDWARE
. USE HARDWARE
. DISPLAY STRUCTURE
Structure for database: C:\DB4\HARDWARE.DBF
Number of data records:        0
Date of last update   : 09/30/88
Field  Field Name  Type       Width    Dec    Index
    1  STOCK_NO    Character     9               N
    2  DIVISION    Character     2               N
    3  TYPE        Character    20               N
    4  COST        Numeric       7      2        N
    5  PRICE       Numeric       7      2        N
** Total **                     46

. _
```

Fig. 3.5. *Copying an existing file structure in a new database file.*

Splitting the Contents of an Existing Database File

3.18 Trick: **Organize your data in a master file.**

With many database-management applications, you can organize your data effectively by storing all the data records for a particular item in one master file. You can then store subsets of the records in their own files. For example, you can store—in a master database PRODUCTS.DBF file—all the products your store carries (see fig. 3.6).

You can split the master database file into two database files—one that saves the data for the hardware items and another that stores information about the software products. For example, you can copy the data structure from PRODUCTS.DBF to two new database files named HARDWARE.DBF and SOFTWARE.DBF:

```
. USE PRODUCTS
. COPY STRUCTURE TO HARDWARE
. COPY STRUCTURE TO SOFTWARE
```

```
. LIST
Record#  STOCK_NO DIVISION TYPE                COST   PRICE
    1    CPQ-SP256 HW      system            1359.00 1895.00
    2    ZEN-SL101 HW      system            1695.00 2399.00
    3    IBM-AT640 HW      system            3790.00 4490.00
    4    ZEN-MM012 HW      monitor             89.00  159.00
    5    NEC-PC660 HW      printer            560.00  820.00
    6    HAY-M1200 HW      modem              269.00  389.00
    7    SEA-HD020 HW      hard disk          390.00  495.00
    8    IOM-HD040 HW      hard disk         2190.00 2790.00
    9    PAR-GC100 HW      graphic card       279.00  389.00
   10    HER-GC100 HW      graphic card       199.00  239.00
   11    ASH-DB300 SW      database           395.00  595.00
   12    ANS-DB110 SW      database           525.00  695.00
   13    CLP-DB100 SW      database compiler  450.00  595.00
   14    WOR-DB100 SW      database compiler  469.00  595.00
   15    LOT-L0123 SW      spread sheet       289.00  359.00
   16    MIC-WS330 SW      word processing    229.00  269.00
   17    MIS-WD300 SW      word processing    229.00  289.00
   18    AST-FW200 SW      integrated         345.00  395.00
   19    MIC-QB100 SW      language            79.00  109.00
   20    BOL-PA300 SW      language            39.50   69.50
```

Fig. 3.6. *Data records in the PRODUCTS.DBF file.*

Once you've created the structures of the HARDWARE.DBF and
SOFTWARE.DBF database files, you can copy selected records in the
master database file and save them in the new files. To do so, use the
following APPEND FROM command and the necessary filtering condition:

. APPEND FROM < *database file*> < *filtering condition*>

The filtering condition determines which set of records will be
affected by the APPEND FROM operation. Following are examples:

. APPEND FROM PRODUCTS FOR RECNO( )>=11
. APPEND FROM PRODUCTS FOR DIVISION="HW"
. APPEND FROM PRODUCTS FOR TYPE="printer"
. APPEND FROM PRODUCTS FOR DIVISION=1"SW" .AND. TYPE="database"
. APPEND FROM PRODUCTS FOR PRICE>=200.00
. APPEND FROM PRODUCTS FOR (PRICE-COST)>100

To copy all the records related to the hardware products from
PRODUCTS.DBF to HARDWARE.DBF, use the FOR DIVISION="HW"
filtering condition in the APPEND FROM command (see fig. 3.7).

Similarly, you use the FOR DIVISION="SW" filtering condition in the APPEND FROM command to copy all the records related to the software items from the master database file to the SOFTWARE.DBF database file (see fig. 3.8).

```
. USE HARDWARE
. LIST

. APPEND FROM PRODUCTS FOR DIVISION="HW"
      10 records added
. LIST
Record#  STOCK_NO  DIVISION  TYPE              COST    PRICE
      1  CPQ-SP256 HW        system         1359.00  1895.00
      2  ZEN-SL181 HW        system         1695.00  2399.00
      3  IBM-AT640 HW        system         3790.00  4490.00
      4  ZEN-MM012 HW        monitor          89.00   159.00
      5  NEC-PC660 HW        printer         560.00   820.00
      6  HAY-M1200 HW        modem           269.00   389.00
      7  SEA-HD020 HW        hard disk       398.00   495.00
      8  IOM-HD040 HW        hard disk      2190.00  2790.00
      9  PAR-GC100 HW        graphic card    279.00   389.00
     10  HER-GC100 HW        graphic card    199.00   239.00
```

Fig. 3.7. *Appending hardware records from the PRODUCTS.DBF database file.*

Using the HISTORY Buffer

The HISTORY buffer is a handy reference file for reviewing the commands you've issued using the dot prompt. When you are creating or modifying a database, the information in the HISTORY buffer can be quite useful. For example, during the data-manipulation process, you might have forgotten the name of the database you created or the name of the index file you used for rearranging the records in a certain file. By listing the contents of the HISTORY buffer, you can retrieve the name of the database and index file.

```
. USE SOFTWARE
. LIST

. APPEND FROM PRODUCTS FOR DIVISION="SW"
     10 records added
. LIST
Record#  STOCK_NO  DIVISION  TYPE                     COST    PRICE
      1  ASH-DB300  SW        database               395.00   595.00
      2  AN3-DB110  SW        database               525.00   695.00
      3  CLP-DB100  SW        database compiler      450.00   595.00
      4  WOR-DB100  SW        database compiler      469.00   595.00
      5  LOT-LO123  SW        spread sheet           289.00   359.00
      6  MIC-WS330  SW        word processing        229.00   269.00
      7  MIS-WD300  SW        word processing        229.00   289.00
      8  AST-FW200  SW        integrated             345.00   395.00
      9  MIC-QB100  SW        language                79.00   109.00
     10  BOL-PA300  SW        language                39.50    69.50
```

Fig. 3.8. *Appending software records from the PRODUCTS.DBF database file.*

Displaying the Contents of the HISTORY Buffer

3.19 Tip: **Use the HISTORY buffer to review previously issued commands.**

Each time you issue a dot prompt command, the program saves the command in a temporary HISTORY buffer. HISTORY is not a disk file, so you cannot assign it a file name.

The default size of the HISTORY buffer is 20 commands. When the buffer is full, new commands replace—in a first-in, first-out order—the ones entered earlier. As a result, while the cursor is at the dot prompt, you can use the LIST HISTORY command to display as many as 20 previously entered commands (see fig. 3.9).

When you issue the LIST HISTORY command, the commands are displayed in the order they were saved in the HISTORY buffer (see fig. 3.9). The first two commands (SET HISTORY TO Ø and SET HISTORY TO 4Ø) clear the contents of the current buffer and prepare to save a set of new commands.

```
. SET HISTORY TO 0
. SET HISTORY TO 40
. USE SOFTWARE
. DISPLAY NEXT 2
Record#  STOCK_NO  DSCRIPTION          TYPE                 COST    PRICE
      1  ASH-DB400 dBASE IV v 1.0       database           495.00  795.00
      2  ANS-DB110 Paradox v.1.1        database           525.00  695.00
. LIST FOR RECNO()=6
Record#  STOCK_NO  DSCRIPTION          TYPE                 COST    PRICE
      6  MIC-WS330 WordStar v3.30       word processing    229.00  269.00

. LIST HISTORY
USE SOFTWARE
DISPLAY NEXT 2
LIST FOR RECNO()=6
LIST HISTORY


. _
```

Fig. 3.9. *Listing the contents of HISTORY.*

3.20 Tip: **Display a selected portion of the HISTORY buffer.**

Use the LAST option of the LIST HISTORY command to specify the number of command lines you want to display. For example, if you want to see only the last eight commands that were issued, use the following command:

. LIST HISTORY LAST 8

Working with the HISTORY Buffer

3.21 Tip: **You can enlarge your HISTORY buffer.**

The default size of the HISTORY buffer is 20 commands. However, you can specify the size you want by using the SET HISTORY TO command:

. SET HISTORY TO < *number of commands*>

You can specify as many as 16,000 commands in SET HISTORY TO.

3.22 Trick: **To clear the HISTORY buffer, first set the buffer size to zero.**

Whenever you want to flush the buffer and begin saving a new stream of commands, set the HISTORY buffer size to zero and then reset the size to a desired number of commands. For example, if the current size of the HISTORY buffer is 40, you can clear the buffer's contents by issuing these commands:

```
. SET HISTORY TO 0
. SET HISTORY TO 40
```

If you set HISTORY to a number less than the number of commands currently in the buffer, the dBASE IV program erases all the existing commands.

Saving HISTORY to a File

3.23 Trick: **Save the HISTORY buffer in a disk file.**

When you issue the SET HISTORY TO 0 command to empty the buffer or issue the QUIT command to leave a session, the program erases the current contents of the HISTORY buffer. You can, however, save the contents of the HISTORY buffer to a file by using the TO FILE option of the LIST HISTORY command:

```
. LIST HISTORY TO FILE < file name>
```

3.24 Tip: **Print the HISTORY buffer.**

You can produce a printed copy of the HISTORY buffer by using the TO PRINTER option of the LIST HISTORY command:

```
. LIST HISTORY TO PRINTER
```

You can also combine the TO PRINTER option or the TO FILE option with the LAST option. For example, to print the last five command lines in the HISTORY buffer, you use the following command:

```
. LIST HISTORY LAST 5 TO PRINTER
```

Modifying Data Structure

When you change the attributes or the number of data fields in a database file, you change the structure of the file. The most direct method for changing the structure of a database file is the MODIFY STRUCTURE command. The tips, tricks, and traps in this section help you change the structure of your database file to meet your needs.

Using the MODIFY STRUCTURE Command

3.25 Tip: **You can change the structure of a database file.**

To modify the structure of the HARDWARE.DBF file, you issue the following commands:

```
. USE HARDWARE
. MODIFY STRUCTURE
```

After executing these commands, the program displays the structure of the active database file on-screen (see fig. 3.10). You then can use the editing keys provided by the program to make the necessary changes. When all the changes are made, press Ctrl-End to save the modified structure in the file.

Converting Character Fields to Numeric Fields

3.26 Trap: **You can lose valuable data while converting a character field to a numeric field.**

If the file whose structure you want to modify has some data records in it, be cautious. The nonnumeric characters in a character field will be dropped if you convert to a numeric field. For example, if the contents of your character field named ACCT_NO (account number) combine character strings and numeric digits (A1234, $123-45-6789, and so on), some or all of the field contents will be lost if you convert the field to a numeric field.

The amount of information you lose depends on the contents of the character field. In general, if the contents of the character field begin with numeric digits (such as 123-45-6789, as in a Social Security

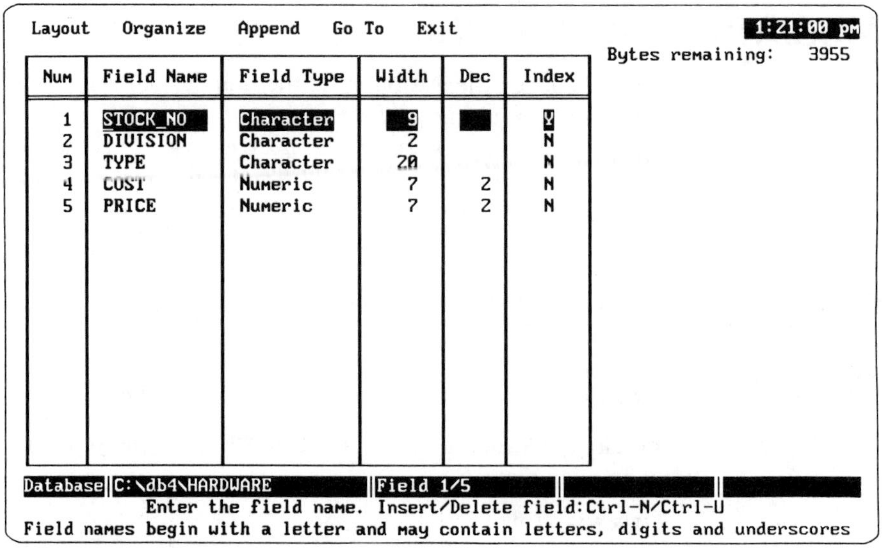

```
 Layout   Organize   Append   Go To   Exit                    1:21:00 pm
                                                 Bytes remaining:    3955
 ┌─────┬────────────┬─────────────┬───────┬──────┬───────┐
 │ Num │ Field Name │ Field Type  │ Width │ Dec  │ Index │
 ├─────┼────────────┼─────────────┼───────┼──────┼───────┤
 │   1 │ STOCK_NO   │ Character   │   9   │      │   Y   │
 │   2 │ DIVISION   │ Character   │   2   │      │   N   │
 │   3 │ TYPE       │ Character   │  2A   │      │   N   │
 │   4 │ COST       │ Numeric     │   7   │  2   │   N   │
 │   5 │ PRICE      │ Numeric     │   7   │  2   │   N   │
 │     │            │             │       │      │       │
 │     │            │             │       │      │       │
 └─────┴────────────┴─────────────┴───────┴──────┴───────┘
 Database C:\db4\HARDWARE          Field 1/5
           Enter the field name. Insert/Delete field:Ctrl-N/Ctrl-U
 Field names begin with a letter and may contain letters, digits and underscores
```

Fig. 3.10. *Modifying the file structure of an existing database file.*

number format), the leading digits (123) are retained. The characters or digits that appear after a nonnumeric character are dropped. (In this case, - is treated as a dash.) However, if the character field value begins with a nonnumeric character, such as A1234, all the characters and digits are lost.

If records are in the existing database file, examine the field contents carefully before you convert a character field to a numeric field.

Making Backup Copies of Data

3.27 Tip: **Keep a backup copy of your original data.**

When you modify a database file, and especially when you convert from one data type to another, keep a backup copy of the original data. You then can compare the original data with the new file to be sure that data was converted correctly.

3.28 Trap: **Be sure that you have adequate disk space before modifying a database file.**

Because MODIFY STRUCTURE creates a new file that has the new attributes specified, a backup copy of the original database file (with the extension .BAK) is made. A backup of memo-field files is also made (with the extension .TBK). If you do not have adequate space available on your data disk, dBASE IV will not be able to create these backup files.

3.29 Trap: **Do not interrupt the file-creation operation.**

MODIFY STRUCTURE adds data to the new file created. If you interrupt this operation by resetting your computer, you may lose some of the data.

Changing Field Attributes

3.30 Trap: **You can lose data if you change a field name and its width at the same time.**

Use caution during file-structure modification: don't change the name and the width of a data field simultaneously when records are already in the database file. If you try, the values in that field may be lost.

To change both the name and the width of a data field, make the changes in steps:

1. Use the MODIFY STRUCTURE command to edit the field name.

2. Save the modified structure in the database file by pressing Ctrl-End.

3. Reissue the MODIFY STRUCTURE command to change the field width.

4. Press Ctrl-End to save the modified file.

Repositioning Existing Data Fields

3.31 Trick: **You can rearrange your data fields.**

In some display operations (such as the Browse operation without using BROWSE FIELDS), the screen width limits the number of data fields you can see on-screen. You can move some of the data fields to the beginning of the file structure so that they can be displayed on the same screen by using the Browse operation.

For example, if you restructure the HARDWARE.DBF database file, you might switch the PRICE and COST data fields so that PRICE appears before COST on your screen. Such a switching operation can be performed by moving the PRICE field to the front of the COST field.

To move a field from its current position in the structure to a new position, follow these steps:

1. Access the appropriate database and issue the MODIFY STRUCTURE command.

2. Delete the field at the current position.

3. Insert a new field at the new position.

4. Define the new field and the field attributes (field name and width, for example) of the field deleted in Step 2.

For example, to move the PRICE field from the current position (field #5) to the front of the COST field (field #4), follow these steps:

1. Place the cursor anywhere in the PRICE field and press Ctrl-U.

   The PRICE field is removed temporarily from the structure, and the cursor moves to the beginning of the COST field (see fig. 3.11).

2. Press Ctrl-N to insert a blank field in the structure (see fig. 3.12).

3. Enter the name, the type, and the field width of the PRICE field in the inserted field.

4. When you see the prompt Should data be COPIED from backup for all fields? (Y/N), press Y.

```
 Layout   Organize   Append   Go To   Exit                    1:22:29 pm
                                               Bytes remaining:    3962
  ┌─────┬────────────┬────────────┬───────┬───────┬───────┐
  │ Num │ Field Name │ Field Type │ Width │  Dec  │ Index │
  ├─────┼────────────┼────────────┼───────┼───────┼───────┤
  │  1  │ STOCK_NO   │ Character  │   9   │       │   Y   │
  │  2  │ DIVISION   │ Character  │   2   │       │   N   │
  │  3  │ TYPE       │ Character  │  20   │       │   N   │
  │  4  │ COST       │ Numeric    │   7   │   2   │   N   │
  │     │            │            │       │       │       │
  │     │            │            │       │       │       │
  │     │            │            │       │       │       │
  │     │            │            │       │       │       │
  │     │            │            │       │       │       │
  │     │            │            │       │       │       │
  │     │            │            │       │       │       │
  └─────┴────────────┴────────────┴───────┴───────┴───────┘
 Database C:\db4\HARDWARE          Field 4/4
          Enter the field name.  Insert/Delete field:Ctrl-N/Ctrl-U
 Field names begin with a letter and may contain letters, digits and underscores
```

Fig. 3.11. *The PRICE data field removed from the file structure.*

```
 Layout   Organize   Append   Go To   Exit                    1:23:29 pm
                                               Bytes remaining:    3962
  ┌─────┬────────────┬────────────┬───────┬───────┬───────┐
  │ Num │ Field Name │ Field Type │ Width │  Dec  │ Index │
  ├─────┼────────────┼────────────┼───────┼───────┼───────┤
  │  1  │ STOCK_NO   │ Character  │   9   │       │   Y   │
  │  2  │ DIVISION   │ Character  │   2   │       │   N   │
  │  3  │ TYPE       │ Character  │  20   │       │   N   │
  │  4  │            │ Character  │       │       │   N   │
  │  5  │ COST       │ Numeric    │   7   │   2   │   N   │
  │     │            │            │       │       │       │
  │     │            │            │       │       │       │
  │     │            │            │       │       │       │
  │     │            │            │       │       │       │
  │     │            │            │       │       │       │
  │     │            │            │       │       │       │
  └─────┴────────────┴────────────┴───────┴───────┴───────┘
 Database C:\db4\HARDWARE          Field 4/5
          Enter the field name.  Insert/Delete field:Ctrl-N/Ctrl-U
 Field names begin with a letter and may contain letters, digits and underscores
```

Fig. 3.12. *Inserting a blank data field into the file structure.*

5. Press Ctrl-End to save the new database structure. When you are prompted to Press Enter to confirm, any other key to resume, press Enter.

   Data then will be copied from the backup file to the current database.

After you have completed these five steps, the PRICE field is repositioned in the structure.

3.32 Trap: **You will lose the field if you leave the restructuring session before the field has been moved.**

The deleted field stays in memory and can be inserted back into the structure as long as you remain in one restructuring session. After you finish a restructuring session by pressing Ctrl-End to save the modified structure, all deleted fields are lost.

3.33 Trap: **Move a field within a structure with caution.**

When you enter the field attributes of the inserted field, the field name and width must be identical to the existing field (which has been temporarily deleted).

Before the program creates a new field, it checks to see whether the field is one that you deleted earlier. The new field is considered a replacement for the old field only if all the field attributes you enter match those of a deleted field. Otherwise, the program may consider the inserted field as a brand new field. All the values in the field you were moving will be lost.

3.34 Trap: **You can lose data if you insert or delete fields and change a field name at the same time.**

When you change field names, MODIFY STRUCTURE takes data from the original file using the field position in that file. When you insert or delete a field, that position may change; you may lose data. Field widths and data types can be altered when you insert or delete fields, but field names cannot be changed in the same operation.

3.35 Trap: **Use the SQL DBDEFINE command before creating or modifying a database.**

Using a database file in SQL (Structured Query Language) mode in dBASE IV requires some adjustments. If you plan to access the database file while in SQL mode, you need to use the SQL DBDEFINE command to update the system catalogs that SQL uses. If you do not do this, you may be unable to use your database file in SQL mode.

See Appendix D for more information on the SQL commands.

Modifying a Memo Field

3.36 Trap: **Changing a memo field to a character field and vice versa can cause the field contents to be lost.**

When you modify the file structure of a database file, do not change a memo field to a character field if the file is not empty. The contents of the memo field may be lost after the file restructuring process. Similarly, do not change a character field to a memo field. If you do, the contents of the character field may be lost as well.

Restoring Damaged Database Files

3.37 Trick: **Use the backup (.BAK) file to restore damaged database files.**

If the data in your file has been damaged during the file-restructuring process, you can restore the original contents to the file.

Every time the program executes the MODIFY STRUCTURE command, the program makes a duplicate copy of the file you are modifying. The duplicate is saved in a disk file with the same name as the active file and a .BAK (for Backup) file extension.

If some or all of your file contents are lost or damaged because of unexpected problems in the structure modification process, you can restore the file to its original form from the information saved in the backup file. To restore the damaged file to its original form, follow these steps:

1. Delete the damaged file by using the ERASE command.

2. Rename the backup file (with .BAK file extension) back to its original form (with a .DBF file extension).

For example, if the contents of the HARDWARE.DBF file are damaged during restructuring, you can restore the contents to those in the HARDWARE.BAK backup file by entering these commands:

```
. USE
. ERASE HARDWARE.DBF
. RENAME HARDWARE.BAK TO HARDWARE.DBF
```

You must close the database file before you erase and rename it because the program does not let you delete an open file. Remember that you can issue the USE command to close the current active file and not open another database file.

If all else fails, you may want to use a commercial software package designed to recover damaged dBASE files, such as QuickFix-2™, published by Hilco Software of Sebastopol, California.

Modifying Database Structure with a Text Editor

3.38 Trick: **To change a large file structure, save it in a text file for easy editing.**

The usual MODIFY STRUCTURE command procedure for changing a database structure might be sufficient for most applications. But to make substantial changes, you can use a more efficient approach—copying the existing database structure to a text file.

Before copying a database structure to a text file, you must copy the structure to a temporary working file. The contents of the working file then are copied to a text file for editing. To copy a database structure to a working file, use the COPY TO...STRUCTURE EXTENDED command:

. COPY TO < *name of working file*> STRUCTURE EXTENDED

The data structure of the working file created by the COPY TO... STRUCTURE EXTENDED command is set automatically by the program.

Figure 3.13 shows a working file (HWSTRUC.DBF) for the HARDWARE.DBF file. Data records in the working file correspond to field definitions in the original file.

```
. USE HARDWARE
. COPY TO HWSTRUC STRUCTURE EXTENDED
. USE HWSTRUC
. DISP STRUC
Structure for database: C:\DB4\HWSTRUC.DBF
Number of data records:      5
Date of last update   : 09/30/88
Field  Field Name  Type        Width    Dec     Index
    1  FIELD_NAME  Character     10               N
    2  FIELD_TYPE  Character      1               N
    3  FIELD_LEN   Numeric        3               N
    4  FIELD_DEC   Numeric        3               N
    5  FIELD_IDX   Character      1               N
** Total **                     19

. LIST
Record#  FIELD_NAME FIELD_TYPE FIELD_LEN FIELD_DEC FIELD_IDX
      1  STOCK_NO   C                  9         0 N
      2  DIVISION   C                  2         0 N
      3  TYPE       C                 20         0 N
      4  COST       N                  7         2 N
      5  PRICE      N                  7         2 N
.
```

Fig. 3.13. *Using the COPY STRUCTURE EXTENDED command.*

The data structure created automatically by the program for this working file contains five fields: FIELD _ NAME, FIELD _ TYPE, FIELD _ LEN (field length), FIELD _ DEC (decimal places), and FIELD _IDX (index flag). Each data field definition in the original database structure is saved as a data record in the working database file.

If the file structure of the Index field was created in dBASE IV, you were given the option of including an index tag for any of the fields in a production index file. A Y in the Index column would indicate that an index tag had been created for that field. (For more information on indexing, see Chapter 6.)

You are now ready to create a text file. Use the COPY TO. . .SDF command, which converts the data records in the active database file to lines of ASCII text (in the SDF standard data format). Issue the following command:

. COPY TO < *name of text file*> SDF

You can convert the contents of your data records when the file is in use by issuing the COPY TO. . .SDF command (see fig. 3.14). The contents of the file are shown in figure 3.15.

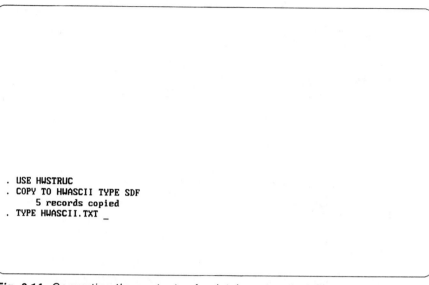

```
. USE HWSTRUC
. COPY TO HWASCII TYPE SDF
      5 records copied
. TYPE HWASCII.TXT _
```

Fig. 3.14. *Converting the contents of a database to a text file.*

```
HWASCII.TXT 09/30/88                                          1

STOCK_NO C  9  0N
DIVISION C  2  0N
TYPE     C 20  0N
COST     N  7  2N
PRICE    N  7  2N
```

Fig. 3.15. *Displaying the contents of the text file.*

3.39 Tip: **Modify your text file with the text editor.**

You can see in figure 3.15 that the text file contains five lines that represent the contents of a record in the HWSTRUC.DBF file. You are now ready to invoke the text editor to modify the structure in the text file. To use the text editor provided by the program, issue the following command:

. MODIFY COMMAND HWASCII.TXT

The contents of the text file are displayed, and you can begin modifying the file (see fig. 3.16).

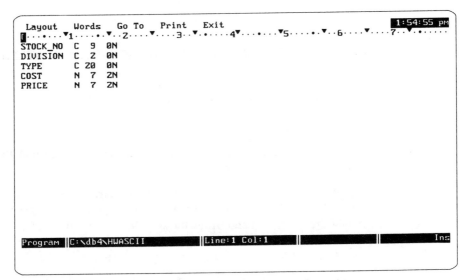

Fig. 3.16. Modifying the contents of the HWASCII.TXT file.

You can make changes to the structure by rearranging the fields, adding new data fields, deleting existing fields, or changing the attributes of the fields (see fig. 3.17). However, the field attributes must be entered in the format defined by the program as shown in the HWSTRUC.DBF file. The field name must be defined within the first 10 spaces, followed by the field type (1 character width), field length (3 characters), and field decimals (3 characters).

Save the edited database structure by pressing Ctrl-W.

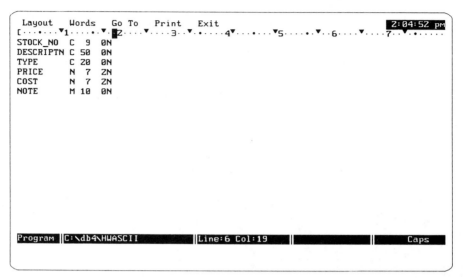

Fig. 3.17. Changing text in the HWASCII.TXT file.

3.40 Tip: **Convert your text file to a database structure to complete the modification of your file.**

Before you convert the text file to a database structure, you must delete the original records in the working file (HWSTRUC.DBF) by issuing the ZAP command. After the working file has been emptied, you can copy the contents of the text file to the working file by using the APPEND FROM...SDF command (see fig. 3.18).

Use the contents of the working file to create a new database file (see fig. 3.19) with the CREATE...FROM command:

. CREATE < *new database file*> FROM < *file containing database structure*>

A new database file with a modified structure is created. To copy some of the information from the original database file, use the APPEND FROM command (see fig. 3.20).

```
. USE HWSTRUC
. ZAP
Zap C:\DB4\HWSTRUC.DBF? (Y/N) Yes
. APPEND FROM HWASCII.TXT TYPE SDF
      6 records added
. LIST
Record#   FIELD_NAME FIELD_TYPE FIELD_LEN FIELD_DEC FIELD_IDX
        1 STOCK_NO   C                  9         0 N
        2 DESCRIPTN  C                 50         0 N
        3 TYPE       C                 20         0 N
        4 PRICE      N                  7         2 N
        5 COST       N                  7         2 N
        6 NOTE       M                 10         0 N
.
```

Fig. 3.18. *Saving the modified structure back to HWSTRUC.DBF.*

```
. CREATE NEWHW FROM HWSTRUC.DBF
. USE NEWHW
. DISPLAY STRUCTURE
Structure for database: C:\DB4\NEWHW.DBF
Number of data records:        0
Date of last update   : 09/30/88
Field  Field Name  Type        Width    Dec    Index
    1  STOCK_NO    Character       9              N
    2  DESCRIPTN   Character      50              N
    3  TYPE        Character      20              N
    4  PRICE       Numeric         7      2       N
    5  COST        Numeric         7      2       N
    6  NOTE        Memo           10              N
** Total **                     104
```

Fig. 3.19. *Creating a new database with the structure of HWSTRUC.DBF.*

```
. USE NEWHW
. APPEND FROM HARDWARE
     10 records added
. LIST STOCK_NO,TYPE,PRICE,COST
Record#  STOCK_NO  TYPE              PRICE    COST
      1  CPQ-SP256 system          1359.00 1895.00
      2  ZEN-SL181 system          1695.00 2399.00
      3  IBM-AT64A system          3790.00 4490.00
      4  ZEN-MM012 monitor           89.00  159.00
      5  NEC-PC660 printer          560.00  820.00
      6  HAY-M1200 modem            269.00  389.00
      7  SEA-HD020 hard disk        398.00  495.00
      8  IOM-HD040 hard disk       2190.00 2790.00
      9  PAR-GC100 graphic card     279.00  389.00
     10  HER-GC100 graphic card     199.00  239.00

.
```

Fig. 3.20. Appending data records from HARDWARE.DBF.

3.41 Trick: **Edit the file structure using Edit or Browse mode.**

You can avoid using a text editor to alter a database structure file by using either Edit or Browse to make the desired changes. After you have used the COPY STRUCTURE EXTENDED command to create a new file that contains the structure of the original database file, USE the new structure file, and then issue the EDIT or BROWSE commands. Press Ctrl-End to save any changes made to the structure file. You then can use the new structure with the CREATE...FROM command.

4

Entering and Editing Data

his chapter presents tips, tricks, and traps to help you enter and
edit data, as well as some shortcuts for designing and modifying a
custom data-entry form using the form design screen. The form design
screen is accessible from the Control Center menu by highlighting
< **create**> or a file in the Forms column, or by issuing the CREATE
SCREEN or MODIFY SCREEN command from the dot prompt.

Creating a Custom Data-Entry Form

Using dBASE IV's form design screen, you can place data fields
anywhere on the screen and provide your own field labels. You also
can add graphic designs such as single- or double-line boxes. From the
form design screen, you can make changes to the layout or the
contents of a data-entry form.

You can make your data-entry form more effective by using a
formatting template that restricts the types of characters entered in
the data field. As you design a data-entry form, you also can define a
valid range for a given data field or include a calculated field.

Designing a Custom Data-Entry Form

4.1 Tip: **Use the form design screen to create a data-entry form.**

Instead of writing a program or a format file, you can use the form design screen to design a custom data-entry form on the layout surface. After you save a data-entry form to disk in a screen file, you can use the form in the EDIT and APPEND operations.

Use the following steps to create a screen file:

1. Select the database file to be used.

2. Call up the form design screen.

3. Modify the field labels and add a title, notes, and boxes.

4. Save the form to a screen file.

You can carry out the first two steps of this operation either by issuing the necessary commands at the dot prompt or by selecting the appropriate options from the Control Center menu.

To create a data-entry form for the EMPLOYEE.DBF database file (in the default disk drive C:), for example, you would type the following commands at the dot prompt:

```
. USE EMPLOYEE
. CREATE SCREEN EMPLOYEE.SCR
```

The file extension (.SCR) is optional. If the extension is left out in the CREATE SCREEN step, the program inserts it automatically.

If you instead choose to use the Control Center menu, select a database file, and then select < **create**> under the Forms column.

From the form design menu, select **Layout**. Then choose **Quick Layout** (see fig. 4.1). The fields from your database appear on the screen in the default Edit format, flush left at the top of the screen (see fig. 4.2).

With all the data fields loaded where you want them, you can modify the field names and add more descriptive information to the form by using the editing keystrokes described in the text that follows. Figure 4.3 shows a finished data-entry form.

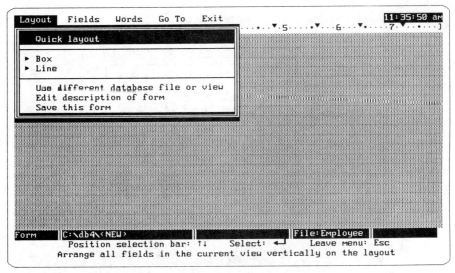

Fig. 4.1. *Loading data fields to the form design surface.*

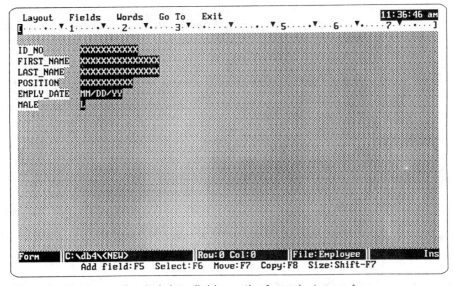

Fig. 4.2. *Displaying loaded data fields on the form design surface.*

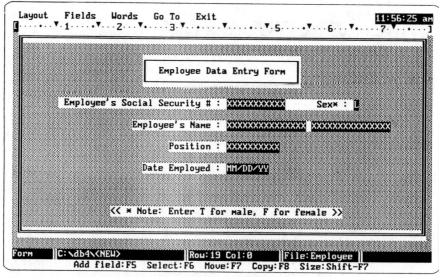

Fig. 4.3. An example of a finished data-entry form.

To save the data-entry form, press Alt-E to select the **Exit** menu, and then choose **Save changes and exit**.

4.2 Tip:

Use single- or double-line boxes to frame a data-entry form.

While designing a data-entry form with the form design screen, you can draw a single- or double-line box by selecting **Box** from the **Layout** menu. Choose S for a single-line box or D for a double-line box.

To draw a box, position the cursor at the top left corner of the box, and then press the Enter key. Next, use the arrow keys to move the cursor to the lower right corner of the box, and press Enter again.

The data-entry form shown in figure 4.3 is framed by a double-line box. The form's title is framed by a single-line box.

4.3 Tip:

Use the arrow keys to adjust the size of an existing box.

After you have drawn a box, you can adjust its size. Place the cursor on the border of the box, and then press Shift-F7 (Size). A "ghost" of the box appears, which you can size by pressing the arrow keys. When the box is the correct size, press Enter.

4.4 Tip: **Use special characters for custom box borders.**

Instead of single- and double-line borders for boxes, you can choose a special character, such as the asterisk (˙) or dollar sign ($). Select **Box** from the **Layout** menu, and then choose **Using specified character.** You can select from a list of available characters by highlighting the character and pressing Enter.

4.5 Tip: **Erase a box by using the Del (Delete) key.**

To erase a box on the layout surface, place the cursor anywhere on the box line. Then press the Del key.

4.6 Tip: **Use the Layout menu to draw lines on the screen.**

If you want to use vertical or horizontal lines, either for emphasis or to divide portions of the screen, select **Line** from the **Layout** menu. You can choose **Single line** or **Double line**, or you can use a specified character. Place the cursor where you want the line to start, and then press Enter. Use the arrow keys to select the position for the end of the line, and then press Enter again. You can edit lines as you would text. For example, to delete a single character, you use the Backspace key.

4.7 Trick: **Blank out areas of the screen with the Blank character.**

Choose the Blank character (ASCII 32) as the specified character for line drawing. The cursor will erase text on the screen as you form your lines.

Modifying a Data-Entry Form

4.8 Tip: **Use the form design screen to modify an existing data-entry form.**

If you want to make changes to the layout or the contents of a data-entry form, you can use the MODIFY SCREEN operation to modify the screen file. To do this from the dot prompt, issue the following command:

. MODIFY SCREEN < *name of screen file* >

To modify an existing screen file from the Control Center menu, highlight the screen file from the Forms column and press Shift-F2 (Design).

4.9 Trick:

Use the form design screen to create a format file.

When you use the form design screen with the CREATE/MODIFY SCREEN operation, information on your data-entry form is saved in a screen file and a format file. The data fields and their display locations are written as dBASE IV commands and saved in the format file automatically. Information needed to convert these commands to the screen display is stored in the screen file. Format and screen files share the same file name but have different file extensions (.FMT and .SCR, respectively).

When the data-entry form shown in figure 4.3 is saved in the screen file (EMPLOYEE.SCR), a format file named EMPLOYEE.FMT is created automatically. This format file contains the dBASE IV commands that specify the layout of the data fields and their labels (see fig. 4.4).

```
*******************************************************************
*-- Name....: EMPLOYEE.FMT
*-- Date....: 9-29-9Ø
*-- Version.: dBASE IV, Format 1.44
*-- Notes...: Format files use "" as delimiters!
*******************************************************************

*-- Format file initialization code ----------------------------

IF SET("TALK")="ON"
   SET TALK OFF
   lc_talk="ON"
ELSE
   lc_talk="OFF"
ENDIF


*-- This form was created in MONO mode
SET DISPLAY TO MONO

lc_status=SET("STATUS")
*-- SET STATUS was ON when you went into the form design.
IF lc_status = "OFF"
   SET STATUS ON
ENDIF
```

```
*-- @ SAY GETS Processing. -------------------------------------

*-- Format Page: 1

@  Ø,1   TO 18,78 DOUBLE
@  2,25  TO 4,54
@  3,26  SAY "  EMPLOYEE DATA ENTRY FORM  "
@  6,9   SAY "Employee's Social Security # : "
@  6,41  GET id_no PICTURE "999-99-9999"
@  6,52  SAY "         Sex* : "
@  6,65  GET male PICTURE "L"
@  8,23  SAY "Employee's Name : "
@  8,41  GET first_name PICTURE "XXXXXXXXXXXXXX"
@  8,56  SAY " "
@  8,57  GET last_name PICTURE "XXXXXXXXXXXXXX"
@ 1Ø,3Ø  SAY "        Position : "
@ 1Ø,41  GET position PICTURE "XXXXXXXXXX"
@ 12,25  SAY " Date Employed : "
@ 12,41  GET emply_date
@ 16,19  SAY " << * Note: Enter T for male, F for female >>"

*-- Format file exit code -------------------------------------

*-- SET STATUS was ON when you went into the form design.
IF lc_status = "OFF"  && Entered form with status off
   SET STATUS OFF      && Turn STATUS "OFF" on the way out
ENDIF

IF lc_talk="ON"
   SET TALK ON
ENDIF

RELEASE lc_talk,lc_fields,lc_status
*-- EOP: EMPLOYEE.FMT
```

Fig. 4.4. *The EMPLOYEE.FMT format file.*

As you can see in the figure, every data field in the data-entry form is defined with an @...SAY...GET statement, which may be written as one or two command lines. The locations and labels of these data fields are clearly identified by using the information in the screen file. Using the form design screen to create a format file is often easier than typing the format statements using a text editor.

Note: The format file is created using the dBASE IV Template Language. Certain system variables (such as lc_talk) are used to set the system environment. Information on using the Template Language is included with the Developer's Edition of dBASE IV.

4.10 Trap: Environment settings in effect when the format file is created are included in the format file.

dBASE IV checks to see what settings are in effect when you enter the form design screen. When a format file is created, these settings are included in the format. For example, if SET TALK ON or SET STATUS ON is in effect when you create the format, this setting will be put into effect when the format is used. Be sure to set the correct environment settings before entering the form design screen.

4.11 Trap: Modifying the format file doesn't affect the screen layout in the screen file.

If you use the CREATE SCREEN or MODIFY SCREEN command to create a format file with the form design screen, dBASE IV allows you to modify the text in the format file independently. Doing so, however, is asking for trouble.

The changes you make to the format file will not be used to modify the corresponding screen file. If you try to examine the screen display from the form design screen, you won't see any of the formatting changes you made. Moreover, if you modify the screen file after you change its corresponding format file, all the changes you made in the format file are lost when you save the screen file.

Validating Data

When you use the form design screen to create a custom data-entry form, each data field specified in the form is represented by a field mask such as XXXXXX (for a character field), 99/99/99 (for a date field), or L (for a logical field).

For example, the field mask for the ID_NO field (Employee's Social Security #) is displayed (using the template symbol X) as XXXXXXXXXXX by the form design screen (refer to fig. 4.3). A value for the field can consist of nine digits and two dashes. With dBASE IV, the default X can be replaced by any character.

4.12 Trap: You can alter data in the field without realizing it has happened.

Because you can substitute any character for the default X, you can make a serious mistake unknowingly. For example, if you mistakenly enter the letter O in place of the number Ø in the ID_NO field, no error message or warning will be given.

4.13 Trick: Prevent errors by adding a PICTURE template to format the data field.

You can avoid entering an invalid value if you use a PICTURE template to restrict the types of characters the data field will accept. To define a PICTURE template on the data-entry form, place the cursor at the data field, and then choose the **Modify field** and **Template** options from the **Fields** menu. The cursor will appear in the template input area, and a list of options will appear below.

For example, you can define a 999-99-9999 PICTURE template for the ID_NO data field, as shown in figure 4.5. Because the template symbol 9 allows only digits to be entered in its place, you can enter only digits and dashes in the ID_NO field. The PICTURE template is displayed also on the data-entry form (see fig. 4.6).

After you define the PICTURE template, suppose that you use the format file to append a new record to the database file, as follows:

```
. USE EMPLOYEE
. SET FORMAT TO EMPLOYEE
. APPEND
```

The ID_NO field (labeled Employee's Social Security # :) is displayed with the PICTURE template (see fig. 4.7). Notice that two dashes have been inserted in the field. You do not have to enter them yourself. Now, the ID_NO field will reject any character that is not a digit.

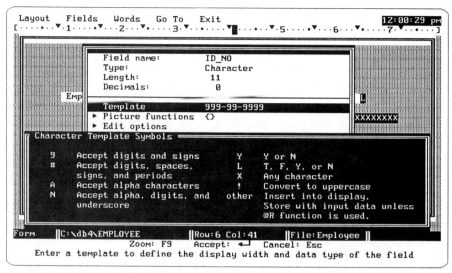

Fig. 4.5. Defining a PICTURE template for the ID_NO field.

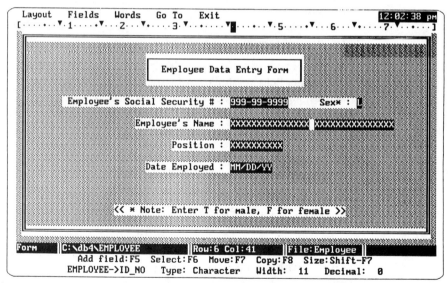

Fig. 4.6. Showing the PICTURE template on the data-entry form.

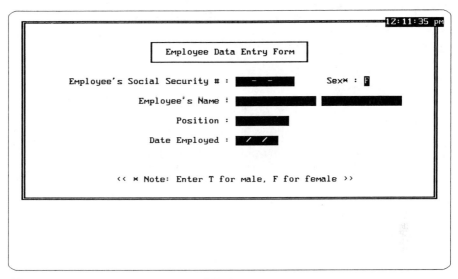

Fig. 4.7. *The result of using the PICTURE template with SET FORMAT TO.*

4.14 Tip: **Use PICTURE template symbols to format data fields in a data-entry form.**

The formatting template plays an important role in the PICTURE clause. By using the appropriate template symbols in the clause, you can restrict the types of characters entered in the data field. These template symbols and their uses are shown in table 4.1.

4.15 Trick: **Use the form design screen's Picture Template to convert lowercase characters to uppercase.**

The **Template** option on the form design screen menu lets you convert one or more characters in a data field to uppercase letters. Position the cursor at the data field, and then choose **Fields** (Alt-F), **Modify field**, and **Template**.

For example, you can ensure that the last name in the data-entry form for the EMPLOYEE.DBF database file always begins with an uppercase letter. To do so, set the template value for the LAST_NAME data field to the ! Picture Template symbol (see fig. 4.8).

Table 4.1
PICTURE Template Symbols

Symbol	Use
X	Allows any character
9	Allows only digits and signs
N	Allows only alpha characters, digits, and underscores
#	Allows only digits, blanks, signs, and periods
A	Allows only alpha characters
Y	Allows only Y or N (Yes or No)
L	Allows only logical data (T or F, Y or N)
!	Converts letters entered to uppercase

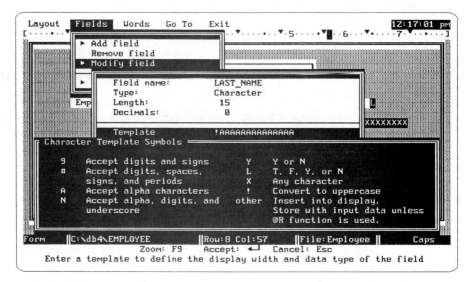

Fig. 4.8. *Defining a Picture Template on the LAST_NAME field.*

If you use PICTURE !AAAAAAAAAAAAA to define the format of the
LAST_NAME field in an @...SAY...GET statement, the first letter you
enter in the field is converted automatically to uppercase.

4.16 Trap: **Templates cannot be used on date fields.**

When entering data into a date field, the date format in effect is used. If you try to specify a template using the form design screen, you could change the field type inadvertently.

4.17 Tip: **Be aware of the date format that will be used when entering data, and set this option before designing your screen.**

Use the SET DATE command to specify the date format to be used. For example, the SET DATE AMERICAN (which is the default) uses the format mm/dd/yy for dates. Other available options are shown in table 4.2.

Table 4.2
Date Formats

Option	Format
ANSI	yy.mm.dd
BRITISH	dd/mm/yy
FRENCH	dd/mm/yy
GERMAN	dd.mm.yy
ITALIAN	dd-mm-yy
JAPAN	yy/mm/dd
USA	mm-dd-yy
MDY	mm/dd/yy
DMY	dd/mm/yy
YMD	yy/mm/dd

Note: When SET CENTURY ON is in effect, the century prefix is displayed in dates. For example, 09/01/1989 rather than 09/01/89 would be displayed for September 1, 1989, when AMERICAN format is used.

Setting Data Ranges

4.18 Tip: **Use the Edit options of the form design screen to define a valid range for numeric and date fields.**

As you design a data-entry form, you can define a valid range for a given data field. Then only values within those limits will be accepted during data entry. Place the cursor on the appropriate field, select **Fields** (Alt-F), choose the **Modify field** and **Edit options**, and then specify the lower and upper values as needed.

For example, you can set the range of applicable employment dates when you design the data-entry form for the EMPLOYEE.DBF file (see fig. 4.9). When you set the range for a date field, the lower and upper limits refer to the earliest and latest dates, respectively. Note that for date fields, values must be entered within curly braces ({}).

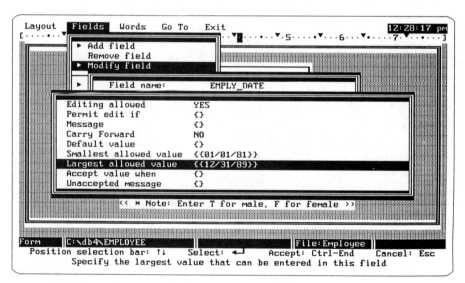

Fig. 4.9. *Setting lower and upper limits for a date field.*

4.19 Trap: **Your keyboard may "lock up" if you enter a value that is not within the specified range.**

When you use a range for a field in a data-entry screen, all values must fall within the specified range. If you enter a value that is not within the specified range, the keyboard appears to lock up. To clear this condition, press the space bar. The cursor will then return to the data-entry field.

4.20 Tip: **You can add fields to the screen form using the Add field option.**

The **Add field** option from the **Fields** menu allows you to place fields from the current database into the form design. Place the cursor where you want the field to be added. Select **Fields** (Alt- F) and **Add field**, and then choose a field from the menu that appears by highlighting the field name and pressing Enter (see fig. 4.10).

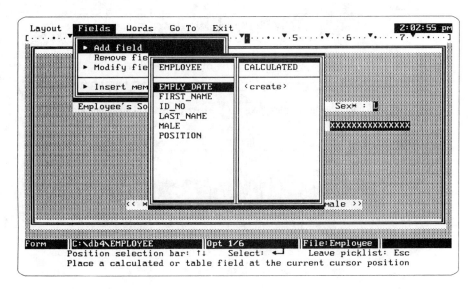

Fig. 4.10. Selecting a field from the Add field menu.

The field description menu then allows you to specify **Picture functions**, **Edit options** such as ranges, and other options. When you have completed the appropriate option selection, press Ctrl-End to save your changes, or press Esc to cancel the operation.

4.21 Trick: **Add a calculated field to the form design.**

You can create calculated fields that will appear on-screen when the screen form is used. Using a valid dBASE IV expression, you can display information derived from other fields. (Calculated fields are discussed in Chapters 5 and 7).

For example, if you have two fields called COST and QUANTITY, you can create a calculated field called TOTAL that shows the amount calculated by multiplying COST and QUANTITY (see figs. 4.11, 4.12, and 4.13). Create a calculated field the same way you would add a field from the current database to the form design, except instead of selecting a field from the menu presented, select < **create**> from the calculated field menu. Enter the expression (for example COST * QUANTITY) for the calculated value and any appropriate PICTURE template options.

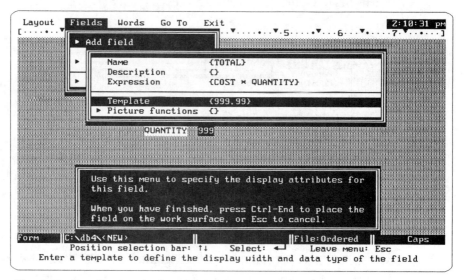

Fig. 4.11. Creating a calculated field.

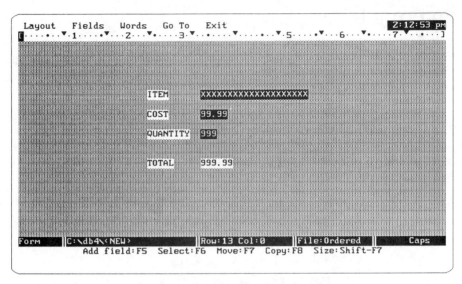

Fig. 4.12. *A calculated field (TOTAL) on the form design screen.*

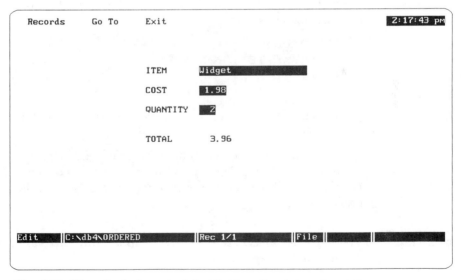

Fig. 4.13. *The effect of a calculated field on the data-entry screen.*

Entering Data

Before you can enter data into a data-entry form, you must select the appropriate form. This section gives you tips, tricks, and traps for selecting a data-entry form, as well as suggestions for entering data by replicating data records and appending data records from another database file.

Selecting a Data-Entry Form

4.22 Tip: **To select a format file, issue the SET FORMAT TO command.**

To select the custom data-entry form you've saved in a format file, select its corresponding database file and then issue the SET FORMAT TO command:

. SET FORMAT TO < *name of format file*>

For example, you can use the data-entry form (EMPLOYEE.FMT) for editing the fifth data record in the EMPLOYEE.DBF database file. Issue the following commands:

. USE EMPLOYEE
. SET FORMAT TO EMPLOYEE
. GOTO 5
. EDIT

The custom data-entry form is displayed, and you can edit the data record (see fig. 4.14).

You also can select a screen form in the current catalog from the Control Center by highlighting the file in the Forms column and pressing Enter. To enter data using the form, highlight the file and press F2 (Data).

4.23 Trap: **You can't tell which record you're working on if the status line is not displayed.**

If the SET STATUS OFF command is in effect when you use the data-entry form to add a new data record or to edit existing records, no information on the record's status is displayed. You can't tell how many records are in the database file or which record you are working on.

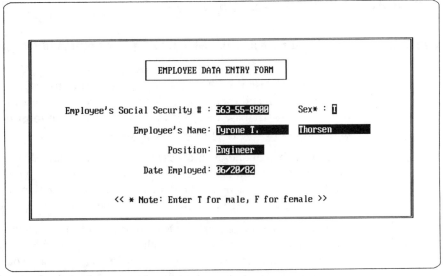

Fig. 4.14. *Editing a data record with a custom data-entry form.*

4.24 Trick: **Use the SET STATUS ON command to show the record number during data entry.**

To display the status line, issue the SET STATUS ON command before entering the form design screen. Then, when you save the screen format file, the status line will be set ON in the format code. The status line shows you the current record number and other information about the database file in use.

You also can bring up the custom data-entry form using the Control Center menu before you carry out the EDIT or APPEND operation. Highlight the form's file name in the Forms column, and then press F2 (Data). The status line always is displayed in the Control Center menu.

Replicating Data Records

4.25 Trick: **Save time by using the SET CARRY ON command to replicate field values.**

You ordinarily use the APPEND or INSERT command to display a blank data-entry form and then type the field values for each record you add to an existing database file. This method works well if most of the field values in these records are different.

If many of the data fields in the records you are adding share the same values, however, you can carry the field values from one record to another—without using the keyboard. The CARRY operation replicates the field values of a data record and saves them in another record.

If you first issue the SET CARRY ON command and then execute the APPEND or INSERT operation, field values from the preceding record are carried over in a new record in the existing database file. For example, if you want to keep track of all the items sold in your store, you can set up a database file named ITEMSOLD.DBF. Figure 4.15 shows the structure and contents of such a database file.

```
. USE ITEMSOLD
. DISP STRU
Structure for database: C:\DB4\ITEMSOLD.DBF
Number of data records:     3
Date of last update    : 09/29/88
Field  Field Name  Type        Width    Dec    Index
    1  INVOICE_NO  Numeric        4              N
    2  DATE_SHIPD  Date           8              N
    3  CLERK_NO    Numeric        2              N
    4  DIVISION    Character      2              N
    5  STOCK_NO    Character      9              N
    6  UNITS_SOLD  Numeric        3              N
    7  PRICE       Numeric        8       2      N
** Total **                      37

. LIST
Record#  INVOICE_NO DATE_SHIPD CLERK_NO DIVISION STOCK_NO  UNITS_SOLD    PRICE
      1        1001 02/07/87        10 SW       MIS-WS300           1   269.00
      2        1001 02/07/87        10 SW       MIS-WS300           1   269.00
      3        1001 02/07/87        10 SW       MIS-WS300           1   269.00
```

Fig. 4.15. The file structure and contents of ITEMSOLD.DBF.

As you can see from figure 4.16, if you issue the SET CARRY ON and APPEND commands after you select the database file (USE ITEMSOLD), the contents of the preceding record (Record No. 3) are carried over to the new record (Record No. 4). The two records now contain the same contents. At this point, you can edit some of the field values before you save the record.

To replicate the field values of the current record, press the PgDn key. When you press PgDn, the contents of the current record are carried over to the next new record.

Fig. 4.16. *Carrying over the contents from the preceding record.*

4.26 Trap: | **Leaving CARRY ON after replicating field values can produce unwanted records.**

When CARRY ON is in effect, the contents of a record are carried over automatically to the next record when you use the INSERT or APPEND operation. Be sure to issue the SET CARRY OFF command when CARRY is no longer needed.

4.27 Trick: | **Use the Carry forward option from the Fields menu to replicate field contents.**

When you use the form design screen to create your screen form, you can choose which fields will contain data "carried forward" from the previous record. To do this, simply highlight the appropriate field on the form design layout screen. Then pull down the **Fields** menu (Alt-F), select **Modify field**, and then choose **Carry forward** from the **Edit Options** submenu. If you set **Carry forward** to YES, the contents of the field in the previous record automatically will be inserted into the field of the new record when you append the file using the data-entry form.

4.28 Trick: **Save the contents of a record to a temporary file, and then append the database from the temporary file.**

You can copy the current record to another file, and then append the current file from the temporary file to add a duplicate record, which can be edited. From the dot prompt, the following commands would accomplish this task:

```
. COPY NEXT 1 TO TEMP.DBF
. APPEND FROM TEMP.DBF
. ERASE TEMP.DBF
. EDIT
```

If you were to place these commands in a program file, you could invoke it from the dot prompt by typing DO followed by the program name . Or, you could assign the commands to a function key, as in the following example:

```
. SET FUNCTION 6 TO "COPY NEXT 1 TO TEMP.DBF;APPEND FROM
  TEMP.DBF;ERASE TEMP.DBF;EDIT;"
```

When you press the F6 (Select) key from the dot prompt, the record is duplicated and the program changes to Edit mode so that any necessary changes can be made to the new record.

Appending Data Records from Another Database File

4.29 Tip: **Use only common fields in a filter to append selected records from an existing database file.**

Often you need to use a data field in a filtering condition when you append selected records from one file to another. In such cases, the data field must be common to both database files. Otherwise, you will have to use a temporary database file or the COPY FIELDS command to append the records.

Creating a new database file that contains a subset of the records in an existing database file can be desirable when you manipulate data. To create such a file, use the APPEND FROM command to add the records instead of typing them from the keyboard.

When you use the APPEND FROM operation, all the records in the source database file are appended to the target file. To append data records selectively from one database file to another, you can add a qualifier condition to the APPEND FROM command. For example, to append the data records for products whose stock levels are near depletion from the inventory database (INVENTRY.DBF) to the active database file (LOWSTOCK.DBF), you can use a qualifier condition (on-hand quantity is two or less) in the APPEND FROM command:

```
. USE LOWSTOCK
. APPEND FROM INVENTRY FOR ON _ HAND  < = 2
```

The operation specified by this command works properly only when both LOWSTOCK.DBF and INVENTRY.DBF have the ON_HAND field in their database structures. Otherwise, no records are appended.

4.30 Trap: **Trying to append selected records by using a field that is not shared by both databases results in an error message.**

If, as shown in figure 4.17, the data field ON_HAND belongs only to INVENTRY.DBF and not to LOWSTOCK.DBF, executing the APPEND FROM command causes the following error message:

```
Variable not found
```

The data field ON_HAND, which is missing from the active database file, is considered an undefined memory variable.

```
. USE INVENTRY
. DISP STRU
Structure for database: D:\DBASE4\OTHER\INVENTRY.DBF
Number of data records:    20
Date of last update   : 01/16/89
Field  Field Name  Type      Width   Dec    Index
    1  STOCK_NO    Character     9                 Y
    2  ON_HAND     Numeric       3                 N
    3  ON_ORDER    Numeric       3                 N
** Total **                     16

. USE LOWSTOCK
. DISP STRU
Structure for database: D:\DBASE4\OTHER\LOWSTOCK.DBF
Number of data records:    5
Date of last update   : 01/16/89
Field  Field Name  Type      Width   Dec    Index
    1  STOCK_NO    Character     9                 Y
** Total **                     10

.
```

Fig. 4.17. *The file structures of INVENTRY.DBF and LOWSTOCK.DBF.*

4.31 Trick: **Use a temporary database file.**

One solution to the problem of not having a common field is to copy the structure from the source database file (INVENTRY.DBF) to a temporary working file (TEMP.DBF) and then to append data records from the inventory file to the temporary file, as follows:

```
. USE INVENTRY
. COPY STRUCTURE TO TEMP
. USE TEMP
. APPEND FROM INVENTRY FOR ON_HAND <= 2
```

Next, delete the unwanted data fields from the structure of the temporary file and add the remaining records to the original target file (LOWSTOCK.DBF), as follows:

```
. USE LOWSTOCK
. APPEND FROM TEMP
. ERASE TEMP.DBF
```

Another solution to the problem is to save the records to be appended to the temporary database file (by using the COPY FIELDS command) and then add them to the target file by using the APPEND FROM command, as follows:

```
. USE INVENTRY
. COPY TO TEMP FIELDS STOCK_NO FOR ON_HAND <= 2
. USE LOWSTOCK
. APPEND FROM TEMP
. ERASE TEMP.DBF
```

Editing Data

This section gives you tips, tricks, and traps for editing data. The text offers suggestions for editing selected records, filtering data records to be edited, editing selected data fields, editing multiple database files simultaneously, and deleting empty records.

Editing Selected Records

4.32 Trick: **To edit a selected set of records, use a search condition in the EDIT command.**

When you issue the EDIT command at the dot prompt, all the records in the active database file are the subject of the editing command. You can select a record in either of two ways. First, you can specify its record number in the EDIT command, as follows:

```
. USE EMPLOYEE
. EDIT RECORD 5
```

Or, second, you can position the record pointer at the record to be edited before you issue the EDIT command, as follows:

```
. GOTO 5
. EDIT
```

You also can use the Edit screen's **Go To** option to select the record to be edited. From the **Go To** menu, you can choose to go to the top record, the last record in the file, or a particular record number, or you can search forward or backward for a record.

From the dot prompt, you can add a search condition to the EDIT command:

```
. EDIT < search condition>
```

For example, to change those records whose POSITION field value is "Sales Rep" in the EMPLOYEE.DBF database file, issue the following commands:

```
. USE EMPLOYEE
. EDIT FOR POSITION="Sales Rep"
```

The first record to meet the qualifying condition is displayed for editing. When you finish editing and you pass beyond the last data field or press the PgDn key, the next data record to meet the search condition is displayed. All records that do not meet the search condition are ignored.

You can use the .AND. and .OR. operators in the search condition:

```
. EDIT FOR MALE .AND. DTOC(EMPLY_DATE) >="Ø1/Ø1/86"
```

And you can filter out the records to be edited by adding to the EDIT command a condition that specifies the scope:

```
. EDIT FOR RECNO( ) >=5
```

Filtering Data Records To Be Edited

4.33 Tip:

Use the SET FILTER TO command to select a subset of the data records in a database file to be edited.

To edit a selected group of data records in the database file, single out a subset of the records by using a filtering command, as follows, instead of using a search condition in the EDIT command:

. SET FILTER TO < *filtering condition*>

Only those records that satisfy the filtering condition are subjected to the EDIT operation. For example, if you want to edit only those records in the PRODUCTS.DBF database file that contain information on products in the software division, you can set the following filter:

. SET FILTER TO DIVISION="SW"

Only records that meet the filter condition are displayed for editing when you use the BROWSE or EDIT commands.

4.34 Trap:

When you are screening data records, dBASE IV allows only one filter condition at a time.

You can use the SET FILTER TO command to screen data records. However, you can set only one filter at a time. When you issue a new filter command, the existing filter condition is erased.

If you want to erase the current filter condition without setting another condition, use the SET FILTER TO command without specifying a filter condition.

4.35 Tip:

To edit selected records using a complex filtering condition, use a query file.

Query files allow you to create a complex set of filtering conditions that can be used for many operations, including editing records. Chapter 7 discusses the creation of a query file.

Editing Selected Data Fields

4.36 Tip:

To edit the contents of selected data fields, specify the field list in the EDIT command.

When you edit the contents of an existing database file, you may need to change only the values in selected data fields. Instead of displaying all the data fields, you can specify in the EDIT command which fields to edit:

. EDIT FIELDS < *fields to be edited* >

For example, if you need to change only the price and cost of the products in the PRODUCTS.DBF database file, you can issue the following commands:

. USE PRODUCTS
. EDIT FIELDS STOCK _ NO,COST,PRICE

Only those data fields specified in the EDIT FIELDS command are displayed for editing. The effect is the same as if you were editing while in the BROWSE FIELDS environment.

You also can edit selected data fields in a subset of data records. Add a search condition to the EDIT FIELDS command:

. USE PRODUCTS
. EDIT FIELDS STOCK _ NO,COST,PRICE FOR TYPE="printer"

4.37 Trap:

The EDIT FIELDS command does not work if you use a custom data-entry screen specified in a SET FORMAT TO command.

If you want to use the selective EDIT function, issue the following command before issuing the EDIT command:

. SET FORMAT TO

This command cancels any format file specified in an earlier SET FORMAT TO command.

Editing Multiple Database Files Simultaneously

To design a good database system, store data (according to function) in several database files instead of saving all the information in one large file. Each of these database files should contain a relatively small number of data fields. You may want to be able to use the EDIT or BROWSE operations to modify the records in these database files simultaneously rather than editing the records in each file separately.

4.38 Tip:

To edit records in multiple database files, link them with the SET RELATION TO command.

To edit the data records in multiple database files simultaneously, you must first use the SET RELATION TO operation to link the files. (Chapter 5 contains a detailed discussion on linking database files.)

For example, assume that you store information about software products in SOFTWARE.DBF, whose structure and records are shown in figure 4.18. You store the inventory level of these software products in another database file named SWSTOCK.DBF (see fig. 4.19).

```
Structure for database: C:\DB4\SOFTWARE
Number of data records:      10
Date of last update  : 09/30/88
Field  Field Name  Type       Width   Dec    Index
    1  STOCK_NO    Character     9              Y
    2  DSCRIPTION  Character    20              N
    3  TYPE        Character    20              N
    4  COST        Numeric       7     2        N
    5  PRICE       Numeric       7     2        N
** Total **                     64

. LIST
Record#  STOCK_NO  DSCRIPTION        TYPE                   COST    PRICE
      1  ASH-DB400 dBASE IV v 1.0    database             495.00   795.00
      2  ANS-DB110 Paradox v.1.1     database             525.00   695.00
      3  CLP-DB100 Clipper DB Compiler database compiler  450.00   595.00
      4  WOR-DB100 WordTech DB Compiler database compiler 469.00   595.00
      5  LOT-L0123 Lotus 1-2-3 Rel 2 spread sheet         289.00   359.00
      6  MIC-WS330 WordStar v3.30    word processing      229.00   269.00
      7  MIS-WD400 Microsoft Word 4.0 word processing     229.00   289.00
      8  ASH-FW300 Framework v.3.0   integrated           345.00   395.00
      9  MIC-QB200 Microsoft QuickBasic language           79.00   109.00
     10  BOL-PA300 Turbo Pascal v.3.0 language             39.50    69.50
.
```

Fig. 4.18. *The file structure and contents of SOFTWARE.DBF.*

Notice that both files include an index tag for the STOCK_NO field. You should set the index order for files to be related to the common key field.

If you want to modify the data records in SOFTWARE.DBF and SWSTOCK.DBF simultaneously, you must first link the two database files. Figure 4.20 shows the commands for linking the two files with the SET RELATION TO command. Notice that you link the two database files by using the common data field STOCK_NO with the SET RELATION TO command.

```
. USE SWSTOCK
. DISP STRU
Structure for database: C:\DB4\SWSTOCK.DBF
Number of data records:      10
Date of last update   : 09/30/88
Field  Field Name  Type       Width    Dec    Index
    1  STOCK_NO    Character      9             Y
    2  ON_HAND     Numeric        3             N
    3  ON_ORDER    Numeric        3             N
** Total **                     16

. LIST
Record#  STOCK_NO  ON_HAND ON_ORDER
      1  ASH-DB400       4        2
      2  ANS-DB110       3        2
      3  CLP-DB100       2        1
      4  WOR-DB100       2        3
      5  LOT-L0123       5        1
      6  MIC-WS330       3        3
      7  MIS-WD400       2        3
      8  ASH-FW300       3        2
      9  MIC-QBZ00       4        1
     10  BOL-PA300       0        2

.
```

Fig. 4.19. *The file structure and contents of SWSTOCK.DBF.*

```
. SELE 1
. USE SWSTOCK ORDER STOCK_NO
Master index: STOCK_NO
. SELE 2
. USE SOFTWARE ORDER STOCK_NO
Master index: STOCK_NO
. SET RELATION TO STOCK_NO INTO A
.
```

Fig. 4.20. *Relating the SOFTWARE.DBF and SWSTOCK.DBF files.*

After you link the database files, you can modify some or all the fields in both files by using the BROWSE FIELDS command:

```
. GO TOP
. BROWSE FIELDS STOCK_NO,DSCRIPTION,COST,PRICE,
   A->ON_HAND,A->ON_ORDER
```

The BROWSE FIELDS command selects fields from these two database files for display and modification. On the BROWSE screen, you can edit simultaneously the field values common to both database files.

You can see the modified results for Record No. 2 (STOCK_NO="ANS-DB110") in the example shown in figure 4.21.

```
 Records      Fields     Go To     Exit                        8:50:11 am
┌──────────┬──────────────────────┬────────┬────────┬────────┬──────────┐
│STOCK_NO  │DSCRIPTION            │ COST   │ PRICE  │ON_HAND │ON_ORDER  │
├──────────┼──────────────────────┼────────┼────────┼────────┼──────────┤
│ANS-DB110 │Paradox v.1.1         │ 425.00 │ 575.00 │      1 │     5    │
│ASH-DB400 │dBASE IV v 1.0        │ 495.00 │ 795.00 │      4 │     2    │
│ASH-FW300 │Framework v.3.0       │ 345.00 │ 395.00 │      3 │     2    │
│BOL-PA300 │Turbo Pascal v.3.0    │  39.50 │  69.50 │      3 │     2    │
│CLP-DB100 │Clipper DB Compiler   │ 450.00 │ 595.00 │      2 │     1    │
│LOT-L0123 │Lotus 1-2-3 Rel 2     │ 289.00 │ 359.00 │      5 │     1    │
│MIC-QB200 │Microsoft QuickBasic  │  79.00 │ 109.00 │      4 │     1    │
│MIC-WS330 │WordStar v3.30        │ 229.00 │ 269.00 │      3 │     3    │
│MIS-WD400 │Microsoft Word 4.0    │ 229.00 │ 289.00 │      2 │     3    │
│WOR-DB100 │WordTech DB Compiler  │ 469.00 │ 595.00 │      2 │     3    │
│          │                      │        │        │        │          │
└──────────┴──────────────────────┴────────┴────────┴────────┴──────────┘
 Browse    C:\db4\SOFTWARE            Rec 2/10          File
                          View and edit fields
```

Fig. 4.21. *Simultaneously editing fields from related databases.*

The values of the COST, PRICE, ON_HAND, and ON_ORDER fields have been changed as follows:

Field	Original Value	New Value
COST	525.00	425.00
PRICE	695.00	575.00
ON_HAND	3	1
ON_ORDER	2	5

These changes are stored in the data records in both database files when you exit the BROWSE operation by using the Ctrl-End key combination. At this point, if you display the contents of the STOCK_NO="ANS-DB11Ø" data record, you will see that its field values have been changed (see fig. 4.22).

```
. SELE 1
. DISP FOR STOCK_NO="ANS-DB110"
Record#  STOCK_NO  ON_HAND ON_ORDER
      2  ANS-DB110        1        5
  .
. SELE 2
. DISP FOR STOCK_NO="ANS-DB110"
Record#  STOCK_NO  DSCRIPTION        TYPE                COST   PRICE
      2  ANS-DB110 Paradox v.1.1     database          425.00  575.00
  .
  .
```

Fig. 4.22. *Showing the modified field values in the related files.*

4.39 Tip:

To edit the records in multiple database files, use a custom data-entry form.

After you've linked database files with the SET RELATION TO operation, you can use the form design screen to create a data-entry form for editing the records in those files. If you want to create a data-entry form for editing simultaneously all the data fields in the SOFTWARE.DBF and SWSTOCK.DBF records, for example, you can create a screen file.

Before you issue the CREATE SCREEN command, however, you must link the files with a SET RELATION TO operation, as shown in figure 4.20. Then use the SET FIELDS TO command to select the data fields from the two database files:

```
. SET FIELDS TO STOCK_NO,DSCRIPTION,TYPE,COST,PRICE,
  A->ON_HAND,A->ON_ORDER
. CREATE SCREEN MULTEDIT
```

Using the SET FIELDS TO command to combine the fields in the two database files you will use in the data-entry form is important. If you don't use this command, only those data fields in the active work area will be used in the form.

Choose the **Quick Layout** option from the form design screen to load all the fields in the custom data-entry form (see fig. 4.23). Figure 4.24 shows a custom data-entry form that contains all the data fields from the two database files.

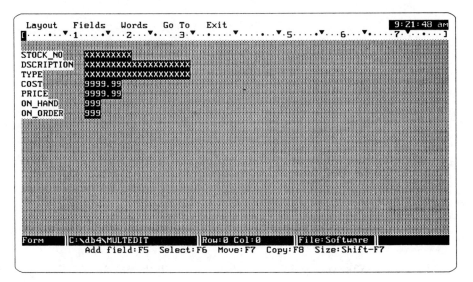

Fig. 4.23. Designing a data-entry form for the linked database files.

After you save the data-entry form in a screen file (as MULTEDIT.SCR) and its corresponding format file (as MULTEDIT.FMT), you can use the form to append data records to the two files simultaneously:

```
. SET FORMAT TO MULTEDIT
. EDIT
```

And you can use the data-entry form to edit simultaneously the contents of the data records common to both database files (see fig. 4.25).

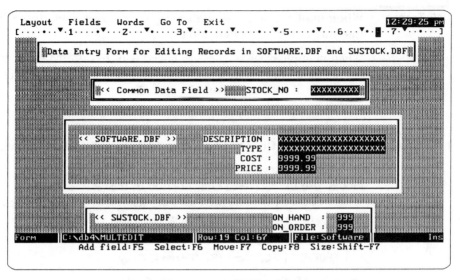

Fig. 4.24. *A custom data-entry form for editing fields in related files.*

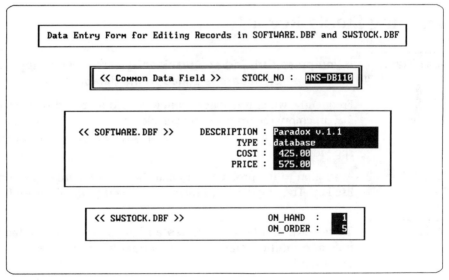

Fig. 4.25. *Editing records from related database files.*

4.40 Trap: **When multiple files are related on an indexed field, do not edit the index field in an individual file.**

When multiple database files are linked with the SET RELATION TO operation, do not attempt to edit the common (linked) data field in an individual database. If you do, records in the database files may be related incorrectly.

4.41 Trick: **Use the Read Only option in the BROWSE FIELDS statement.**

If you want to keep a field from being edited in the Browse or Edit modes, use the /R (Read Only) option in the BROWSE FIELDS statement. For example, the following statement displays the Name, Address, and City fields, but it does not allow editing of the Name field:

. BROWSE FIELDS Name /R, Address, City

Calculated fields always are read-only fields.

Deleting Empty Records

4.42 Trap: **If you press Ctrl-End at a blank entry screen while appending data, an empty record is added to the database file.**

Frequently, when you append a new record to an existing database file, an empty record is saved by accident. This can occur when you press Ctrl-End at a blank entry screen after a new record has been appended.

A solution to the problem is to exit the blank record by pressing the Esc key. The empty record then is not saved to the database file.

4.43 Trick: **To remove empty records, use a blank space surrounded by a pair of quotation marks (" ") as a qualifier in the DELETE command.**

To delete blank records in an existing database file, you can use a blank string enclosed by a pair of quotation marks as the condition in a FOR qualifier of the DELETE command. Be sure to include at least one blank space between the quotation marks. Otherwise, any nonblank data fields are considered a match.

Suppose, for example, that you issue the following command:

. DELETE FOR ID _ NO=" "

All nonblank records in the database file are marked for deletion.

You may want to test this first by using the following command:

. DISPLAY FOR ID _ NO=" "

If the desired records are displayed, then you can feel free to delete them. In any case, if you use the DELETE command before you pack the records, you can recover them by using the RECALL ALL command. However, if you issue the PACK command to remove all records marked for deletion now, these records are lost permanently.

5

Organizing Data

dBASE IV provides powerful file-management tools. You can group disk files in an applications or project catalog. And you can link files by their records and data fields in small, easily managed database files.

Some restrictions are imposed on the use of these functions, however, and traps are hidden in their operations. This chapter provides tips to help you use these tools effectively—and tricks to circumvent the traps and restrictions.

Using Catalogs To Organize Data

Catalogs let you access only the files you need for a particular application. This section gives you tips, tricks, and traps about catalog basics: the structure of a catalog, its contents, its functions, and the master catalog. The section also tells you how to create and use catalogs, as well as how to a edit a catalog file.

Understanding Catalog Files

5.1 Tip: **To organize data effectively, save files (by application) in catalogs.**

When you design a sizable database management system, you work with many data tables and their associated disk files. But you rarely use all the files at the same time. You may need only a subset of these files.

For example, when you work with the invoicing function in your data management operation, you have to access only the files needed for that particular function. dBASE IV provides a catalog file for just such a purpose.

A catalog file, similar in many ways to a regular database file, is defined with a file structure and consists of a set of records, each holding information about disk files to be included in the catalog. To process the contents of a catalog file, you use most of the commands (such as LIST, DISPLAY, DISPLAY STRUCTURE, EDIT, and APPEND) provided by dBASE IV for manipulating a database file.

Structure of a Catalog File

5.2 Tip: **To use a catalog file, you should understand its structure.**

Catalog and database files consist of the same types of field attributes: Field Name, Type, and Width. Unlike a regular database file, however, a catalog file has a data structure that is not defined by the user. dBASE IV specifies the structure of a catalog file with a standard set of data fields and prespecified field attributes. The file structure of the sample SOFTWARE.CAT catalog file is shown in figure 5.1.

```
. SELE 10
. USE SOFTWARE.CAT
. DISP STRUC
Structure for database: C:\DB4\SOFTWARE.CAT
Number of data records:      21
Date of last update   : 10/04/88
Field  Field Name  Type       Width    Dec    Index
    1   PATH        Character    70             N
    2   FILE_NAME   Character    12             N
    3   ALIAS       Character     8             N
    4   TYPE        Character     3             N
    5   TITLE       Character    80             N
    6   CODE        Numeric       3             N
    7   TAG         Character     4             N
** Total **                     181
.
```

Fig. 5.1. *The file structure of the SOFTWARE.CAT catalog file.*

The following attributes of the disk file are saved in data fields in a record of the catalog file:

❏ The PATH field tells dBASE IV where in the directory path to find the file.

❏ The fields FILE_NAME and ALIAS are used to identify the disk file. If you do not assign an alias, dBASE IV assigns the file name to the ALIAS field.

❏ The type of disk file is defined in the TYPE field.

❏ You can save in the TITLE field a label (up to 80 characters long) to describe the disk file.

❏ The CODE field is used by dBASE IV to store an internal file code, which is of no significance to most users.

❏ The last field, TAG, is not used.

Contents of a Catalog File

5.3 Tip: **Only certain types of disk files can be included in a catalog.**

A catalog file is useful for holding the disk files related to a given database management application. You can include the following disk files in a catalog:

❏ Database files (.DBF), which contain the actual data from your database

❏ Index files (.NDX), separate dBASE III Plus–type index files that determine the order of your database file when used

❏ Format files (.FMT) and Screen files (.SCR), which specify the design of a screen input form to be used

❏ Label files (.LBL), which contain specifications for label printing

❏ Report files (.FRM), which specify the design of reports to be printed

❏ View Query files (.QBE), dBASE IV Query-By-Example files that determine how your data will be displayed

❏ View files (.VUE), dBASE III Plus–type view files

❏ Update Query files (.UPD), dBASE IV queries that perform updates on database files

❏ Program files (.PRG) and Application (.APP) files, which contain program instruction commands

❏ SQL program files (.PRS), which contain dBASE/SQL instruction commands

Figure 5.2 shows the contents of a sample catalog file (SOFTWARE.CAT).

```
. SELE 10
. USE SOFTWARE.CAT
. LIST FOR RECNO()<=5
Record# PATH
FILE_NAME    ALIAS    TYPE TITLE
                          CODE TAG
       1 C:software.dbf
SOFTWARE.dbf SOFTWARE dbf  Software product description, type, cost and price
                          3
       2 SWINPUT.fmt
SWINPUT.fmt  SWINPUT  fmt  Data entry form for SOFTWARE.DBF
                          3
       3 SWLIST.lbl
SWLIST.lbl   SWLIST   lbl  Software product list
                          3
       4 SWREPORT.frm
SWREPORT.frm SWREPORT frm  Software product report
                          3
       5 SWSEARCH.qry
SWSEARCH.qry SWSEARCH qry  Query to find database compiler software
                          3

.
```

Fig. 5.2. *The contents of the SOFTWARE.CAT catalog file.*

Functions of a Catalog File

A catalog file's primary function is to group the data files for a database management application so that you can better segregate your files. A catalog file also lets you keep track of all the files associated with an open database file.

5.4 Trick: **If you forget a file's name, use the query operator (?) to select the file from the catalog.**

You can use the query operator (?) when you've forgotten a file's name because the ? can be used in place of the file name. For example, if you need to open a database file in the current catalog (SOFTWARE.CAT) and you do not remember the name of the file, you can use the query operator in the USE command:

> . USE ?

dBASE IV displays a list of all the disk files that are accessible by the command (in this case, all the database files). You select the file you want (see fig. 5.3). As you can see in the figure, a list of database files in the current catalog is shown in a "pop-up" picklist menu.

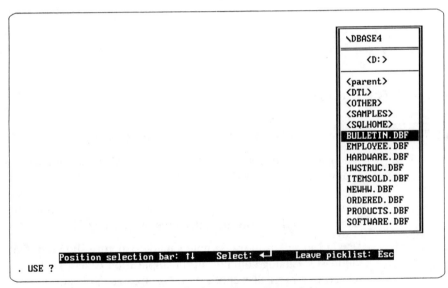

Fig. 5.3. *Selecting a database file from the active catalog.*

When you attempt to select a file from the Control Center menu, you see on-screen only the files in the current catalog. For example, you can select a format file for the active database (SOFTWARE.DBF). Only the format files associated with the active database in the current catalog are displayed (see fig. 5.4).

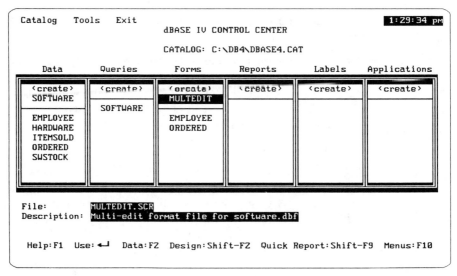

Fig. 5.4. *Selecting a format file from the active catalog.*

The Master Catalog

5.5 Tip: **All catalog files are saved in a master catalog.**

When you create your first catalog file, dBASE IV automatically sets up a master catalog named CATALOG.CAT. This master file, which organizes all the catalog files in a data management system, has the same data structure as a regular catalog file. Each record in the master catalog is used to store the attributes of a catalog file.

As you can see from the sample catalog structure shown in figure 5.5, the master catalog contains all the application catalogs. The disk files related to a particular application (such as an application for processing personnel information) are grouped under a separate catalog (such as EMPLOYEE.CAT).

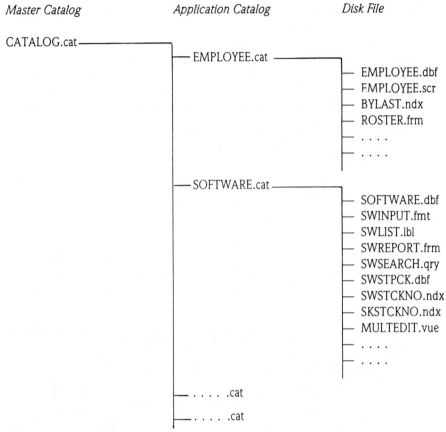

Master Catalog   *Application Catalog*   *Disk File*

CATALOG.cat ———————————————

——— EMPLOYEE.cat ———————————

— EMPLOYEE.dbf
— EMPLOYEE.scr
— BYLAST.ndx
— ROSTER.frm
— . . . .
— . . . .

——— SOFTWARE.cat ———————————

— SOFTWARE.dbf
— SWINPUT.fmt
— SWLIST.lbl
— SWREPORT.frm
— SWSEARCH.qry
— SWSTPCK.dbf
— SWSTCKNO.ndx
— SKSTCKNO.ndx
— MULTEDIT.vue
— . . . .
— . . . .

——— . . . . . .cat

——— . . . . . .cat

Fig. 5.5. *The structure of catalog files.*

Creating a Catalog File

5.6 Tip: **Use the SET CATALOG TO command to create a catalog file.**

As mentioned previously, you do not have to create the master catalog (CATALOG.CAT) because dBASE IV sets it up automatically. To create a catalog file, you first assign a name to the file by using the SET CATALOG TO command at the dot prompt:

. SET CATALOG TO < *name of catalog file*>

For example, the catalog file SOFTWARE.CAT was created with the following command:

```
. SET CATALOG TO SOFTWARE
```

Issuing the SET CATALOG TO command activates the master catalog, which will hold the catalog file you are creating. dBASE IV sets up the master catalog file (CATALOG.CAT) and places it in work area 10.

You are asked whether you are creating a new catalog:

```
Create new file catalog? (Y/N)
```

In response to this prompt, type Y. You then are asked to give a title to the catalog file:

```
Edit the description of this .cat file:
```

After you assign the title "Product division, type, cost, and price" to the catalog file, a new record is appended to the master catalog file (CATALOG.CAT) and the new catalog file is loaded into work area 10. Now you can save the data files related to your application in the catalog file.

When you set up a new catalog file, the following message is displayed when you execute the SET CATALOG TO command:

```
File catalog is empty
```

At this point, SOFTWARE.CAT becomes the current catalog in work area 10. If you were to examine the contents of the master catalog, the data record in the master catalog file (CATALOG.CAT) would look like the one shown in figure 5.6.

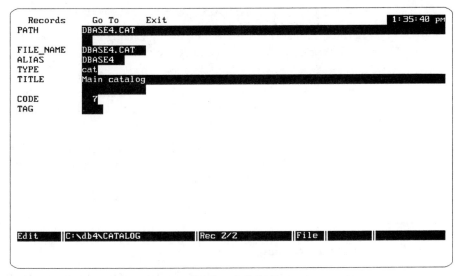

Fig. 5.6. *Editing a record in the CATALOG.CAT master catalog.*

Using a Catalog File

This section gives you tips, tricks, and traps on using a catalog file. The text gives you suggestions about activating an existing catalog file, terminating the cataloging operation, and displaying the contents of a catalog file.

Activating an Existing Catalog File

5.7 Tip:

Use the SET CATALOG TO command to activate and deactivate a catalog.

You can use the SET CATALOG TO command to create a catalog file or to select an existing catalog file. To activate the catalog file you want, specify the name of the file in the command line. If the catalog file exists, it is loaded in work area 10. Otherwise, a new catalog file is created and added to the master catalog.

If SOFTWARE.CAT is the active catalog in work area 10, for example, you can use the SET CATALOG TO command to switch to another catalog (EMPLOYEE.CAT):

. SET CATALOG TO EMPLOYEE.CAT

Because EMPLOYEE.CAT is an existing catalog file, it is loaded into work area 10 and becomes the active catalog.

A catalog remains active until you deactivate it by selecting another catalog or by issuing the SET CATALOG OFF command. Issue the SET CATALOG ON command to activate a catalog that has been selected previously with the SET CATALOG TO command.

Note: SET CATALOG TO names the file that holds the catalog information, and SET CATALOG ON indicates that you now want to use the catalog named in the SET CATALOG ON statement. The SET CATALOG TO command, then, must be used before the SET CATALOG ON command.

5.8 Trick:

If you forget a catalog's name, use the query operator (?) to select the catalog.

You can use the query operator (?) when you've forgotten a catalog's name because the ? can be used in place of the catalog name. A pop-up picklist menu lets you select from the available catalogs (see fig. 5.7).

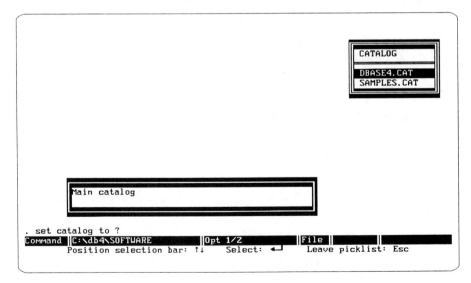

Fig. 5.7. Selecting a catalog.

5.9 Tip: **You can add new disk files to an existing catalog.**

One way to build the contents of a catalog file is to add new disk files as you create them. After you activate a catalog file (by using the SET CATALOG TO or SET CATALOG ON command), a new entry is added to the active catalog when you access or create a file using any of the following commands (if the file is not already in the catalog):

```
COPY STRUCTURE
COPY STRUCTURE EXTENDED
COPY TO
CREATE
CREATE FROM
CREATE/MODIFY LABEL
CREATE/MODIFY QUERY
CREATE/MODIFY REPORT
CREATE/MODIFY SCREEN
CREATE/MODIFY VIEW
IMPORT FROM
INDEX
JOIN
SET FILTER TO FILE
SET FORMAT
SET VIEW
SORT
TOTAL
USE
```

For example, to add the existing database file (SOFTWARE.DBF) and its format file (SWINPUT.FMT) to the SOFTWARE.CAT catalog, enter the following series of commands at the dot prompt (all file extensions are optional):

```
. SET CATALOG TO SOFTWARE.CAT
. SELECT 1
. USE SOFTWARE.DBF
. SET FORMAT TO SWINPUT.FMT
```

5.10 Trap: **If you use work area 10 to manipulate data while a catalog is active, the catalog file will be closed.**

When you use a catalog, remember that dBASE IV holds the active catalog file in work area 10. If you use work area 10 for creating a new disk file or performing other data manipulation operations, the catalog file will be removed from work area 10.

5.11 Trick: **To avoid losing the active catalog file, create a new disk file in another work area.**

Select another work area (from 1 to 9) in which to create a new disk file:

```
. SET CATALOG TO SOFTWARE.CAT
. SELECT 1
. CREATE ACCOUNT
```

5.12 Trap: **If you try to activate the master catalog file with the SET CATALOG TO CATALOG.CAT command, a new catalog file is created and saved in the master file.**

When the first catalog file is created, dBASE IV sets up the master catalog CATALOG.CAT to hold the attributes of the catalog files. Whenever you add a new catalog file to the master file, the program appends to the master file a new record describing the new catalog file.

Because you don't need to "activate" the master catalog before you create a new catalog file, any name you specify in the SET CATALOG TO command is treated as a catalog file. Therefore, issuing the SET CATALOG TO CATALOG.CAT command at the dot prompt creates a catalog file named CATALOG.CAT and saves it as a new catalog in the master file.

Terminating the Cataloging Operation

5.13 Tip: **Selecting a new catalog closes the current catalog automatically.**

When you select a new catalog with the SET CATALOG TO command, the active catalog is closed and removed from work area 10.

5.14 Trick: **Use the SET CATALOG TO command to close an active catalog.**

To terminate the active catalog without selecting another catalog, issue the SET CATALOG TO command without specifying the name of a catalog.

5.15 Tip: **Use SET CATALOG OFF to halt the catalog operation temporarily.**

If you want to stop adding data files to the active catalog in work area 10, issue the SET CATALOG OFF command at the dot prompt. You can reactivate the catalog by issuing the SET CATALOG ON command.

Displaying the Contents of a Catalog File

5.16 Tip: **Use normal display commands to display the contents of a catalog file.**

Except for the file structure, which is defined by dBASE IV, a catalog file can be treated as a regular database file. To display the contents of a catalog file, use one of the following commands:

```
BROWSE
DISPLAY
DISPLAY STRUCTURE
LIST
```

5.17 Tip: **Select work area 10 for displaying the contents of a catalog.**

Remember that the active catalog file is held in work area 10. If you want to display the contents of the active catalog file, you must select this work area before you issue the DISPLAY command. To display the catalog, use the following sequence of commands:

```
. SELECT 1Ø
. DISPLAY STRUCTURE
. . . . .
. LIST
. GOTO 3
. DISPLAY
```

Editing a Catalog File

This section gives you tips, tricks, and traps on editing a catalog file. The suggestions here can help you edit the contents of an existing catalog, edit records in the master catalog, delete an existing catalog, and remove disk files from a catalog.

Editing the Contents of an Existing Catalog

5.18 Tip: **Use normal editing commands to edit the contents of a catalog file.**

You can edit the contents of the records in a catalog file with the same procedures you use to modify a database file. For example, to edit the records in the SOFTWARE.CAT file, you could use the EDIT or BROWSE commands:

```
. SELECT 1Ø
. EDIT RECORD 3
 . . . . .
. BROWSE
```

Editing Records in the Master Catalog

5.19 Tip: **To change the attributes of an existing catalog, edit its corresponding record in the master catalog.**

Each record in the master catalog contains information on the attributes of a catalog file. If you need to modify the attributes of an existing catalog file, you can edit the contents of its corresponding records in the master catalog. You must, however, put the master catalog in work area 10 (by issuing the USE command) before you edit its records.

For example, if the master catalog's third record contains information on the attributes of a given catalog file, the following commands allow you to edit the contents of that record after you select the master catalog (USE CATALOG.CAT) in work area 10 (SELECT 1Ø):

```
. SELECT 1Ø
. USE CATALOG.CAT
. EDIT 3
```

5.20 Trap: **You can lose a record from a catalog if you change the names and the order of the fields in the file structure.**

Never change the names and order of the fields in the catalog file structure. Although dBASE IV does not prevent you from modifying the structure of a catalog file, doing so may cause records referring to your disk files to be removed from a catalog without warning.

5.21 Trap: **Do not select work areas 1 through 9 for holding the master catalog.**

You should not put the master catalog file in work areas 1 through 9 for editing operations. If you do, any file selected in these areas when an active catalog is in use will be treated as a new catalog file. Work area 10 is reserved for holding catalog files until they are needed.

Deleting an Existing Catalog

5.22 Tip: **Delete a catalog file as you would a database file.**

To remove an existing catalog from your file directory, simply use the ERASE command. To remove the SOFTWARE.CAT file from the directory, for example, you would issue the following command at the dot prompt:

```
. ERASE SOFTWARE.CAT
```

5.23 Trap: **You cannot delete an open catalog file.**

If you try to delete an open catalog file, the following error message appears on-screen:

```
Cannot erase open file
```

You can choose to Cancel the command, Edit the command, or get Help.

5.24 Trick: **Close a catalog you intend to delete from the master catalog.**

To close a catalog file, use one of the following commands:

```
SET CATALOG TO (without a file name)
CLOSE ALL
CLEAR ALL
```

Use the SET CATALOG TO command if you want to close only the catalog file (but not other disk files). As their names imply, the CLOSE ALL and CLEAR ALL commands close all the disk files and memory variables—not just the catalog file.

5.25 Trick:

To erase a catalog file, delete its corresponding record from the master catalog.

When you erase a catalog file, dBASE IV automatically deletes from the master catalog (CATALOG.CAT) the data record that describes the catalog file. One way to remove a catalog file from the master catalog is to delete from the master catalog the record related to that catalog file.

To remove the SOFTWARE.CAT catalog file from the master catalog, for example, use the following commands:

```
. SELECT 1Ø
. USE CATALOG.CAT
. DELETE FOR FILE_NAME="SOFTWARE.CAT"
. PACK
```

You also can delete a record by its record number.

An alternative method is to use the BROWSE or EDIT command to delete a record by using the Ctrl-U key combination, followed by the PACK command.

5.26 Trick:

To delete all the catalogs from the directory, use the DOS ERASE command.

The dBASE IV ERASE command allows you to delete only one file at a time. To delete a group of catalog files, use the DOS ERASE command:

```
. RUN ERASE *.CAT
```

or

```
. ! ERASE *.CAT
```

Of course, you also can use the **Operations** menu from the **DOS utilities** in the **Tools** menu to delete files.

Removing Disk Files from a Catalog

5.27 Trap: **If you delete a disk file with the dBASE IV ERASE command, the erased file is removed from the catalog file and the file directory.**

If you want to use a file for other applications, that file must remain in the file directory. Do not use the dBASE IV ERASE command if you want to remove a file from the catalog but not from the file directory.

5.28 Trick: **To remove a disk file from a catalog, delete its corresponding record from the catalog file.**

When you add a disk file to a catalog, a record that describes the disk file is appended to the catalog file. If you want to remove a disk file from the catalog, simply delete its corresponding record from the catalog file. In this way, the disk file remains in the file directory and can be used for other applications.

5.29 Tip: **Use the Control Center menu to update your catalog.**

Using the Control Center menu, you easily can add files to and delete files from the current catalog. To add a file, simply press Alt-C to choose the **Catalog** menu, and then select **Add file to catalog**. A list of available files appears. Choose the file to be added and press Enter (see fig. 5.8).

To remove a file, first highlight the file in the files column on the Control Center screen. Then choose **Remove highlighted file from catalog** from the **Catalog** menu.

5.30 Trap: **Only files of the type specified can be added from the Control Center.**

The types of files you can add to your catalog from the Control Center are determined by the column in which the cursor is placed. For example, when you want to add a forms file, place the cursor in the Forms column, and then choose **Add file to catalog** from the **Catalog** menu. The picklist will contain forms files in the current directory. Similarly, if you want to add a database file, you place the cursor in the Data column before initiating the **Add file to catalog** operation.

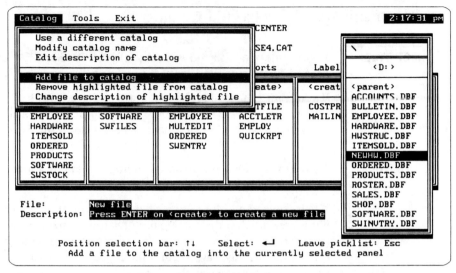

Fig. 5.8. *Adding a file to the current catalog.*

5.31 Trick: **Use the DISPLAY STATUS command to monitor the program's status.**

When you are using more than one work area for data manipulation operations and for setting up a catalog, you can use the DISPLAY STATUS command to monitor the program's status. To find out which operations are being performed and which database and catalog are active in the work areas, use the DISPLAY STATUS command.

As you can see from figure 5.9, the database and index files currently being used in all the work areas are described when you execute the DISPLAY STATUS command. The status of the printer and function keys also is displayed.

```
. DISPLAY STATUS

Select area:  1, Database in Use: C:\DB4\SOFTWARE.DBF   Alias: SOFTWARE
Production   MDX file:  C:\DB4\SOFTWARE.MDX
          Index TAG:      STOCK_NO Key: STOCK_NO

Currently Selected Database:
Select area:  2, Database in Use: C:\DB4\SWSTOCK.DBF   Alias: SWSTOCK
Production   MDX file:  C:\DB4\SWSTOCK.MDX
          Index TAG:      STOCK_NO Key: STOCK_NO

Select area: 10, Database in Use: C:\DB4\DBASE4.CAT   Alias: CATALOG

File search path:
Default disk drive: C:
Print destination:  PRN:
Margin =      0
Refresh count =     0
Reprocess count =    0
Number of files open =    8
Current work area =    2

ALTERNATE  - OFF   DELIMITERS - OFF   FULLPATH   - OFF   SAFETY    - ON
AUTOSAVE   - OFF   DESIGN     - ON    HEADING    - ON    SCOREBOARD - ON
Press any key to continue...
```

Fig. 5.9. *Monitoring program status with the DISPLAY STATUS command.*

Linking Database Files

Information in two or more database files can be linked in a number of ways. You can link databases vertically by adding records from one database file to another. You also can combine data fields from several database files by linking them horizontally, using the dBASE IV RELATION operation.

Combining Data Records in Two Database Files

5.32 Tip: **To combine data records in two database files with an identical structure, use the APPEND FROM command.**

The simplest way to combine records in two different database files with an identical file structure is to use the APPEND FROM command. This command adds all the records from the source file to the target file.

For example, if sales data for departments A and B are stored in two database files (SALES_ A.DBF and SALES_B.DBF), and the two files share the same file structure, you can combine all the records in SALES_ A.DBF and SALES_B.DBF by using the APPEND FROM command:

```
. USE SALES _ A
. APPEND FROM SALES _ B
```

The APPEND FROM command adds all the records in the source database file (SALES_B.DBF) to the target file (SALES_A.DBF). As a result, the target file holds the combined records while the source file remains unchanged.

5.33 Trick: **Use a new database file to hold combined records.**

To combine the records of two database files with an identical file structure and save them in a new file, copy the records of one file to the new file, and then use the APPEND FROM command. When you use the APPEND FROM command to combine records from two database files, all the combined records will reside in the target database file.

For example, to combine all the records in SALES_ A.DBF and SALES_B.DBF and save them in a new database file ALLSALES.DBF, issue the following commands:

```
. USE SALES _ A
. COPY TO ALLSALES
. USE ALLSALES
. APPEND FROM SALES _ B
```

When you use APPEND FROM to add records from the source database file to the target file, you won't have any problems if the two database files share an identical file structure. However, if the two database files have different file structures, APPEND FROM adds to the target file only records with fields that are common to both files.

5.34 Trap: **Be careful when you use the APPEND FROM command to combine two database files with different file structures.**

Only records with fields that are common to both files are added from the source file to the target file when you use the APPEND FROM command. Figure 5.10, for example, shows two database files with different file structures: one (EMPLOYEE.DBF) has six data fields, and the other (ROSTER.DBF) has three data fields.

Because the structures of the source database file (EMPLOYEE.DBF) and the target file (ROSTER.DBF) are different, only some of the fields from the source file's records are added to the target file when you execute the following commands:

```
. USE ROSTER
. APPEND FROM EMPLOYEE
```

In figure 5.11, the records that have been added from the EMPLOYEE.DBF file to the ROSTER.DBF file contain only those data fields that are common to both files.

To add records selectively from one database file to another, include a qualifier in the APPEND FROM command, as in the following example:

```
. USE OFFICERS
. APPEND FROM EMPLOYEE FOR POSITION="President"
.OR. POSITION="VP"
```

In this example, the data field POSITION is used to select those records in the source file that meet the qualifying conditions for the APPEND operation.

```
. DISP STRUC
Structure for database: C:\DB4\EMPLOYEE.DBF
Number of data records:        0
Date of last update   : 09/29/88
Field  Field Name  Type       Width    Dec    Index
    1  ID_NO       Character     11             N
    2  FIRST_NAME  Character     15             N
    3  LAST_NAME   Character     15             N
    4  POSITION    Character     10             N
    5  EMPLY_DATE  Date           8             N
    6  MALE        Logical        1             N
** Total **                      61

. USE ROSTER
. DISP STRUC
Structure for database: C:\DB4\ROSTER.DBF
Number of data records:       10
Date of last update   : 10/04/88
Field  Field Name  Type       Width    Dec    Index
    1  FIRST_NAME  Character     15             N
    2  LAST_NAME   Character     15             N
    3  POSITION    Character     10             N
** Total **                      41

.
```

Fig. 5.10. *The file structures of the EMPLOYEE.DBF and ROSTER.DBF files.*

```
. USE ROSTER
. APPE FROM EMPLOYEE
      10 records added
. LIST
Record#  FIRST_NAME    LAST_NAME      POSITION
      1  Thomas T,     Smith          President
      2  Tina Y,       Thompson       VP
      3  Peter F,      Watson         Manager
      4  Doris Y,      Taylor         Sales Rep
      5  Tyrone T,     Thorson        Engineer
      6  Cathy J,      Faust          Secretary
      7  Vincent M,    Corso          Sales Rep
      8  Jane W,       Kaiser         Accountant
      9  Tina K,       Davidson       Trainee
     10  James J,      Smith          Trainee
```

Fig. 5.11. Records appended from EMPLOYEE.DBF to ROSTER.DBF.

5.35 Trap: **If the search field is not common to both database files, no record will be appended and an error message will appear.**

You cannot add the records of all the male employees in EMPLOYEE.DBF to ROSTER.DBF (their structures are shown in fig. 5.10) by using the following commands:

```
. USE ROSTER
. APPEND FROM EMPLOYEE FOR MALE
```

Because the target file (ROSTER.DBF) is active and the field MALE is not one of its data fields, the field is treated as an undefined variable. A Variable not found error message appears, and the APPEND operation halts.

5.36 Trap: **You can't use a logical field as a character string comparison condition for appending a data record.**

When you use a logical field or logical memory variable, the value of the field or variable must be either .T. or .F. Because the value of .T. or .F. is not considered a character string, you cannot use it in a FOR qualifier in a dBASE IV command for evaluating a logical field or variable.

For example, the value specified for the logical field MALE in the following APPEND and LIST commands will not be evaluated correctly:

```
. USE MALES
. APPEND FROM EMPLOYEE FOR MALE=.T.
. LIST FOR MALE=.T.
```

The correct method is as follows:

```
. USE MALES
. APPEND FROM EMPLOYEE FOR MALE
. LIST FOR MALE
```

To specify the opposite condition, the syntax would be as follows:

```
. APPEND FROM EMPLOYEE FOR .NOT. MALE
```

Filtering Out Deleted Records

5.37 Trick: **Before appending records from one database file to another, use SET DELETED ON to filter selected records.**

With the APPEND operation, one way to screen records in the source file before adding them to a target file is to mark unwanted records temporarily with deletion marks. To mark selected records, you can use any legitimate qualifying condition in the DELETE command.

For example, if you want to add to the ROSTER.DBF database file only the EMPLOYEE.DBF records for male employees, you should first mark with deletion marks the records for female employees. As you can see from figure 5.12, the records are marked with asterisks (*).

Then issue the SET DELETED ON command to filter out the marked records. Because all the marked records will be ignored by most dBASE IV commands, including the APPEND FROM command, only the unmarked EMPLOYEE.DBF records are appended to the ROSTER.DBF file (see fig. 5.13).

As you can see from figure 5.13, executing the SET DELETED ON command excludes the marked records from the LIST and APPEND FROM commands. As a result, only the five unmarked records are appended by the APPEND FROM command.

After appending the records, issue the RECALL ALL command to remove the temporary deletion marks.

```
. USE EMPLOYEE
. DELE FOR .NOT. MALE
      5 records deleted
. LIST
Record#  ID_NO        FIRST_NAME    LAST_NAME    POSITION    EMPLY_DATE MALE
      1  123-45-6789 Thomas T.     Smith        President   03/01/81   .T.
      2 *254-63-5691 Tina Y.       Thompson     VP          09/22/82   .F.
      3  467-34-6789 Peter F.      Watson       Manager     10/12/82   .T.
      4 *732-08-4589 Doris Y.      Taylor       Sales Rep   08/14/83   .F.
      5  663-55-8900 Tyrone T.     Thorsen      Engineer    06/20/82   .T.
      6 *823-46-6213 Cathy J.      Faust        Secretary   04/15/83   .F.
      7  554-34-7893 Vincent M.    Corso        Sales Rep   07/20/84   .T.
      8 *321-65-9087 Jane W.       Kaiser       Accountant  11/22/82   .F.
      9 *560-56-9321 Tina K.       Davidson     Trainee     05/16/86   .F.
     10  435-54-9876 James J.      Smith        Trainee     01/23/86   .T.
```

Fig. 5.12. *Using a qualifier to mark records to be deleted.*

```
. SET DELETED ON
. LIST
Record#  ID_NO        FIRST_NAME    LAST_NAME    POSITION    EMPLY_DATE MALE
      1  123-45-6789 Thomas T.     Smith        President   03/01/81   .T.
      3  467-34-6789 Peter F.      Watson       Manager     10/12/82   .T.
      5  563-55-8900 Tyrone T.     Thorsen      Engineer    06/20/82   .T.
      7  554-34-7893 Vincent M.    Corso        Sales Rep   07/20/84   .T.
     10  435-54-9876 James J.      Smith        Trainee     01/23/86   .T.

. USE ROSTER
. APPE FROM EMPLOYEE
      5 records added
.
```

Fig. 5.13. *Hiding deleted records from the APPEND operation.*

5.38 Trap: **If you forget to SET DELETED OFF, marked records cannot be displayed.**

After using the SET DELETED ON command, remember to issue the SET DELETED OFF command. Otherwise, the records you marked for deletion will be hidden from view when you issue the LIST, DISPLAY, or BROWSE command.

5.39 Tip: **Use the query design surface to mark records for deletion or to specify records to be appended.**

Access the query design surface by selecting < **create**> from the Queries column on the Control Center screen. Or, type CREATE QUERY at the dot prompt.

Setting up query and view files are discussed in more detail later in this chapter and in Chapter 7. For now, be aware that the **Update** menu offers four operations to perform on your files based on the filtering criteria you specify: **Replace values**, **Append records**, **Mark records for deletion**, and **Unmark records** (see fig. 5.14). Using a query file to mark records for deletion allows you to save a complex series of filtering conditions in a query file that can be used over and over again as needed.

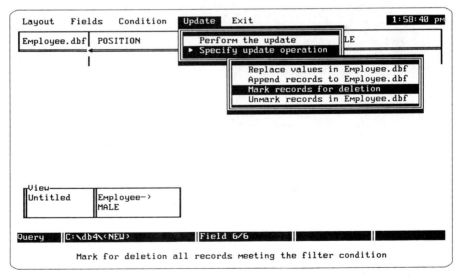

Fig. 5.14. *Creating a view file to mark records for deletion.*

Merging Data Fields

This section gives you tips, tricks, and traps on merging data fields in multiple database files. You will learn techniques for using the JOIN command to combine data fields from two or more database files.

Merging Data Fields from Two Database Files

5.40 Trick: **To combine data fields from two different databases, use the JOIN command.**

If you want to form a new database by combining some or all the data fields in two database files, use the JOIN command. The JOIN command lets you merge data fields from two database files by using a linking field to find the values common to both database files.

For example, software product information is stored in SOFTWARE.DBF, and inventory data is saved in the SWSTOCK.DBF database file. The file structures of these files are shown in figure 5.15. Notice that both files have an index tag for the STOCK_NO field. (See Chapter 6 for more information on index tags.)

```
. USE SOFTWARE
. DISP STRUC
Structure for database: C:\DB4\SOFTWARE.DBF
Number of data records:     10
Date of last update   : 09/30/88
Field  Field Name  Type       Width   Dec    Index
    1  STOCK_NO    Character      9            Y
    2  DSCRIPTION  Character     20            N
    3  TYPE        Character     20            N
    4  COST        Numeric        7     2      N
    5  PRICE       Numeric        7     2      N
** Total **                      64

. USE SWSTOCK
. DISP STRUC
Structure for database: C:\DB4\SWSTOCK.DBF
Number of data records:     10
Date of last update   : 09/30/88
Field  Field Name  Type       Width   Dec    Index
    1  STOCK_NO    Character      9            Y
    2  ON_HAND     Numeric        3            N
    3  ON_ORDER    Numeric        3            N
** Total **                      16

.
```

Fig. 5.15. The file structures of the SOFTWARE.DBF and SWSTOCK.DBF files.

To create an inventory list that contains some of the data fields from both files, use the STOCK_NO as the linking field in the JOIN command. Assuming that you have created an index tag for a common field in both files, the method for using the JOIN command follows:

> . SELECT 1
> . USE < *name of file to be joined* > ORDER < *index tag* >
> . SELECT 2
> . USE < *name of active database* > ORDER < *index tag* >
> . JOIN WITH < *ALIAS of file to be joined* > TO < *new file* >
> FOR < *joining condition* > FIELDS < *list of merged fields* >

The joining operation examines each record in the active file and tries to match the records in the joined file according to the value of the linking field. If a match is found, the values in the records of the two files are merged to form a record in the new database file.

As mentioned before, the two files you want to join must first be indexed on their linking fields. As you can see from figure 5.16, the database files have index tags for the STOCK_NO linking field. The fields that are to be created in the new database file (SWINVTRY.DBF) are specified with the FIELDS clause.

```
. SELE 1
. USE SOFTWARE ORDER STOCK_NO
Master index: STOCK_NO
. SELE 2
. USE SWSTOCK ORDER STOCK_NO
Master index: STOCK_NO
. JOIN WITH A TO SWINVTRY FOR STOCK_NO=A->STOCK_NO FIELDS STOCK_NO,A->DSCRIPTION
,ON_HAND,A->COST
      10 records joined
.
```

Fig. 5.16. *Joining records in SOFTWARE.DBF with SWSTOCK.DBF.*

The two database files are then joined by using the linking field in the JOIN command. The records resulting from the joining operation are saved in the SWINVTRY.DBF file, whose contents are shown in figure 5.17. Notice that SWINVTRY.DBF contains data fields from both the SOFTWARE.DBF and SWSTOCK.DBF files.

```
. USE SWINVTRY
. LIST
Record#   STOCK_NO  DSCRIPTION           ON_HAND    COST
      1   ANS-DB110 Paradox v.1.1            1    525.00
      2   ASH-DB400 dBASE IV v 1.0           4    495.00
      3   ASH-FW300 Framework v.3.0          3    345.00
      4   BOL-PA300 Turbo Pascal v.3.0       0     39.50
      5   CLP-DB100 Clipper DB Compiler      2    450.00
      6   LOT-LO123 Lotus 1-2-3 Rel 2        5    289.00
      7   MIC-QB200 Microsoft QuickBasic     4     79.00
      8   MIC-WS330 WordStar v3.30           3    229.00
      9   MIS-WD400 Microsoft Word 4.0       2    229.00
     10   WOR-DB100 WordTech DB Compiler     2    469.00
```

Fig. 5.17. *Displaying the joined records.*

5.41 Trap: **To avoid confusion with dBASE IV's ALIAS names, do not use the single letters A through M as names for database files to be joined.**

When you link database files with the JOIN command, do not use the single letters A through M as names for database files to be joined. These letters are reserved for ALIAS names. In general, do not use single-letter names for database files.

Merging Data Fields in Multiple Database Files

5.42 Trick:

To merge data fields from more than two database files, perform the JOIN operations in sequence.

Because you can join only two database files at one time, you need to perform the file-joining operation more than once if you want to combine database fields from several database files. To merge fields in three database files (FILE_A.DBF, FILE_B.DBF, and FILE_C.DBF), for example, follow these steps:

```
. SELECT 1
. USE FILE _ A ORDER < index tag>
. SELECT 2
. USE FILE _ B ORDER < index tag>
. JOIN WITH A TO TEMP FOR < condition>
. USE TEMP ORDER < index tag>
. SELECT 1
. USE FILE _C ORDER < index tag>
. JOIN WITH B TO NEWFILE FOR < condition>
. CLOSE DATABASE
. ERASE TEMP.DBF
```

5.43 Tip:

Allocate sufficient disk space before you join files.

When you join files, the resulting database file may contain many records. Before carrying out the JOIN operations, be sure to provide enough disk space for saving the resulting file.

When you join two database files, the number of records in the resulting database depends on the the number of unique records in the two database files. If each record in the active file matches only one record in the joining file according to the value in the linking field, the new database file that results will contain the same number of records as the active file. However, if a record in the active file matches several records in the joining file, the new database file will contain many more records than the active file.

Relating Data

This section gives you tips, tricks, and traps on relating data in multiple database files. You will learn techniques for using the SET RELATION command to link two or more database files.

Relating Data in Two Database Files

5.44 Tip: **When you need to access data simultaneously in multiple database files, use the SET RELATION command to link the files.**

You can save time and disk space when you need to access data simultaneously in multiple database files. Link the files with the SET RELATION TO command instead of joining them in a permanent file.

Because joining two database files is time-consuming and the database file created by the JOIN command may take up a great deal of disk space, the JOIN command may not be appropriate for many applications. Unless you need to create a permanent database file for holding the combined records, the JOIN command is an inefficient way to merge the data fields from two database files.

You may need to access information from more than one database file during a single operation. To access these files simultaneously, you can merge them temporarily with the SET RELATION TO command. The records in the individual files are saved back to the disk rather than to a new database file.

Relating one database file to another is similar to joining files. To relate two database files based on a key field, use the following sequence of commands:

```
. SELECT 1
. USE < name of file to be related > ORDER < index tag >
. SELECT 2
. USE < name of active file > ORDER < index tag >
. SET RELATION TO < key field > INTO < ALIAS of file to be related >
```

If the database file has already been indexed and has an existing index file, you can combine the USE and INDEX commands into one command:

. USE < *name of file*> INDEX < *name of existing index file*>

Use the SET FILTER TO command to specify the condition for record selection. Only records that meet the filter condition are included in the SET RELATION operation.

After using the SET RELATION TO command to relate the two files, you can select the data fields you want to access. As shown in figure 5.18, the combined fields are displayed when you list the records.

```
. SELE 1
. USE SOFTWARE ORDER STOCK_NO
Master index: STOCK_NO
. SELE 2
. USE SWSTOCK ORDER STOCK_NO
Master index: STOCK_NO
. SELE 1
. SET RELATION TO STOCK_NO INTO B
. SET FIELDS TO STOCK_NO,DSCRIPTION,COST,B->ON_HAND
. SET FILTER TO COST>=200
. LIST
Record#   STOCK_NO   DSCRIPTION            COST ON_HAND
      2   ANS-DB110  Paradox v.1.1        525.00       1
      1   ASH-DB400  dBASE IV v 1.0       495.00       4
      8   ASH-FW300  Framework v.3.0      345.00       3
      3   CLP-DB100  Clipper DB Compiler  450.00       2
      5   LOT-L0123  Lotus 1-2-3 Rel 2    289.00       5
      6   MIC-WS330  WordStar v3.30       229.00       3
      7   MIS-WD400  Microsoft Word 4.0   229.00       2
      4   WOR-DB100  WordTech DB Compiler 469.00       2
.
```

Fig. 5.18. Linking SOFTWARE.DBF and SWSTOCK.DBF with SET RELATION TO.

In addition to LIST, you can use DISPLAY, EDIT, and BROWSE to manipulate the contents of records that contain merged fields. At this point, you can define and invoke a custom data-entry form for the combined data fields by using the SET FORMAT TO command.

5.45 Trap: **Because related files are merged temporarily, closing them erases the merged data fields.**

Note that when two database files are linked with SET RELATION, no new data records are created. The data fields are merged only temporarily for the LIST, DISPLAY, EDIT, and BROWSE operations. If you close all the database files in work areas 1 and 2, records containing the merged data fields are erased.

5.46 Trick: **To save information from related database files, create a view file.**

Once defined, the relation between the database files can be saved in a view file for later use. For example, you can save the relation between the SOFTWARE.DBF and SWSTOCK.DBF files by using the CREATE VIEW...FROM ENVIRONMENT command:

```
. CREATE VIEW SWFILES.VUE FROM ENVIRONMENT
```

5.47 Tip: **To relate previously related database files, save time and work by setting up the view file.**

Once you save the relation information in a view file, you can repeat the relation operation by setting up the view file:

```
. SET VIEW TO  < name of existing view file>
```

You don't have to enter the commands for selecting, indexing, and relating the files. For example, when you issue the SET VIEW TO SWFILES command, the SOFTWARE.DBF and SWSTOCK.DBF files are again related according to the procedure described in the view file (see fig. 5.19).

```
. CLOSE ALL
. SET VIEW TO SWFILES
Master index: STOCK_NO
Master index: STOCK_NO
. LIST
Record#  STOCK_NO  DSCRIPTION              COST ON_HAND
      2  ANS-DB110 Paradox v.1.1          525.00       1
      1  ASH-DB400 dBASE IV v 1.0         495.00       4
      8  ASH-FW300 Framework v.3.0        345.00       3
      3  CLP-DB100 Clipper DB Compiler    450.00       2
      5  LOT-L0123 Lotus 1-2-3 Rel 2      289.00       5
      6  MIC-WS330 WordStar v3.30         229.00       3
      7  MIS-WD400 Microsoft Word 4.0     229.00       2
      4  WOR-DB100 WordTech DB Compiler   469.00       2
.
```

Fig. 5.19. *Relinking the database files by activating the view file.*

The CLOSE ALL command closes all the database files and clears all the work areas. The LIST command verifies that no database file is in use. By selecting a view file (SWFILES) with the SET VIEW TO command, you relink the database files from the information contained in the view file. Then, with the LIST command, display the records from the related SOFTWARE.DBF and SWSTOCK.DBF files.

5.48 Tip:

To relate database files with no common key field, use the RECNO( ) function.

If the two database files do not share a common key field, you can link the files with their record numbers (RECNO( )). Simply use the RECNO( ) function in place of a key field in the SET RELATION TO command:

```
. SET RELATION TO RECNO( ) INTO...
```

As a result, because the records from both files are matched by their sequential record numbers, you do not need to index the files before you relate them:

```
. SELECT 1
. USE FILE_A
. SELECT 2
. USE FILE_B
. SELECT 1
. SET RELATION TO RECNO( ) INTO B
```

Relating Multiple Database Files

5.49 Tip:

To relate more than two database files, create a continuous linking chain.

You can simultaneously access data fields from more than two files. To do so, create a relation chain that links the files through a common index field or by record number.

Put the master file in work area 1 and each of the other database files in separate work areas. If you want to relate the files by a key data field (KEYFIELD), first index all but the master file:

```
. USE DBFILE2
. INDEX ON KEYFIELD TO NDXFILE2
. USE DBFILE3
```

```
. INDEX ON KEYFIELD TO NDXFILE3
. . . . .
. . . . .
. SELECT 1
. USE DBFILE1
. SELECT 2
. USE DBFILE2 INDEX NDXFILE2
. SELECT 3
. USE DBFILE3 INDEX NDXFILE3
. . . . .
. . . . .
. . . . .
```

The relation chain begins with the master file. Each of the other database files is linked in subsequent steps:

```
. SELECT 1
. SET RELATION TO KEYFIELD INTO DBFILE2
. SELECT 2
. SET RELATION TO KEYFIELD INTO DBFILE3
. . . . .
. . . . .
```

Figure 5.20 shows how to relate three database files: HWLIST.DBF (the master file), HWCOST.DBF, and HWSTOCK.DBF. As you can see from the figure, the three files are related in two steps. First, the HWLIST.DBF file is linked with the HWCOST.DBF file. The HWSTOCK .DBF file is then related to the linked files.

After you index the files on the common data field STOCK_NO, you relate the master file HWLIST.DBF in work area 1 to HWCOST.DBF in work area 2 (alias B). Finally, you add the third database file HWSTOCK.DBF in work area 3 (alias C) to the relation chain. You use the LIST command to display the selected fields of the records resulting from the relation operations.

5.50 Trick: **Link more than one file to the master file with the SET RELATION TO command.**

dBASE IV allows "multiple child" relations in one statement. This means that more than one file can be related to the master file using one SET RELATION TO command. The format is as follows:

```
, SELE 1
, USE HWLIST
, SELE 2
, USE HWCOST INDE HCSTCKNO
, SELE 3
, USE HWSTOCK INDE HSSTCKNO
, SELE 1
, SET RELATION TO STOCK_NO INTO B
, SELE 2
, SET RELATION TO STOCK_NO INTO C
, SELE 1
, SET FIELDS TO STOCK_NO,DSCRIPTION,B->COST,C->ON_HAND
, LIST
Record#  STOCK_NO  DSCRIPTION                        COST ON_HAND
       1  CPQ-SP256 Compaq 256, desk top, 512K RAM 1359.00       3
       2  ZEN-SL181 Zenith Z-181 lap top, 640K RAM 1695.00       5
       3  IBM-AT640 IBM AT 640K, 1.2MB FD + 20MB    3790.00       4
       4  ZEN-MM012 Zenith monochrome monitor         89.00       2
       5  NEC-PC660 NEC 660 printer                  560.00      10
       6  HAY-M1200 Hayes 1200 BAUD internal modem   269.00       5
       7  SEA-HD020 Seagate 20MB internal harddisk   398.00       2
       8  IOM-HD040 Iomega Bernoulli 20+20 system   2190.00       4
       9  PAR-GC100 Paradise CGA graphic card        279.00      10
      10  HER-GC100 Hercules monochrome card         199.00       6
```

Fig. 5.20. *Relating more than two database files.*

. SET RELATION TO < *expression 1*> INTO < *alias 1*>,
< *expression 2*> INTO < *alias 2*> ...

As an example, if you had a master file named FILE1 and wanted to link the STOCK_ NO field with both FILE2 and FILE3, these commands would relate the files:

. SET RELATION TO STOCK _ NO INTO B, STOCK _ NO INTO C

5.51 Trap: Don't create a circular relation chain.

One important point to remember in relating database files is that you should not create a circular relation chain in which the last database file is linked back to the master file. This can cause unpredictable results and prevent data from being linked correctly.

5.52 Trap: You can't save records that contain data fields from more than one work area.

When you relate two database files, the contents of these files are held in two different work areas (such as 1 and 2). The active data fields for these files are specified by the SET FIELDS TO command. Because each of these work areas contains only the data fields of one database file, you cannot save to a database file the set of records that contains data fields from more than one work area.

5.53 Trick:

To relate multiple database files quickly and easily, create a view file from the query design screen.

Most users prefer to relate two or more database files by selecting a set of options from the query design screen. Because this approach allows you to view on-screen all the databases, their index files, and data fields, you don't have to remember their names and file structures when you relate them. And you can enter the filter condition and the key field directly from the keyboard or select from a list of options. The approach used by dBASE IV in the creation of queries and views is called Query By Example (QBE), and the file normally created by this operation has the extension .QBE.

To merge the data fields in the SOFTWARE.DBF and SWSTOCK.DBF files, for example, you can select a series of menu options from the query design menus. The process is illustrated in detail by figures 5.21 through 5.33.

As you can see in figure 5.21, to create a new query or view, you select < **create**> from the Queries column on the Control Center screen. From the query design screen, you choose the **Layout** menu by pressing Alt-L, and then you select **Add file to query** to specify the first file to be included (see fig. 5.22). The file skeleton, showing the name of the database files and its fields, appears (see fig. 5.23). Repeat this procedure for the second file (see figs. 5.24 and 5.25).

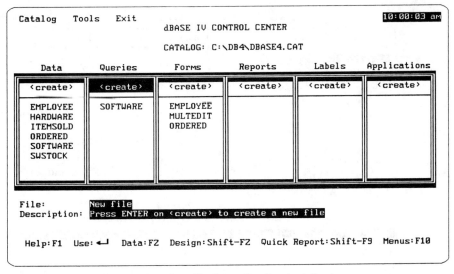

Fig. 5.21. *Creating a query/view file from the Control Center.*

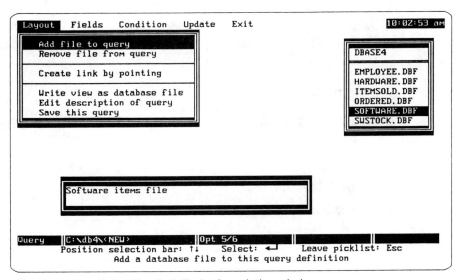

Fig. 5.22. *Specifying the first file in the relation chain.*

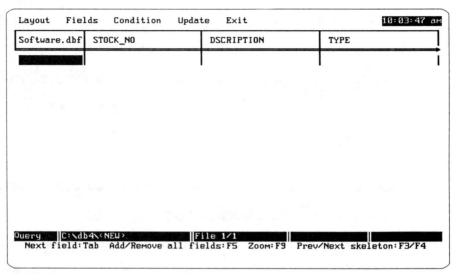

Fig. 5.23. *The file skeleton for SOFTWARE.DBF.*

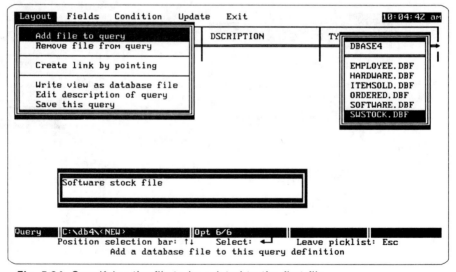

Fig. 5.24. *Specifying the file to be related to the first file.*

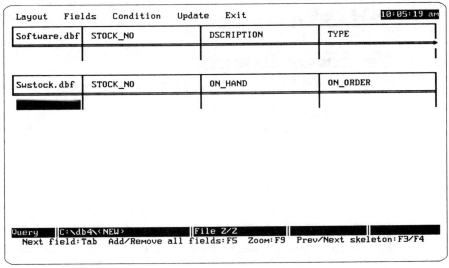

Fig. 5.25. *The file skeletons for SOFTWARE.DBF and SWSTOCK.DBF.*

You can link the files by selecting the **Create link by pointing** option from the **Layout** menu. In the example, you would follow these steps:

1. Position the cursor in the STOCK_NO field in the SOFTWARE.DBF file skeleton. Use the F3 (Previous) and F4 (Next) keys to move between file skeletons. Use the Tab and Shift-Tab keys to move between fields.

2. Pull down the **Layout** menu by pressing Alt-L, select **Create link by pointing**, and press Enter (see fig. 5.26). LINK1 will appear in the field.

3. Move the cursor to the STOCK_NO field in the SWSTOCK.DBF skeleton by pressing F4 (Next). Press Enter, and LINK1 will appear in the field (see fig. 5.27).

You can link on multiple fields by repeating the process (LINK2, LINK3, and so forth). You also can accomplish the same task by entering a common variable name in the linked fields. For instance, if you type the variable name MFIELD in both STOCK_NO fields, the two will be linked.

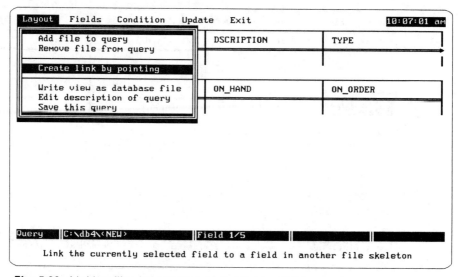

Fig. 5.26. Linking files by pointing to the linking field.

```
 Layout   Fields   Condition   Update   Exit              10:11:01 am
┌────────────┬────────────────────┬─────────────────┬────────────────┐
│Software.dbf│ STOCK_NO           │ DSCRIPTION      │ TYPE           │
├────────────┤                    │                 │                ├──→
│            │ LINK1              │                 │                │
│            └────────────────────┴─────────────────┴────────────────┘
├────────────┬────────────────────┬─────────────────┬────────────────┐
│Swstock.dbf │ STOCK_NO           │ ON_HAND         │ ON_ORDER       │
├────────────┤                    │                 │                │
│            │ LINK1              │                 │                │
└────────────┴────────────────────┴─────────────────┴────────────────┘



 Query   ║C:\db4\<NEW>            ║Field 1/3
   Prev/Next field:Shift-Tab/Tab   Data:F2   Pick:Shift-F1   Prev/Next skel:F3/F4
```

Fig. 5.27. File skeletons showing the linked field.

To specify selected data fields from the two database files that are being related, move the cursor to a field and press F5 (Field). A copy of the field moves to the bottom of the screen and is added to the view skeleton (see figs. 5.28 and 5.29). Conversely, if you press F5 on a field in the view skeleton, the field is removed from the view.

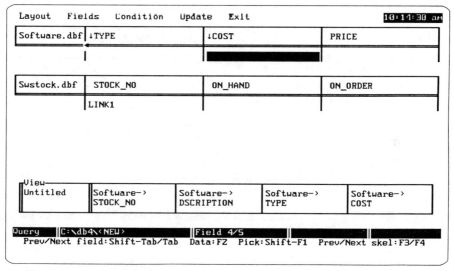

Fig. 5.28. *Selecting fields from the first file.*

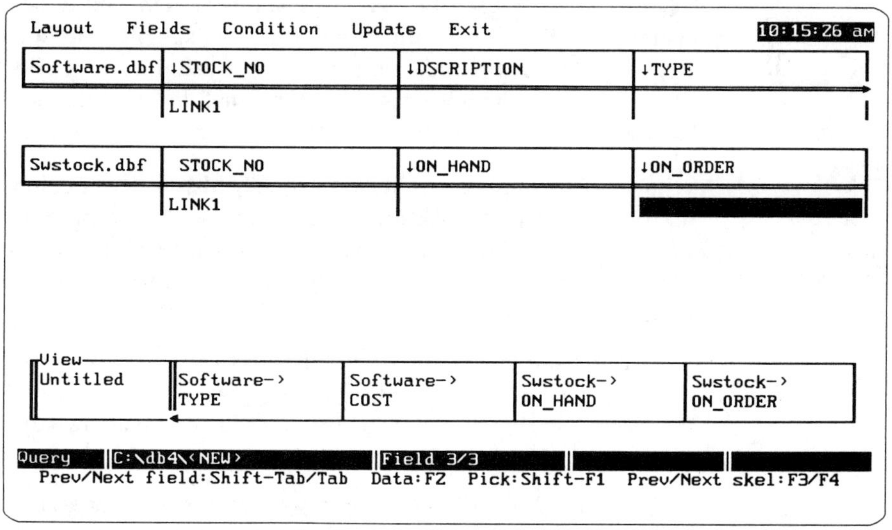

Fig. 5.29. *Selecting fields from the second file.*

You can use a filter condition (such as COST>2ØØ) if you want to select only certain records. You can type the condition in the appropriate skeleton column, or you can press Shift-F1 (Pick) to select filtering conditions from a menu (see fig. 5.30).

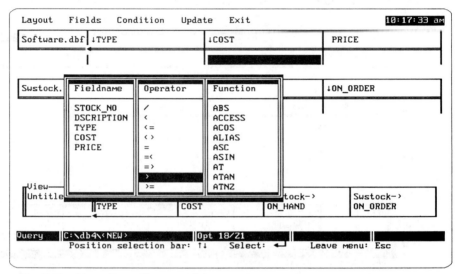

Fig. 5.30. *Choosing a filter condition operator.*

Because dBASE IV uses a Query-By-Example system, you don't need to reenter the field name in the condition. For example, you don't need to type COST>2ØØ. Instead, you simply enter >2ØØ in the COST column. This system gives you a better visual image of the filtering conditions than a series of long dBASE commands (see fig. 5.31).

If you have a complex condition to specify, the skeleton column will pan to the right to accommodate long statements. Or, press F9 (Zoom) in the column to open a window that will allow you to type a long statement, and then press F9 again to zoom back to the original column size.

You can list several criteria on one line if they normally would be joined by an .AND. clause. Put criteria that would be separated by an .OR. clause on separate lines by pressing the down-arrow key (↓) to create a new line. See Chapter 7 for more information on queries.

When you finish creating the view, you can test it by pressing F2 (Data) to see the data on-screen in the new format (see fig. 5.32). If you press Esc to exit, you are asked whether you want to save the view file. Then you are returned to the Control Center.

```
 Layout   Fields   Condition   Update   Exit              10:18:11 am
┌─────────────┬────────────────┬──────────────────┬────────────────────┐
│Software.dbf │↓TYPE           │↓COST             │PRICE               │
│             ├────────────────┼──────────────────┼────────────────────┤
│             │                │>200              │                    │
│             │                │                  │                    │
└─────────────┴────────────────┴──────────────────┴────────────────────┘
┌─────────────┬────────────────┬──────────────────┬────────────────────┐
│Sustock.dbf  │STOCK_NO        │↓ON_HAND          │↓ON_ORDER           │
│             ├────────────────┼──────────────────┼────────────────────┤
│             │LINK1           │                  │                    │
└─────────────┴────────────────┴──────────────────┴────────────────────┘


 ┌View────┬─────────┬──────────┬──────────┬──────────┐
 │Untitled│Software→│Software→ │Sustock→  │Sustock→  │
 │        │TYPE     │COST      │ON_HAND   │ON_ORDER  │
 └────────┴─────────┴──────────┴──────────┴──────────┘
 Query   C:\db4\<NEW>
 Prev/Next field:Shift-Tab/Tab   Data:F2   Pick:Shift-F1   Prev/Next skel:F3/F4
```

Fig. 5.31. *Setting the condition for filtering data records.*

```
 Records     Fields      Go To     Exit              10:21:12 am
┌─────────┬────────────────────┬──────────────────┬───────┬────────┬─────────┐
│STOCK_NO │DSCRIPTION          │TYPE              │COST   │ON_HAND │ON_ORDER │
├─────────┼────────────────────┼──────────────────┼───────┼────────┼─────────┤
│ASH-DB400│dBASE IV v 1.0      │database          │495.00 │      4 │    2    │
│ANS-DB110│Paradox v.1.1       │database          │525.00 │      1 │    5    │
│CLP-DB100│Clipper DB Compiler │database compiler │450.00 │      2 │    1    │
│WOR-DB100│WordTech DB Compiler│database compiler │469.00 │      2 │    3    │
│LOT-LO123│Lotus 1-2-3 Rel 2   │spread sheet      │289.00 │      5 │    1    │
│MIC-WS330│WordStar v3.30      │word processing   │229.00 │      3 │    3    │
│MIS-WD400│Microsoft Word 4.0  │word processing   │229.00 │      2 │    3    │
│ASH-FW300│Framework v.3.0     │integrated        │345.00 │      3 │    2    │
│         │                    │                  │       │        │         │
│         │                    │                  │       │        │         │
│         │                    │                  │       │        │         │
│         │                    │                  │       │        │         │
│         │                    │                  │       │        │         │
└─────────┴────────────────────┴──────────────────┴───────┴────────┴─────────┘
 Browse   C:\db4\SOFTWARE           Rec 1/10        File  ReadOnly
                         View and edit fields
```

Fig. 5.32. *Viewing data using the query.*

To save your file from the query design screen, as shown in figure 5.33, you select the **Exit/Save changes and exit** option and specify a file name for the view file. You then are returned to the Control Center, where the new file should appear in the Queries columns (see fig. 5.34). Note that the file has the extension .QBE, for Query By Example.

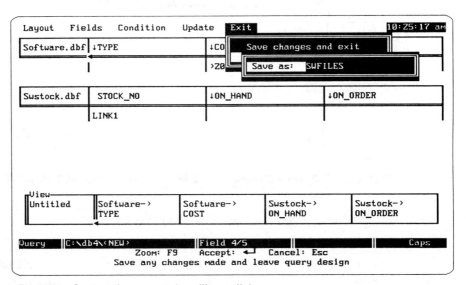

Fig. 5.33. *Saving the query/view file to disk.*

5.54 Tip: **Set up a view file quickly with the Control Center menu.**

After you create a view file for saving the information about how two database files are related, you can set it up to relate the files again. Simply select the file from the Queries column in the Control Center (see fig. 5.34).

To view data using the view, highlight the file and press F2 (Data). The data from the related files appears on-screen (see fig. 5.35).

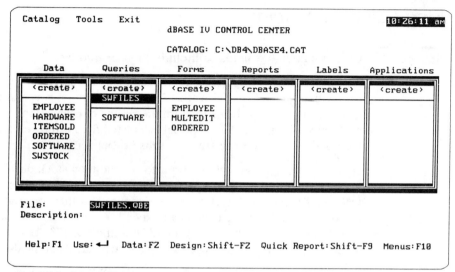

```
 Catalog   Tools   Exit                                      10:26:11 am
                          dBASE IV CONTROL CENTER

                          CATALOG: C:\DB4\DBASE4.CAT

       Data        Queries      Forms       Reports     Labels    Applications
   ┌───────────┬───────────┬───────────┬───────────┬───────────┬───────────┐
   │ <create>  │ <create>  │ <create>  │ <create>  │ <create>  │ <create>  │
   │           │ SWFILES   │           │           │           │           │
   │ EMPLOYEE  │           │ EMPLOYEE  │           │           │           │
   │ HARDWARE  │ SOFTWARE  │ MULTEDIT  │           │           │           │
   │ ITEMSOLD  │           │ ORDERED   │           │           │           │
   │ ORDERED   │           │           │           │           │           │
   │ SOFTWARE  │           │           │           │           │           │
   │ SWSTOCK   │           │           │           │           │           │
   │           │           │           │           │           │           │
   └───────────┴───────────┴───────────┴───────────┴───────────┴───────────┘

   File:        SWFILES.QBE
   Description:


  Help:F1  Use: ◄┘  Data:F2  Design:Shift-F2  Quick Report:Shift-F9  Menus:F10
```

Fig. 5.34. *A new file displayed in the Queries column.*

```
 Records     Fields     Go To     Exit                       10:27:03 am
 ┌─────────┬──────────────────┬──────────────────┬────────┬────────┬────────┐
 │STOCK_NO │ DSCRIPTION       │ TYPE             │ COST   │ON_HAND │ON_ORDER│
 ├─────────┼──────────────────┼──────────────────┼────────┼────────┼────────┤
 │ASH-DB400│ dBASE IV v 1.0   │ database         │ 495.00 │   4    │   2    │
 │ANS-DB110│ Paradox v.1.1    │ database         │ 525.00 │   1    │   5    │
 │CLP-DB100│ Clipper DB Compiler│database compiler│ 450.00 │   2    │   1    │
 │WOR-DB100│ WordTech DB Compiler│database compiler│ 469.00│  2    │   3    │
 │LOT-L0123│ Lotus 1-2-3 Rel 2│ spread sheet     │ 289.00 │   5    │   1    │
 │MIC-WS330│ WordStar v3.30   │ word processing  │ 229.00 │   3    │   3    │
 │MIS-WD400│ Microsoft Word 4.0│ word processing │ 229.00 │   2    │   3    │
 │ASH-FW300│ Framework v.3.0  │ integrated       │ 345.00 │   3    │   2    │
 │         │                  │                  │        │        │        │
 │         │                  │                  │        │        │        │
 │         │                  │                  │        │        │        │
 │         │                  │                  │        │        │        │
 │         │                  │                  │        │        │        │
 │         │                  │                  │        │        │        │
 └─────────┴──────────────────┴──────────────────┴────────┴────────┴────────┘
 Browse    C:\db4\SWFILES           Rec 1/10        View  ReadOnly
                          View and edit fields
```

Fig. 5.35. *Viewing data using the query/view file.*

Using Calculated Fields

5.55 Tip: **Create calculated fields to include in your queries.**

dBASE IV allows you to create calculated fields for use in viewing your data with a query. This means that instead of having to waste disk space with additional fields to store the results of calculations performed on other fields, a special calculated field can be created in your query view file to see these results as data is examined.

For example, suppose that you want to see the total stock quantity for each item in the SWSTOCK database, derived by adding the ON_HAND and ON_ORDER figures. Suppose also that you want to see the markup, or margin, you can expect on each item sold, derived by subtracting the COST from the PRICE in the SOFTWARE database. To accomplish these tasks, you can create two calculated fields.

For this example, create a query linking the SWSTOCK and SOFTWARE database files on the STOCK_NO field, as described in the preceding paragraph. This time, however, call the new query SOFTSTOK, and let the view contain the fields STOCK_NO, ON_HAND, and ON_ORDER, plus two calculated fields, ALLSTOCK and MARGIN.

After you have added the SWSTOCK and SOFTWARE file skeletons to the work surface, add the STOCK_NO, ON_HAND, and ON_ORDER fields to the view skeleton using the **Add field to view** option from the **Fields** menu, as described earlier. You now are ready to create and add the two new calculated fields.

Pull down the **Fields** menu (Alt-F) and select the **Create calculated field** option (see fig. 5.36). The first time you create a calculated field, a new skeleton labeled Calc'd Flds appears below the file skeletons. All calculated fields are added to this skeleton.

When the first field in the calculated fields skeleton appears, you can type the expression in the highlighted box. For example, to calculate the total stock by adding the ON_HAND stock to the ON_ORDER stock, you type the following in the expression box:

```
ON_HAND + ON_ORDER
```

Repeat these steps to create another calculated field. This time, to calculate the margin of each item, enter the following in the expression box:

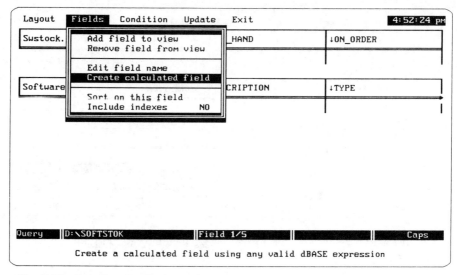

Layout	Fields	Condition	Update	Exit	4:52:24 PM

Swstock. | Add field to view | HAND | ↓ON_ORDER
Remove field from view

Edit field name
Create calculated field

Software | | CRIPTION | ↓TYPE
Sort on this field
Include indexes NO

Query | D:\SOFTSTOK | Field 1/5 | Caps

Create a calculated field using any valid dBASE expression

Fig. 5.36. *Creating a calculated field.*

        PRICE – COST

Now, to see the results in your view, you need to add them to your view skeleton.

Position the cursor on the expression box for the first calculated field, and then press F5 (Field). When you are prompted for a name, type a name for the field—in this case, ALLSTOCK—and press Enter. The field is added to the view skeleton. Do the same for the second calculated field, naming it MARGIN (see fig. 5.37). Figure 5.38 shows the view skeleton with the calculated fields added. To view data using the new query, press F2 (Data). Figure 5.39 shows data displayed using the SOFTSTOK view query.

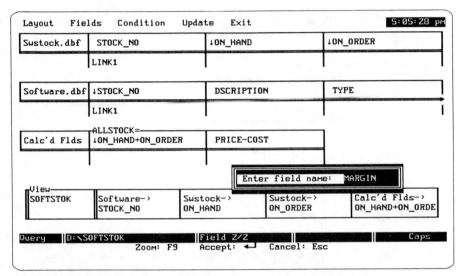

Fig. 5.37. *Entering the name for a calculated field added to the view.*

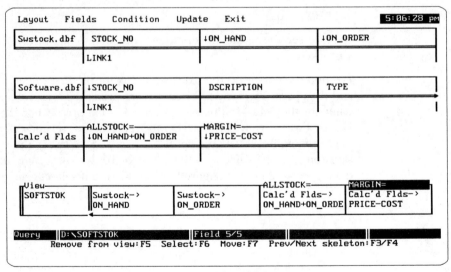

Fig. 5.38. *The view skeleton for the SOFTSTOK query.*

```
 Records      Fields     Go To     Exit                     5:07:11 PM
┌──────────┬────────┬─────────┬─────────────────────┬────────────────────┐
│STOCK_NO  │ON_HAND │ON_ORDER │ALLSTOCK             │MARGIN              │
├──────────┼────────┼─────────┼─────────────────────┼────────────────────┤
│ASH-DB400 │      4 │       2 │             6.00    │          300.00    │
│ANS-DB110 │      1 │       5 │             6.00    │          170.00    │
│CLP-DB100 │      2 │       1 │             3.00    │          145.00    │
│WOR-DB100 │      2 │       3 │             5.00    │          126.00    │
│LOT-L0123 │      5 │       1 │             6.00    │           70.00    │
│MIC-WS330 │      3 │       3 │             6.00    │           40.00    │
│MIS-WD400 │      2 │       3 │             5.00    │           60.00    │
│ASH-FW300 │      3 │       2 │             5.00    │           50.00    │
│MIC-QBZ00 │      4 │       1 │             5.00    │           30.00    │
│BOL-PA300 │      0 │       2 │             2.00    │           30.00    │
│          │        │         │                     │                    │
│          │        │         │                     │                    │
│          │        │         │                     │                    │
│          │        │         │                     │                    │
│          │        │         │                     │                    │
└──────────┴────────┴─────────┴─────────────────────┴────────────────────┘
 Browse   ║D:\SOFTSTOK       ║        ║Rec 1/10     ║ ║View ║ReadOnly║
                              View and edit fields
```

Fig. 5.39. Viewing data using the SOFTSTOK query.

6

Sorting and Indexing Data

This chapter focuses on ways to make the most of the sorting and indexing capabilities provided by dBASE IV. Although the processes are similar, differences in design philosophy impose varying restrictions. Each operation has its own strengths and weaknesses. The tips, tricks, and traps discussed here will help you take advantage of their strengths and circumvent their restrictions.

Sorting versus Indexing

This section gives you tips, tricks, and traps to help you learn the differences between sorting and indexing. The suggestions here also show you how to use the two types of index files and how to sort records with multiple numeric key fields.

6.1 Tip: **Use SORT if you do not update your database often.**

If you want to see data in a particular order, but you will not be updating the data often, you may want to sort the file. This process creates a new file sorted by one or more fields. The syntax of the SORT command is as follows:

> . SORT TO < *sorted file*> ON < *field*>

or

> . SORT ON < *field* > TO < *sorted file*>

Both are used in the following example:

```
. USE EMPLOYEE
. SORT ON LAST_NAME TO SORTED
. SORT TO ROSTER ON LAST_NAME, FIRST_NAME
```

6.2 Trap: **Sorting large files can use a lot of disk space.**

Because both a new file and a temporary work file are created by SORT, be sure that you have adequate disk space to hold these files. This is of particular concern if you have an extremely large database. You should have about double the size of the database available for sorting and for the new file. For example, if you have a database file that is one million bytes, you should have about two million bytes of free space on your disk before performing the sort.

6.3 Tip: **Use INDEX if you update a file often or want to find information quickly.**

When you index a file, a separate index file is created which contains pointers that tell dBASE IV where to find records in the database. The actual database file itself is not altered. When index files are active, the index is updated whenever changes are made to the records in the database. The file, therefore, always appears to be sorted by the key field.

Using the FIND or SEEK commands with an indexed file allows you to find a record instantly, rather than having dBASE IV scan through a long file to find a particular record. To make the file appear to be sorted by another field, or to search by another field, you can change index files at any time. This offers great versatility and alleviates the need to re-sort the file.

Using Two Types of Index Files

dBASE IV offers two kinds of index files:

❑ Index files, which have a file extension of .NDX. These function the same as index files used in dBASE III Plus. A separate .NDX file must be created and maintained for each key field to be indexed.

❑ Multiple index files, which have a file extension of .MDX. Each of these files can contain up to 47 index tags. Each tag represents an indexed key field.

Each time you create a database file, you are given the opportunity to create an index tag for one or more fields. If you answer Y in the

Index column of the database design screen for any field, a production index file is automatically created. This is an .MDX file that is used automatically as the default index when you USE the associated database file. For example, when the SOFTWARE.DBF file is created (fig. 6.1), to include multiple index tags in the production index for the key fields STOCK_NO and TYPE, you place a Y in the Index column for those fields.

```
  Layout    Organize    Append    Go To    Exit                      9:46:37 am
                                                            Bytes remaining:    3937
 ┌──────┬──────────────┬──────────────┬───────┬───────┬────────┐
 │ Num  │ Field Name   │ Field Type   │ Width │  Dec  │ Index  │
 ├──────┼──────────────┼──────────────┼───────┼───────┼────────┤
 │  1   │ STOCK_NO     │ Character    │   9   │       │   Y    │
 │  2   │ DSCRIPTION   │ Character    │  20   │       │   N    │
 │  3   │ TYPE         │ Character    │  20   │       │   Y    │
 │  4   │ COST         │ Numeric      │   7   │   2   │   N    │
 │  5   │ PRICE        │ Numeric      │   7   │   2   │   N    │
 │      │              │              │       │       │        │
 │      │              │              │       │       │        │
 │      │              │              │       │       │        │
 │      │              │              │       │       │        │
 │      │              │              │       │       │        │
 │      │              │              │       │       │        │
 └──────┴──────────────┴──────────────┴───────┴───────┴────────┘
 Database C:\db4\SOFTWARE            Field 3/5
              Enter the field name.  Insert/Delete field:Ctrl-N/Ctrl-U
 Field names begin with a letter and may contain letters, digits and underscores
```

Fig. 6.1. *Specifying production indexing keys for the SOFTWARE.DBF file.*

Normally, using the production multiple index (.MDX) file is most convenient. Sometimes, however, you need a special index file to perform a particular function, such as printing labels or report data in a certain order. In those cases, you may prefer to create a temporary .NDX file (see fig. 6.2).

6.4 Tip: Understand the basic INDEX command.

Indexing arranges the records in a database file according to the value of the indexing key. The indexing key can be a single key field, a set of key fields, or an expression.

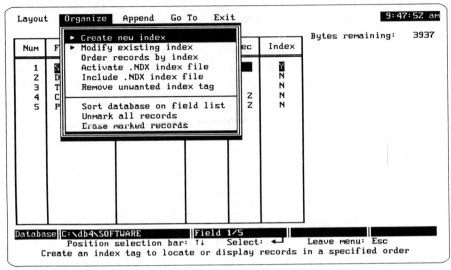

Fig. 6.2. Creating a new index for an existing database file.

If you are creating an .NDX file, the format of the INDEX command is

. INDEX ON < *indexing key*> TO < *name of index file*>

or

. INDEX TO < *name of index file*> ON < *indexing key*>

If you are creating an index tag for a multiple index (.MDX) file, the format is

. INDEX ON < *indexing key*> TAG < *tag name*>

The default file is the production index file. If you want to use a different .MDX file, you can use the OF clause:

. INDEX ON < *indexing key*> TAG < *tag name*>
OF < *name of .MDX file*>

6.5 Tip: **Indexing is usually a better approach than sorting for organizing data records.**

Indexing has several advantages over sorting. As mentioned, you can find a record much faster in an indexed file than in a sorted file. In addition, when changes are made to records in an indexed database file, the corresponding, active index file is automatically updated. Also, an index file takes up much less disk storage space than a sorted file because a duplicate of the database is not created.

Indexed files can be linked with the SET RELATION TO operation. Records from two or more files can be accessed simultaneously with a view file. And, arithmetic expressions can be used as indexing keys. Sorting, on the other hand, arranges records in ASCII order so that numbers appear before uppercase letters, which normally appcar before lowercase letters.

6.6 Tip: To arrange records with a single key field, use the INDEX command.

When you use a single data field as the key for arranging the records in a database file, you can use either SORT or INDEX. Records sequenced by either method are arranged in the same order.

Using STOCK_ NO as the key field, you could use the following SORT operation to arrange the records in the SOFTWARE.DBF file:

```
. USE SOFTWARE
. SORT ON STOCK_NO TO SORTED
```

But the indexing operation takes less time and disk storage space:

```
. INDEX ON STOCK_NO TO SWSTCKNO
```

The major difference is that SORT saves the sorted records in a .DBF file, which takes up more disk space than an index file.

6.7 Trap: INDEX does not produce a database file for sorted records.

If you need to create a database file for sorted records, you can copy the indexed records to a database file.

6.8 Trick: Create a file for indexed records.

To create a database file for indexed records, simply follow these steps:

```
. USE < name of database file>
. INDEX ON . . . TO . . .
. COPY TO < name of database file for saving ordered records>
```

Using the data from the previous example, the commands would be as follows:

```
. USE SOFTWARE
. INDEX ON STOCK _ NO TO SWSTCKNO
. COPY TO SORTED
```

6.9 Tip: **Use the INDEX command to sequence records with multiple character key fields.**

You can specify several character fields as separate key fields in a SORT command or as an expression in an INDEX command. Either procedure arranges data records in the same order.

If you want to order the records in the EMPLOYEE.DBF file, for example, you can use either method.

You could index with the following commands:

```
. USE EMPLOYEE
. INDEX ON LAST _ NAME + FIRST _ NAME TO BYNAMES
```

Indexing is much faster and takes up less storage space than sorting does:

```
. USE EMPLOYEE
. SORT ON LAST _ NAME , FIRST _ NAME TO ROSTER
```

Sorting Records with Multiple Numeric Key Fields

6.10 Trap: **When you use multiple numeric fields as keys for arranging records, the results you get with SORT and INDEX can be quite different.**

If you use more than one numeric field as a key for arranging records with SORT, the fields must be specified as separate sorting keys. With INDEX, the fields must be combined as an arithmetic expression.

You can, for example, arrange the records in the SALEITEM.DBF file. Figure 6.3 shows what happens with both sorting and indexing. Each operation arranges the records in a different order.

```
. USE SALEITEM
. SORT ON PRICE,COST TO SORTED
  100% Sorted           4 Records sorted
. USE SORTED
. LIST
Record#  STOCK_NO    PRICE    COST
      1  A1001      100.00   80.00
      2  A1002      100.00   90.00
      3  A1003      110.00   60.00
      4  A1004      120.00   50.00

. USE SALEITEM
. INDEX ON PRICE+COST TO VALUES
  100% indexed          4 Records indexed
. LIST
Record#  STOCK_NO    PRICE    COST
      3  A1003      110.00   60.00
      4  A1004      120.00   50.00
      1  A1001      100.00   80.00
      2  A1002      100.00   90.00
```

Fig. 6.3. *Rearranging data records, using multiple numeric fields as a key.*

You can sort the records with PRICE as the primary sorting field and COST as the secondary sorting field. You use the following commands:

. USE SALEITEM
. SORT ON PRICE,COST TO SORTED

SORT arranges the records in two ways: by the values in the PRICE field and then by the values in the COST field (see fig. 6.3).

To index these same records, you must combine the two fields in the form of an expression. Then use the expression as an indexing key in the INDEX command:

. USE SALEITEM
. INDEX ON PRICE + COST TO VALUES

As you can see in figure 6.3, records are arranged in ascending order by the combined value of PRICE + COST.

6.11 Trick: **To save disk space, index records on partial fields.**

If you have a very large database file and if your key field is a long character field, you may be able to save disk space by indexing on part of the key field. For example, if you have a field called Company that is 40 characters in length, you are not likely to type all 40 characters when searching for a record. To FIND a record containing the company "Smith, Jones, Johnson & Burkholtz," you might use the command:

. FIND "Smith, Jones"

By indexing on the maximum length used in a FIND or SEEK command, or the maximum length required to keep the database in the correct order, you create a smaller index file than indexing on the entire field. For instance, to index by the 12 leftmost characters of the Company field, use the following command:

. INDEX ON LEFT(Company,12) TO COMPANY.NDX

Arranging Records in Descending Order

The tips, tricks, and traps in this section show you how to arrange records in descending order. The text gives you suggestions on sorting records and indexing records in descending order. You also learn to use a date key field to arrange records in descending order.

Sorting Records in Descending Order

6.12 Tip: **Use the / D option to sort records in descending order.**

The /D option may be added to the SORT command to have records sorted in descending order by any field. For example, to sort in descending order by Age, then in ascending order by Name, use the following command syntax:

. SORT TO < *file name*> ON Age /D, Name /A

Indexing Records in Descending Order

6.13 Trap: **Using INDEX with .NDX files always arranges data records in ascending order.**

Unlike the SORT command's /D operator, .NDX files provide no means to arrange records in descending order.

6.14 Trick: **To arrange data records in descending order with a numeric field, use its negative value as the indexing key.**

If you use a numeric field as the indexing field, you can put the records in descending order. To do so, index the file on the negative value of the key field. The procedure is shown in figure 6.4. As you can see in the figure, the records are arranged quite differently with COST and –COST as the indexing keys.

```
. USE SALEITEM
. INDEX ON COST TO BYCOST
  100% indexed            4 Records indexed
. LIST
Record#  STOCK_NO    PRICE    COST
      4  A1004      120.00   50.00
      3  A1003      110.00   60.00
      1  A1001      100.00   80.00
      2  A1002      100.00   90.00

. INDEX ON -COST TO BYCOST
  100% indexed            4 Records indexed
. LIST
Record#  STOCK_NO    PRICE    COST
      2  A1002      100.00   90.00
      1  A1001      100.00   80.00
      3  A1003      110.00   60.00
      4  A1004      120.00   50.00
```

Fig. 6.4. Indexing, using the negative value of a numeric field as a key.

Using a Date Key Field To Arrange Records in Descending Order

You can use a date field as a key for arranging data records with both SORT and INDEX. With SORT, the records can be arranged in either ascending or descending order. With INDEX, however, records always are arranged in ascending order.

6.15 Trick: **Use a multiple index file to index in descending order.**

If you use an .MDX file, whether it is the production index file or another file, you can create index tags in descending ASCII order using the DESCENDING option:

. INDEX ON < *key expression* > TAG < *tag name* > DESCENDING

6.16 Trap: **The DESCENDING option can be used only with the entire key expression.**

If you create a key expression from more than one element, such as multiple fields, the entire key expression is used to index in descending order. You cannot index in descending order by part of the expression (such as one field) and in ascending order by the rest of the expression.

Sorting Records Chronologically

6.17 Tip: **To arrange data records chronologically in descending order, use the SORT command with the / D option.**

When you issue the SORT command with a date field as the sort key field, records in the active database file are arranged in ascending order by default (see fig. 6.5). To arrange records in descending order according to the values in a date field, include the /D operator in the SORT command (see fig. 6.6).

```
, USE EMPLOYEE
, SORT ON EMPLY_DATE TO SORTED
  100% Sorted            10 Records sorted
, USE SORTED
, LIST ID_NO, LAST_NAME, FIRST_NAME, EMPLY_DATE
Record#  ID_NO       LAST_NAME     FIRST_NAME      EMPLY_DATE
      1  123-45-6789 Smith         Thomas T.       03/01/81
      2  563-55-8900 Thorsen       Tyrone T.       06/20/82
      3  254-63-5691 Thompson      Tina Y.         09/22/82
      4  467-34-6789 Watson        Peter F.        10/12/82
      5  321-65-9087 Kaiser        Jane W.         11/22/82
      6  823-46-6213 Faust         Cathy J.        04/15/83
      7  732-08-4589 Taylor        Doris Y.        08/14/83
      8  554-34-7893 Corso         Vincent M.      07/20/84
      9  435-54-9876 Smith         James J.        01/23/86
     10  560-56-9321 Davidson      Tina K.         05/16/86
```

Fig. 6.5. *Sorting records chronologically with a date key field.*

```
, USE EMPLOYEE
, SORT ON EMPLY_DATE/D TO SORTED
  100% Sorted            10 Records sorted
, USE SORTED
, LIST ID_NO, LAST_NAME, FIRST_NAME, EMPLY_DATE
Record#  ID_NO       LAST_NAME     FIRST_NAME      EMPLY_DATE
      1  560-56-9321 Davidson      Tina K.         05/16/86
      2  435-54-9876 Smith         James J.        01/23/86
      3  554-34-7893 Corso         Vincent M.      07/20/84
      4  732-08-4589 Taylor        Doris Y.        08/14/83
      5  823-46-6213 Faust         Cathy J.        04/15/83
      6  321-65-9087 Kaiser        Jane W.         11/22/82
      7  467-34-6789 Watson        Peter F.        10/12/82
      8  254-63-5691 Thompson      Tina Y.         09/22/82
      9  563-55-8900 Thorsen       Tyrone T.       06/20/82
     10  123-45-6789 Smith         Thomas T.       03/01/81
```

Fig. 6.6. *Sorting records chronologically in descending order.*

Indexing Records Chronologically

6.18 Trap: **INDEX normally arranges records in ascending order.**

As mentioned, INDEX normally arranges records in ascending order according to the original value of the key. For example, when you use a date field as an indexing key, the earliest date is the first record and the most recent date is the last record (see fig. 6.7).

```
. USE EMPLOYEE
. INDEX ON EMPLY_DATE TO EMPLDATE
  100% indexed          10 Records indexed
. LIST ID_NO, LAST_NAME, FIRST_NAME, EMPLY_DATE
Record#  ID_NO       LAST_NAME     FIRST_NAME     EMPLY_DATE
      1  123-45-6789 Smith         Thomas T.      03/01/81
      5  563-55-8900 Thorsen       Tyrone T.      06/20/82
      2  254-63-5691 Thompson      Tina Y.        09/22/82
      3  467-34-6789 Watson        Peter F.       10/12/82
      8  321-65-9087 Kaiser        Jane W.        11/22/82
      6  823-46-6213 Faust         Cathy J.       04/15/83
      4  732-08-4589 Taylor        Doris Y.       08/14/83
      7  554-34-7893 Corso         Vincent M.     07/20/84
     10  435-54-9876 Smith         James J.       01/23/86
      9  560-56-9321 Davidson      Tina K.        05/16/86
```

Fig. 6.7. Indexing records chronologically with a date key field.

6.19 Trick: **To arrange records chronologically in descending order with INDEX, convert the date fields to a numeric expression.**

The simplest approach to arranging records in descending order is to create an index tag in descending order using a multiple index file. However, if you will be using an .NDX file, after you convert the date field to a numeric expression, you can use the expression's negative value as the indexing key (see fig. 6.8).

To form the numeric expression used as a key in the indexing operation shown in figure 6.8, follow these steps:

1. Use the DTOC() function to convert a date field into a character field.

2. Use the RIGHT(), LEFT(), and SUBSTR() functions to rearrange and combine the substrings of the character field that correspond to the year, month, and day of the original date fields.

3. Convert the character string into a numeric expression.

4. Use the negative value of the numeric expression as the indexing key.

For example, if you use these steps to convert the date value in Record No. 9 (05/16/86) to a key value of –860516, and to change the date value of Record No. 10 (01/23/86) to –860123, INDEX will arrange these records in descending order.

6.20 Trick: **To arrange records chronologically in descending order, convert the date to a numeric value.**

Another way to arrange records chronologically in descending order is to convert the date to a numeric value that represents the number of days between the date and a future date (such as 12/31/99). As you can see in figure 6.9, dBASE IV lets you compute the number of days between two given dates by taking the difference between these dates. There are 4,977 days between DATE3 (12/31/99) and DATE1 (5/16/86). The figure shows that these dates have been stored as memory variables.

```
. USE EMPLOYEE
. INDEX ON -VAL(RIGHT(DTOC(EMPLY_DATE),2)+LEFT(DTOC(EMPLY_DATE),2)+SUBSTR(DTOC(E
MPLY_DATE),4,2)) TO EMPLDATE
   100% indexed          10 Records indexed
. LIST ID_NO, LAST_NAME, FIRST_NAME, EMPLY_DATE
Record#  ID_NO         LAST_NAME      FIRST_NAME      EMPLY_DATE
      9  560-56-9321 Davidson         Tina K.         05/16/86
     10  435-54-9876 Smith            James J.        01/23/86
      7  554-34-7893 Corso            Vincent M.      07/20/84
      4  732-08-4589 Taylor           Doris Y.        08/14/83
      6  823-46-6213 Faust            Cathy J.        04/15/83
      8  321-65-9087 Kaiser           Jane W.         11/22/82
      3  467-34-6789 Watson           Peter F.        10/12/82
      2  254-63-5691 Thompson         Tina Y.         09/22/82
      5  563-55-8900 Thorsen          Tyrone T.       06/20/82
      1  123-45-6789 Smith            Thomas T.       03/01/81
.
```

Fig. 6.8. *Indexing records chronologically in descending order.*

```
. DATE1={05/16/86}
05/16/86
. DATE2={01/23/86}
01/23/86
. DATE3={12/31/99}
12/31/99
. ?"Days between DATE1 and DATE3 =",DATE3-DATE1
Days between DATE1 and DATE3 =      4977
. ?"Days between DATE2 and DATE3 =",DATE3-DATE2
Days between DATE2 and DATE3 =      5090
.
```

Fig. 6.9. Computing the number of days between two dates.

You can arrange the records in EMPLOYEE.DBF chronologically in descending order according to the value in the EMPLY_DATE field. Use the negative value of the number of days between the value in EMPLY_DATE and a future date (see fig. 6.10).

```
. USE EMPLOYEE
. INDEX ON -(EMPLY_DATE - {12/31/99}) TO EMPLDATE
  100% indexed          10 Records indexed
. LIST ID_NO, LAST_NAME, FIRST_NAME, EMPLY_DATE
Record#  ID_NO        LAST_NAME      FIRST_NAME      EMPLY_DATE
     9  560-56-9321 Davidson        Tina K.         05/16/86
    10  435-54-9876 Smith           James J.        01/23/86
     7  554-34-7893 Corso           Vincent M.      07/20/84
     4  732-08-4589 Taylor          Doris Y.        08/14/83
     6  823-46-6213 Faust           Cathy J.        04/15/83
     8  321-65-9087 Kaiser          Jane W.         11/22/82
     3  467-34-6789 Watson          Peter F.        10/12/82
     2  254-63-5691 Thompson        Tina Y.         09/22/82
     5  563-55-8900 Thorsen         Tyrone T.       06/20/82
     1  123-45-6789 Smith           Thomas T.       03/01/81
.
```

Fig. 6.10. Indexing records chronologically in descending order.

The records in figure 6.10 are ordered according to the negative value of the number of days between December 31, 1999, and the dates in the EMPLY_DATE field. The indexing operation places the record with the earliest employment date at the end of the file because that record has the largest negative value in the indexing key. If you use this approach, the expression's future date (12/31/99, for example) must be beyond the most recent date in the date field that you index.

6.21 Tip: **Use the SET CENTURY ON command to show the century prefix of a date.**

If you use December 31, 2000, as the future date, be sure to include the century prefix (12/31/2000) and to use the SET CENTURY ON command. Otherwise, as you can see from figure 6.11, the date is treated as 12/31/1900.

```
. DATEA={12/31/1900}
12/31/00
. DATEB={12/31/2000}
12/31/00
. ?DATEA, DATEB
12/31/00 12/31/00
. SET CENTURY ON
. ?DATEA, DATEB
12/31/1900 12/31/2000
.
```

Fig. 6.11. *Showing the century prefix in date variables.*

Arranging Records Based on Fields

The tips, tricks, and traps in this section show you how to arrange records based on fields. You will learn how to index a logical field, how to ignore case when you sort or index character fields, how to ignore records with duplicate key field values, and how to index on mixed data fields.

Indexing a Logical Field

6.22 Trick: **To use a logical field as an indexing key, use the IIF() function to convert the key to a character string.**

To use a logical field as an indexing key, you must convert the field's value (.T. or .F.) to a character string. Then use that string as a character key in the INDEX command.

To convert the value of a logical field to a character string, use the dBASE IV IIF() function in the following format:

. IIF(< *logical field*>, < *first expression*>,< *second expression*>)

When the value of the logical field is true (.T.), the IIF() function returns the value of the first expression; otherwise, the value of the second expression is returned.

The following function, for example, returns a character string of Y if the value of the logical field MALE is true:

. IIF (MALE,"Y","N")

If the value of the logical field is false (.F.), the character string N is returned.

Figure 6.12 shows how to arrange records in the EMPLOYEE.DBF file. Use the IIF() function in the INDEX command, with the logical field MALE in the function argument.

```
. USE EMPLOYEE
. INDEX ON IIF(MALE,"Y","N") TO BYSEX
  100% indexed           10 Records indexed
. LIST ID_NO, LAST_NAME, MALE
Record#  ID_NO        LAST_NAME      MALE
     2   254-63-5691  Thompson       .F.
     4   732-88-4589  Taylor         .F.
     6   823-46-6213  Faust          .F.
     8   321-65-9087  Kaiser         .F.
     9   560-56-9321  Davidson       .F.
     1   123-45-6789  Smith          .T.
     3   467-34-6789  Watson         .T.
     5   563-55-8900  Thorsen        .T.
     7   554-34-7893  Corso          .T.
    10   435-54-9876  Smith          .T.
```

Fig. 6.12. *Using a logical field for indexing records.*

Or, as shown in figure 6.13, you can use the IIF() function to convert the value of the logical field to a numeric value. Then you can use the numeric value to sequence data records with an INDEX command.

Ignoring Case When Sorting or Indexing Character Fields

When you use a character field as a key in a sorting or indexing operation, records in the database file normally are arranged according to their ASCII order (see Appendix A). This places values beginning with uppercase letters before those beginning with lowercase letters.

```
. USE EMPLOYEE
. INDEX ON IIF(MALE,1,2) TO BYSEX
  100% indexed          10 Records indexed
. LIST ID_NO, LAST_NAME, MALE
Record#  ID_NO        LAST_NAME      MALE
      1  123-45-6789  Smith          .T.
      3  467-34-6789  Watson         .T.
      5  563-55-8900  Thorsen        .T.
      7  554-34-7000  Corso          .T.
     10  435-54-9876  Smith          .T.
      2  254-63-5691  Thompson       .F.
      4  732-88-4589  Taylor         .F.
      6  823-46-6213  Faust          .F.
      8  321-65-9887  Kaiser         .F.
      9  560-56-9321  Davidson       .F.
```

Fig. 6.13. *Another example of using a logical field for indexing records.*

6.23 Trick: To ignore the case, use the /C option when sorting.

You can have SORT ignore the case of letters in a field by using the /C option. In other words, lowercase letters are treated as their uppercase equivalents; therefore, the file is not sorted in strict ASCII order. The format of the command is

. SORT TO NEWFILE ON NAME /C

As an example, the following names have been sorted using the /C option:

davidson
Johnston
ROBINSON
WASHINGTON

In contrast, when you sort the same names without the /C option, the following list is produced:

Johnston
ROBINSON
WASHINGTON
davidson

6.24 Tip: Combine multiple sort options.

You can combine sort options in one statement. In this case, you need only one slash (/) for each set of options. For example, to combine the **Case** and **Ascending** options on Name, and the **Case** and **Descending** options on State, you would use a statement similar to the following:

. SORT TO < *file name*> ON Name /AC, State /DC

6.25 Trick: **To ignore case while indexing a character field, convert the field values to lowercase or uppercase values with the LOWER() or UPPER() function.**

If you want to treat lowercase and uppercase character strings the same, convert the lowercase strings to uppercase by using the UPPER( ) function (see fig. 6.14). Otherwise, data is indexed according to case, and all lowercase records follow uppercase records.

```
, USE NAMES
, INDEX ON UPPER(FIRST_NAME) TO FIRST
   100% indexed           10 Records indexed
, LIST
Record#  FIRST_NAME
      6  Cathy J.
      4  Doris Y.
     10  James J.
      8  Jane W.
      3  Peter F.
      1  Thomas T.
      9  Tina K.
      2  Tina Y.
      5  Tyrone T.
      7  Vincent M.
,
```

Fig. 6.14. *Arranging records regardless of case.*

If you convert all the characters in the FIRST_ NAME field to uppercase letters, or if you convert all characters to lowercase, case no longer plays a part in the indexing operation. As you can see from figure 6.14, first names are arranged alphabetically regardless of case.

Ignoring Records with Duplicate Key Field Values

When you index a file with a key field, all the records with key fields that contain the same value are arranged consecutively. As you can see from the first set of records in figure 6.15, for example, records 1 and 4 contain the same name but different addresses.

```
. USE MAILLIST
. INDEX ON NAME TO BYNAME
  100% indexed           5 Records indexed
. LIST
Record#  NAME            ADDRESS             CITY_ST
      1  John J. Smart   123 Main Street     New York, N.Y. 10020
      4  John J. Smart   3506 Broadway S.    New York, N.Y. 10022
      2  Mary Jane Doe   2450 Front Avenue   Portland, OR 97203
      3  Peter A. Great  99909 First Avenue  Seattle, Wa. 98615
      5  Thomas Peterson 25968 N. W. 21th Ave Vancouver, WA. 98665

. SET UNIQUE ON
. INDEX ON NAME TO BYNAME
  100% indexed           4 Records indexed
. LIST
Record#  NAME            ADDRESS             CITY_ST
      1  John J. Smart   123 Main Street     New York, N.Y. 10020
      2  Mary Jane Doe   2450 Front Avenue   Portland, OR 97203
      3  Peter A. Great  99909 First Avenue  Seattle, Wa. 98615
      5  Thomas Peterson 25968 N. W. 21th Ave Vancouver, WA. 98665
```

Fig. 6.15. Indexing records with unique keys.

6.26 Trick: **To index records with unique keys, use the SET UNIQUE ON command.**

To display each record with unique keys only once, issue the SET UNIQUE ON command before you carry out the indexing operation (see fig. 6.15). Note that when SET UNIQUE ON is in effect, only records with unique values in the key field are displayed.

This approach is handy for eliminating duplicated records from the database and is an easy way to update the records in a file. With this method, existing records are ignored when a record with new field values is entered into the file.

Note also that after the SET UNIQUE ON command is executed, the first record with duplicated field values is retained. If you want to use this approach to update your mailing list, for example, be sure to insert the new record at the beginning of the database file. You can save the updated mailing list to a new file (NEWLIST.DBF) by using the COPY TO command:

    . COPY TO NEWLIST

6.27 Tip: **Use the UNIQUE option of the INDEX command to create an index of unique records.**

Instead of issuing the SET UNIQUE ON command before indexing, you can add the UNIQUE option to the INDEX command. Use the following syntax:

. INDEX ON < *key expression*> TO < *file name*> UNIQUE

Indexing on Mixed Data Fields

6.28 Tip: **To index a file using multiple data fields of different types as an indexing key, combine the fields into an expression.**

If you need to use several data fields of different types as a key for the indexing operation, combine these fields into an expression and then use dBASE IV's built-in functions to convert the fields into one type. In most applications, you can convert all the indexing fields into character fields and include them in a character expression. Or you can use a built-in function to convert a character field into a numeric field.

To convert from a numeric value to a character string, use the STR( ) function. The syntax is as follows:

STR(*numeric expression, length, decimal*)

For example, to convert the value in PRICE to a string of 6 characters with 2 decimal places, you use the following format:

STR(PRICE,6,2)

To convert from a date to a character string, use the DTOC( ) function with the following syntax:

DTOC(*date expression*)

For example, to convert the value in a field called DATE, you use this format:

DTOC(DATE)

To convert from a character representation of a number to a numeric value, use the VAL( ) function with the following syntax:

VAL(*character expression*)

For example, to convert the string "456" to a number, you can use this function:

VAL("456")

To sequence the data records in the SOFTWARE.DBF file in figure 6.16, you can combine a character field (TYPE) and a numeric field (PRICE) as a character expression key in the INDEX command. As you can see from the figure, the built-in function STR() is used to convert the value of the numeric field PRICE to a character string. Then PRICE is combined with the character field TYPE to form the character expression.

```
, USE SOFTWARE
, INDEX ON TYPE+STR(PRICE,6,2) TO BYPRICE
  100% indexed          10 Records indexed
, LIST STOCK_NO, TYPE, PRICE
Record#  STOCK_NO  TYPE                  PRICE
      2  AMS-DB110 database             575.00
      1  ASH-DB300 database             595.00
      3  CLP-DB100 database compiler    595.00
      4  WOR-DB100 database compiler    595.00
      8  AST-FW200 integrated           395.00
     10  BOL-PA300 language              69.50
      9  MIC-QB100 language             109.00
      5  LOT-L0123 spread sheet         359.00
      6  MIC-WS330 word processing      269.00
      7  MIS-WD300 word processing      289.00
```

Fig. 6.16. *Combining character and numeric fields as an indexing key.*

6.29 Trap: **Using the YEAR( ), MONTH( ), and DAY( ) functions to convert a date field into a numeric field causes problems.**

Even though you can convert the year, month, and day of a given date to numeric values with the YEAR(), MONTH(), and DAY() functions, the leading zeros in these values are dropped when you combine these numeric values into a numeric expression.

As you can see from figure 6.17, the numeric value 2002 converted from the first date ("04/15/83") is smaller than the value 2004 converted from the second date ("10/12/82"). Therefore, if you use such a numeric expression as a key for indexing, the records in the database file are not arranged correctly (see fig. 6.18).

```
. DATE1=CTOD("04/15/83")
04/15/1983
. ?YEAR(DATE1),MONTH(DATE1),DAY(DATE1)
  1983   4   15
. ?YEAR(DATE1)+MONTH(DATE1)+DAY(DATE1)
   2002
. DATE2=CTOD("10/12/82")
10/12/1982
. ?YEAR(DATE2),MONTH(DATE2),DAY(DATE2)
  1982  10   12
. ?YEAR(DATE2)+MONTH(DATE2)+DAY(DATE2)
   2004
.
```

Fig. 6.17. Incorrect ways to convert dates to numeric values.

```
. USE EMPLOYEE
. INDEX ON YEAR(EMPLY_DATE)+MONTH(EMPLY_DATE)+DAY(EMPLY_DATE) TO EMPLDATE
  100% indexed        10 Records indexed
. LIST ID_NO, LAST_NAME, FIRST_NAME, EMPLY_DATE
Record#  ID_NO        LAST_NAME      FIRST_NAME      EMPLY_DATE
      1  123-45-6789 Smith          Thomas T.       03/01/1981
      6  823-46-6213 Faust          Cathy J.        04/15/1983
      3  467-34-6789 Watson         Peter F.        10/12/1982
      4  732-08-4589 Taylor         Doris Y.        08/14/1983
      9  560-56-9321 Davidson       Tina K.         05/16/1986
      5  563-55-8900 Thorsen        Tyrone T.       06/20/1982
     10  435-54-9876 Smith          James J.        01/23/1986
      7  554-34-7893 Corso          Vincent M.      07/20/1984
      2  254-63-5691 Thompson       Tina Y.         09/22/1982
      8  321-65-9087 Kaiser         Jane W.         11/22/1982
```

Fig. 6.18. An incorrect way to index records with a date key field.

6.30 Trick: **When indexing with date values, use the DTOS( ) function with character values.**

The DTOS( ) function converts a date expression to a standard format:

CCYYMMDD

This format is used regardless of the SET CENTURY or SET DATE settings. When indexing using a date value, the best practice is to use the DTOS( ) function to convert the date to a string before using it as an indexing key.

For example, to index by EMPLY_ DATE, you can use the following statement:

. INDEX ON DTOS(EMPLY _ DATE) TO EMPLDATE

6.31 Tip: **Use curly braces to indicate dates.**

As shown in figure 6.17, the CTOD( ) function is used to convert the string representation of a date to a date value. dBASE IV provides a shortcut for representing date values: curly braces ({}). The following two commands are equivalent:

. MYDATE={Ø7/Ø4/89}
. MYDATE=CTOD("Ø7/Ø7/89")

6.32 Tip: **To speed data manipulation, index a file before using it.**

The indexing operation is a powerful tool. If a database file has been indexed on a key field, finding a specific record in that file is much faster than finding the record before you index the file.

Indexing a database file takes time up-front, but the amount of time needed to rebuild or reset an index is minimal. And although the index file created by the operation uses disk and RAM storage space, the amount of space is minimal. For most applications, the access time saved by using an indexed file is far greater than the time spent indexing the file.

Using an Index File

This section suggests ways you can use an index file. The tips, tricks, and traps show what can happen if you use the wrong index file, how to select the master index file, and how to display an indexing key.

6.33 Tip: **Always index a database file with an existing index file before accessing the database file.**

Before using a database file that has been indexed on a key, use the previously created index file to rearrange the file's records. You don't need to index the file from scratch.

As mentioned previously, using the production multiple index file that was created when you designed your database is usually most convenient. This index file is put into use automatically when you access the database file with the USE command.

To select an index tag from the multiple index file, include the ORDER clause in the USE command:

. USE < *name of database file*> ORDER < *tag name*>

To use another existing index file to rearrange the records in a database file, include the INDEX keyword in the USE command:

. USE < *name of database file*>
INDEX < *name of existing index file*>

For example, after you index the SOFTWARE.DBF file and create the SWSTCKNO.NDX file, you can use the index file to rearrange the records in the database file:

. USE SOFTWARE INDEX SWSTCKNO

Using the Wrong Index File

6.34 Trap: **If you use the wrong index file to index a database file, some or all the records in that database file will not be shown.**

Before you issue the USE...INDEX command to index a database file with an existing index file, be careful to identify the correct index file. If you use the wrong index file, two scenarios are possible. In the less severe case, the index operation is not carried out and you are warned with an error message. In the more severe case, some or all data records are excluded without warning. The greatest loss occurs when the indexing key used in the wrong index file is present in the database file you want to index.

For example, suppose that you mistakenly use the index file SWSTCKNO.NDX (created by using the STOCK_ NO key field when you indexed SOFTWARE.DBF) to index EMPLOYEE.DBF:

. USE EMPLOYEE INDEX SWSTCKNO

dBASE IV returns the following error message:

Index file does not match database.

The program then stops the indexing operation because EMPLOYEE.DBF does not contain the indexing key field STOCK_NO.

If the indexing key used to create the correct index file happens to have the same name as a field in the file you want to index, you will have other problems. dBASE IV can't tell which is the correct database file. As a result, the information in the wrong index file is used to sort the records in the database file. The results of such an operation are unpredictable. As you can see in figure 6.19, some records can be lost.

```
. USE SALEITEM
. LIST
Record#   STOCK_NO  DSCRIPTION             TYPE                  COST    PRICE
      1   ASH-DB300 dBASE III Plus v1.01 database              395.00   595.00
      2   CLP-DB100 Clipper DB Compiler   database compiler    450.00   595.00
      3   AST-FW200 Framework v2.0         integrated           345.00   349.00
      4   MIC-QB100 Microsoft QuickBasic language              79.00   109.00
      5   LOT-LO123 Lotus 1-2-3 v2.0       spread sheet         289.00   359.00
      6   MIC-WS330 Wordstar v3.30         word processing      229.00   269.00

. USE SALEITEM INDEX SWSTCKNO
. LIST
Record#   STOCK_NO  DSCRIPTION             TYPE                  COST    PRICE
      2   CLP-DB100 Clipper DB Compiler   database compiler    450.00   595.00
      1   ASH-DB300 dBASE III Plus v1.01 database              395.00   595.00
```

Fig. 6.19. *Effects of using the wrong index file.*

6.35 Trick: **To keep track of the correct index files for a database file, catalog the disk files.**

One of the powerful functions of a file catalog is that it keeps track of all database files and their associated index (.NDX), format (.FMT), label (.LBL), and form (.FRM) files. While you're using a database file, you can use the query operator (?) to find the name of its associated files in a particular operation.

To find the names of all index files you've created for indexing a given database file, for example, issue the SET INDEX TO ? command:

> . SET CATALOG TO SOFTWARE
> . USE SOFTWARE
> . SET INDEX TO ?

In response to the query operator (?), all the index files related to the SOFTWARE.DBF file are displayed on-screen. The list of index files is displayed in a box in the upper right corner of the screen (see fig. 6.20). To select an index file, simply use a cursor key to highlight the file, and then press Enter.

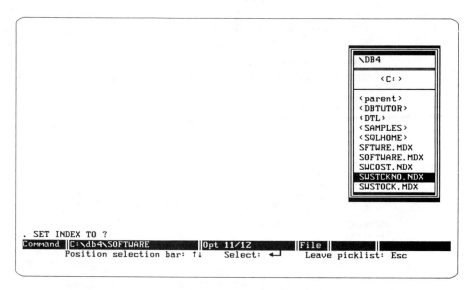

Fig. 6.20. *Using the query operator (?) to select an index field.*

From the Control Center, you can add an index file to the active catalog. Highlight the database file, and then press Shift-F2 (Design). Choose **Include .NDX index file** from the **Organize** menu (see fig. 6.21), and then select the appropriate index file.

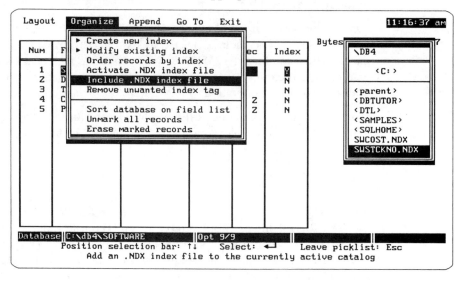

Fig. 6.21. *Adding an index file to the active catalog.*

To select a new index file for the current database, start from the database design screen. Then choose **Activate .NDX index file** from the **Organize** menu (see fig. 6.22)

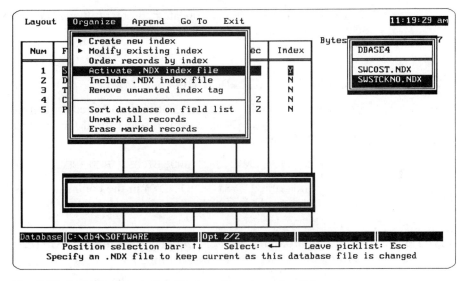

Fig. 6.22. *Selecting an index file from the current catalog.*

6.36 Trap: **To avoid corruption of an index file, index a database file with an existing index file before you edit the database file.**

Be sure to activate the index file before adding records to or removing records from an indexed database file. Otherwise, the index file becomes obsolete and data may be lost.

When you select an indexed database file with the USE...INDEX command, the index file is updated automatically whenever the contents of the file are changed. Therefore, when you set up an existing database file that has been indexed with an indexing key, activating the index file is highly recommended. If you don't activate the index file, it will not reflect any changes you make in the database file. Information stored in the index file won't match the edited contents of the database file. If you then use the index file to rearrange the records in the database file, you may lose access to valuable information.

If the database file has been indexed with more than one index file, you can activate all of its index files with the USE command:

```
. USE SOFTWARE INDEX SWSTCKNO, BYCOST, BYPRICE
```

The activated index files are updated automatically whenever you change the contents of the database file.

Selecting the Master Index File

To maintain multiple index files that you've created for a given database file, activate them when you select the database file with the USE...INDEX command:

```
. USE SOFTWARE INDEX SWSTCKNO, BYCOST, BYPRICE
```

The first index file (SWSTCKNO.NDX) in the command is used as the master index for arranging the records in the database file.

6.37 Tip: **While maintaining multiple indexes, use the SET ORDER TO command to specify the master index file.**

If you want to specify a file other than the first as the master index file, use the SET ORDER TO command. For example, if you want to index the records in the database file and specify the second index file, issue the following command:

```
. SET ORDER TO 2
```

The second index file becomes the master index file (see fig. 6.23).

If you are using a multiple index file, you can change the order to a different index tag by including the TAG clause:

```
. SET ORDER TO TAG < tag name>
```

6.38 Tip: **To maintain the integrity of data in an indexed database file, always update your index file.**

The information in your index files should be kept up-to-date at all times. For this reason, you normally should use the production multiple index file, which dBASE IV automatically updates when changes are made to your database file.

```
. USE SOFTWARE INDEX SWSTCKNO, BYCOST, BYPRICE
. SET ORDER TO 2
Master index: C:BYCOST.ndx
. LIST
Record#  STOCK_NO  DSCRIPTION             TYPE                 COST    PRICE
      1  ASH-DB300 dBASE III Plus v1.01 database             395.00  595.00
      2  ANS-DB110 Paradox v1.1          database             425.00  575.00
      3  CLP-DB100 Clipper DB Compiler   database compiler    450.00  595.00
      4  WOR-DB100 Wordtech DB Compiler  database compiler    469.00  595.00
      8  AST-FW200 Framework v2.A        integrated           345.00  395.00
     10  BOL-PA300 Turbo Pascal v3.0     language              39.50   69.50
      9  MIC-QB100 Microsoft QuickBasic  language              79.00  109.00
      5  LOT-L0123 Lotus 1-2-3 Release2  spread sheet         289.00  359.00
      6  MIC-WS330 Wordstar v3.30        word processing      229.00  269.00
      7  MIS-WD300 Microsoft Word v3.0   word processing      229.00  289.00

. SET ORDER TO 1
Master index: C:SWSTCKNO.ndx
. SET ORDER TO 3
Master index: C:BYPRICE.ndx
.
```

Fig. 6.23. *Specifying the master index with the SET ORDER TO command.*

When using .NDX files, however, if you're not sure whether an index file has been updated, update it to match the records in the current database file before you use the index file. Use the REINDEX command with the following syntax:

. USE < *name of database file*>
. SET INDEX TO < *name of index file*>
. REINDEX

The following is an example of how the preceding syntax is applied:

. USE EMPLOYEE
. SET INDEX TO BYFIRST
. REINDEX
Rebuilding index – C:BYFIRST.ndx
100% indexed   10 Records indexed

Displaying an Indexing Key

When you index a database file, the index file contains information about the indexing key. But you can't identify the indexing key by listing the contents of the index file.

6.39 Trick: **Use DISPLAY STATUS to display the indexing key of the indexing file you're using.**

If you want to identify the indexing key during a dBASE IV session, first activate the index file with the SET INDEX TO command. After activating the index file, use the DISPLAY STATUS command to display all the information about the active files in the current work area. As you can see from figure 6.24, displaying the status identifies both the indexing key and the master index.

```
Currently Selected Database:
Select area:  1, Database in Use: C:\DB4\SOFTWARE.DBF   Alias: SOFTWARE
     Master Index file:  C:\DB4\SWCOST.NDX  Key: type+str(cost,6,2)
Production   MDX file:  C:\DB4\SOFTWARE.MDX
             Index TAG:    STOCK_NO  Key: STOCK_NO

File search path:
Default disk drive: C:
Print destination:  PRN:
Margin =     0
Refresh count =    0
Reprocess count =    0
Number of files open =    6
Current work area =    1

ALTERNATE  - OFF   DELIMITERS - OFF   FULLPATH   - OFF   SAFETY     - ON
AUTOSAVE   - OFF   DESIGN     - ON    HEADING    - ON    SCOREBOARD - ON
BELL       - ON    DEVELOP    - ON    HELP       - ON    SPACE      - ON
CARRY      - OFF   DEVICE     - SCRN  HISTORY    - ON    SQL        - OFF
CATALOG    - OFF   ECHO       - OFF   INSTRUCT   - ON    STATUS     - ON
Press any key to continue...
Command  C:\db4\SOFTWARE          Rec 1/10          File
```

Fig. 6.24. *Using DISPLAY STATUS to identify the indexing key.*

6.40 Trap: **Marking records for deletion doesn't exclude them from the indexing operation.**

When you index a database file, data records you've marked for deletion are included in the operation. When the DELETE command is executed, records to be "deleted" are marked with a deletion symbol (*). Until you issue the PACK command, these records remain in the file. The deletion marks do not affect many dBASE IV operations, including the indexing operation.

As you can see in figure 6.25, all the records marked for deletion have been indexed. You can't exclude the "deleted" records from the indexing operation.

```
. USE EMPLOYEE
. DELETE FOR MALE
      5 records deleted
. LIST
Record# ID_NO        FIRST_NAME    LAST_NAME    POSITION    EMPLY_DATE MALE
      1 *123-45-6789 Thomas T.     Smith        President   03/01/1981 .T.
      2  254-63-5691 Tina Y.       Thompson     VP          09/22/1982 .F.
      3 *467-34-6789 Peter F.      Watson       Manager     10/12/1982 .T.
      4  732-08-4589 Doris Y.      Taylor       Sales Rep   08/14/1983 .F.
      5 *563-55-8900 Tyrone T.     Thorsen      Engineer    06/20/1982 .T.
      6  823-46-6213 Cathy J.      Faust        Secretary   04/15/1983 .F.
      7 *554-34-7893 Vincent M.    Corso        Sales Rep   07/20/1984 .T.
      8  321-65-9087 Jane W.       Kaiser       Accountant  11/22/1982 .F.
      9  560-56-9321 Tina K.       Davidson     Trainee     05/16/1986 .F.
     10 *435-54-9876 James J.      Smith        Trainee     01/23/1986 .T.

. INDEX ON ID_NO TO BYINDNO
  100% indexed           10 Records indexed
.
```

Fig. 6.25. *Deleted records included in the indexing operation.*

6.41 Trick:

To hide records you've marked for deletion, use the SET DELETED ON command before issuing the DISPLAY command.

If you want to hide records you've marked for deletion, issue the SET DELETED ON command before you issue the DISPLAY command. Figure 6.26 shows that all 10 records in the EMPLOYEE.DBF database file were indexed. Although the records marked for deletion (DELETE FOR MALE) are not excluded from the indexing operation, the SET DELETED ON command did hide the deleted records from the LIST operation.

6.42 Trap:

While SET DELETED ON is in effect, you can't recall a record you've marked for deletion.

Although the SET DELETED ON command is useful for excluding certain "deleted" records from some dBASE IV operations, the command may sometimes cause confusion. Figure 6.27 shows the kind of confusion caused by the SET DELETED ON command.

If you forget to issue the SET DELETED OFF command before you issue the RECALL ALL command, the program displays the following message:

```
No records recalled
```

```
. USE EMPLOYEE
. RECALL ALL
      5 records recalled
. DELETE FOR MALE
      5 records deleted
. SET DELETED ON
. INDEX ON ID_NO TO BYIDNO
   100% indexed          10 Records indexed
. LIST
Record#  ID_NO      FIRST_NAME    LAST_NAME     POSITION   EMPLY_DATE MALE
      2  254-63-5691 Tina Y.       Thompson      UP         09/22/1982 .F.
      8  321-65-9087 Jane W.       Kaiser        Accountant 11/22/1982 .F.
      9  560-56-9321 Tina K.       Davidson      Trainee    05/16/1986 .F.
      4  732-08-4589 Doris Y.      Taylor        Sales Rep  08/14/1983 .F.
      6  823-46-6213 Cathy J.      Faust         Secretary  04/15/1983 .F.

.
```

Fig. 6.26. *Using SET DELETED ON to exclude records from the indexing operation.*

```
                                          Caps




. USE EMPLOYEE
. LIST
Record#  ID_NO       FIRST_NAME   LAST_NAME     POSITION   EMPLY_DATE MALE
      1 *123-45-6789 Thomas T.    Smith         President  03/01/1981 .T.
      2  254-63-5691 Tina Y.      Thompson      UP         09/22/1982 .F.
      3 *467-34-6789 Peter F.     Watson        Manager    10/12/1982 .T.
      4  732-08-4589 Doris Y.     Taylor        Sales Rep  08/14/1983 .F.
      5 *563-55-8900 Tyrone T.    Thorsen       Engineer   06/20/1982 .T.
      6  823-46-6213 Cathy J.     Faust         Secretary  04/15/1983 .F.
      7 *554-34-7093 Vincent M.   Corso         Sales Rep  07/20/1984 .T.
      8  321-65-9087 Jane W.      Kaiser        Accountant 11/22/1982 .F.
      9  560-56-9321 Tina K.      Davidson      Trainee    05/16/1986 .F.
     10 *435-54-9876 James J.     Smith         Trainee    01/23/1986 .T.

. SET DELETED ON
. RECALL ALL
No records recalled
.
```

Fig. 6.27. *Effects of the SET DELETED ON command on the RECALL operation.*

You may mistakenly interpret this message as meaning that no more "deleted" records remain in the file. When you no longer need to hide the "deleted" records, you can avoid confusion by issuing the SET DELETED OFF command.

Displaying Data

d BASE IV commands allow you to display the contents of your database files and information about their structure and directories. You can use the power of these commands to enhance your work. This chapter focuses on tips and tricks that make the dBASE IV commands more flexible and powerful by using their special features.

Using Directories

Using directories is an effective way to keep track of your files. This section gives you suggestions on how to display and print directories using dot-prompt commands and the Control Center's DOS utilities.

Displaying a File Directory

There are several ways to list the files in a directory. Among the techniques covered in the text that follows are suggestions for using the dBASE IV DIR and LIST FILES commands, as well as using wild cards.

7.1 Tip: **To list only database files in a directory, use the dBASE IV DIR command.**

The dBASE IV DIR command displays the name, number of records, and size (in bytes) of each database file and the date of each file's most recent update. If you want to interrupt a listing, press Esc.

241

7.2 Tip:

To produce a summary listing of files other than database files, use wild cards (* and ?) in the dBASE IV DIR command.

By default, the DIR command lists only the current directory's database files. If you want to list other types of files, you need to specify their file extensions.

To list all the files of a certain type, use an asterisk (*) and the file extension in the DIR command. (The asterisk is a global symbol, or wild card, that causes all file names to be selected.)

To list all of a directory's index files, for example, use either of the following commands:

    . DIR *.NDX

or

    . DIR *.MDX

To list certain files in a directory, use the question mark (?) as a wild card in the DIR command. (The question mark is used to denote a character in a file name.)

Figure 7.1 illustrates how to use wild cards in the DIR command to list different types of files with names that share certain common characters. The first command, in which an asterisk replaces the file extension, lists all EMPLOYEE files:

    . DIR EMPLOYEE.*

In the second command, the six question marks cause all the index files whose names begin with SW to be displayed:

    . DIR SW??????.NDX

The third command lists all files with names of up to six letters that begin with SW:

    . DIR SW????.*

7.3 Trap:

All files may not be displayed if you use question marks in the dBASE IV DIR command.

Consider the following command:

    . DIR SW????.DBF

```
. DIR EMPLOYEE.*
EMPLOYEE.DBF        EMPLOYEE.FMT        EMPLOYEE.DIF        EMPLOYEE.TXT
EMPLOYEE.CAT        EMPLOYEE.BAK        EMPLOYEE.SCR        EMPLOYEE.DAT
EMPLOYEE.WKS        EMPLOYEE.WK1

    9703 bytes in     10 files.
8331264 bytes remaining on drive.

. DIR SW??????.MDX
SWSTCKNO.MDX        SWCOST.MDX

    2048 bytes in      2 files.
8331264 bytes remaining on drive.

. DIR SW????.*
SWLIST.DBF         SWCOST.MDX         SWLIST.LBL

    2620 bytes in      3 files.
8331264 bytes remaining on drive.
```

Fig. 7.1. *Displaying disk files of different types by using the * and ?*
wild-card characters.

This command uses only four question marks, lists only database files with names beginning with SW and followed by up to four characters. This command does not display a file such as SWSTOCK.DBF, even though the file exists.

7.4 Tip: **To display a file list in the current directory, use either the LIST FILES command or the DIR command.**

You can substitute the LIST FILES command for the dBASE IV DIR command. Both commands produce the same result. Even if you use wild cards (˙ or ?) with the DIR and LIST FILES commands, file attributes (such as file size and update information) are not displayed for nondatabase files.

Note: Scrolling of the screen display in LIST-type commands can be stopped by pressing the Ctrl-S key combination, and restarted by pressing any key.

7.5 Tip: **Use the DISPLAY FILES command to view large directories.**

If you have a directory that contains a large number of files, you can use the DISPLAY FILES command (instead of LIST FILES) to view the directory one screen at a time.

7.6 Trick: **For a detailed listing of files, use the DOS DIR command with the dBASE IV RUN (or !) command.**

From within dBASE IV, use the RUN command at the dot prompt to issue DOS commands. With RUN, you can execute a DOS command as if it were part of the dBASE IV system. (For a detailed discussion of the RUN command, refer to Chapter 1.)

Note: The RUN command works only if the DOS COMMAND.COM command file is in the root directory when you start the computer. Also, because that file should be accessible by the system, you need to place the directory containing the COMMAND.COM file in your search path in DOS.

If you want to list all the screen files in the file directory, issue the following command at the dot prompt:

. RUN DIR *.SCR

To list selected disk files, use the * and ? wild cards in the command. As you can see from figure 7.2, the RUN DIR command gives more detailed information than the simple dBASE IV DIR command.

Printing a File Directory

7.7 Trap: **To avoid error messages and possible loss of data, be sure to turn on the printer before you send output to it.**

If the printer is not turned on when you issue a dBASE IV display command that includes the TO PRINT or SET PRINT ON instructions, you will see a Printer not ready error message. The display operation stops, and the system may appear to lock up. Because you may need to reboot the system and reenter dBASE IV in order to recover from this situation, you run the risk of losing valuable data. Be sure to turn on the printer before you issue commands that require its use.

```
. RUN DIR *.SCR


  Volume in drive C is DBASE_DISK1
  Directory of  C:\DBASE\DBFILES

  EMPLOYEE SCR     1120    1-26-87  11:00a
  PAYROLL  SCR      649    1-26-87  11:05a
  MULTEDIT SCR     1257    2-15-87  12:16p
         3 File(s)   8323072 bytes free


. ! DIR SW????.NDX


  Volume in drive C is DBASE_DISK1
  Directory of  C:\DBASE\DBFILES

  SWCOST   NDX     1024    2-28-87   9:05p
         1 File(s)   8323072 bytes free
```

Fig. 7.2. *Displaying disk files with the DOS DIR command.*

7.8 Tip:

To print a file directory, use the TO PRINT clause.

Use the dBASE IV keywords TO PRINT to print the screen display generated by some commands. If you want to print the contents of an active data record, for example, issue the DISPLAY TO PRINT command. You cannot print a file directory by using the DIR. . .TO PRINT command.

7.9 Trick:

To print a file directory, use the LIST FILES...TO PRINT command.

Use the LIST FILES. . .TO PRINT command, for example, to print a listing of the names of all index files in the directory:

    . LIST FILES *.NDX TO PRINT

7.10 Trap:

When you use the TO PRINT option, all of your copy may not be printed.

When you direct output to a printer by using the TO PRINT option in a command, the last line of the output is not always printed. Sometimes the last line of the output remains in the printer buffer and is printed only with the next batch of output.

7.11 Trick: **To flush the printer buffer, use the SET PRINT ON command.**

The simplest way to print the last line in the printer buffer is to activate the printer with the SET PRINT ON command. The contents of the printer buffer will be flushed out. To deactivate the printer, issue the SET PRINT OFF command.

Alternatively, the EJECT command entered at the dot prompt will cause any output held in the print buffer to be printed, and the paper to advance to the top of the next page.

7.12 Trap: **Using the SET PRINT ON and RUN DIR commands to print a file directory produces an undesirable format.**

One way to print a set of files is to turn on the printer (SET PRINT ON) before issuing the DIR or LIST FILES command. Then turn off the printer after printing:

. SET PRINT ON
. DIR
. SET PRINT OFF

This approach, however, produces listings with an undesirable format. As you can see in figure 7.3, when a listing is too long to fit on one screen, the message Press any key to continue is inserted in the list. And when you turn off the printer, the command SET PRINT OFF is printed.

7.13 Trick: **To direct output to a printer, use the output redirection symbol (>) in the DOS command.**

If you want to print a file directory, using the following DOS DIR command from the dot prompt is preferable to using the SET PRINT ON and dBASE IV DIR commands:

. RUN DIR. . . >LPT1:

You use the greater than sign (>), called an output redirection symbol, to specify the destination of the directory list. LPT1 designates the printer connected to the first printer port. (If you have another printer connected to a different printer port, such as LPT2, you would use >LPT2: to display the results of the RUN DIR command.)

```
Press any key to continue...
CUSTOMER.DBF       6    03/02/87      284
PRODSOLD.DBF      20    03/05/87     1206
ALLSTOCK.DBF      20    03/03/87     1258
HWLIST.DBF        20    03/05/87     1230
HWCOST.DBF        10    03/05/87      512
PRODLIST.DBF      20    03/05/87     1230
PRODSTCK.DBF      20    03/05/87      450
SALARY.DBF        10    04/02/87      788
STAFF.DBF         10    03/14/87      836
JOINFILE.DBF      10    03/30/87      494
BULLETIN.DBF       1    01/06/87      224
SORTLAST.DBF      10    01/06/87      836
SRTFIRST.DBF       8    01/06/87      714
BARDATA.DBF        5    04/15/87      512
PERSONAL.DBF      21    04/23/87     1507
SORTED.DBF        10    02/16/87      836
NAMES.DBF         10    02/16/87      226
SALEITM.DBF        4    02/16/87      250

   27600 bytes in     40 files.
8314880 bytes remaining on drive.

. SET PRINT OFF
```

Fig. 7.3. Using the dBASE IV DIR command with SET PRINT ON.

To print a directory listing of all the index files, for example, enter the following command at the dot prompt:

. RUN DIR *.NDX >LPT1:

The name, size, and update information for each file is included in the printed directory.

Saving a File Directory to a Text File

7.14 Trick: **To save the file directory to a text file, use the output redirection symbol (>) in a DOS DIR command.**

You can save the output produced by a DOS DIR command to a text file by including in the command an output redirection symbol (>) followed by the name of the text file. If you want to save the directory of all the index files to a text file named INDEXES.TXT, for example, enter the following command at the dot prompt:

. RUN DIR *.NDX >INDEXES.TXT

The greater than sign (>), or output redirection symbol, specifies the destination of output from the RUN DIR command. When you specify a text file as the destination, the results of the command are redirected to that text file.

To display on-screen the contents of the text file, use the following command:

. TYPE INDEXES.TXT

To print the contents of the text file, use either of the following commands:

. TYPE INDEXES.TXT TO PRINT

. RUN TYPE INDEXES.TXT >LPT1:

Using the DOS Utilities Menu
To Display a File Directory

7.15 Tip: **Use DOS utilities to view file directories.**

From the Control Center, select the **Tools** menu by pressing Alt-T. Then choose **DOS utilities** (see fig. 7.4).

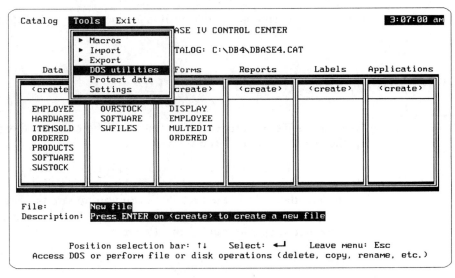

Fig. 7.4. Selecting the DOS utilities option from the Control Center menu.

A window containing the names of files in the current directory appears. To specify files to be displayed, pull down the **Files** menu by pressing Alt-F, and then select **Display only**. You are prompted for a file specification. You can use wild cards (' and ?) or leave the input blank to see all files, which is the same as entering *.*. For example, to see all index files with the extension .NDX, enter *.NDX at the prompt (see fig. 7.5).

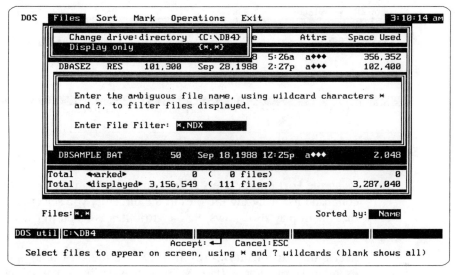

Fig. 7.5. *Using the Display only option to specify files to display.*

The files you requested are displayed, along with subdirectories accessible from the current directory (see fig. 7.6). To see the files in a subdirectory, move the highlighter to that directory and press Enter. To view the files in the next higher directory, select the < **parent**> directory and press Enter.

7.16 Tip: **Organize your directory using the DOS utilities Sort option.**

dBASE IV allows you to view directories sorted by one of four criteria:

Name	(file name, the default)
Extension	(file extension)
Date & Time	(date and time that file was last updated)
Size	(size of file in bytes)

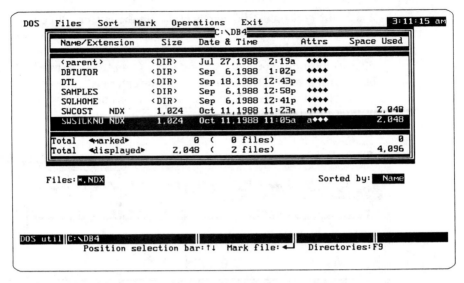

Fig. 7.6. *Displaying .NDX files with the DOS utilities screen.*

Using the **Sort** option offers greater versatility than the DOS DIR command for analyzing the files in the directory you selected. Note that the display also shows the file attributes assigned to each file (Archive, Read only, Hidden, or System).

Access the **Sort** menu by pressing Alt-S, and then select an option. For example, if you choose **Date & Time**, that option is marked ON, and the files are displayed in that order (see fig. 7.7).

When you exit the DOS utilities screen (by pressing Alt-E and Enter), the default settings are restored and you are returned to the Control Center screen.

Displaying Data Records

You can display the contents of active database files by using the LIST, DISPLAY, and BROWSE commands. These commands are commonly used for displaying the contents of data records in an active database file. When combined with the appropriate search and scope conditions, these commands can be used to display the contents of selected records in the database file. You also can display selected records by using a filtering command with a display command.

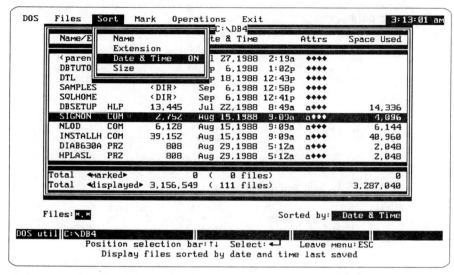

Fig. 7.7. *Using the Sort option to display files by date and time.*

Filtering Data Records before Displaying Them

7.17 Trick: **Use the SET FILTER TO command to screen records that you want to display.**

Instead of using a search or scope condition in a display command, use the SET FILTER TO command to display a subset of the data records in an active database file:

. SET FILTER TO < *filtering condition*>

As you can see from the examples in figure 7.8, the filtering condition specified in the command instructs dBASE IV to filter out records that do not meet the condition.

7.18 Trap: **After you impose a filtering condition on the data records, only records that match the filtering condition are available for additional dBASE IV operations.**

When you issue the LIST command after imposing a filtering condition with the SET FILTER TO MALE command, you do not see all the contents of the file. As shown in figure 7.8, the contents of

```
, USE EMPLOYEE
, SET FILTER TO EMPLY_DATE>=CTOD("1/1/84")
, LIST
Record#  ID_NO       FIRST_NAME     LAST_NAME     POSITION    EMPLY_DATE MALE
      7  554-34-7893 Vincent M.     Corso         Sales Rep   07/20/84   .T.
      9  560-56-9321 Tina K.        Davidson      Trainee     05/16/86   .F.
     10  435-54-9876 James J.       Smith         Trainee     01/23/86   .T.

, SET FILTER TO MALE
, LIST
Record#  ID_NO       FIRST_NAME     LAST_NAME     POSITION    EMPLY_DATE MALE
      1  123-45-6789 Thomas T.      Smith         President   03/01/81   .T.
      3  467-34-6789 Peter F.       Watson        Manager     10/12/82   .T.
      5  563-55-8900 Tyrone T.      Thorsen       Engineer    06/20/82   .T.
      7  554-34-7893 Vincent M.     Corso         Sales Rep   07/20/84   .T.
     10  435-54-9876 James J.       Smith         Trainee     01/23/86   .T.

, SET FILTER TO EMPLY_DATE>=CTOD("1/1/84") .AND. MALE
, LIST
Record#  ID_NO       FIRST_NAME     LAST_NAME     POSITION    EMPLY_DATE MALE
      7  554-34-7893 Vincent M.     Corso         Sales Rep   07/20/84   .T.
     10  435-54-9876 James J.       Smith         Trainee     01/23/86   .T.
```

Fig. 7.8. *Screening data records with the SET FILTER TO command.*

EMPLOYEE.DBF are displayed as if the file contained only records of male employees.

7.19 Tip: **Use only one FILTER command at a time.**

FILTER commands are not cumulative. The FILTER command entered most recently supersedes those issued earlier.

Displaying Specific Data Records

7.20 Tip: **To display the contents of data records based on an exact field value, use the SET EXACT command.**

To display CUSTOMER.DBF records in which "Jo" is the value for the FIRST_NAME, issue the following commands:

```
. USE CUSTOMER
. LIST FOR FIRST_NAME="Jo"
```

As you can see in figure 7.9, the qualifier FOR FIRST_NAME="Jo" does not produce an exact match with the field value. Instead, the LIST operation selects all first names that begin with "Jo". dBASE IV compares the characters in the qualifying condition with those characters of the file's field values. If all the characters in the condition are present in the field values, the names are considered a match.

```
. USE CUSTOMER
. LIST FOR FIRST_NAME="Jo"
Record#  FIRST_NAME      LAST_NAME
      1  John            Smith
      2  Jo              Mason
      3  Jonathan        Walter

. SET EXACT ON
. LIST FOR FIRST_NAME="Jo"
Record#  FIRST_NAME      LAST_NAME
      2  Jo              Mason

.
```

Fig. 7.9. *Listing data records with "Jo" in the FIRST_NAME data field.*

To ensure that only those records that exactly match the qualifying condition are listed, use the SET EXACT ON command before you issue the LIST command (see fig. 7.9). When SET EXACT ON is in effect, only the records with a field that exactly matches the qualifying condition are listed.

Storing Complex Search Conditions in a Query File

The tips, tricks, and traps in this section show you how to store complex search conditions in a query file. You learn how to select records that meet certain conditions, how to filter records before displaying them, and how to display specific records.

7.21 Trick:

To select records that meet a set of complex search conditions, store the conditions in a query file.

If you define complex search conditions that are tedious to enter from the keyboard, save those conditions in a query file. Then, whenever you need to impose those conditions in a display operation, you can activate the query file with a simple command.

To display the less profitable, over-stocked items in the PRODUCTS.DBF inventory file shown in figure 7.10, for example, you define the following search conditions for these items:

1. In the hardware division (DIVISION="HW")

2. Less profitable: profit (PRICE–COST) is less than 40% of cost, or ((PRICE–COST)/COST)) < 0.4

3. Over-stocked: ON _HAND >= 3 or (ON _HAND + ON _ORDER) >=4

```
. use a:products.dbf
. disp stru
Structure for database: A:\PRODUCTS.DBF
Number of data records:      10
Date of last update   : 10/16/88
Field  Field Name  Type      Width    Dec    Index
    1  STOCK_NO    Character      9             N
    2  DIVISION    Character      2             N
    3  DSCRIPTION  Character     40             N
    4  COST        Numeric        7      2      N
    5  PRICE       Numeric        7      2      N
    6  ON_HAND     Numeric        3             N
    7  ON_ORDER    Numeric        3             N
** Total **                     72
.
Command  A:\PRODUCTS               Rec 1/10          File
```

Fig. 7.10. *The file structure of PRODUCTS.DBF.*

Then you incorporate these search conditions in a LIST command with a FOR qualifier:

. LIST FOR (DIVISION="HW" .AND. ((PRICE–COST)/COST) < .4)
  .AND. (ON _HAND >=3 .OR. (ON _HAND + ON _ORDER)>=4)

Although this LIST command with its complex search condition produces the appropriate list of records, having to enter the condition whenever you want to examine these selected records would be tedious. As a shortcut, you can define the search conditions in a query file and save it on disk. Then recall the file to impose the conditions whenever you choose.

Creating a Query File

dBASE IV uses a system called Query By Example (QBE) that allows you to create view queries. Those queries specify the files, fields, and records that will be viewed on-screen or printed.

You can create a query file by issuing the CREATE QUERY command at the dot prompt:

. CREATE QUERY < *name of query file*>

For example, to create a query file named OVRSTOCK.QBE for the set of search conditions described in the preceding trick, you issue the following command:

. CREATE QUERY OVRSTOCK

7.22 Tip: **Use the Control Center menu to create a query file.**

Creating a query file is easy if you use the Control Center menu. To create the file, select the < **create**> option from the Queries column.

If no database file is in use, you can choose the name of the database file on which this query will operate. From the **Layout** menu, select **Add file to query**, and then choose the database file from the picklist (see fig. 7.11)

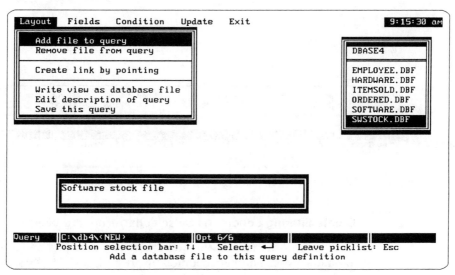

Fig. 7.11. *Choosing a database file for the query.*

A file skeleton for the database file and a file skeleton for the view appear, with a column for each field. To move from one field to another, use the Tab and Shift-Tab keys. To move between skeletons, use the F3 (Previous) and F4 (Next) keys.

You can add additional files to the view if you will be relating two or more databases. See Chapter 5 for a discussion of linking files using a view query.

7.23 Tip: **Define the filtering conditions.**

Specify filtering conditions by placing the expressions in the appropriate field columns. The filtering conditions specified can be any valid dBASE IV expression. Because dBASE IV uses the Query-By-Example approach, you don't need to repeat the field name in the expression. For example, to specify DIVISION="HW", you need only to type HW in the DIVISION field column (see fig. 7.12).

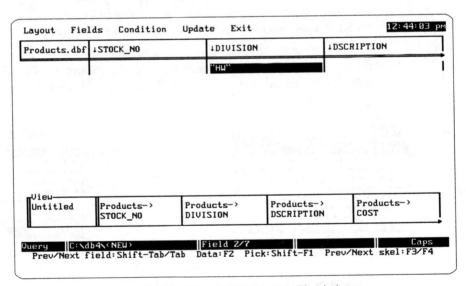

Fig. 7.12. Entering the first search condition in the file skeleton.

7.24 Tip: **Create filtering conditions by selecting from the picklist.**

You can choose from a list of available fields, operators, and functions in building your filtering condition by pressing Shift-F1 (Pick). Choose the appropriate item from the list presented, and it will be added to your expression (see fig. 7.13). Use the up-arrow (↑) and down-arrow (↓) keys to scroll through the lists of operators and functions.

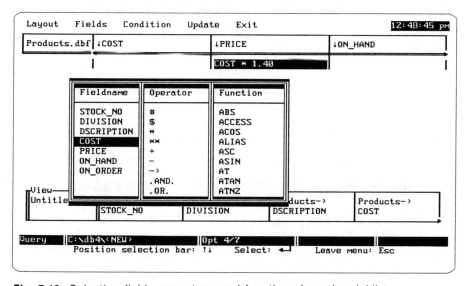

Fig. 7.13. *Selecting fields, operators, and functions from the picklist.*

7.25 Tip: **List multiple conditions on one line if all conditions must be met.**

You can list several conditions that must be met in one field on a single line. Each condition should be separated by a comma. As you type, the column will scroll horizontally to accommodate your list of expressions. This approach is equivalent to using the .AND. operator in an expression.

For example, the condition PRICE <1ØØ .AND PRICE>5ØØ can be specified by typing thee following in the PRICE field column (see fig. 7.14):

>1ØØ, <5ØØ

7.26 Tip: **Use multiple lines to define .OR. conditions.**

If you need to specify "OR" conditions, equivalent to using the .OR. operator, specify them on a separate line. Press the down-arrow (↓) key to add a line to the file skeleton.

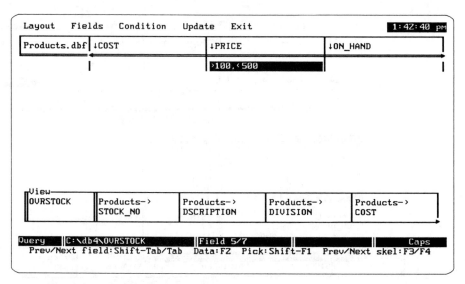

Fig. 7.14. *Listing multiple conditions on one line.*

For example, consider the following condition:

```
PRICE  < 100 .OR. PRICE > 200
```

This condition would show records in which either PRICE is greater than 200 or PRICE is less than 100. Simply type the following on one line under the PRICE field column:

```
< 100
```

Press the down arrow (↓), and then type the following on the next line under the same column (see fig. 7.15):

```
>200
```

7.27 Tip: **Test the query conditions before saving them to a file.**

Before saving the defined search or filtering conditions, test them. To instruct dBASE IV to display the records that meet the defined conditions, press F2 (Data). The first record that meets the defined filtering conditions is displayed (see fig. 7.16).

Press PgDn to display the next record that meets the conditions. You can toggle between Edit and Browse modes by pressing F2 (Data).

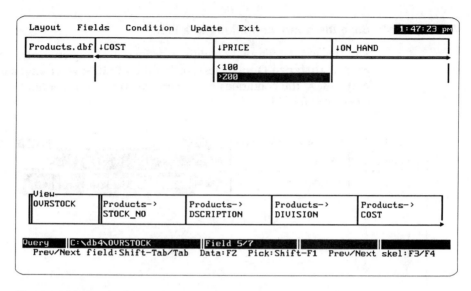

Fig. 7.15. Placing "OR" conditions on separate lines.

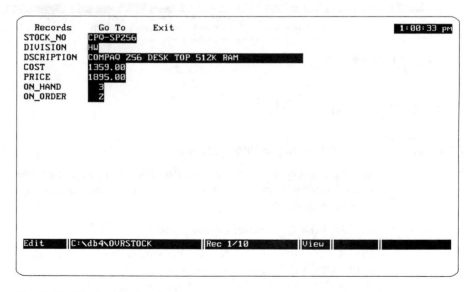

Fig. 7.16. Displaying the first record meeting query conditions.

7.28 Tip: **Save the query conditions to a file.**

After testing the filtering conditions defined in the query table, select **Exit/Transfer to Query Design**, and then **Exit/Save changes and exit** to save the conditions in a query file. You are prompted for a file name (see fig. 7.17).

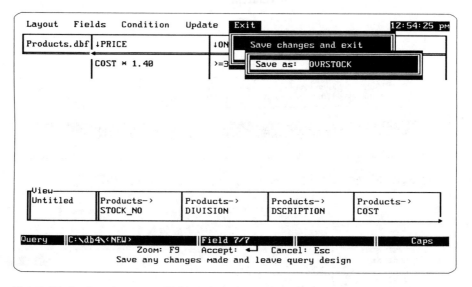

```
 Layout    Fields   Condition    Update   Exit               12:54:25 PM
┌───────────┐                         ┌──────────────────────────────────┐
│Products.dbf│ ↓PRICE          │↓ON  │ Save changes and exit            ║
│           │                  │     ├─┬──────────────────────────────┐ ║
│           │ COST × 1.40      │>=3  │ │ Save as:   OVRSTOCK          │ ║
│           │                  └─────┴─┴──────────────────────────────┘ ║


┌─View─────────────────────────────────────────────────────────────────
║Untitled   ║┌Products─>   ┬Products─>   ┬Products─>   ┬Products─>
║           ║│STOCK_NO     │DIVISION     │DSCRIPTION   │COST
┌──────────┬────────────────┬──────────────┬─────────────────────────────
│Query     ║C:\db4\<NEW>    ║Field 7/7     ║            ║           Caps
            Zoom: F9    Accept: ↵   Cancel: Esc
          Save any changes made and leave query design
```

Fig. 7.17. *Saving the query file.*

Activating a Query File

7.29 Tip: **Use a query file to filter records.**

Activate a query file to display the database file records that meet the search condition you defined in the query file. You can use the SET VIEW TO command:

. SET VIEW TO < *name of query file*>

For example, you can use the SET VIEW TO command to display records in PRODUCTS.DBF that meet the search or filtering conditions defined and saved in the OVRSTOCK.QBE file (see fig. 7.18).

```
. USE A:PRODUCTS
. SET VIEW TO OVRSTOCK
. LIST STOCK_NO, DIVISION, COST, PRICE, ON_HAND, ON_ORDER
Record#  STOCK_NO  DIVISION    COST   PRICE ON_HAND ON_ORDER
      1  CPQ-SP256 HW        1359.00 1895.00       3        2
      3  IBM-AT640 HW        3790.00 4300.00       4        0
      7  SEA-HD020 HW         398.00  495.00       2        3
      9  PAR-GC100 HW         279.00  390.00      10        0
     10  HER-GC100 HW         199.00  289.00       6        4
.
Command  A:\PRODUCTS                 Rec EOF/10         File
```

Fig. 7.18. *Displaying data records with the SET VIEW command.*

7.30 Tip: **Use the Control Center to activate a query file.**

From the Control Center, simply highlight the query file you want to use in the Queries column, and then press Enter. If you want to view the data selected by the query, highlight the query file in the Queries column and press F2 (Data).

Displaying Selected Data

The tips, tricks, and traps in this section show you how to display selected data. You will learn how to hide deleted records from display, how to select fields for display, and how to eliminate field headings from displays.

Hiding Deleted Records from Display

When you remove data records from a database file by using the DELETE command, the records are marked with an asterisk (*). Because these "deleted" records remain in the file until you PACK the file, they are still accessible by many dBASE IV operations. For example, if you issue the LIST or DISPLAY command after having marked the data records for deletion, the records are still displayed as active records.

7.31 Trick: **Use the SET DELETED ON command to hide records.**

To exclude marked records from a display operation, issue the SET DELETED ON command. As you can see from figure 7.19, while the SET DELETED ON command is in effect, the records that have been marked for deletion are not displayed by the LIST command.

```
. USE EMPLOYEE
. DELE FOR MALE
       5 records deleted
. LIST
Record#  ID_NO        FIRST_NAME   LAST_NAME   POSITION    EMPLY_DATE MALE
       1 *123-45-6789 Thomas T.    Smith       President   03/01/81   .T.
       2  254-63-5691 Tina Y.      Thompson    VP          09/22/82   .F.
       3 *467-34-6789 Peter F.     Watson      Manager     10/12/82   .T.
       4  732-08-4589 Doris Y.     Taylor      Sales Rep   08/14/83   .F.
       5 *563-55-8900 Tyrone T.    Thorsen     Engineer    06/20/82   .T.
       6  823-46-6213 Cathy J.     Faust       Secretary   04/15/83   .F.
       7 *554-34-7893 Vincent M.   Corso       Sales Rep   07/20/84   .T.
       8  321-65-9087 Jane W.      Kaiser      Accountant  11/22/82   .F.
       9  560-56-9321 Tina K.      Davidson    Trainee     05/16/86   .F.
      10 *435-54-9876 James J.     Smith       Trainee     01/23/86   .T.
. SET DELETED ON
. LIST
Record#  ID_NO        FIRST_NAME   LAST_NAME   POSITION    EMPLY_DATE MALE
       2  254-63-5691 Tina Y.      Thompson    VP          09/22/82   .F.
       4  732-08-4589 Doris Y.     Taylor      Sales Rep   08/14/83   .F.
       6  823-46-6213 Cathy J.     Faust       Secretary   04/15/83   .F.
       8  321-65-9087 Jane W.      Kaiser      Accountant  11/22/82   .F.
       9  560-56-9321 Tina K.      Davidson    Trainee     05/16/86   .F.
```

Fig. 7.19. The effects of SET DELETED ON on listing data records.

Selecting Fields for Display

7.32 Trick: **To display selected data fields, use the SET FIELDS TO command.**

To select the data fields to be displayed, use the dBASE IV SET FIELDS TO command like a FILTER command:

. SET FIELDS TO < *list of fields to be displayed* >

Specify in the command the fields you want to display. Data fields that are not listed are hidden from display (see fig. 7.20). As you can see from the figure, you can use more than one SET FIELDS TO command to add data fields to the list.

```
                                    Caps
, USE EMPLOYEE
, SET FIELDS TO ID_NO, POSITION, LAST_NAME, FIRST_NAME
, LIST
Record#   ID_NO      FIRST_NAME    LAST_NAME     POSITION
     1    123-45-6789 Thomas T.    Smith         President
     2    254-63-5691 Tina Y.      Thompson      VP
     3    467-34-6789 Peter F.     Watson        Manager
     4    732-88-4589 Doris Y.     Taylor        Sales Rep
     5    563-55-8900 Tyrone T.    Thorsen       Engineer
     6    823-46-6213 Cathy J.     Faust         Secretary
     7    554-34-7893 Vincent M.   Corso         Sales Rep
     8    321-65-9087 Jane W.      Kaiser        Accountant
     9    560-56-9321 Tina K.      Davidson      Trainee
    10    435-54-9876 James J.     Smith         Trainee
, SET FIELDS TO EMPLY_DATE
, SET FILTER TO .NOT. MALE
, LIST
Record#   ID_NO      FIRST_NAME    LAST_NAME     POSITION   EMPLY_DATE
     2    254-63-5691 Tina Y.      Thompson      VP         09/22/82
     4    732-88-4589 Doris Y.     Taylor        Sales Rep  08/14/83
     6    823-46-6213 Cathy J.     Faust         Secretary  04/15/83
     8    321-65-9087 Jane W.      Kaiser        Accountant 11/22/82
     9    560-56-9321 Tina K.      Davidson      Trainee    05/16/86
```

Fig. 7.20. *Selecting data fields with the SET FIELDS TO command.*

7.33 Trap: **The effects of SET FIELDS TO commands are cumulative.**

When you issue more than one SET FIELDS TO command, all the data fields specified by those commands remain selected because the effects of SET FIELDS TO commands are cumulative.

7.34 Trick: **To remove data fields from the list, repeat the selection process.**

To remove selected data fields from the field list, start over. You need to repeat the field-selection process, selecting the database file with the USE command (as in USE EMPLOYEE). You can clear all the selected fields by issuing the SET FIELDS TO command with no fields specified.

7.35 Trick: **Use a calculated field with the SET FIELDS command.**

You can create a calculated field using a dBASE IV expression and add the field to your fields list. For example, if you have fields called Cost and Quantity, you can create a calculated field called Amount using the expression Cost*Quantity:

. SET FIELDS TO Cost,Quantity,Amount=Cost*Quantity

Figure 7.21 illustrates the difference between using the two fields Cost and Quantity alone and adding the calculated field Amount.

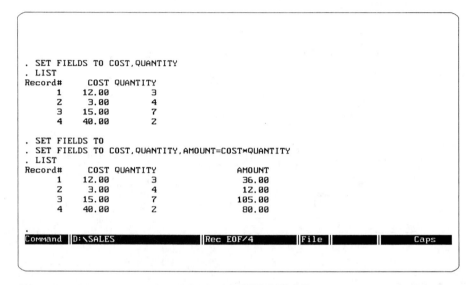

```
. SET FIELDS TO COST,QUANTITY
. LIST
Record#      COST QUANTITY
       1    12.00        3
       2     3.00        4
       3    15.00        7
       4    40.00        2

. SET FIELDS TO
. SET FIELDS TO COST,QUANTITY,AMOUNT=COST×QUANTITY
. LIST
Record#      COST QUANTITY             AMOUNT
       1    12.00        3              36.00
       2     3.00        4              12.00
       3    15.00        7             105.00
       4    40.00        2              80.00

.
Command  D:\SALES                    Rec EOF/4      File            Caps
```

Fig. 7.21. *Adding a calculated field with SET FIELDS.*

Eliminating Field Headings from Displays

7.36 Tip: **To exclude field headings while you display data records, use the SET HEADINGS OFF command.**

Whenever you execute the LIST and DISPLAY commands, the field headings are displayed as well as the contents of the records. Because these field headings sometimes clutter the screen, you may prefer to remove them. Issue the SET HEADINGS OFF command before you use the LIST and DISPLAY commands.

Using the Browse Operation's Powerful Features

Use the Browse menu options to enhance the power of the BROWSE command. Four menus are available in the Browse operation: **Records, Fields, Go To,** and **Exit** (see fig. 7.22). To pull down one of the menus, press the Alt-key with the first letter of the menu name.

For example, to pull down the **Go To** menu, press Alt-G. To cancel the menu, press Esc.

```
   Records      Fields      Go To      Exit                    1:12:47 PM
  ┌──────────┬─────────┬──────────────────────────────┬─────────┬─────────┬────┐
  │STOCK_NO  │DIVISION │DSCRIPTION                    │COST     │PRICE    │ON  │
  ├──────────┼─────────┼──────────────────────────────┼─────────┼─────────┼────┤
  │CPU-SP256 │HW       │COMPAQ 256 DESK TOP 512K RAM  │1359.00  │1895.00  │    │
  │ZEN-SL181 │HW       │ZENITH Z181 LAP TOP 640K RAM  │1695.00  │1998.00  │    │
  │IBM-AT640 │HW       │IBM AT 640K 1.2MB FD 20 MB HD │3790.00  │4300.00  │    │
  │ZEN-MM012 │HW       │ZENITH MONO MONITOR           │  89.00  │ 110.00  │    │
  │NEC-PC660 │HW       │NEC 660 PRINTER               │ 560.00  │ 690.00  │    │
  │HAY-M1200 │HW       │HAYES 1200 BAUD INT MODEM     │ 269.00  │ 350.00  │    │
  │SEA-HD020 │HW       │SEAGATE 20MB INT HD           │ 398.00  │ 495.00  │    │
  │10M-HD040 │HW       │IOMEGA BERNOULLI 20+20 SYSTEM │2190.00  │2890.00  │    │
  │PAR-GC100 │HW       │PARADISE CGA GRAPHIC CARD     │ 279.00  │ 390.00  │    │
  │HER-GC100 │HW       │HERCULES MONO CARD            │ 199.00  │ 289.00  │    │
  │          │         │                              │         │         │    │
  │          │         │                              │         │         │    │
  │          │         │                              │         │         │    │
  │          │         │                              │         │         │    │
  ├──────────┴──┬──────┴───────────────┬──────────────┴─┬───────┴──┬──────┴────┤
  │Browse     ║ │C:\db4\OURSTOCK       ║ │Rec 1/10      ║ │View  ║  │       ║  │
  └─────────────┴──────────────────────┴────────────────┴──────────┴───────────┘
                           View and edit fields
```

Fig. 7.22. *Using the Browse operation.*

Freezing Fields

7.37 Trick: **Freeze a data field in the Browse operation.**

The **Freeze field** option is very useful for editing data during a Browse operation. When you freeze a field, you can move up and down within the field as you edit. The cursor's movement is restricted within the column that corresponds to the frozen field.

Select the **Fields** menu by pressing Alt-F, and then select **Freeze field** and press Enter. Enter the field name as shown in figure 7.23. To edit only the COST field, for example, enter COST as the field to be frozen. The cursor is placed in the COST field so that the movement of the cursor is restricted to that field. By using the up-arrow (↑) and down-arrow (↓) keys, you can move up and down within the field column to make your changes.

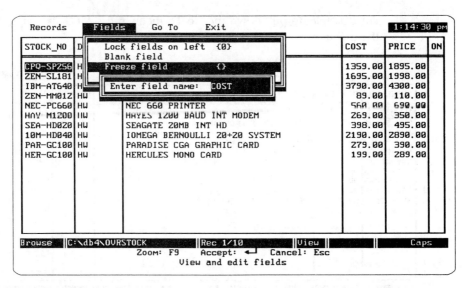

```
   Records      Fields      Go To     Exit                        1:14:30 pm
  ┌─────────────┬──────────────────────────────────┬──────┬────────┬───────┬────┐
  │ STOCK_NO   │D│ Lock fields on left   {0}       │      │ COST   │ PRICE │ ON │
  │            │ │ Blank field                     │      │        │       │    │
  │ CPQ-SP256 │H│ Freeze field          {}        │      │1359.00 │1895.00│    │
  │ ZEN-SL181 │H│ ┌───────────────────────────────┐│      │1695.00 │1998.00│    │
  │ IBM-AT640 │H│ │ Enter field name:    COST     ││      │3790.00 │4300.00│    │
  │ ZEN-MM01Z │HW│ └───────────────────────────────┘      │  89.00 │ 110.00│    │
  │ NEC-PC660 │HW│ NEC 660 PRINTER                        │ 560.00 │ 690.00│    │
  │ HAY M1200 │HW│ HAYES 1200 BAUD INT MODEM              │ 269.00 │ 350.00│    │
  │ SEA-HD020 │HW│ SEAGATE 20MB INT HD                    │ 398.00 │ 495.00│    │
  │ 10M-HD040 │HW│ IOMEGA BERNOULLI 20+20 SYSTEM          │2190.00 │2890.00│    │
  │ PAR-GC100 │HW│ PARADISE CGA GRAPHIC CARD              │ 279.00 │ 390.00│    │
  │ HER-GC100 │HW│ HERCULES MONO CARD                     │ 199.00 │ 289.00│    │
  │            │ │                                        │        │       │    │
  │            │ │                                        │        │       │    │
  │            │ │                                        │        │       │    │
  │            │ │                                        │        │       │    │
  └────────────┴─┴────────────────────────────────┴──────┴────────┴───────┴────┘
  Browse   │C:\db4\OVRSTOCK        ││Rec 1/10      ││View ││         │ Caps    │
               Zoom: F9    Accept: ◄┘   Cancel: Esc
                      View and edit fields
```

Fig. 7.23. *Specifying a field to freeze.*

7.38 Tip: **Use a dot prompt command to freeze a field in the BROWSE operation.**

From the dot prompt, you can select the field to be frozen during the BROWSE operation by including a FREEZE option in the BROWSE command. For example, to freeze the ZIP field while you browse the records of the ACCOUNTS.DBF file, issue the following commands:

    . USE ACCOUNTS
    . GO TOP
    . BROWSE FREEZE ZIP

7.39 Trap: **You can't unfreeze a field from the Browse screen if the field was frozen by a dot-prompt command.**

After you have used the BROWSE FREEZE command to freeze a field, the **Freeze field** option of the Fields menu in the Browse screen is disabled. To unfreeze a field in this case, you must return to the dot prompt and enter the BROWSE command *without* the FREEZE option.

Displaying Hidden Fields with BROWSE

7.40 Tip: **To "pan" data fields in a Browse operation, use the Home and End keys.**

During a Browse operation, if the database file you're examining has more fields than can be displayed on-screen, use the Home and End keys to "pan" the displayed fields. Home shows the leftmost fields; End shows the rightmost fields.

In figure 7.24, the STOCK_NO field is not shown because it scrolled off the screen to the left when the End key was pressed. The five rightmost fields appear.

```
   Records      Fields     Go To     Exit                      1:16:07 PM
  ┌────────────────────────────────┬─────────┬─────────┬─────────┬─────────┐
  │ DSCRIPTION                     │ COST    │ PRICE   │ ON_HAND │ ON_ORDER│
  ├────────────────────────────────┼─────────┼─────────┼─────────┼─────────┤
  │ COMPAQ 256 DESK TOP 512K RAM   │ 1359.00 │ 1895.00 │    3    │    2    │
  │ ZENITH Z181 LAP TOP 640K RAM   │ 1695.00 │ 1998.00 │    5    │    5    │
  │ IBM AT 640K 1.2MB FD 20 MB HD  │ 3790.00 │ 4300.00 │    4    │    0    │
  │ ZENITH MONO MONITOR            │   89.00 │  110.00 │    2    │    2    │
  │ NEC 660 PRINTER                │  560.00 │  690.00 │   10    │    0    │
  │ HAYES 1200 BAUD INT MODEM      │  269.00 │  350.00 │    5    │    5    │
  │ SEAGATE 20MB INT HD            │  398.00 │  495.00 │    2    │    3    │
  │ IOMEGA BERNOULLI 20+20 SYSTEM  │ 2190.00 │ 2890.00 │    4    │    0    │
  │ PARADISE CGA GRAPHIC CARD      │  279.00 │  390.00 │   10    │    0    │
  │ HERCULES MONO CARD             │  199.00 │  289.00 │    6    │    4    │
  │                                │         │         │         │         │
  └────────────────────────────────┴─────────┴─────────┴─────────┴─────────┘
  Browse   C:\db4\OURSTOCK         Rec 1/10         View
                         View and edit fields
```

Fig. 7.24. *Displaying the last five data fields in a Browse operation.*

If you have a large number of fields, you can move between them by pressing Tab or Shift-Tab.

Locking Data Fields in a Browse Operation

7.41 Trap: **If fields are hidden from view, knowing which record you are looking at is difficult.**

One of the problems associated with using Home or End in the Browse operation is that panning hides data fields. As you saw from figure 7.24, panning to the right hid the STOCK_NO field. This makes knowing which record you are examining or editing difficult.

7.42 Trick: **To create a window effect while browsing data, lock certain data fields.**

You can create a window effect by locking certain data fields (to exclude them from panning) so that they remain displayed. Choose the **Lock fields on left** option from the **Fields** menu and indicate the number of columns to be locked.

For example, you can lock the first two data fields (STOCK_NO and DIVISION) so that they are displayed at all times. Use the Shift-Tab or Home keys to pan the data fields to the left. When the two fields appear in the first and second columns, press Alt-F (for **Fields**), and then choose the **Lock fields on left** option from the menu. The program displays the following prompt:

Enter number of fields to remain stationary:

At this prompt, enter 2 as the number of data fields to be locked (see fig. 7.25).

Now the two locked fields will remain on-screen when you pan left or right. In the example, if you press End, the STOCK_NO and DIVISION fields are displayed along with the last four fields (see fig. 7.26).

7.43 Trap: **When you lock a number of columns, you lock the displayed data fields.**

If you specify 2 as the number of columns to be locked, the first two data fields that are currently displayed are locked. These two fields are not necessarily the first two in the database file.

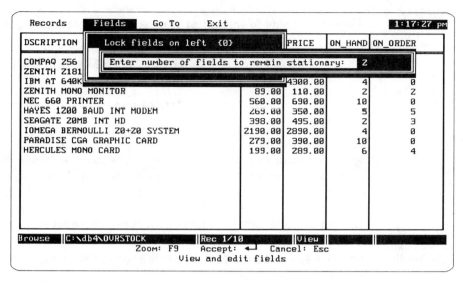

```
 Records        Fields      Go To      Exit                         1:17:27 PM
┌──────────────────────────────────────────────────────────────────────────┐
│ DSCRIPTION   │ Lock fields on left  {0}          │PRICE  │ON_HAND│ON_ORDER │
│ COMPAQ 256   ┌──────────────────────────────────────────────┐             │
│ ZENITH Z181  │  Enter number of fields to remain stationary:  Z │         │
│ IBM AT 640K  └──────────────────────────────────────────────┘4300.00│  4│    0│
│ ZENITH MONO MONITOR                      89.00│ 110.00│  2│    2│
│ NEC 660 PRINTER                         560.00│ 690.00│ 10│    0│
│ HAYES 1200 BAUD INT MODEM               269.00│ 350.00│  5│    5│
│ SEAGATE 20MB INT HD                     398.00│ 495.00│  2│    3│
│ IOMEGA BERNOULLI 20+20 SYSTEM          2190.00│2890.00│  4│    0│
│ PARADISE CGA GRAPHIC CARD               279.00│ 390.00│ 10│    0│
│ HERCULES MONO CARD                      199.00│ 289.00│  6│    4│
│                                                                            │
│                                                                            │
│                                                                            │
│                                                                            │
├────────────────────────────────────────────────────────────────────────────
│Browse  │C:\db4\OURSTOCK        │Rec 1/10      │View │                      │
           Zoom: F9     Accept: ┘   Cancel: Esc
                     View and edit fields
```

Fig. 7.25. *Locking data fields in Browse.*

```
 Records        Fields      Go To      Exit                         1:18:52 PM
┌──────────────────────────────────────────────────────────────────────────┐
│ STOCK_NO │ DIVISION│COST    │ PRICE  │ON_HAND│ON_ORDER                     │
│ CPQ-SPZ56│ HW      │1359.00 │1895.00 │   3│  2                            │
│ ZEN-SL181│ HW      │1695.00 │1998.00 │   5│  5                            │
│ IBM-AT640│ HW      │3790.00 │4300.00 │   4│  0                            │
│ ZEN-MM012│ HW      │  89.00 │ 110.00 │   2│  2                            │
│ NEC-PC660│ HW      │ 560.00 │ 690.00 │  10│  0                            │
│ HAY-M1200│ HW      │ 269.00 │ 350.00 │   5│  5                            │
│ SEA-HD020│ HW      │ 398.00 │ 495.00 │   2│  3                            │
│ 10M-HD040│ HW      │2190.00 │2890.00 │   4│  0                            │
│ PAR-GC100│ HW      │ 279.00 │ 390.00 │  10│  0                            │
│ HER-GC100│ HW      │ 199.00 │ 289.00 │   6│  4                            │
│                                                                            │
│                                                                            │
│                                                                            │
│                                                                            │
│                                                                            │
├────────────────────────────────────────────────────────────────────────────
│Browse  │C:\db4\OURSTOCK        │Rec 1/10      │View │                      │
                     View and edit fields
```

Fig. 7.26. *Panning the unlocked data fields in Browse.*

7.44 Trick: **Place data fields to the left of your screen before locking them.**

To avoid hiding data fields, pan the fields so that they appear in the screen's leftmost columns. You then can lock all the data fields.

7.45 Trap: **In the Browse operation, you cannot pan to the left of locked data fields.**

One of the restrictions imposed on locking fields in the Browse operation is that you cannot pan to the left beyond the locked data fields. When you lock a number of data fields in the Browse operation, those fields to the left of the locked fields are hidden from the Browse operation. You can't reveal them by panning unless you rearrange the order of the fields before beginning the Browse operation.

7.46 Trick: **Use the BROWSE FIELDS command to rearrange the order of the data fields.**

With the BROWSE FIELDS command, you can rearrange the order of the data fields so that the fields to be locked appear in the screen's leftmost columns. Then you will be able to pan the data fields that appear to the right of the locked fields.

7.47 Tip: **Use the BROWSE FIELDS command to select and arrange the data fields to be browsed.**

If a database file contains more data fields than can be displayed simultaneously, use the BROWSE FIELDS command to browse selected fields. For example, you can select and rearrange the fields in the ACCOUNTS.DBF file for the BROWSE operation. Issue the following command:

```
. BROWSE FIELDS MAX _CREDIT,ACCOUNT _ NO,NAME,AREA _CODE,
  PHONE _ NO,ADDRESS,CITY,STATE,ZIP
```

The data fields are displayed in the order specified in the command.

Using Views To Select and Arrange Fields

7.48 Tip: **Use a view query to specify which fields are to be displayed in either Browse or Edit mode.**

As mentioned earlier, query files can be used not only to filter records but also to relate files and to display selected fields. To create a view query, you do not have to specify filtering conditions. To eliminate certain fields from view, you can simply remove them from the view skeleton on the query design screen. There are two easy ways to do this:

Press F3 (Previous) or F4 (Next) to select the database file skeleton, and then press Tab or Shift-Tab to choose the field to remove. Press Alt-F to pull down the **Fields** menu, and then select **Remove field from view** and press Enter (see fig. 7.27).

or

Select the view skeleton, press Tab or Shift-Tab to choose the field to remove, and then press F5 (Field).

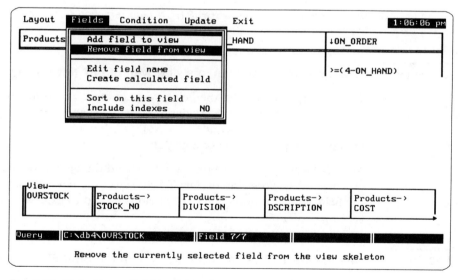

Fig. 7.27. *Selecting a field to delete from the view.*

To view data, press F2 (Data). Press F2 again to switch between Browse and Edit modes. Figure 7.28 shows a record displayed in Edit mode with the DSCRIPTION field removed from the view.

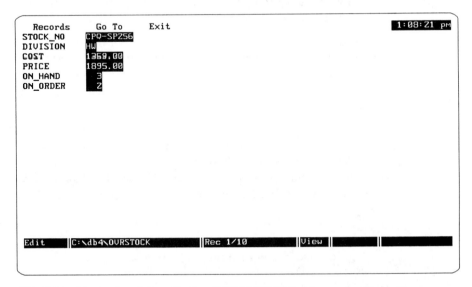

Fig. 7.28. Displaying data with the DSCRIPTION field removed from the view.

7.49 Trick: **Change a field's location in a view with the F7 (Move) key.**

To rearrange the order of the fields, you can move a field to a new location in a view in the query design screen. Select the view skeleton by pressing F3 (Previous) or F4 (Next), and then choose the field to be moved by pressing Tab or Shift-Tab.

Next, press F7 (Move). A box appears around the field to be moved (see fig. 7.29). Press Tab or Shift-Tab to select the new location for the field, and then press Enter. The field is moved to its new location (see fig. 7.30).

7.50 Trick: **Change the width of a field display with the Shift-F7 (Size) key.**

To change the display width of a field in Browse, highlight the field, press the Shift-F7 (Size) key, use the right-arrow (→) and left-arrow (←) keys to adjust the width of the field column, and then press Enter

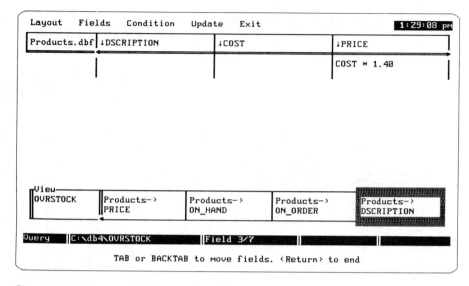

Fig. 7.29. *Moving a field to another position in the view.*

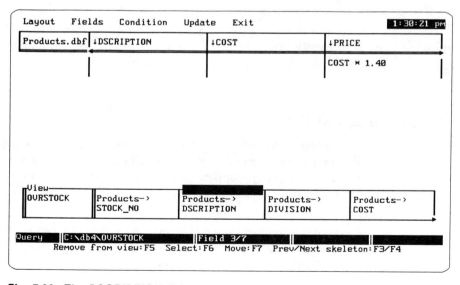

Fig. 7.30. *The DSCRIPTION field moved to its new location.*

(see fig. 7.31). This method allows you to fit more fields on-screen by narrowing a long field, or to display fewer fields by widening a field. The maximum display width for a single field is 78 characters.

```
 Records      Fields      Go To      Exit                    1:23:27 PM

 STOCK_NO  DIVISION DSCRIPTION              COST   PRICE   ON_HAND ON_ORDER

 CPQ-SP256 HW       COMPAQ 256 DESK TOP 512K 1359.00 1895.00      3       2
 ZEN-SL181 HW       ZENITH Z181 LAP TOP 640K 1695.00 1998.00      5       5
 IBM-AT640 HW       IBM AT 640K 1.2MB FD 20 M 3790.00 4300.00      4       0
 ZEN-MM012 HW       ZENITH MONO MONITOR        89.00  110.00      2       2
 NEC-PC660 HW       NEC 660 PRINTER           560.00  690.00     10       0
 HAY-M1200 HW       HAYES 1200 BAUD INT MODEM  269.00  350.00      5       5
 SEA-HD020 HW       SEAGATE 20MB INT HD        398.00  495.00      2       3
 10M-HD040 HW       IOMEGA BERNOULLI 20+20 SY 2190.00 2890.00      4       0
 PAR-GC100 HW       PARADISE CGA GRAPHIC CARD  279.00  390.00     10       0
 HER-GC100 HW       HERCULES MONO CARD         199.00  289.00      6       4




 Browse   ||C:\db4\OURSTOCK      ||Rec 1/10       ||View ||      ||      ||
          Change current column width:  ↔     End sizing:  ↵
```

Fig. 7.31. *Using Shift-F7 (Size) to change the display width of a field.*

Note that this process does not alter the actual width of the field in your database file. The process temporarily changes the amount of the field that is displayed while in a Browse session.

Displaying Data in Color

Depending on the type of monitor you have, you can display data on the screen in either monochrome or color mode. If you have a color monitor with the appropriate graphics adapter card, you can use the SET COLOR TO command to choose a number of colors for displaying data.

Text, lines, and graphics symbols are displayed in one color (foreground color) over another (background color). There are two types of text: standard and enhanced.

Use standard text to display the following:

❏ The dBASE IV command at the dot prompt

❏ The direction of cursor movement in the navigation line

❏ Information on the message line

❏ Field labels

❏ Double- and single-line boxes

❏ Menu options in the Control Center menu (except for the highlighted option)

❏ The contents of data records displayed with the DISPLAY and LIST commands

❏ The listing of data records in the Browse operation (except for the current record)

The following items are displayed in enhanced text:

❏ The text in the status bar

❏ The highlighted option on the menu bar of the Control Center menu

❏ The contents of the current record displayed with the Browse operation

❏ The contents of the data record being edited in the Edit or Append operations

The foreground and background colors for standard and enhanced text can be set independently, as can the color of the screen's border. See Chapter 2 for information on specifying colors in your CONFIG.DB.

7.51 Tip: **Use a one- or two-letter code to define the foreground, background, and border colors.**

To specify the colors you want in a screen display, use the following letter codes:

Color	Letter Code
Black	N or blank
White	W
Blue	B
Green	G
Cyan	BG
Red	R
Magenta	RB
Brown	GR
Yellow	GR +
Gray	N +
Blank	X

To display text in blinking color, add an asterisk (*) after the letter code. For example, specify B* for blinking blue text. To display a color in high intensity, add a plus sign (+) after the letter code. Specify R + for bright red, for instance.

Note: Not all the colors listed here are available to all graphic adapters and color monitors. For example, if you use an EGA card, you cannot set a high-intensity color for the background. Also, a border color may not be set when using EGA.

7.52 Tip: **Use the SET COLOR TO command to set foreground, background, and border colors.**

You can select the screen color at the dot prompt by issuing the SET COLOR TO command in the following format:

. SET COLOR TO < *color of standard text/background color*>,
   < *color of enhanced text/background color*>, < *border color*>

7.53 Tip: **Define foreground and background colors in pairs.**

If your display adapter permits setting different colors for standard and enhanced text, you can define foreground and background colors in pairs. Specify the code for the foreground color, and then type a slash (/) followed by the code for the background color.

For example, to display standard text as white letters on a blue background and enhanced text as bright red letters on a white background with a green border, issue the following command at the dot prompt:

. SET COLOR TO W/B, R +/W, G

7.54 Trick: **To eliminate the border, set the border color to the background color of the standard text.**

If you prefer not to show a border, set the border color to match the background color of the standard text:

. SET COLOR TO W/B, R +/W, B

7.55 Tip: **To select the default colors, do not specify colors in the SET COLOR TO command.**

The default color setting is W/N, N/W, N. In this default setting, standard text is displayed as white letters on a black background, and enhanced text is displayed as black letters on a white background (in reverse video) with no border.

To switch to the default color setting at any point during processing, issue the SET COLOR TO command without specifying colors:

. SET COLOR TO

7.56 Tip: **Use SET COLOR ON/OFF or the SET DISPLAY command to switch from a monochrome to a color monitor.**

The color combinations described here can be displayed only on a color monitor. If you have both a monochrome monitor and a color monitor, you can switch from one to the other with the following commands:

. SET COLOR ON

or

. SET COLOR OFF

On a color monitor, the whole screen may go blank if you issue the SET COLOR OFF command. If this happens, use the SET COLOR ON command to return to the default color setting.

You can use SET DISPLAY if you have an EGA graphics card that supports a 43-line display. In this case, you can specify a color or monochrome monitor and the number of lines to display. The format of the command is as follows:

. SET DISPLAY TO < *option*>

The following options are available:

MONO	Monochrome monitor
COLOR	Color monitor
EGA25	EGA monitor, 25-line display
EGA43	EGA monitor, 43-line display
MONO43	Monochrome monitor, 43-line display

Because of the differences among the variety of monitors and adapter cards, the results of these commands can be unpredictable. Experiment with your equipment.

7.57 Trick:

Use the form design screen to specify colors and text attributes.

As mentioned in Chapter 4, screen forms can be created to customize the way your data appears on-screen. One advantage to using forms is the ability to change the colors or attributes of individual components on the screen. For example, you could make one field appear in bold, another blinking, and have a field description underlined.

From the form design screen, select the text or field you want to change using the F6 (Select) key. Use the arrow keys to move to the end of the area to be changed and press Enter. Press Alt-W to pull down the **Words** menu, select **Display**, and then choose the attribute for the text area selected (see fig. 7.32).

If you use a monochrome monitor, you can select from **Intensity (Bold)**, **Underline**, **Reverse**, and **Blink**, or any combination of these. If you use a color monitor, a menu showing available foreground and background colors appears, and you can select the appropriate colors from the list.

In the example in figure 7.33, notice the data displayed using the form. The Item and Total field contents are in normal text, the Cost and Quantity field contents are in reverse video, and the Total field label is underlined.

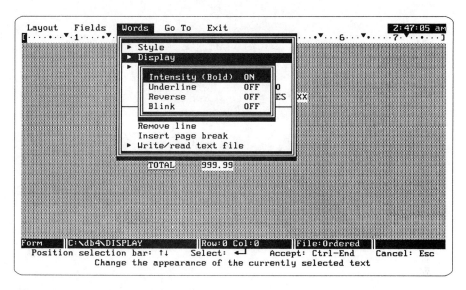

Fig. 7.32. *Setting display attributes from the form design screen for a monochrome monitor.*

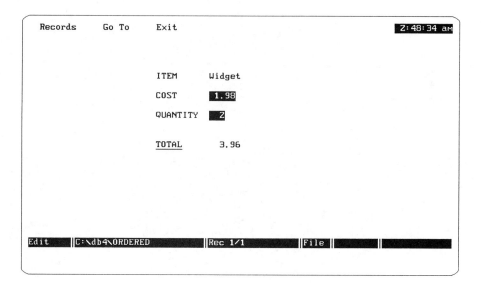

Fig. 7.33. *Viewing data with new display attributes.*

8

Generating Mailing Lists and Reports

Y ou can use dBASE IV's powerful and flexible label and report
generator to produce mailing lists as well as complex reports
with sophisticated formats. This chapter presents tips, tricks, and traps
that will help you make the most of the dBASE IV label and report
generator.

Producing Mailing Labels

dBASE IV has one of the most useful functions a database can offer: the
capability of producing mailing labels. You can easily format and
produce a mailing list by creating a label file. The tips, tricks, and traps
in this section cover the basics of designing and creating a label file.

Designing Mailing Labels

8.1 Tip: **Design a mailing label with the CREATE LABEL command.**

To access the label design screen from the dot prompt, use the CREATE
LABEL command after you've set up the database file.

To produce a mailing list from the names and addresses in the
ACCOUNTS.DBF file, for example, create a label file (MAILING.LBL)
with the following dot prompt commands:

```
. USE ACCOUNTS
. CREATE LABEL MAILING
```

Then use the label design screen to format the label.

281

8.2 Tip:

Access the label design screen from the Control Center.

To create a new label format, first select a database file from the current catalog by highlighting the file in the **Data** column on the Control Center screen; then press Enter. Next, highlight < **create**> in the Labels column and press Enter (see fig. 8.1).

To modify an existing label format, highlight the label file and press Shift-F2 (Design).

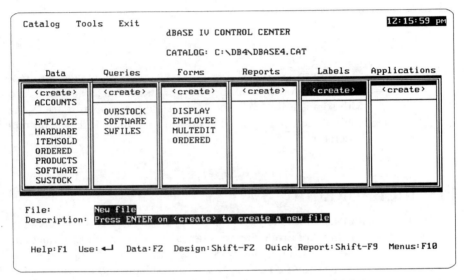

Fig. 8.1. *Accessing the label design screen from the Control Center.*

8.3 Tip:

Position fields in the label format by using the Fields menu.

It is easy to position fields in their appropriate places on the label design screen. Place the cursor in the label box where the field is to appear, press Alt-F to pull down the **Fields** menu, select **Add field**, and press Enter (see fig. 8.2).

A list of available database fields appears, as well as calculated and predefined fields. Select a field and press Enter (see fig. 8.3).

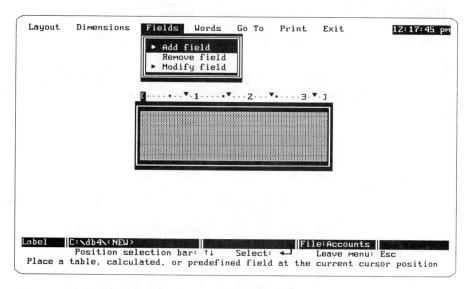

Fig. 8.2. *Adding a field to the label layout surface.*

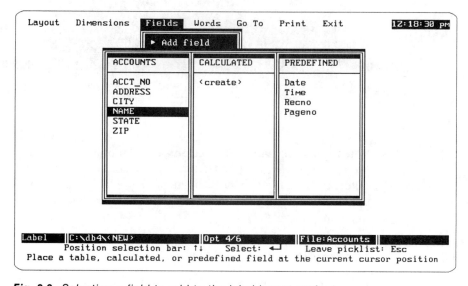

Fig. 8.3. *Selecting a field to add to the label layout surface.*

8.4 Tip: **Use a Template or Picture function to specify how the field will be printed.**

As mentioned in Chapter 4, dBASE IV offers various **Template** and **Picture** functions that determine the length and content of fields for data input. The label design screen also enables you to use templates to format your data. To specify a data template for a field, enter the information at the Template prompt, or press Ctrl-End to accept the default (see fig. 8.4).

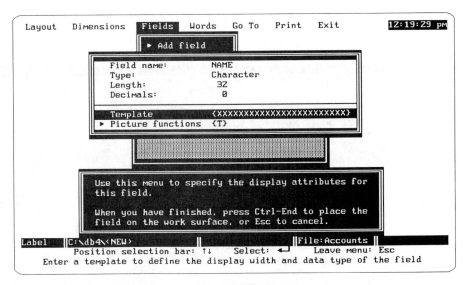

Fig. 8.4. *Specifying the data template for the field.*

When you select **Picture functions**, a menu of functions available for the field type appears. Choose the appropriate function and press Enter, or press Esc to cancel the menu. For example, to convert to uppercase all alphabetic characters in a character field, select the **!** function (see fig. 8.5).

8.5 Tip: **Use the Dimensions menu to specify the label size.**

Pull down the **Dimensions** menu by pressing Alt-D. **Predefined Size** is highlighted as the default (see fig. 8.6). When you press Enter, a submenu of predefined label sizes appears.

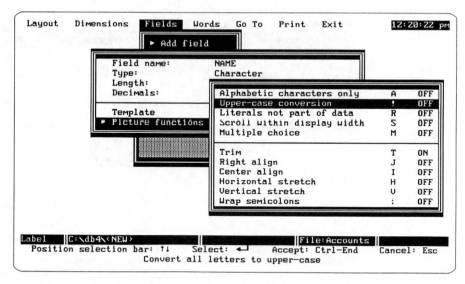

```
 Layout   Dimensions  Fields   Words   Go To   Print   Exit          12:20:22 pm
                      ┌──────────────────────┐
                      │  ▶ Add field         │
          ┌───────────────────────────────────────────────────────┐
          │  Field name:       NAME                                │
          │  Type:             Character                           │
          │  Length:        ┌─────────────────────────────────────┐
          │  Decimals:      │ Alphabetic characters only    A  OFF │
          │                 │ Upper-case conversion         !  OFF │
          │  Template       │ Literals not part of data     R  OFF │
          │ ▶ Picture functions│ Scroll within display width  S  OFF │
          │                 │ Multiple choice               M  OFF │
          │                 ├─────────────────────────────────────┤
          │                 │ Trim                          T  ON  │
          │                 │ Right align                   J  OFF │
          │                 │ Center align                  I  OFF │
          │                 │ Horizontal stretch            H  OFF │
          │                 │ Vertical stretch              V  OFF │
          │                 │ Wrap semicolons               ;  OFF │
          │                 └─────────────────────────────────────┘
 Label  ║C:\db4\<NEW>                      ║    ║File:Accounts ║
    Position selection bar: ↑↓     Select: ◄┘     Accept: Ctrl-End   Cancel: Esc
                      Convert all letters to upper-case
```

Fig. 8.5. *Selecting Picture functions for the field.*

Once you have selected a predefined size, you can still override certain defaults (such as **Width of label** {35}). To modify the label format (label size, number of labels across a page, margins, and so forth), select the item to change from the **Dimensions** menu, press Enter, and then type the new information (see fig. 8.6).

8.6 Trick: Enhance the appearance of your labels by using special fonts.

You can make selected text appear in various fonts, including bold, underlined, italic, superscript, and subscript, if your printer supports these fonts. Also, you can use any special fonts that you installed for your printer. (See Chapter 2 for information on printer font installation.)

To specify a font, first select the text to be enhanced. Position the cursor at the beginning of the text or field, press F6 (Select), move to the end of the text or field, press Enter, pull down the **Words** menu (Alt-W), choose **Style**, and then select the appropriate font (see fig. 8.7). Any special fonts you have installed (up to five) are shown on the list of available fonts.

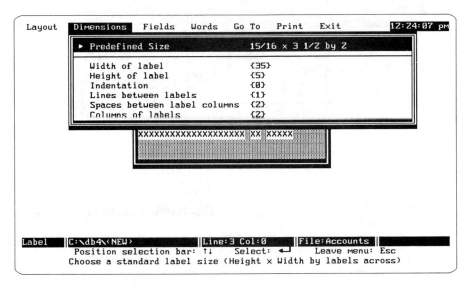

Fig. 8.6. *Specifying the label size.*

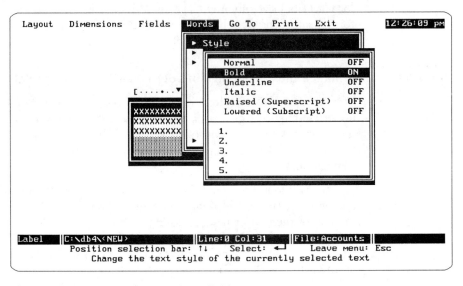

Fig. 8.7. *Choosing a font style for a field.*

8.7 Tip: **Preview labels on-screen before saving your label-format file.**

To ensure that your design is correct before you print any labels, you can view the labels on-screen. From the label design screen, pull down the **Print** menu (Alt-P) and select **View labels on screen** (see fig. 8.8). The labels will appear in the format you have specified, one screen at a time (see fig. 8.9).

You can make changes to the format as needed. Once you have determined that the format is correct, save the file. Choose the **Exit** menu (Alt-E), select **Save changes and exit**, and then name the file (see fig. 8.10).

8.8 Trick: **Use a calculated field in your label format.**

Chapter 4 discusses techniques for creating calculated fields for screen forms. You can use the same techniques for labels and reports. You use the calculated fields to print data derived from the information in your database.

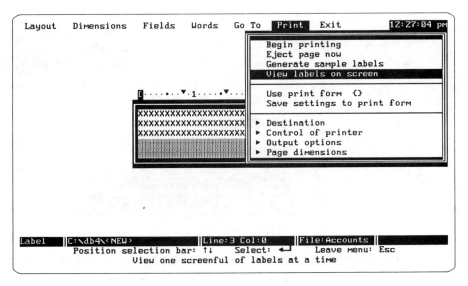

Fig. 8.8. *Choosing the option to view labels on-screen.*

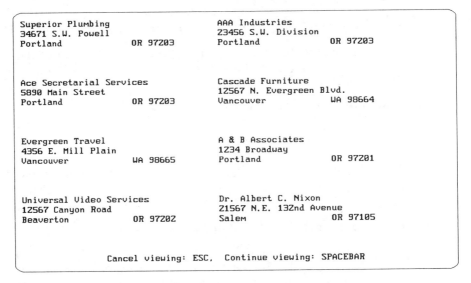

Fig. 8.9. *Displaying labels on-screen.*

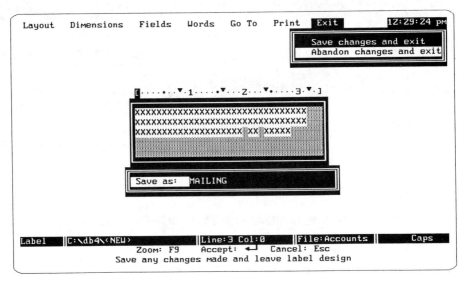

Fig. 8.10. *Saving the label-format file.*

For example, suppose that the SOFTWARE.DBF file contains two numeric fields called PRICE and COST. To print labels that contain the price and cost of each item, as well as the difference between these two figures, you can create a new calculated field called DIFFERENCE.

From the **Fields** menu, select **Add field**. From the list of fields, highlight < **create**> in the Calculated column, and then fill in the information about the field when prompted (see fig. 8.11).

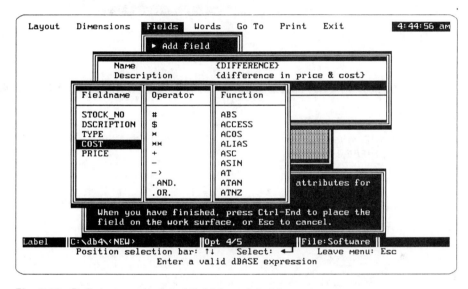

Fig. 8.11. *Defining a calculated field for a label format.*

At the Expression prompt, you can either type a valid dBASE IV expression or build one by selecting fields, operators, and functions from the picklist by pressing Shift-F1 (Pick), highlighting your choice, and pressing Enter.

Figure 8.12 shows a completed label format with the COST and PRICE fields and the DIFFERENCE calculated field, which is the PRICE minus the COST. Figure 8.13 shows the labels printed on-screen using the label format.

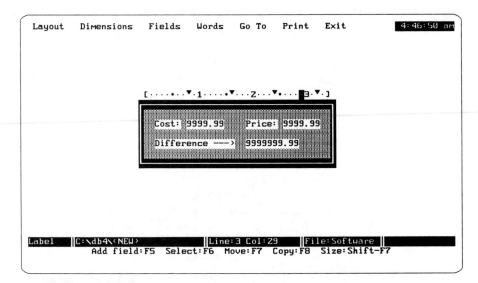

Fig. 8.12. *A label format showing COST, PRICE, and the calculated field, DIFFERENCE.*

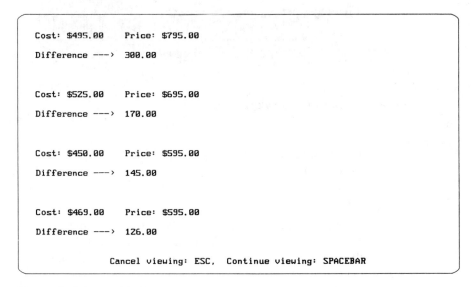

Fig. 8.13. *Printing labels on-screen.*

Using the LABEL FORM Command

8.9 Tip: **Use the LABEL FORM command to display names and addresses as a mailing list.**

You can access a label format from the dot prompt with the LABEL FORM command. The default displays the label format on the screen. For example, you can use the following command to select the label file and display the output on-screen:

```
. USE ACCOUNTS
. LABEL FORM MAILING
```

8.10 Tip: **To align labels on the printer, test the label before producing the mailing list.**

Before you produce a mailing list, it is good practice to print a sample label. Then use this sample to align the labels correctly on the printer. You can use either of two ways to produce a sample label: the SAMPLE option of the LABEL FORM command or the **Print** menu from the label design screen. Both methods are discussed in the next few tips.

8.11 Tip: **Use the SAMPLE option to produce a sample label.**

One way to produce a sample mailing label for aligning the printer is to use the SAMPLE option of the LABEL FORM command:

```
. USE ACCOUNTS
. LABEL FORM MAILING SAMPLE TO PRINT
```

The contents of the mailing label are displayed and printed as a set of asterisks rather than as normal characters (see fig. 8.14).

After you print one row of labels and adjust the printer, you can see other sample labels by pressing Y at the prompt:

```
Do you want more samples? (Y/N)
```

Press N to print the mailing list. (You can interrupt printing at any time by pressing Esc.)

```
, USE ACCOUNTS
, LABEL FORM MAILING SAMPLE TO PRINT
  ****************************    *******************************
  ****************************    *******************************
  ****************************    *******************************
  ****************************    *******************************

Do you want more samples? (Y/N)
```

Fig. 8.14. Sample mailing labels.

8.12 Tip: **Use the Print menu from the label design screen to print sample labels.**

Before you save the label format, make sure that the printer is on and the paper is aligned properly. Then pull down the label design screen's **Print** menu (Alt-P), select **Generate sample labels**, and press Enter. A row of labels will print.

8.13 Tip: **To produce a mailing list of selected records, use a qualifier in the LABEL FORM command.**

To produce a small set of sample labels, set the record range to only a few data records by using a qualifying condition (FOR ...) in the LABEL FORM command:

```
. USE ACCOUNTS
. LABEL FORM MAILING FOR RECNO( ) <=4 TO PRINT
```

The preceding commands print only the first four records.

To include only the names and addresses of certain data records, use an appropriate qualifier in the LABEL FORM command to select the records. For example, to select only addresses where the ZIP code is 97203 or is between 98660 and 98669, specify those ZIP codes as a search condition (see fig. 8.15).

```
. USE ACCOUNTS
. LABEL FORM MAILING FOR ZIP="97203" .OR. ZIP="9866"
                         A0002                                A0003
      Superior Plumbing                  AAA Industries
      34671 S.W. Powell                  23456 S.W. Division
      Portland, OR  97203                Portland, OR  97203


                         B0001                                B0002
      Ace Secreterial Services           Cascade Furniture
      5890 Main Street                   12567 N. Evergreen Blvd.
      Portland, OR  97203                Vancouver, WA  98664


                         B0003
      Evergreen Travel
      4356 E. Mill Plain
      Vancouver, WA  98665
```

Fig. 8.15. *Printing a mailing list with selected ZIP codes.*

The search condition ZIP="9866" finds and includes all ZIP codes that begin with 9866. To search for a specific ZIP code, use the SET EXACT ON command. (See Chapter 3 for more information on the SET EXACT command.)

8.14 Tip: **To facilitate mail handling, index your data records by ZIP code.**

To produce a mailing list in ZIP-code order, use the ZIP field as the index key. When you created the database structure, if you entered Y in the Index column for the ZIP field, an index tag was created in the production multiple index file. (See Chapter 6 for more information on indexing.) To activate the tag before printing labels, use the following command:

    . USE ACCOUNTS ORDER ZIP

8.15 Tip: **Use a WHILE clause to select records in a LABEL FORM command.**

You can use a search condition (such as FOR ...) in a LABEL FORM command to select the records to display. However, because each record in the file is checked to see whether the condition is met, processing a large set of records can be slow and cumbersome.

You can use a shortcut: Once you have indexed the file on the appropriate field, position the record pointer at the beginning of the first correct record by using the FIND command. Then use the WHILE clause in the LABEL FORM command to process records only while a certain condition exists.

For example, you can display a mailing list for all the ACCOUNTS.DBF records with "OR" as the STATE code. First, index the file on the STATE field. This groups all records with the same STATE codes. Next, skip unwanted records by using the FIND command to place the record pointer at the beginning of the records you need. Then issue the LABEL FORM command with the WHILE clause. Records will be selected until the condition is no longer satisfied (see fig. 8.16).

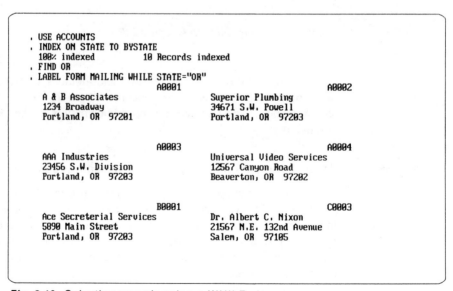

Fig. 8.16. *Selecting records using a WHILE clause.*

Eliminating Duplicate Entries from a Mailing List

8.16 Trick: **To exclude duplicate records, use the SET UNIQUE ON command.**

In some cases, more than one record in the database file can belong to the same subject (an individual or a company account, for example). You can exclude duplicate records in the mailing list by indexing the database file with the SET UNIQUE ON function in effect.

You can ensure, for example, that each company is listed only once in the mailing list by indexing the database file on the company's name before printing the list:

```
. USE ACCOUNTS
. SET UNIQUE ON
. INDEX ON NAME TO ACCTNAME
. LABEL FORM MAILING TO PRINT
```

Likewise, if SET UNIQUE ON is in effect when a multiple index (.MDX) file is created, only unique keys are indexed.

8.17 Trap: **You cannot manipulate duplicate-key records.**

After you have executed the SET UNIQUE ON and INDEX ON NAME TO ACCTNAME commands, you cannot manipulate the records excluded by this operation—even though those records are still part of the file. If you REINDEX, the index file is maintained as though SET UNIQUE ON were still in effect.

To make non-unique records available, you must either deactivate the index file using SET INDEX TO with no file or tag specified, or use the INDEX ON command to re-create an index with SET UNIQUE OFF in effect.

Excluding Inactive Records from a Mailing List

8.18 Trick: **Use the SET DELETED ON command to exclude inactive records from the mailing list.**

At times, you want to exclude inactive entries from a mailing list. You may not want to remove these records permanently from the database file, however. You can mark the inactive records by pressing Ctrl-U in the Edit or Browse operation. After these records have been "deleted," issue the SET DELETED ON command to exclude them from the LABEL FORM command.

When the mailing list has been produced, you can reactivate the "deleted" records. Recall them with a RECALL ALL command.

Producing Reports

dBASE IV includes a flexible report generator that can produce many types of reports: standard or customized columnar and form reports, as well as mail-merge format reports for printing custom form letters. A basic report that you can create with dBASE IV is shown in figure 8.17.

```
Page No.        1
05/29/88
                            MONTHLY SALES REPORT
                        Hardware and Software Divisions
                          Month ending March 31, 1988

  Stock No    Product Type         Units Sold       Price      Total Sales

  CPQ-SP256   system                       2     1895.00          3790.00
  ZEN-SL181   system                       1     2399.00          2399.00
  IBM-AT640   system                       3     4490.00         13470.00
  ZEN-MM012   monitor                      2      159.00           318.00
  NEC-PC660   printer                      3      820.00          2460.00
  HAY-M1200   modem                        4      389.00          1556.00
  SEA-HD020   hard disk                    3      495.00          1485.00
  IOM-HD040   hard disk                    2     2790.00          5580.00
  PAR-GC100   graphic card                 2      389.00           778.00
  HER-GC100   graphic card                 3      239.00           717.00
  ASH-DB300   database                     3      595.00          1785.00
  ANS-DB110   database                     4      695.00          2780.00
  CLP-DB100   database compiler            2      595.00          1190.00
  WOR-DB100   database compiler            1      595.00           595.00
  LOT-L0123   spreadsheet                  4      395.00          1436.00
  MIC-WS330   word processing              2      269.00           538.00
  MIS-WS330   word processing              2      289.00           578.00
  AST-FW200   integrated                   2      395.00           790.00
  MIC-QB100   language                     1      109.00           109.00
  BOL-PA300   language                     2       69.50           139.00
*** Total ***
                                         48                      42493.00
```

Fig. 8.17. *A sample horizontal tabulating report.*

Using the Quick Report Feature

8.19 Tip: **Use Shift-F9 (Quick Report) to produce standard reports quickly.**

You can use dBASE IV to produce a standard columnar report without accessing the form design screen. Simply highlight a database file from the Control Center; then press Shift-F9 (Quick Report). The **Print** menu appears, and you can set various printing options (see fig. 8.18).

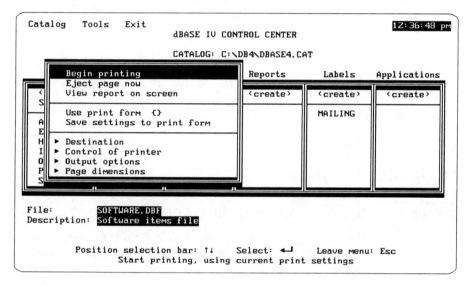

Fig. 8.18. *Producing a Quick Report from the SOFTWARE.DBF file.*

Make sure that your printer is on; then select **Begin printing**. To display the report on-screen, select **View report on screen**. Figure 8.19 shows a standard columnar Quick Report displayed on-screen.

```
Page No.    1
10/17/88

STOCK_NO   DSCRIPTION          TYPE                COST      PRICE

ASH-DB400  dBASE IV v 1.0      database            495.00    795.00
ANS-DB110  Paradox v.1.1       database            525.00    695.00
CLP-DB100  Clipper DB Compiler database compiler   450.00    595.00
WOR-DB100  WordTech DB Compiler database compiler   469.00    595.00
LOT-L0123  Lotus 1-2-3 Rel 2   spread sheet        289.00    359.00
MIC-WS330  WordStar v3.30      word processing     229.00    269.00
MIS-WD400  Microsoft Word 4.0  word processing     229.00    289.00
ASH-FW300  Framework v.3.0     integrated          345.00    395.00
MIC-QB200  Microsoft QuickBasic language            79.00    109.00
BOL-PA300  Turbo Pascal v.3.0  language             39.50     69.50
                                                  3149.50   4170.50



                Cancel viewing: ESC,   Continue viewing: SPACEBAR
```

Fig. 8.19. *Displaying the Quick Report on-screen.*

Designing a Report

8.20 Tip: **Design a report form with the CREATE REPORT command.**

The first step in creating a new report form is to assign a name to the report (.FRM) file. The .FRM file stores the format and contents of the report.

To create a new report form, select the database file to which the report will apply, and then issue the CREATE REPORT command at the dot prompt:

    . USE SALES
    . CREATE REPORT SALERPT1

You can also use the Control Center to create a report. Select the database file by highlighting it in the Data column and pressing Enter. Move the cursor to < **create**> in the Reports column and press Enter again. The report design screen appears; you are ready to design your report.

8.21 Tip: Understand the basic bands in a report.

dBASE IV breaks the various components of a report into *bands*. The following basic bands appear on the report design screen when you create a new report:

Band	Description
Page Header Band	The area at the top of each page of the report; can include the page number, date, and column headings
Report Intro Band	Includes information printed at the beginning of a report, such as an introductory paragraph or cover letter
Detail Band	Contains the data from your database file
Report Summary Band	Includes information printed at the end of the report, such as comments, final totals, counts, or averages
Page Footer Band	The area at the bottom of each page of the report, such as a running title or identification

Figure 8.20 shows the report design screen with all basic bands open. Only open bands will print, so use the **Open all bands** option from the **Bands** menu to make all bands available.

Figure 8.21 shows a sample report called ITEMS, which was created from the SOFTWARE database. The figure illustrates the basic bands.

The Page Header Band displays the current page number, system date, field column headings, and the title Software Items Stocked. The Report Intro Band contains a message to be printed only on the first page of the report. The Detail Band contains the printed fields from the SOFTWARE database, and the Report Summary Band includes totals for the numeric fields. The Page Footer Band is used to print a message at the bottom of each page. A sample report, printed using the ITEMS report design, is shown in figure 8.22.

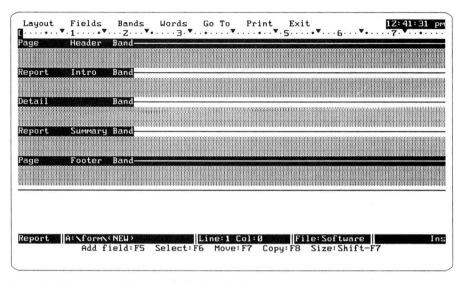

Fig. 8.20. A report design screen showing basic bands.

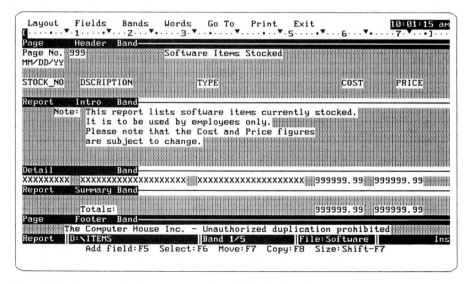

Fig. 8.21. A report design screen using all basic bands.

```
Page No.   1              Software Items Stocked                          ⎤
12/01/88                                                                  ⎥ Page Header Band
                                                                         ⎦
STOCK_NO   DSCRIPTION           TYPE                      COST    PRICE

           Note: This report lists software items currently stocked.    ⎤
                 It is to be used by employees only.                    ⎥ Report Intro Band
                 Please note that the Cost and Price figures           ⎦
                 are subject to change.

ASH-DB400  dBASE IV v 1.0       database               495.00   795.00  ⎤
ANS-DB110  Paradox v.1.1        database               525.00   695.00  ⎥
CLP-DB100  Clipper DB Compiler  database compiler      450.00   595.00  ⎥
WOR-DB100  WordTech DB Compiler database compiler      469.00   595.00  ⎥
LOT-LO123  Lotus 1-2-3 Rel 2    spread sheet           289.00   359.00  ⎥ Detail Band
MIC-WS330  WordStar v3.30       word processing        229.00   269.00  ⎥
MIS-WD400  Microsoft Word 4.0   word processing        229.00   289.00  ⎥
ASH-FW300  Framework v.3.0      integrated             345.00   395.00  ⎥
MIC-QB200  Microsoft QuickBasic language                79.00   109.00  ⎥
BOL-PA300  Turbo Pascal v.3.0   language                39.50    69.50  ⎦

           Totals:                                    3149.50  4170.50  ⎤ Report Summary Band
                                                                         ⎦

     The Computer House Inc. - Unauthorized duplication prohibited       ⎤ Page Footer Band
                                                                         ⎦
```

Fig. 8.22. *A printed ITEMS report form showing all basic bands.*

Using the Quick Layout Option

8.22 Tip: **To design reports quickly, use the Quick layout option.**

The simplest way to create a new report is to select **Quick layout** from the **Layout** menu. **Quick layout** offers three layout options:

Column layout A standard columnar report. The same as using **Quick Report** from the Control Center.

Form layout Data is displayed with each field on a new line, flush left. Similar to the default Edit screen layout.

Mailmerge layout Used to produce form letters, in which data will be merged with other text.

Using Column Layout

8.23 Tip: **To produce a standard columnar report, select Column layout.**

From the **Quick layouts** menu, select **Column layout** for a standard columnar report (see fig. 8.23). A standard columnar form design is shown in figure 8.24.

Notice the contents of the Header Band shown in figure 8.24. The contents include a Page No. caption, followed by a data template (999) representing the current page number of the report. The Header Band also includes a date template (MM/DD/YY) that represents the system date in effect when the report is printed. Column headings for each field are also included in the Header Band for each field. Also note that templates for each field automatically appear in the Detail Band area.

To save the report without making any changes, pull down the **Exit** menu (Alt-E), select **Save changes and exit**, and then give the report file a name (see fig. 8.25).

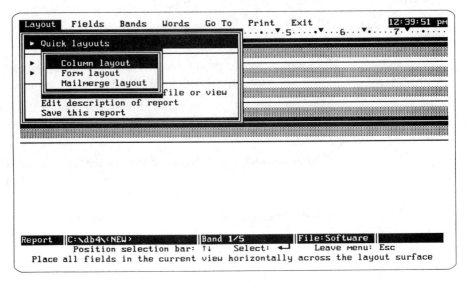

Fig. 8.23. Selecting the Quick layouts option for a default form.

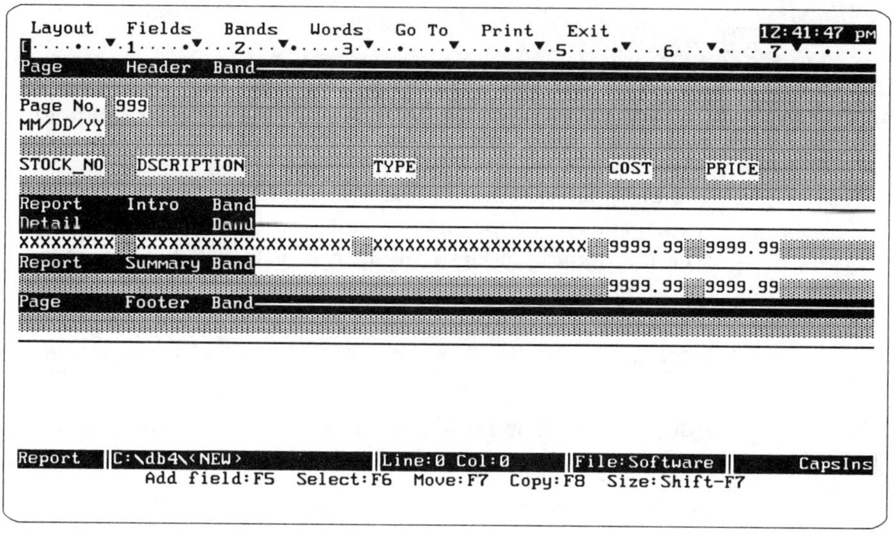

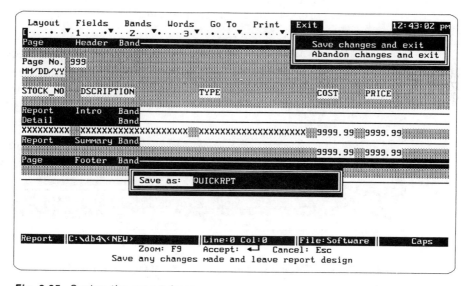

Fig. 8.24. *A standard columnar form design.*

Fig. 8.25. *Saving the report form.*

Using Form Layout

8.24 Tip: **Use the Form layout option to produce a list of items in a single column.**

The **Form layout** option from the **Quick layout** menu produces a report similar in appearance to the default screen form used in the Edit and Append modes (see fig. 8.26). The **Form layout** option can be useful when you want to make a printed client list or directory easier to read. Figure 8.27 illustrates a Form layout report printed on-screen.

8.25 Tip: **Add, delete, or move fields to customize the format of your report.**

To remove a field from the layout surface, move the cursor to the field template. Then press Del (Delete) or select **Remove field** from the **Fields** menu.

To reposition an item, use the F6 (Select) key to select a field or block of text to be moved, press the F7 (Move) key, move the cursor to the appropriate location, and press Enter.

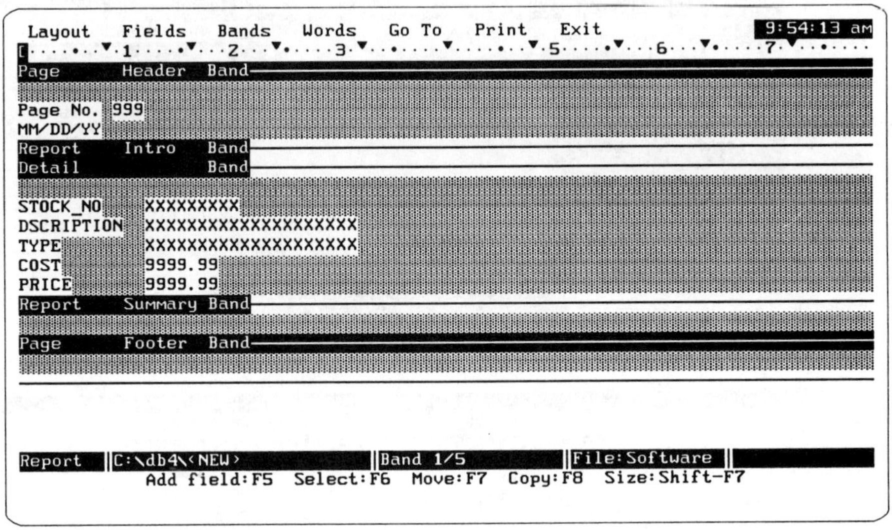

Fig. 8.26. *Using the Form layout option.*

```
Page No.    1
10/20/88

STOCK_NO    ASH-DB400
DSCRIPTION  dBASE IV v 1.0
TYPE        database
COST        495.00
PRICE       795.00

STOCK_NO    ANS-DB110
DSCRIPTION  Paradox v.1.1
TYPE        database
COST        525.00
PRICE       695.00

STOCK_NO    CLP-DB100
DSCRIPTION  Clipper DB Compiler
TYPE        database compiler
COST        450.00
PRICE       595.00

STOCK_NO    WOR-DB100
DSCRIPTION  WordTech DB Compiler
          Cancel viewing: ESC,   Continue viewing: SPACEBAR
```

Fig. 8.27. *Viewing data using the Form layout report form.*

To add a field, move the cursor to the location where the field is to be placed; then select **Add field** from the **Fields** menu.

8.26 Trap: **You can erase text from the layout surface if you add fields when Insert mode is off.**

Pressing the Ins (Insert) key toggles Insert mode on and off. In Insert mode, when you type text or add a field to the work surface, existing text moves to the right to make room for the inserted material. If Insert is off, however, anything under the added material is erased. Therefore, be sure that there is room for a field before adding it to the work surface unless Insert is on.

Using Horizontal Stretch

8.27 Trick: **Use the Horizontal stretch option to fit data into your document.**

dBASE IV offers a powerful feature to make your data fit within surrounding text without printing extra blank spaces. The Horizontal stretch feature expands or contracts the width of a field automatically and can give your reports a professional appearance.

Without Horizontal stretch, if the Name field is 30 characters wide, a form letter to Jane Doe might look like the following:

Congratulations, XXXXXXXXXXXXXXXXXXXXXXXXXXXXXX, you
have won our grand prize of $1000!

The resulting letter would be printed as follows:

Congratulations, Jane Doe   , you
have won our grand prize of $1000!

Using Horizontal stretch, the blank space is eliminated:

Congratulations, Jane Doe, you
have won our grand prize of $1000!

The field to which Horizontal stretch is applied has a fixed length of five characters on the report layout surface, represented by HHHHH:

Congratulations, HHHHH, you
have won our grand prize of $1000!

When you add a field to the work surface, simply select **Horizontal stretch** from the **Picture functions** menu (see fig. 8.28).

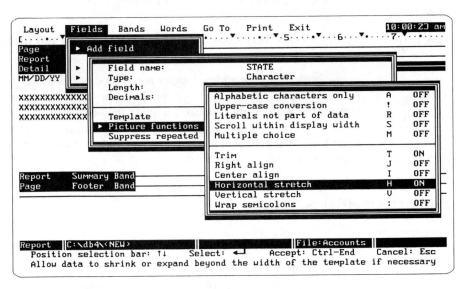

Fig. 8.28. *Choosing the Horizontal stretch option.*

Note: The **Horizontal stretch** function is automatically applied to fields added to a Mailmerge layout.

Using Mailmerge Layout

8.28 Tip: **Use the Mailmerge layout option for producing form letters and long text documents.**

dBASE IV's report generator makes it easy to produce form letters and long text documents. You can use data from dBASE IV database files without having to export data to an external word processor. The **Mailmerge layout** option essentially turns the Detail Band into a word processor.

You can type text anywhere on the work surface, just as with other word processing programs. You can embed data by adding fields at the appropriate places. Simply pull down the **Fields** menu (Alt-F), select **Add field**, and then choose the field (see fig. 8.29).

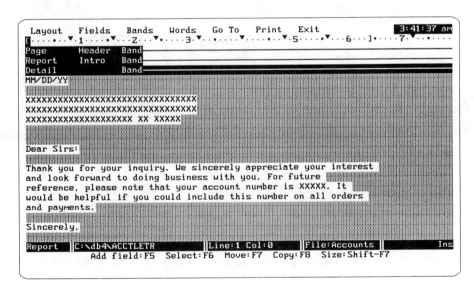

Fig. 8.29. A form letter created with Mailmerge layout.

8.29 Trick: **To avoid retyping long documents, use the Read text from file option.**

To include in your report an existing document or block of text, perhaps something created with an external word processing program, be sure that the text has been saved as an ASCII text file. Then position the cursor on the work surface where the text is to be merged.

Pull down the **Words** menu (Alt-W) and select **Write/read text file**. Then select **Read text from file** and specify the file name of the text to be imported (see fig. 8.30).

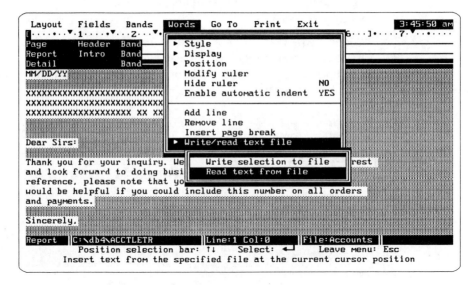

Fig. 8.30. *Including text in a report from an external file.*

Likewise, when you have created a document with the dBASE IV reports design surface, you can select text by using the F6 (Select) key and selecting the **Write selection to file** option to save the text to a disk file for future use in other reports or documents. If you do not select text, the entire document is saved.

8.30 Trick: **Predefined fields save time when you are updating mail-merge documents.**

You can use the predefined Date and Time fields to enter the current date or time in a document. For example, if you place the predefined Date field at the head of a letter, the correct date will be printed when the letter is printed, assuming that you entered the date when you turned on your computer or that your system has a built-in clock/calendar.

Four predefined fields are available: **Date**, **Time**, **Recno** (record number), and **Pageno** (page number). Select any of the fields from the PREDEFINED column in the **Add field** menu (see fig. 8.31).

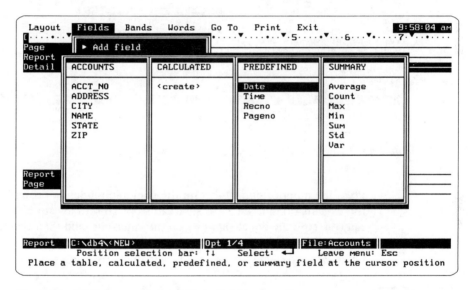

Fig. 8.31. *Adding a predefined Date field to a mail-merge report form.*

Defining Margins, Columns, and Headings

8.31 Tip: **Set the margins for your report using the Modify ruler option.**

You use the **Modify ruler** option in the **Words** menu to set margins, paragraph indentations, and tab stops for your document. When you select this option, the cursor is moved to the ruler line at the top of the screen. To set the margins, move the cursor to the correct location and press the left bracket ([) to set the left margin or the right bracket (]) to set the right margin (see fig. 8.32).

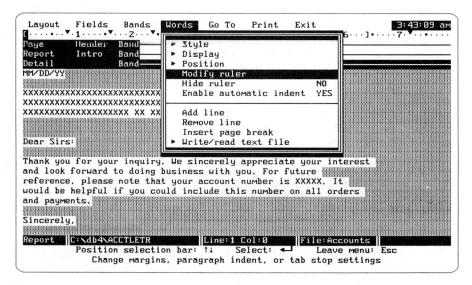

Fig. 8.32. *Using the Modify ruler option to set margins.*

Press the number sign (#) to set the paragraph indentation, and press the exclamation mark (!) to set a tab stop. To set tabs at a certain interval, type the equal sign (=) on the ruler line, and then type the interval when prompted. For example, to set tabs every 10 spaces, enter 10 for the number of spaces between tabs.

8.32 Tip: **Use Word wrap mode to make text automatically wrap from one line to the next.**

Reports have two available editing modes: Layout mode and Word wrap mode. In Layout mode, objects appear exactly where you place them. Like most word processors, in Word wrap mode, text wraps automatically to the next line when the right margin is reached. The default mode for the Mailmerge layout is Word wrap mode, while the default for the Column layout and Form layout is Layout mode.

To use Word wrap mode in any band, move the cursor to the appropriate band, pull down the **Bands** menu (Alt-B), and select **Word wrap band**. YES or NO appears by the selection to indicate whether Word wrap is on or off (see fig. 8.33). Press Enter.

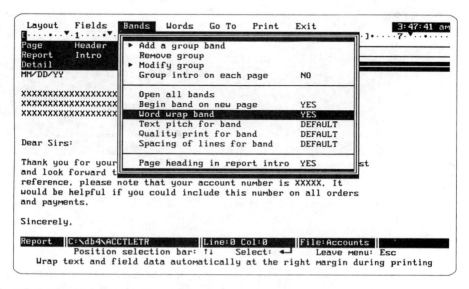

Fig. 8.33. *Selecting Word wrap mode for the Detail Band.*

Notice that the texture in the layout surface disappears when the band is in Word wrap mode. This feature indicates in which mode you are working.

8.33 Tip: **Define report columns.**

You can change the width of a column by changing the length of the template. Move the cursor to the field to be changed, pull down the **Fields** menu (Alt-F), select **Modify field**, then select **Template**, press Enter, and finally edit the length of the field template to suit your needs (see fig. 8.34).

For example, if the TYPE field is 20 characters long but you want only 8 characters to be displayed, remove 12 characters from the end of the template. Press Enter; then press Ctrl-End to accept the new format.

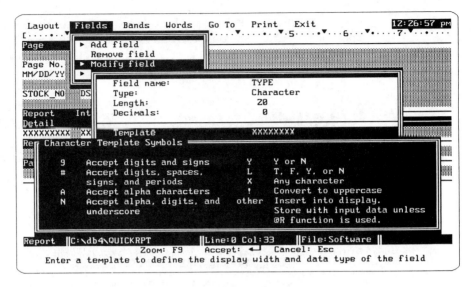

Fig. 8.34. Changing the field width with Modify field.

8.34 Tip: **Define the report title.**

To design a report heading (called the *page title*), move the cursor into the Header Band and type the desired text. You can position text by typing it where you want it to appear, or use the **Words** menu to position it flush left, centered, or flush right. To do this, select the text using the F6 (Select) key and then pull down the **Words** menu. Select **Position**; then choose **Left**, **Center**, or **Right**, and press Enter to reposition the selected text (see fig. 8.35).

8.35 Trap: **If the margins are not set, titles may be improperly positioned.**

When you use the **Words/Position** menu to position text, the current margin settings are used. Be sure that you have set the right margin before repositioning text. (See Tip 8.31 on modifying the ruler.)

For example, to center the report title, set the right margin to 80 (or another width), and then select the text and center it with the **Words/Position** menu. An example of a title centered on a report layout surface is shown in figure 8.36.

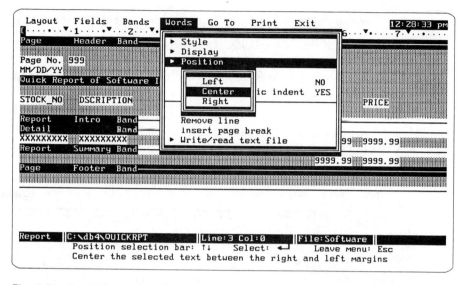

Fig. 8.35. *Centering a title for the report.*

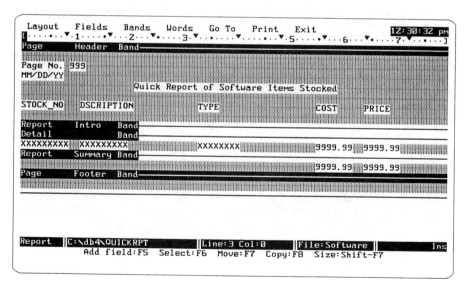

Fig. 8.36. *A report layout with the title centered in the Header Band.*

8.36 Tip: **Move fields or headings to make your report easier to read.**

You can reposition fields, text, or headings on the report layout surface by selecting the field or text using the F6 (Select) key and the F7 (Move) key. You can use this procedure to take up blank space left when you shorten field lengths or column headings.

For example, you can shorten the DSCRIPTION and TYPE fields, and then move the COST and PRICE fields and column headings to the left to take up the empty space (see fig. 8.37).

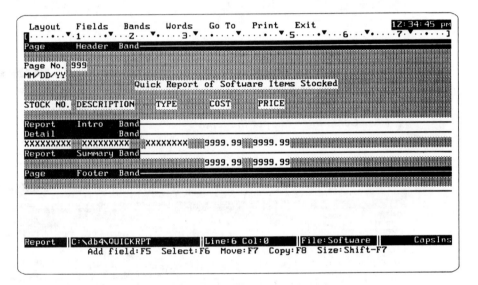

Fig. 8.37. A report layout with fields and headings moved.

You can also retype the STOCK_NO and DSCRIPTION headings as STOCK NO. and DESCRIPTION to make them easier to read. The modified report form, printed on-screen, is shown in figure 8.38.

```
Page No.    1
10/26/88
                        Quick Report of Software Items Stocked

STOCK NO. DESCRIPTION    TYPE      COST      PRICE

ASH-DB400  dBASE IV      database  495.00    795.00
ANS-DB110  Paradox v     database  525.00    695.00
CLP-DB100  Clipper D     database  450.00    595.00
WOR-DB100  WordTech      database  469.00    595.00
LOT-LO123  Lotus 1-2     spread s  289.00    359.00
MIC-WS330  WordStar      word pro  229.00    269.00
MIS-WD400  Microsoft     word pro  229.00    289.00
ASH-FW300  Framework     integrat  345.00    395.00
MIC-QB200  Microsoft     language   79.00    109.00
BOL-PA300  Turbo Pas     language   39.50     69.50
                                   3149.50   4170.50




              Cancel viewing: ESC,  Continue viewing: SPACEBAR
```

Fig. 8.38. *The modified report printed on-screen.*

Modifying a Report Form

8.37 Tip: | **For safety's sake, make a backup copy of your report file before modifying it.**

To change the layout or contents of a report, you can either issue the MODIFY REPORT command or highlight the report name in the Control Center menu's Reports column and press Shift-F2 (Design).

Because changes made to the report file are permanent, make the changes in a copy of the report file (a backup file). You can then go back to the original report file if you make any mistakes in the backup file. When you are satisfied with the modified report, delete the original file and rename the backup file.

To copy a report file, use the COPY FILE command:

. COPY FILE SALERPT1.FRM TO SALERPT2.FRM

Be sure to include the file extension (.FRM).

Formatting a Numeric Value

8.38 Trap: **A numeric value is normally displayed as a series of digits and a decimal point.**

When you specify a numeric value (the value of either a numeric field or a formula), that value is displayed as a series of digits and decimal points, such as 123456.78. The report generator doesn't place a dollar sign in front of a monetary value nor does it add commas to conform to the format of a business report (for example, $123,456.78) unless you specify otherwise.

8.39 Trick: **To display a numeric or monetary value in conventional business format, use the Template or Picture functions.**

You can modify a numeric field for a specific display format by moving the cursor to that field on the reports layout surface and accessing the **Fields** menu (Alt-F). Select **Modify field**; then specify the format in the Template and Picture function input lines.

For example, to display a leading zero as a dollar sign ($), use the **Template** option (see fig. 8.39). To specify that numbers are to be displayed as currency, select **Financial format** from the **Picture functions** menu (see fig. 8.40).

Setting Printer Options

8.40 Tip: **Use the SET PRINTER TO command or the Print Options menu to select a printer.**

If you issue the REPORT FORM command directly from the dot prompt, the **Print Options** menu does not appear. Before printing your report, you should specify the printer port with the SET PRINTER TO command, as in the following:

    . SET PRINTER TO LPT2:

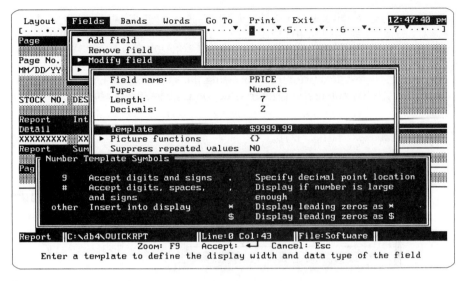

Fig. 8.39. *Using the Template option to format monetary amounts.*

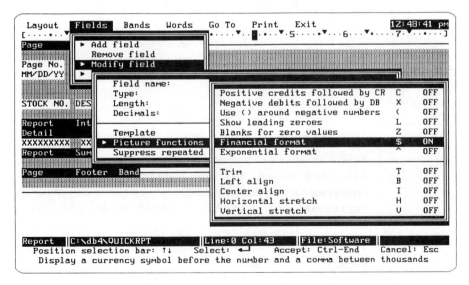

Fig. 8.40. *Using the Picture functions option to format monetary amounts.*

When you select **Print** from the report design screen, or if you choose **Quick Report** or print a report from the Control Center, the **Print Options** menu appears. Select **Destination** to choose the printer. In the **Printer model** line, you can select among various previously installed printers by pressing the space bar or Enter (see fig. 8.41). To complete the printer selection process, press either Esc or Ctrl-End.

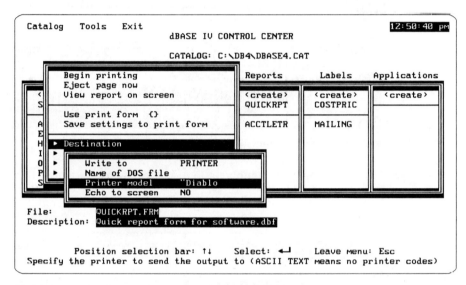

Fig. 8.41. *Using the Print menu to select a printer.*

8.41 Trick: **To save space, print wide reports in compressed mode.**

Most dot-matrix printers enable you to print text in compressed mode, a very useful option for printing wide reports. A report printed in compressed mode takes up much less space than a normal report. Figure 8.42 shows an example of a report printed in compressed mode.

To select the type pitch for an entire band, you can select **Text pitch for band** from the **Bands** menu. This lets you print a band in Pica (10 pitch), Elite (12 pitch), Condensed (compressed) type, or the default pitch for the document.

MONTHLY SALES REPORT
Hardware and Software Divisions
Month ending March 31, 1988

Stock No	Product Type	Units Sold	Unit Price	Unit Cost	Unit Profit	Total Sales	Total Profit
CPQ-SP256	system	2	$1895.00	$1,359.00	$ 536.00	$ 3790.00	$1,072.00
ZEN-SL181	system	1	$2399.00	$1,695.00	$ 704.00	$ 2399.00	$ 704.00
IBM-AT640	system	3	$4490.00	$3,790.00	$ 700.00	$ 13470.00	$2,100.00
ZEN-MM012	monitor	2	$ 159.00	$ 89.00	$ 70.00	$ 318.00	$ 140.00
NEC-PC660	printer	3	$ 820.00	$ 560.00	$ 260.00	$ 2460.00	$ 780.00
HAY-M1200	modem	4	$ 389.00	$ 269.00	$ 120.00	$ 1556.00	$ 480.00
SEA-HD020	hard disk	3	$ 495.00	$ 398.00	$ 97.00	$ 1485.00	$ 291.00
IOM-HD040	hard disk	2	$2790.00	$2,190.00	$ 600.00	$ 5580.00	$1,200.00
PAR-GC100	graphic card	2	$ 389.00	$ 279.00	$ 110.00	$ 778.00	$ 220.00
HER-GC100	graphic card	3	$ 239.00	$ 199.00	$ 40.00	$ 717.00	$ 120.00
ASH-DB300	database	3	$ 595.00	$ 395.00	$ 200.00	$ 1785.00	$ 600.00
ANS-DB110	database	4	$ 695.00	$ 525.00	$ 170.00	$ 2780.00	$ 680.00
CLP-DB100	database compiler	2	$ 595.00	$ 450.00	$ 145.00	$ 1190.00	$ 290.00
WOR-DB100	database compiler	1	$ 595.00	$ 469.00	$ 126.00	$ 595.00	$ 126.00
LOT-L0123	spreadsheet	4	$ 395.00	$ 289.00	$ 70.00	$ 1436.00	$ 280.00
MIC-WS330	word processing	2	$ 269.00	$ 229.00	$ 40.00	$ 538.00	$ 80.00
MIS-WS330	word processing	2	$ 289.00	$ 229.00	$ 60.00	$ 578.00	$ 120.00
AST-FW200	integrated	2	$ 395.00	$ 345.00	$ 50.00	$ 790.00	$ 100.00
MIC-QB100	language	1	$ 109.00	$ 79.00	$ 30.00	$ 109.00	$ 30.00
BOL-PA300	language	2	$ 69.50	$ 39.50	$ 30.00	$ 139.00	$ 60.00

*** Total ***

48

Fig. 8.42. *Printing a report in compressed mode.*

8.42 Tip: **Use the Style option to specify fonts for selected text.**

dBASE IV has several font-style options, including bold, underlined, italic, superscript, and subscript. These options enable you to enhance selected text in your printouts if your printer supports them.

To change a printer font, select the text to be changed using the F6 (Select) key; then choose **Style** from the **Words** menu and select the appropriate font.

Grouping Data in a Report

8.43 Tip: **You can summarize data in common groups.**

Use the dBASE IV report generator to group data by a field, expression, or record number. For example, to group products by the contents of the TYPE field, you can create a group band.

Position the cursor inside a band (such as the Report Intro or Page Header Band) that is above the Detail Band. If you previously created a group band, you can put the cursor there to create a second group band.

Pull down the **Bands** menu (Alt-B), choose **Add a group band**, and then select the type of grouping: **Field value**, **Expression value**, or **Record count**. To group by an interval of records (for example, every 10 records), select **Record count**. To group by the TYPE field value, select the field from the menu and press Enter (see fig. 8.43).

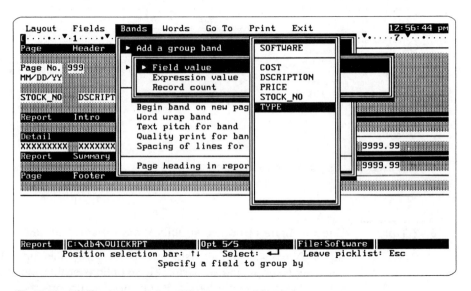

Fig. 8.43. *Adding a group band to the report layout.*

Figure 8.44 shows the report layout with the group band added. Notice that both a Group 1 Intro Band and a Group 1 Summary Band were automatically placed on the work surface. You then can summarize or total data by group as well as for the entire report. Figure 8.45 shows the report printed to the screen using the group bands.

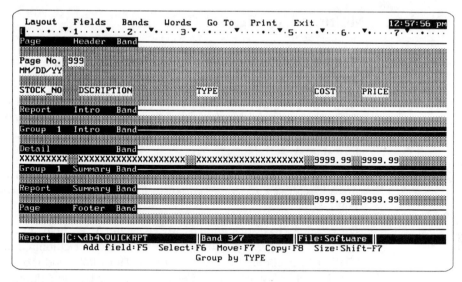

Fig. 8.44. *Group Intro and Group Summary Bands added to the layout.*

```
Page No.    1
10/26/88

STOCK_NO  DSCRIPTION        TYPE              COST     PRICE


ASH-DB400  dBASE IV v 1.0    database          495.00   795.00
ANS-DB110  Paradox v.1.1     database          525.00   695.00


CLP-DB100  Clipper DB Compiler database compiler  450.00   595.00
WOR-DB100  WordTech DB Compiler database compiler  469.00   595.00


LOT-L0123  Lotus 1-2-3 Rel 2  spread sheet      289.00   359.00


MIC-WS330  WordStar v3.30    word processing   229.00   269.00
MIS-WD400  Microsoft Word 4.0  word processing   229.00   289.00


ASH-FW300  Framework v.3.0    integrated        345.00   395.00

          Cancel viewing: ESC,  Continue viewing: SPACEBAR
```

Fig. 8.45. *A report printed on-screen with data grouped by TYPE.*

Displaying Multiple-Line Report Columns

8.44 Tip: **Reposition fields or headings to display them in a multi-line format.**

In most reports, the contents of each data field or expression are shown horizontally in a single line. You can, however, display the contents of several fields or expressions vertically in a multiple-line format.

Select an item to be repositioned using the F6 (Select) key. Then press F7 (Move), move the cursor to the new location, and press Enter.

For example, to display the DSCRIPTION and TYPE fields in one column, and the COST and PRICE fields in another column, move the TYPE field to the line below the DSCRIPTION field, and move the PRICE field below the COST field. You can retype the column headings to indicate the new arrangement.

You can even place totals or subtotals in separate columns by moving the fields in the Summary Band and typing appropriate headings in the Header Band (see fig. 8.46). Figure 8.47 shows the multi-line report format printed on-screen.

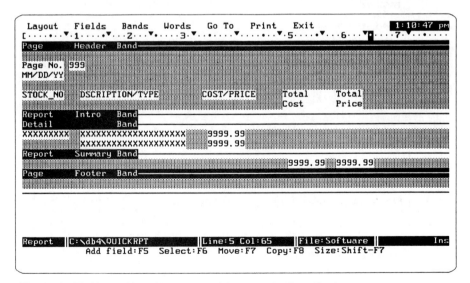

Fig. 8.46. Fields and headings moved for a multi-line display.

```
Page No.    1
10/26/88

STOCK_NO    DSCRIPTION/TYPE          COST/PRICE    Total      Total
                                                   Cost       Price
ASH-DB400   dBASE IV v 1.0             495.00
            database                   795.00
ANS-DB110   Paradox v.1.1              525.00
            database                   695.00
CLP-DB100   Clipper DB Compiler        450.00
            database compiler          595.00
WOR-DB100   WordTech DB Compiler       469.00
            database compiler          595.00
LOT-LO123   Lotus 1-2-3 Rel 2          289.00
            spread sheet               359.00
MIC-WS330   WordStar v3.30             229.00
            word processing            269.00
MIS-WD400   Microsoft Word 4.0         229.00
            word processing            289.00
ASH-FW300   Framework v.3.0            345.00
            integrated                 395.00
MIC-QB200   Microsoft QuickBasic        79.00
            language                   109.00
            Cancel viewing: ESC,  Continue viewing: SPACEBAR
```

Fig. 8.47. *A report with a multi-line display printed on-screen.*

Using Logical Fields in a Report

8.45 Trap: **Because its value can be only .T. or .F., a logical field rarely provides adequate descriptive information.**

If you use the field MALE in a database to describe the sex of an employee, a .T. can represent a male, and an .F. can represent a female. However, to make your reports easier to read and interpret, you can change the logical value to something more meaningful, such as the word Male or Female.

8.46 Trick: **Use the IIF( ) function to display the value of a logical data field in a report.**

You can create a calculated field and use the dBASE IV IIF( ) function to interpret the meaning of a logical field and display the appropriate information. This function can convert the logical value to different expressions, depending on the value.

For example, to display Male when the value of the logical field MALE is .T. and Female when the value is .F., use the IIF() function:

IIF(SEX,"Male","Female")

Select **Add field** from the **Fields** menu; then choose < **create**> from the Calculated column. Select the IIF() function from the picklist by pressing Shift-F1 (Pick) (see fig. 8.48). Or type the function at the **Expression** line (see fig. 8.49).

Set the length of the template to the maximum length to be displayed. For this example, because Female takes up 6 characters, you set the template to XXXXXX. You can also change the field label from MALE to SEX on the layout surface to make the information more meaningful to the reader (see fig. 8.50). Figure 8.51 shows the report printed on-screen using the new calculated field to display Male or Female for each record.

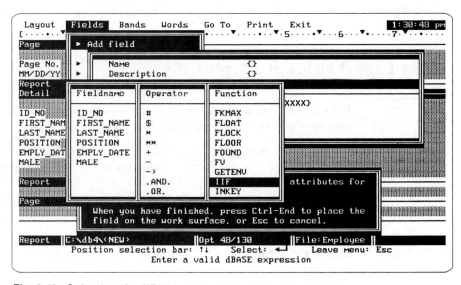

Fig. 8.48. *Selecting the IIF( ) function for a calculated field.*

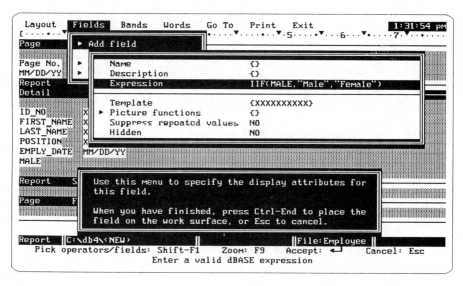

Fig. 8.49. *Using the IIF( ) function in a calculated expression.*

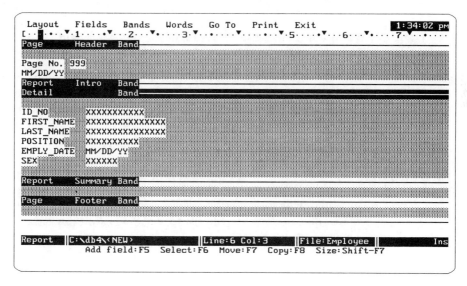

Fig. 8.50. *A report layout with a calculated field for SEX.*

```
Page No.    1
10/26/88

ID_NO       12345
FIRST_NAME  John
LAST_NAME   Davis
POSITION    assembly
EMPLY_DATE  01/15/88
SEX         Male


ID_NO       34566
FIRST_NAME  Mary
LAST_NAME   Smith
POSITION    secretary
EMPLY_DATE  09/17/87
SEX         Female


ID_NO       45677
FIRST_NAME  Kirk
LAST_NAME   Matthews
POSITION    sales
             Cancel viewing: ESC,  Continue viewing: SPACEBAR
```

Fig. 8.51. *Data viewed using a report form with a calculated SEX field.*

8.47 Trap: When you define the contents of a calculated field in the Expression line, a long expression can be partially hidden.

After you enter a long expression for a calculated field, only the first portion of the expression is displayed. To view the entire expression, use the arrow keys to scroll back and forth on the Contents line.

8.48 Trick: To view or edit the expression for a calculated field, use the Zoom key.

If you press F9 (Zoom) in the **Expression** line when creating a calculated field, the input line is displayed at the bottom of the screen where you can view and edit it (see fig. 8.52). You can see up to 80 characters at one time.

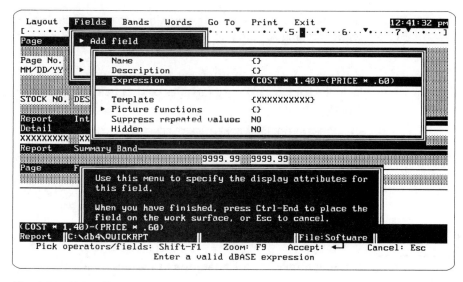

Fig. 8.52. *Using Zoom to enter an expression for a calculated field.*

Adding Report Headings at Time of Reporting

8.49 Trap: **When you specify a report heading in a report form, that heading remains fixed for all subsequent reports.**

Text entered in the Header Band is displayed at the top of every report page. You can change this text only by modifying a report format, which can be time-consuming.

8.50 Trick: **Use the HEADING option to display dynamic report headings.**

To display a dynamic report heading at the time of reporting, use the HEADING option in the REPORT FORM command. You can then display a new heading without modifying the report form.

To enter the heading, use the HEADING option in the REPORT FORM command. You can add multiple lines to the report heading by using semicolons as line separator characters:

```
. USE PRODSOLD
. REPORT FORM SALERPT1 HEADING "MONTHLY SALE REPORT" +";" +
   "Hardware and Software Divisions" +";" +
   "For the month of March, 1987"
```

When the report is produced, these lines of text are added above the report heading specified in the report form's Header Band. Each line is centered automatically.

You also can use the HEADING option in the REPORT FORM command to include character memory variables or data field values as part of the report heading:

```
. LINE1="THE GREAT NORTHWEST COMPUTER STORE"
. LINE2="SALE SUMMARY REPORT"
. LINE3="Period Ending "
. RPTDATE="4/30/87"
. USE SALEDATA
. REPORT FORM SALERPRT HEADING LINE1 +";" +LINE2 +";" +
    LINE3 +";" +RPTDATE
```

8.51 Trick: **Store dynamic report headings in memory variables.**

You can store the values of memory variables in a memory file and recall them whenever you need them.

To save memory variables to a file (REPTVARS.MEM), use the SAVE TO command after you have entered the values for the variables:

```
. LINE1="THE GREAT NORTHWEST COMPUTER STORE"
. LINE2="SALE SUMMARY REPORT"
. LINE3="Period Ending "
. RPTDATE="4/30/87"
. SAVE TO REPTVARS
```

When you need to recall the variables from the memory file, issue the RESTORE FROM...ADDITIVE command:

```
. RESTORE FROM REPTVARS ADDITIVE
```

After recalling the memory variables from the memory file and adding them to memory, use the DISPLAY MEMORY command to examine their values. To change the value of a specific memory variable, you can alter it and save it back to the memory file (see fig. 8.53).

```
. RESTORE FROM REPTVARS ADDITIVE
. DISP MEMORY
LINE1       pub   C   "THE GREAT NORTHWEST COMPUTER STORE"
LINE2       pub   C   "SALE SUMMARY REPORT"
LINE3       pub   C   "Period Ending "
RPTDATE     pub   D   04/30/87
     4 variables defined,        82 bytes used
   252 variables available,   5918 bytes available

. RPTDATE=CTOD("5/31/87")
05/31/87
. SAVE TO REPTVARS
REPTVARS.mem already exists, overwrite it? (Y/N) Yes
.
.
```

Fig. 8.53. *Recalling memory variables from a memory file.*

Selecting Records for a Report

8.52 Trap: **You cannot specify filtering conditions in the report design screen.**

To print only records that meet a certain condition, you can use a FOR or WHILE condition clause in your REPORT FORM command or use the SET FILTER TO command before issuing the REPORT FORM command.

8.53 Tip: **Use a query file to print selected records.**

Instead of selecting a database file before creating a report design, you can select a view query from the Queries column on the Control Center screen. Then select < **create**> from the Reports column. The report format is then associated with a query file that can specify simple or complex conditions that must be met for records to be included in the report. (Chapter 7 discusses the creation of query files.)

8.54 Trick: **To use data records from multiple database files, combine the records with the APPEND operation.**

To produce a report using data records from more than one database file, combine the records in a database file. Then use that file to produce your report. To combine these records, create a new database file and then use the APPEND operation to add records from the existing database files.

For example, to produce a report for the sales of two regional offices (REGION1.DBF and REGION2.DBF), create a database file (ALLSALES.DBF) for the combined records of the two database files. Then append records from the regional database files:

```
. USE ALLSALES
. APPEND FROM REGION1
. APPEND FROM REGION2
```

Using the records in the ALLSALES.DBF file, you can design a custom report form.

8.55 Trick: **To use data fields from multiple database files, link the files with the SET RELATION operation.**

The dBASE IV report generator allows the use of only one database file for a report. To combine data fields from multiple database files in the same report, you must first link the files.

One way to link several data fields from different database files is to use the SET RELATION operation. For example, to use selected data fields from the SOFTWARE.DBF and SWSTOCK.DBF database files, link the files with the following SET RELATION commands:

```
. SELECT 1
. USE SOFTWARE
. INDEX ON STOCK_NO TO SWSTCKNO
. SELECT 2
. USE SWSTOCK
. INDEX ON STOCK_NO TO SKSTCKNO
. SELECT 1
. SET RELATION TO STOCK_NO INTO B
```

You can select data fields from the linked files by using the SET FIELDS command. For example, you can select STOCK_NO, PRICE, and COST from SOFTWARE.DBF in active work area 1, and ON_HAND and ON_ORDER from SWSTOCK.DBF in work area 2 (alias B), with the following command:

. SET FIELDS TO STOCK_NO,COST,PRICE,B->ON_HAND,B->ON_ORDER

At this point, you can invoke the report generator (CREATE REPORT) to design a report form based on the data fields specified with the SET FIELDS command:

. CREATE REPORT INVREPRT

If you expect to link the two database files again, save (in a view file) the information about relating the files. You can create such a view file while the files are being related by using the CREATE VIEW < *name of view file*> FROM ENVIRONMENT command:

. CREATE VIEW INVREPRT FROM ENVIRONMENT

To produce the report, you can relink the database files by using the SET VIEW TO command before selecting the report form:

. SET VIEW TO INVREPRT
. REPORT FORM INVREPRT

Or, from the Control Center, you can select a view from the Queries column instead of selecting a file from the Data column. Then select a report form from the Reports column. The report uses the files and fields specified in the view file.

8.56 Trick:

To use records from multiple database files with different file structures in a report, create a joined database file.

You can use data fields from more than one database file in a report. One way is to link the fields with the JOIN operation before producing the report. A JOIN operation combines selected data fields from two database files, using a common field as a linking key field.

For example, you can join the data fields from SOFTWARE.DBF and SWSTOCK.DBF by using the common STOCK_NO data field:

```
. SELECT 1
. USE SOFTWARE
. SELECT 2
. USE SWSTOCK
. JOIN WITH A TO JOINFILE FOR STOCK_NO=A->STOCK_NO
    FIELDS STOCK_NO,A->COST,A->PRICE,ON_HAND,ON_ORDER
```

Then use the report generator to design a custom report form with the records in JOINFILE.DBF, which combines the data fields from the two database files:

```
. USE JOINFILE
. CREATE REPORT
```

8.57 Trick: **Rearrange data records with the SORT or INDEX operation before producing reports.**

To display the records in a specific order in a report, use the SORT or INDEX operation to rearrange the records in the database file.

To list products in ascending order according to their prices in a monthly sales report, for example, index the file on the PRICE field before issuing the REPORT FORM command sequence:

```
. USE PRODSOLD
. INDEX ON PRICE TO BYPRICE
. REPORT FORM SALERPT1 TO PRINT
```

Or, if you have previously created a multiple index tag for the PRICE field, you can use the following command sequence:

```
. USE PRODSOLD ORDER PRICE
. REPORT FORM SALERPT1 TO PRINT
```

Part III

Programming and Advanced Topics

Includes

Using Basic Programming Techniques

Using Advanced Programming Techniques

Exploring Advanced Topics

9

Using Basic Programming Techniques

Although not developed to be a general-purpose language, the dBASE IV command language includes many powerful programming tools. Using these tools, you can design and develop a powerful, yet user-friendly data management system.

This chapter focuses on tips and tricks for program design. Specifically, you learn about program editing, memory variables, screen design, and menu design. The chapter also shows you how to use color to enhance your screen displays.

Creating and Editing a Program

A program or command file (with a .PRG file extension) consists of a set of instructions. It can be created and edited with a text editor. To use the dBASE IV text editor, enter CREATE COMMAND or MODIFY COMMAND at the dot prompt.

Viewing a Program

9.1 Trick: **Use the TYPE command to view a program.**

An easy way to view a program is to issue the TYPE command at the dot prompt. If the program is more than one screen long, use the Ctrl-S key combination to halt the listing temporarily. Press any key to resume the listing operation.

9.2 Tip: **Use the TYPE . . . TO PRINT command to print a program listing.**

If you want to direct a program listing to the printer, add the TO PRINT option to the TYPE command at the dot prompt:

   . TYPE MAIN.PRG TO PRINT

9.3 Tip: **Use the DOS utilities screen to view a program file.**

To view a program file from the Control Center, you can use the **DOS utilities Operations** menu. From the Control Center, pull down the **Tools** menu (Alt-T), and then select **DOS utilities**. Highlight the file you want to view in the files window. Pull down the **Operations** menu (Alt-O) and select **View** (see fig. 9.1).

```
 DOS   Files   Sort   Mark   Operations   Exit              10:33:53 am
     ┌──────────────────────┬──────────────┬─────────────────────────┐
     │ Name/Extension     S │► Delete  Time │     Attrs   Space Used  │
     │                      │► Copy        │                         │
     │   SWENTRY   SCR    1,│► Move   1988 10:28a  a♦♦♦      2,048    │
     │   SWFILES   QBE    3,│► Rename 1988 12:16p  a♦♦♦      4,096    │
     │   SWFILES   QBO      │  View   1988  1:11p  a♦♦♦      2,048    │
     │   SWFILES   VUE      │  Edit   1988  2:45p  a♦♦♦      2,048    │
     │   SWINVTRY  DBF      │        1988  2:20p  a♦♦♦      2,048    │
     │   SWMENU    APP    1,095   Oct 28,1988 10:31a  a♦♦♦      2,048    │
     │   SWMENU    PRG   15,364   Oct 28,1988 10:31a  a♦♦♦     16,384    │
     │   SWSTCKNO  NDX    1,024   Oct 11,1988 11:05a  a♦♦♦      2,048    │
     │   SWSTOCK   DBF      290   Sep 30,1988 10:15a  a♦♦♦      2,048    │
     │   SWSTOCK   MDX    4,097   Sep 30,1988 10:10a  a♦♦♦      6,144    │
     │  _RWPRINT   FMT    1,479   Oct 14,1988  2:47a  a♦♦♦      2,048    │
     ├──────────────────────┴──────────────┴─────────────────────────┤
     │ Total  ◄marked►           0 (    0 files)                   0   │
     │ Total  ◄displayed► 3,240,611 (  136 files)          3,401,728   │
     └────────────────────────────────────────────────────────────────┘

     Files:*.*                              Sorted by: Name

 DOS util C:\DB4
              Position selection bar:↑↓  Select:◄┘   Leave menu:ESC
              Display the contents of the currently selected file
```

Fig. 9.1. *Viewing a program file with the DOS utilities Operations.*

The text file will be displayed, one screen at a time. You can press a key to view the next screen, or press Esc to exit to the DOS utilities screen.

Programming Conventions

9.4 Tip: **Standardize the representation of data fields, memory variables, and command words in a program.**

A program is a set of instructions that includes dBASE IV commands and keywords. Memory variables are used for storing values (which may be entered from the keyboard) or for saving the intermediate results of computations.

To make these program elements easily identifiable, you need to standardize the way in which commands, memory variables, and keywords are represented in your program. dBASE IV has no universal rules, or conventions. Just be consistent. In this book, for example, the following program elements are represented in uppercase letters:

❑ dBASE IV commands (USE, INDEX, DISPLAY, IF...ENDIF)

❑ Names of database files (EMPLOYEE.DBF, SOFTWARE.NDX)

❑ Names of programs or procedures (MAIN.PRG, FINDRECD.PRG)

❑ Names of data fields (LAST_NAME, COST, PRICE)

The names of memory variables begin with *m*, followed by an assigned name in both upper- and lowercase letters, as in mTotalCost and mChoice.

Comment and remark lines begin with an asterisk (˙) on a separate line or double ampersands (&&) following an instruction:

```
* This is a remark line
USE EMPLOYEE    && Select the database file
```

9.5 Tip: **Use comments and remarks to make a program more readable.**

When you are developing a program for data management, using remarks or comments is good practice. Remarks and comments describing the nature of the program and the important components and procedures you've used make reading and understanding the program easier.

At the beginning of the program, include a general description of the program task. Also, define the important memory variables you use in the process, and add blank spaces in command lines to make them more readable. The following program illustrates how you might develop a program to find and display a record in a database file:

```
*** FINDRECD.PRG
* Find and display a data record in a given database file
*
* Use mDBF,mNDX to store name of .DBF and .NDX files
* mKeyValue stores the searching key value
PARAMETERS mDBF,mNDX, mKeyValue
*
* Display parameters passed from LOCATE.PRG
CLEAR                          && clear the screen
@ 5,2Ø SAY " >> Search parameters specified <<"
@ 7,1Ø SAY "Name of the database file (.dbf): " GET mDBF
@ 9,1Ø SAY "   Name of the index file (.ndx): " GET mNDX
@11,1Ø SAY "          Value for the key field: " GET mKeyValue
*
USE &mDBF INDEX &mNDX    && select and index .dbf file
SEEK mKeyValue           && find the record by the key value
IF FOUND()
    @15,1Ø SAY "The record found:"
    ?
    DISPLAY
ELSE
    @15,3Ø SAY "No such record!"
ENDIF
@22,1
WAIT                     && pause
RETURN                   && return to the calling LOCATE.PRG
```

Despite their value, excessive remarks and blank spaces can be costly. Storing them takes up disk space, and execution time is slightly slower, even though they are ignored during execution. You must balance the benefits of these remarks with their cost in time and space.

Using Memory Variables

9.6 Tip: **Understand the basic functions of a memory variable.**

A memory variable represents a memory location that is used for storing a piece of information. Depending on the type of memory variable, that piece of information can be a character string, a numerical value, a date, or a logical value.

The basic functions of memory variables are as follows:

❏ Storing the values of variables in a formula

❏ Storing the result of a computation

❏ Passing values among different program modules and procedures

❏ Storing the value of a counter or an accumulator

❏ Storing parameters for controlling a program loop

❏ Storing values for branching operations

These functions are discussed in separate sections in this chapter.

Naming Memory Variables

9.7 Tip: **Name memory variables properly.**

When you name a memory variable, try to assign a descriptive, easily identified name. To store the value of the unit cost, for example, use unit_cost instead of x.

A memory variable's name can be as many as 10 characters long. But many punctuation marks and special symbols (such as @, #, $, %, &, *, ?, /, and \) are not allowed. Use only the letters A through Z (and a through z) and the numerals 0 through 9 to name a memory variable. The name must begin with a letter.

You can use both uppercase and lowercase letters (as in TotalCost) because case is ignored in a memory variable name. If you need to group characters in a name, use the underscore symbol (_), as in Total_Cost.

9.8 Trap: **When you use a large set of memory variables in a program, searching for and identifying all of them may be time-consuming.**

Keeping track of a large set of memory variables can be time-consuming if you don't do some preplanning. If you adopt a convention for naming variables, however, you can find them quickly. Use the search-and-find features offered by most text editors or word processors, including the dBASE IV editor.

9.9 Trick: **To minimize search time, begin all memory variable names with an m.**

You can minimize search time by beginning all memory variable names with the letter m, as in the following examples:

```
mTotalCost
mHourlyPay
mQty_Sold
mUnitPrice
```

You then can ask the text editor or word processor to search the program for all strings that begin with m.

9.10 Trap: **Do not use reserved words, dBASE IV commands, or the single letters A through J for naming memory variables.**

When you name memory variables, be sure not to use any reserved words or dBASE IV commands as names. For example, using any of the following summary commands as a memory variable may result (without warning) in erroneous answers:

```
Total
Count
Sum
Average
```

The single letters A through J are reserved as aliases for database files in the work areas.

9.11 Trick: Use the STORE command to assign the value of a memory variable, and the equal (=) assignment operator to change it.

The value of a memory variable can be assigned by the STORE command or by using the equal (=) arithmetical operator. If you are using a large set of memory variables in a program, you may want to find out where and when they were set up in the program. To do so, adopt a convention for assigning values to these variables.

Use STORE to assign the memory variables, and use the equal (=) operator to change their values as needed. Then use the search-and-find features of a text editor or word processor to identify the STORE command easily.

For example, values are assigned to mAnswer, mCost, mBirthDate, and mPaid by the following STORE commands:

```
STORE "Yes" TO mAnswer
STORE 299.5Ø TO mCost
STORE {Ø7/Ø4/87} TO mBirthDate
STORE .T. TO mPaid
```

The same set of values can be assigned to the memory variables by the following commands:

```
mAnswer="Yes"
mCost=299.5Ø
mBirthDate={Ø7/Ø4/87}
mPaid=.T.
```

9.12 Trick: Do not change a variable from one type to another.

In many programming languages, different syntax rules are used for naming different types of variables. When you program in BASIC, for instance, numeric and alphanumeric (character) variables are named differently. In the dBASE IV command language, however, all variables are named with the same syntax rules. The variable type is determined by the value assigned to it.

For example, a character string (such as "John") assigned to a memory variable (mVar) becomes a character variable. It remains a character variable until you assign a different type of value to it. Likewise, if you assign a numeric value to the variable, it becomes a numeric variable.

Although dBASE IV allows you to change a variable's type within a program, this is not good practice and should be avoided. Using one variable to store different types of data in the same program can cause confusion because determining the data type of the variable at any given point in the program may become difficult.

Allocating Memory for Memory Variables

9.13 Tip: **Reserve additional memory if you need to use a large set of memory variables.**

The maximum number of memory variables of all types that can be used in a program is determined by the MVMAXBLKS (memory variable maximum blocks) and MVBLKSIZE (memory variable block size) settings in your CONFIG.DB file. The default settings are the following:

```
MVMAXBLKS = 10
MVBLKSIZE = 50
```

To calculate the number of memory variables you can have, multiply these two figures. In other words, the default would be 500 memory variables (50 × 10). Because each memory variable in a block uses 64 bytes of memory, this procedure reserves 32,000 bytes of memory for use by memory variables. This amount is adequate for most applications. However, if you anticipate using a greater number of variables, you can reserve more memory for variables by increasing one of the values. For example, suppose that you want to reserve 64,000 bytes of memory for use by up to 1,000 memory variables:

20 × 50 = 1,000 variables × 64 bytes = 64,000 bytes

You would use the following setting:

```
MVMAXBLKS = 20
```

The MVMAXBLKS setting must be between 1 and 25, and the MVBLKSIZE setting must be between 25 and 1,000.

Entering Values for Memory Variables

9.14 Tip: **Use the WAIT command to assign a single keystroke value to a memory variable.**

When you design an interactive program, you frequently need to add prompts to tell the user how to proceed. Use the dBASE IV WAIT command for this purpose.

Executing the WAIT command causes the following prompt to appear:

Press any key to continue...

As its name implies, the WAIT command waits for a key to be pressed at the prompt. As soon as that key is pressed, the program proceeds to the next instruction.

Use a WAIT command to display a prompt message and save the keystroke to a memory variable:

WAIT "< *prompt message*>" TO < *name of memory variable*>

For example, after processing a data item, you may want to ask:

"Is the item entered correctly [Y/N]?"

To save a single-key answer (Y or N) to a memory variable (mAnswer) to determine the next processing step, use the following command:

WAIT "Is the item entered correctly [Y/N]?" TO mAnswer

As soon as a keystroke is entered, it is assigned to the memory variable specified in the WAIT command. The command accepts only the first keystroke entered; subsequent keystrokes are ignored.

9.15 Tip: **Use the INPUT command to assign a value to a memory variable when the program is executed.**

If you need to get a value from a keyboard entry at the time the program is executed and assign it to a memory variable, use the INPUT command. The INPUT command can be used with a prompt describing the value to be entered:

INPUT < *prompt*> TO < *name of memory variable*>

The following program illustrates the use of INPUT commands for assigning values to memory variables:

```
*** INPUTDAT.PRG
* Assign values to memory variables from keyboard entry
SET TALK OFF
SET ECHO OFF
CLEAR
* Get variable values from keyboard entries
  @5,1
  INPUT SPACE(5) +"Enter: Account number . . . " TO mAcctNo
  ?
  INPUT SPACE(5) +"        Invoice date . . . . " TO mInvDate
  ?
  INPUT SPACE(5) +"        Amount of sale . . . " TO mSale
  ?
  INPUT SPACE(5) +"        A COD sale [T/F] ?    " TO mCOD
* Display contents of these memory variables
  @15,10 SAY " >> Values assigned to memory variables << "
  @17,15 SAY "    mAcctNo: " GET mAcctNo
  @18,15 SAY "   mInvDate: " GET mInvDate
  @19,15 SAY "      mSale: " GETmSale
  @20,15 SAY "       mCOD: " GETmCOD
RETURN
```

Any type of data can be stored in a memory variable with the INPUT command. The variable type is determined by the type of data entered in response to the INPUT command.

The values to be assigned to the memory variables by using INPUTDAT.PRG are shown in figure 9.2. In the figure, the character string to be assigned to mAcctNo is enclosed in a pair of quotation marks. A date value can be entered by using either the CTOD( ) function or the curly-brace date delimiters to assign the value to the date variable mInvDate. The numeric variable mSale is assigned a value, and the .T. logical value is stored in the mCOD logical variable.

9.16 Trap: **To store a character string in a memory variable with an INPUT command, be sure to enclose the string in a pair of quotation marks.**

When you use the INPUT command, any type of data can be assigned to a memory variable. The variable type is determined by the type of

```
Enter:    Account number ... "A-123-4567"

          Invoice date ..... {07/07/89}

          Amount of sale ... 895

          A COD sale [T/F] ? .T.


    >> Values assigned to memory variables <<

          mAcctNo :  A-123-4567
          mInvDate :  07/07/89
            mSale :        895
             mCOD :  T
.
Command
```

Fig. 9.2. *Assigning data to memory variables with INPUT commands.*

data you enter in response to the INPUT command. The INPUT command is best used for entering numeric data.

If you intend to assign a character string to a memory variable, you must enclose the string in a pair of quotation marks. Otherwise, the character string will be considered a variable.

For example, you can use the following INPUT command to get a first name from a keyboard entry and assign it to the memory variable mFirstName:

```
INPUT "Enter customer's first name . . ." TO mFirstName
```

If the first name to be assigned to the variable is "JOHN", you must enter it (enclosed in quotation marks) at the INPUT prompt:

```
Enter customer's first name . . . "JOHN"
```

If you enter the character string without the quotation marks, the error message Variable not found will be displayed.

This happens because you can enter the name of another memory variable at the INPUT prompt.

9.17 Tip: **Use the ACCEPT command to assign a character string to a memory variable.**

The ACCEPT command is used primarily to assign (with or without a prompt) a character string or the contents of another character variable to a memory variable:

> ACCEPT < *prompt*> TO < *name of memory variable*>

The command is designed to assign a character string to a memory variable from a keyboard entry at the time of program execution. It functions like the INPUT command except that only character data can be used with the ACCEPT command.

For example, the following command can be used in a program file to get the name of a customer and assign it to the memory variable mCustomer:

> ACCEPT "Enter name of customer : " TO mCustomer

Be sure to enclose in quotation marks the character string to be assigned to the memory variable mCustomer:

> Enter name of customer : "John J. Smith"

Without the quotation marks, the first character string (John) will be mistakenly interpreted as the name of another variable.

9.18 Tip: **Use the @...SAY...GET command for storing a value in a memory variable.**

You can store a value in a memory variable in several ways. One way is to use the INPUT or ACCEPT command to assign a value to a memory variable. A better approach is to use the @...SAY...GET command for getting the value that is entered from the keyboard. This command gives you the freedom to place an input prompt anywhere on the screen. In addition, the command allows you to select the type of data (character, numeric, date, or logical) you want to assign to the variable.

For example, the following commands display, at the screen's 5th row and 10th column, a message requesting that a character string be entered:

```
STORE SPACE(1Ø) TO mAcctName
@5,1Ø SAY "Enter name of the account: " GET mAcctName
READ
```

When these commands are executed, the memory variable's current contents are displayed in reverse video following the prompt (see fig. 9.3).

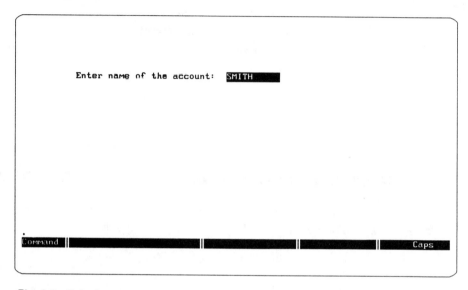

Fig. 9.3. *Entering an account name in a reverse video prompt.*

Because the memory variable mAcctName has been initialized with 10 blank spaces (SPACE(1Ø)) by using the STORE command, an entry block of 10 blank characters is displayed for data entry.

In figure 9.4, the contents of the date, logical, and numerical memory variables are displayed in the appropriate format.

The screen shown in figure 9.4 was generated by executing the following program:

```
*** PROMPTS.PRG
* Prompt for different types of memory variables
CLEAR
STORE CTOD(" / / ") TO mInv_Date
STORE Ø.Ø TO mAmount
STORE .T. TO mCOD
@5,1Ø SAY "Enter    Invoice date : " GET  mInv_Date
@7,1Ø SAY "        Invoice amount : " GET mAmount
@9,1Ø SAY "   Is it a COD sale ? : " GET mCOD
READ
```

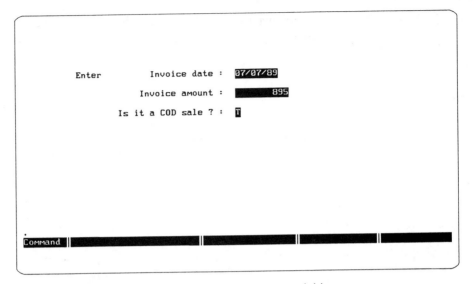

```
        Enter        Invoice date  :   07/07/89

                   Invoice amount  :             895

                Is it a COD sale ? :   T




  .
 Command
```

Fig. 9.4. *Entering the values of different memory variables.*

9.19 Tip: **Use the READ command to accept data from a data-entry screen.**

Notice that the @...GET routines in previous examples end with a READ statement. This allows you to accept user input from a series of @...GET statements simultaneously and lets you take advantage of the full-screen editing capabilities.

9.20 Trick: **Add a PICTURE template to @...SAY...GET to format the input value of a memory variable.**

When you are using the @...SAY...GET command to store a value in a memory variable, you can also add a PICTURE template. Doing so will ensure that the data is entered in the format you want.

For example, when the following program is executed, the data values to be stored in the memory variables must conform to the formats specified by the PICTURE templates:

```
*** PICTURE.PRG
* Format input values in picture templates
CLEAR
STORE SPACE(11) TO mIdb_No
STORE SPACE(1Ø) TO mFirst
STORE SPACE(2)  TO mInit
STORE SPACE(1Ø) TO mLast
STORE Ø TO mSalary
@ 5,1Ø SAY "Employee's Id. No. : " GET mId_No   PICTURE "###-##-####"
@ 7,1Ø SAY "       First Name : " GET mFirst    PICTURE "!AAAAAAAAA"
@ 9,1Ø SAY "   Middle Initial : " GET mInit     PICTURE "!."
@11,1Ø SAY "        Last Name : " GET mLast      PICTURE "!!!!!!!!!!"
@13,1Ø SAY "    Annual Salary : " GET mSalary    PICTURE "##,###.##"
READ
```

The program produces prompts that request values for the memory variables (see fig. 9.5). The symbols in the employee's identification number, middle initial, and salary are inserted in the entry block.

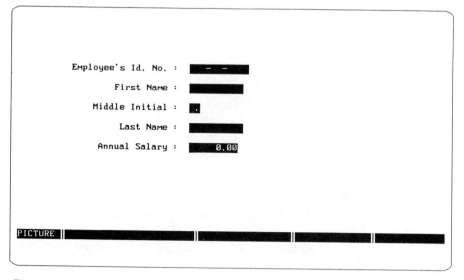

Fig. 9.5. *Formatting input values with PICTURE templates.*

The masking symbols (!, #, and A) specified in the PICTURE templates determine the types of characters allowed in their places. For example, the A symbol permits only a letter of the alphabet to be entered in its place. Only numbers are allowed where a # is specified. A letter entered in place of an ! is converted to uppercase.

As a result, an employee's identification number is entered at the prompt as a series of digits separated by two dashes. Only letters are accepted for the middle initial and last names, and they are converted to uppercase. Each first name will begin with an uppercase letter. The salary figure is displayed in conventional business format, with a comma after every third digit (see fig. 9.6).

```
Employee's Id. No. :  123-45-6789

       First Name :  James

   Middle Initial :  J.

        Last Name :  SMITH

    Annual Salary :  59,590.00
```

Fig. 9.6. *Displaying formatted input values on the entry form.*

9.21 Tip: **Use a macro function with a memory variable as a file name at the time of program execution.**

One way to select a database file is to specify the name of the file in the USE command. For example, to display the structure and records in EMPLOYEE.DBF, select the file by including the USE command in your program before you display the contents of the file:

```
USE EMPLOYEE
DISPLAY STRUCTURE
LIST
```

Although you can use this program segment to select only EMPLOYEE.DBF, you can convert the commands to a general-purpose program.

You can display the contents of any database file by specifying the name of the file at the time of execution. To do this, add a command that requests the name of the database file before you execute the DISPLAY and LIST commands. You can store the name of the file in a memory variable such as mFileName:

```
STORE SPACE(8) TO mFileName
@10,5 SAY "Enter name of the file : " GET mFileName
READ
```

After the name of the file has been saved in the memory variable, use the & macro function to supply the name to the USE command:

```
USE &mFileName
```

The & macro function tells dBASE IV to use the contents of the variable (instead of the actual string mFileName) in place of the file name in the USE command.

You can use the & macro function (with a memory variable) also as a name for other types of disk files, as in the following examples:

```
USE &mDBF INDEX ON &mNDX
SET FORMAT TO &mFMT
LABEL FORM &mLBL
REPORT FORM &mFRM
TYPE &mTXT
MODIFY COMMAND &mPRG
SET VIEW TO &mVUE
MODIFY SCREEN &mSCR
```

Controlling the Screen Display

To enhance the screen displays that your programs produce, you can include special formats for prompts and messages. You also can control the colors of the output on the screen.

Displaying Prompts and Messages

9.22 Trick: **Use @ and SPACE( ) to position a WAIT prompt at a given point on the screen.**

When you execute the WAIT command, the prompt message is displayed at the beginning of the line in which the cursor is situated. If you want to reposition the prompt message, use the @ command to specify a row position for the prompt message.

To display the prompt message at line 10, for example, use the following @ command:

```
@1Ø,1
WAIT "Is the item entered correctly [Y/N]? " TO mAnswer
```

The prompt message always will be displayed at the beginning of the specified line, regardless of the column number designated in the @ command. Even if you specify @1Ø,2Ø, the message will be displayed at the beginning of line 10.

If you want the WAIT command's prompt message to appear in a specific column position on the screen, you need to add the appropriate number of blank spaces to the message. An easy way to do this is to use the SPACE() function. This function, with a number enclosed in the parentheses, displays the specified number of blank spaces in the message.

For example, the following commands display a prompt message for the WAIT operation at the 21st column of the 10th line on the screen:

```
@1Ø,1
WAIT SPACE(2Ø) +"Is the item entered correctly [Y/N]? "
TO mKey
```

Note: Because the first row of the screen is designated as line 0, line 10 is actually the 11th row on the screen. However, the screen is divided into 80 columns that are designated as 1 through 80. The first display position is column 1, not 0.

9.23 Trick: **Eliminate status messages from the screen.**

When you are working in dBASE IV, messages describing the processing status are shown on the status line (line 22) or at the top of the screen, depending on whether STATUS is ON or OFF. When you display program output, you may not want these messages to appear in certain applications.

To eliminate the status line (line 22) from the screen, issue the SET STATUS OFF command before displaying output. Even when STATUS is OFF, however, certain messages (such as the status of the Insert and Caps Lock keys) are displayed at the top of the screen (line 0). To eliminate the messages from line 0, issue the SET SCOREBOARD OFF command.

Displaying Output in Colors

9.24 Tip: **Use the SET COLOR TO command to display color output.**

If you have a color monitor that is connected to a color graphics card, you can display text and graphic symbols in a number of colors. Refer to Chapter 7 for a detailed discussion of setting screen colors with the SET COLOR TO command.

dBASE IV uses colors for enhanced text to display data and text in such operations as DISPLAY, EDIT, and APPEND. When you are writing a program to display output in color text and graphs, you are concerned mainly with the colors for standard text and its background. Specify the colors in the first pair:

```
SET COLOR TO W/B
SET COLOR TO R/G
SET COLOR TO RB/BG
```

After you set the standard text and its background to a given color combination (such as W/B for white text on a blue background), any text or graphics symbols will be displayed in the specified color on the specified background. You can change the colors when you want a different combination.

You can display sections of text or graphs in different colors by resetting the text and its background colors for each section.

To produce a sample color text screen, use the following program:

```
*** COLRTEXT.PRG
* Program to display sample color text
SET TALK OFF
SET ECHO OFF
CLEAR
SET COLOR TO W/B
? "Text in white on blue background               "
SET COLOR TO R/B
? "Text in red on blue background                 "
SET COLOR TO G/B
? "Text in green on blue background               "
SET COLOR TO RB/B
? "Text in magenta on blue background             "
SET COLOR TO BG/B
```

```
? "Text in cyan on blue background            "
SET COLOR TO GR/B
? "Text in brown on blue background           "
SET COLOR TO B/W
? "Text in blue on white background           "
SET COLOR TO R/W
? "Text in red on white background            "
SET COLOR TO G/W
? "Text in green on white background          "
SET COLOR TO RB/W
? "Text in magenta on white background        "
SET COLOR TO BG/W
? "Text in cyan on white background           "
SET COLOR TO B/R
? "Text in blue on red background             "
SET COLOR TO W/R
? "Text in white on red background            "
SET COLOR TO BG/R
? "Text in cyan on red background             "
SET COLOR TO GR/R
? "Text in brown on red background            "
SET COLOR TO B/BG
? "Text in blue on cyan background            "
SET COLOR TO R/BG
? "Text in red on cyan background             "
SET COLOR TO RB/BG
? "Text in magenta on cyan background         "
SET COLOR TO W/G
@ 1,41 SAY "Text in white on green background     "
SET COLOR TO R/G
@ 2,41 SAY "Text in red on green background       "
SET COLOR TO RB/G
@ 3,41 SAY "Text in magenta on green background   "
SET COLOR TO GR/G
@ 4,41 SAY "Text in brown on green background     "
SET COLOR TO R/GR
@ 5,41 SAY "Text in red on brown background       "
SET COLOR TO G/GR
@ 6,41 SAY "Text in green on brown background     "
SET COLOR TO RB/GR
@ 7,41 SAY "Text in magenta on brown background   "
```

```
SET COLOR TO BG/GR
@ 8,41 SAY "Text in cyan on brown background      "
SET COLOR TO W/RB
@ 9,41 SAY "Text in white on magenta background   "
SET COLOR TO G/RB
@10,41 SAY "Text in green on magenta background   "
SET COLOR TO BG/RB
@11,41 SAY "Text in cyan on magenta background    "
SET COLOR TO GR/RB
@12,41 SAY "Text in brown on magenta background   "
SET COLOR TO W/GR +
@13,41 SAY "Text in white on yellow background    "
SET COLOR TO R/GR +
@14,41 SAY "Text in red on yellow background      "
SET COLOR TO G/GR +
@15,41 SAY "Text in green on yellow background    "
SET COLOR TO RB/GR +
@16,41 SAY "Text in magenta on yellow background "
SET COLOR TO BG/GR +
@17,41 SAY "Text in cyan on yellow background     "
SET COLOR TO GR/GR +
@18,41 SAY "Text in brown on yellow background    "
SET COLOR TO W/B
@19,1
? "Color     Letter Code     Color     Letter Code  "
? "Blue          B           Green          G       "
? "Cyan          BG          Red            R        "
? "Magenta       RB          Brown          GR       "
? "Yellow        GR +        White          W        "
SET COLOR TO R/B
@19,47 TO 23,79
@20,48 SAY "  Poor color combinations:      "
@21,48 SAY "GR/W, RB/R, G/BG, R/RB, GR/BG "
@22,48 SAY "BG/G, W/GR, BG/W, GR/G         "
SET COLOR TO W/B
RETURN
```

Designing Menus

The tips, tricks, and traps in this section give you suggestions on designing menus. You will learn how to design a simple menu with the dBASE IV command language, as well as how to create menus quickly with the dBASE IV Applications Generator.

Designing a Simple Menu with the Command Language

9.25 Trick: **Design a menu program to execute your program modules.**

When you develop a complete database management system, organize the system into a number of program modules—each to perform a specific task. After you have designed and tested the programs, you can link them into a complete system by using a set of menus. Figure 9.7 shows a sample menu.

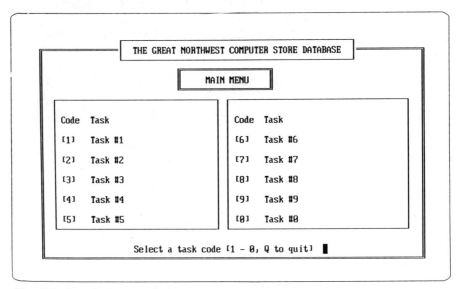

THE GREAT NORTHWEST COMPUTER STORE DATABASE

MAIN MENU

Code	Task		Code	Task
[1]	Task #1		[6]	Task #6
[2]	Task #2		[7]	Task #7
[3]	Task #3		[8]	Task #8
[4]	Task #4		[9]	Task #9
[5]	Task #5		[0]	Task #0

Select a task code [1 - 0, Q to quit]

Fig. 9.7. *A typical menu design.*

You select a specific task by entering a task code (0 through 9). Depending on the task code you enter, a specific program module is called and executed from the MAINMENU.PRG program:

```
*** MAINMENU.PRG
* A typical main menu
SET STATUS OFF
SET SCOREBOARD OFF
SET TALK OFF
SET ECHO OFF
STORE " " TO mChoice
* Set up loop to display menu choices
DO WHILE UPPER(mChoice) <> "Q"
   CLEAR
   @ 2,Ø  TO 23,79 DOUBLE  && draw a double-line box
   @ 4,29 TO  6,48 DOUBLE
   @ 1,17 TO  3,65         && draw a single-line box
   @ 7,3  TO 2Ø,37
   @ 7,39 TO 2Ø,76
   @ 2,18 SAY "THE GREAT NORTHWEST COMPUTER STORE DATABASE"
   @ 5,35 SAY "MAIN MENU"
   @ 9,5  SAY "Code   Task"
   @11,5  SAY "[1]  Task #1"
   @13,5  SAY "[2]  Task #2"
   @15,5  SAY "[3]  Task #3"
   @17,5  SAY "[4]  Task #4"
   @19,5  SAY "[5]  Task #5"
   @ 9,41 SAY "Code   Task"
   @11,41 SAY "[6]  Task #6"
   @13,41 SAY "[7]  Task #7"
   @15,41 SAY "[8]  Task #8"
   @17,41 SAY "[9]  Task #9"
   @19,41 SAY "[Ø]  Task #Ø"
   mChoice=SPACE(1)
   DO WHILE.T.  && program loop for selecting a task code
      @22,2Ø SAY "Select a task code [1 - Ø, Q to quit]";
         GET mChoice
```

```
READ
DO CASE
   CASE mChoice="Q" .OR. mChoice="q"
      EXIT
   CASE mChoice="1"
      DO TASK1
      EXIT
   CASE mChoice="2"
      DO TASK2
      EXIT
   CASE mChoice="3"
      DO TASK3
      EXIT
   CASE mChoice="4"
      DO TASK4
      EXIT
   CASE mChoice="5"
      DO TASK5
      EXIT
   CASE mChoice="6"
      DO TASK6
      EXIT
   CASE mChoice="7"
      DO TASK7
      EXIT
   CASE mChoice="8"
      DO TASK8
      EXIT
   CASE mChoice="9"
      DO TASK9
      EXIT
   CASE mChoice="Ø"
      DO TASKØ
      EXIT
   ENDCASE
ENDDO        && end of task selection loop
ENDDO        && end of menu display loop
RETURN
```

In the MAINMENU.PRG, a memory variable (mChoice) is used to store the task code. The task code is entered and assigned to the memory variable by the @...SAY...GET command within a program loop (between the DO WHILE .T. and ENDDO commands).

The program loop is set up by using CASE statements to get a valid task code. In other words, if the task code meets one of the conditions specified in the CASE statements, a specified program module is called. Otherwise, the prompt is displayed repeatedly until a valid task code is entered.

After you enter a valid task code, the code is used to determine which program module is to be called. For example, pressing 1 at the task selection prompt causes the command DO TASK1 to be executed. At this point, program control is transferred to the TASK1.PRG program module. After the instructions in TASK1.PRG are executed and the program encounters the RETURN command, program control returns to the calling program:

```
*** TASK1.PRG
* A program module called from MAIN MENU.prg
.....
.....
RETURN    && pass control back to the calling program
```

When you return from TASK1.PRG, program execution begins from the MAINMENU.PRG command immediately after DO TASK1 (in this case, the EXIT command). As a result, the program exits the task-selection program loop and returns to MAINMENU.PRG. The menu screen is displayed, and you can select another task.

9.26 Tip:

Use RETURN TO MASTER to return to the main program.

The RETURN command is used in a program module to transfer control back to the preceding calling program. Each time you execute a RETURN command, program control is passed back to the program module that called the current module. Use a series of RETURN commands to return to the main program from a module several levels below it.

If you do not need to pass data values to these intermediate program modules, you can return directly to the main program. To do so, use the RETURN TO MASTER command in the program module. Whenever the RETURN TO MASTER command is executed, program control is passed directly to the main calling program, regardless of which program module you are in.

9.27 Tip: **Group menu options by applications.**

As you plan your menu layout on the screen, you may want to group in one area the menu options related to a particular application. These options can be framed by a single- or double-line box for a better visual presentation. If you are using a color monitor, you can display menu boxes in different colors. Figure 9.8 shows a sample menu design.

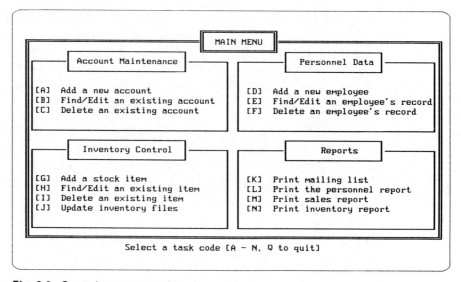

Fig. 9.8. Grouping menu options by application.

The following program produced the menu layout:

```
*** MENU.PRG
* Group menu options by applications
SET STATUS OFF
SET TALK OFF
SET ECHO OFF
SET SCOREBOARD OFF
STORE " " TO mChoice
DO WHILE UPPER(mChoice) <>"Q"  && displaying menu
    CLEAR
    SET COLOR TO R+/B,,B
    @ 2,1  TO 22,79 DOUBLE      && frame the menu screen
    @ 1,34 TO 3,48 DOUBLE       && frame main menu heading
```

```
@ 2,35 SAY "  MAIN MENU        "
SET COLOR TO G/B,,B
@ 4,2   TO 11,39    && frame account maintenance options
@ 4,41  TO 11,78    && frame personnel data options
@13,2   TO 21,39    && frame inventory control options
@13,41  TO 21,78    && frame reports options
SET COLOR TO GR/B,,B
@ 3,9   TO  5,31    && frame account maintenance heading
@ 4,10  SAY " Account Maintenance "
@ 7,3   SAY "[A] Add a new account"
@ 8,3   SAY "[B] Find/Edit an existing account"
@ 9,3   SAY "[C] Delete an existing account"
@ 3,50  TO  5,68    && frame personnel data heading
@ 4,51  SAY " Personnel Data "
@ 7,43  SAY "[D] Add a new employee"
@ 8,43  SAY "[E] Find/Edit an employee's record"
@ 9,43  SAY "[F] Delete an employee's record"
SET COLOR TO W/B,,B
@12,9   TO 14,31    && frame inventory control heading
@13,10  SAY " Inventory Control"
@16,3   SAY "[G] Add a stock item"
@17,3   SAY "[H] Find/Edit an existing item"
@18,3   SAY "[I] Delete an existing item"
@19,3   SAY "[J] Update inventory files"
SET COLOR TO RB/B,,B
@12,50  TO 14,68    && frame reports heading
@13,51  SAY " Reports "
@16,43  SAY "[K] Print mailing list"
@17,43  SAY "[L] Print the personnel report"
@18,43  SAY "[M] Print sales report"
@19,43  SAY "[N] Print inventory report"
STORE "  "  TO mChoice
DO WHILE.T.         && loop for task code selection
   SET COLOR TO R+/B,R+/B,B
   @23,20 SAY "Select a task code [A - N, Q to quit]";
      GET mChoice PICTURE"!"
   READ
   DO CASE
      CASE mChoice="Q"
      EXIT
    CASE mChoice="A"
      DO ADDACCT
```

```
                    EXIT
              CASE mChoice="B"
                 DO EDITACCT
                 EXIT
              CASE mChoice="C"
                 DO DELTACCT
                 EXIT
              CASE mChoice="D"
                 DO ADDEMPL
                 EXIT
              CASE mChoice="E"
                 DO EDITEMPL
                 EXIT
              CASE mChoice="F"
                 DO DELTEMPL
                 EXIT
              CASE mChoice="G"
                 DO ADDITEM
                 EXIT
              CASE mChoice="H"
                 DO EDITITEM
                 EXIT
              CASE mChoice="I"
                 DO DELTITEM
                 EXIT
              CASE mChoice="J"
                 DO UPDATINV
                 EXIT
              CASE mChoice="K"
                 DO MAILLIST
                 EXIT
              CASE mChoice="L"
                 DO EMPLREPT
                 EXIT
              CASE mChoice="M"
                 DO SALEREPT
                 EXIT
              CASE mChoice="N"
                 DO INVNREPT
                 EXIT
           ENDCASE
        ENDDO      && end of task selection loop
     ENDDO         && end of menu display loop
     RETURN
```

Creating Menus with the Applications Generator

You have seen one way to create a simple menu program using the dBASE IV command language. With dBASE IV, you also can create such applications using a menu-driven system to specify the options you want to use in your program. The Applications Generator automatically generates dBASE IV program code based on your specifications. This code can be modified or customized at any time. Creating menus is particularly easy using the Applications Generator.

9.28 Tip:

Use the Applications Generator to create simple dBASE IV programs and menus quickly.

To access the Applications Generator from the Control Center, highlight < **create**> in the Applications column, and then press Enter. An instruction box asks whether you want to create a dBASE program using the command editor or whether you want to use the Applications Generator (see fig. 9.9). Highlight the second choice and press Enter to invoke the Applications Generator.

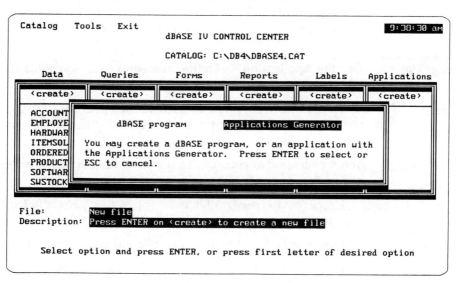

Fig. 9.9. *Accessing the Applications Generator.*

To reach the Applications Generator from the dot prompt, use the following command:

. CREATE APPLICATION < *file name of application*>

9.29 Trap: **You must plan before using the Applications Generator.**

If you do not have information about all files related to your application, you cannot complete the generation of an application. You will need to abort the creation of your application until you have this information. Some things you will need to determine before creating a new application are listed here:

- ❏ The database or view to be used
- ❏ The index file or index tags to be used with the database
- ❏ The name of the application
- ❏ The functions the application is to perform
- ❏ The program files (if any) to be accessed by the application
- ❏ The label and report form files to be used
- ❏ The screen form files to be used

Jot down this information so that you can have it handy when you are creating your application. Be sure that you have created all the necessary files before trying to use them in your applications.

9.30 Tip: **Use the Application Definition screen to enter specifications for a new application.**

When you invoke the Applications Generator to create a new application, the first screen to appear is the Application Definition screen (see fig. 9.10).

You are required to enter a certain amount of information before proceeding:

- ❏ Application name: A file name (up to 8 characters in length) that will identify this application
- ❏ Description: A phrase to describe this application (optional)
- ❏ Main menu type: For the Main menu, you can select from three types of menus:

    BAR—a horizontal bar, such as a menu at the top of the dBASE IV screen

    POP-UP—a vertical pop-up window type of menu

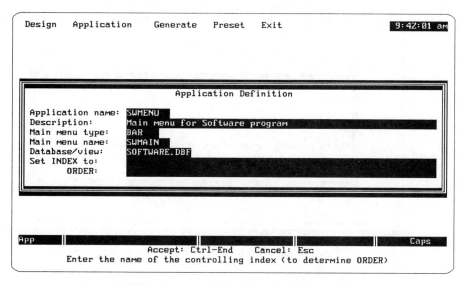

Fig. 9.10. *Entering the Application Definition specifications.*

BATCH—a series of actions or commands that are to be performed when your application is run

Press the space bar to change your selection for the Main menu type.

❏ Main menu name: A short name (up to 8 characters) to refer to the Main menu

❏ Database/view: The database file or view query that will be associated with the application

❏ Set INDEX to: If an index file is being used, the name of the file. You can specify more than one index file, separating the file names with commas.

❏ ORDER: If more than one index file is used or if multiple index tags are available in a multiple index file, the name or number of the index file or tag that will determine the index order for the file

After you have completed the Application Definition screen, press Ctrl-End to accept the values entered. The Applications Generator work surface appears, containing an application object (see fig. 9.11).

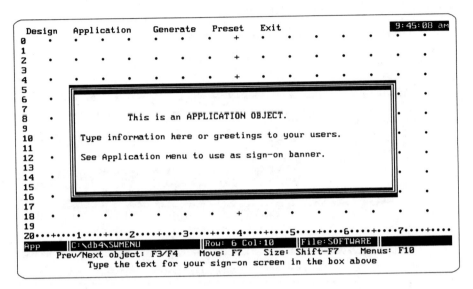

Fig. 9.11. *The Applications Generator work surface.*

9.31 Tip:

Modify the application object to create an opening screen.

The application object represents the application itself. Therefore, it is always present on the work surface, whether it is actually visible or not. The application object makes a handy opening screen for your applications, which can contain a greeting, a special notice, or instructions. When your application is run, the object appears briefly on the screen.

To change the text in the object box, simply type the new information. For example, you may want to put your program title, copyright notice, or other information on the opening screen (see fig. 9.12).

9.32 Tip:

Set display options for your applications.

The Applications Generator has several options that are preset as defaults for the applications you create. These can be modified to apply to your entire application. Then, you can override the settings by changing them for any individual object in your application.

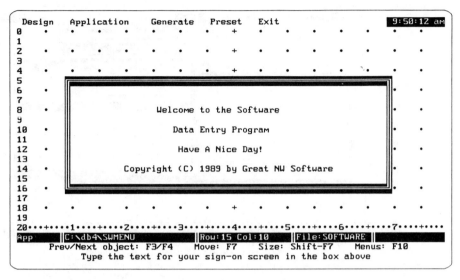

```
   Design   Application    Generate    Preset   Exit                 9:50:12 am
0        •        •       •       •        •       •       +      •       •       •       •       •       •       •
1
2        •        •       •       •        •       •       •       +      •       •       •       •       •       •
3
4        •        •       •       •        •       •       •       +      •       •       •       •       •       •
5
6        •    ┌─────────────────────────────────────────────────────────┐       •       •
7             │                                                         │
8        •    │              Welcome to the Software                    │       •       •
9             │                                                         │
10       •    │                Data Entry Program                       │       •       •
11            │                                                         │
12       •    │                 Have A Nice Day!                        │       •       •
13            │                                                         │
14       •    │         Copyright (C) 1989 by Great NW Software         │       •       •
15            │                                                         │
16       •    └─────────────────────────────────────────────────────────┘       •       •
17
18       •        •       •       •        •       •       •       +      •       •       •       •       •       •
19
20 ••••+••••1••••+••••2••••+••••3••••+••••4••••+••••5••••+••••6••••+••••7••••+••••
┌────┐┌──────────────────┐┌────────────┐┌──────────────┐
│App ││C:\db4\SWMENU     ││Row:15 Col:10││File:SOFTWARE ││
└────┘└──────────────────┘└────────────┘└──────────────┘
        Prev/Next object: F3/F4    Move: F7    Size: Shift-F7    Menus: F10
              Type the text for your sign-on screen in the box above
```

Fig. 9.12. *An application object used for an opening screen.*

For example, the display options can be set so that text, boxes, and other objects appear in the colors you specify if you are using a color monitor. To set the display options, pull down the **Preset** menu (Alt-P), and then select **Display options**. You can set colors for **Standard** items, such as text, messages, and titles, and **Enhanced** items, such as boxes, fields, and other highlighted items (see fig. 9.13).

9.33 Tip: **Establish the environment settings for your applications using the Preset menu.**

The **Preset** menu also lets you set several environment settings. This menu generates certain SET commands as part of the application code to set your program environment. Several of these SET commands are discussed in previous chapters.

For example, to set the BELL ON, pull down the **Preset** menu (Alt-P), select **Environment settings** and **Set BELL**, press the space bar to select ON, and then tab over to the **(to ___,__)** field. You can enter the frequency and duration of the tone used when the bell is sounded (see fig. 9.14). Other options that can be set include **Set CARRY, Set CENTURY, Set CONFIRM, Set ESCAPE, Set SAFETY,** and **Set DELIMITERS**.

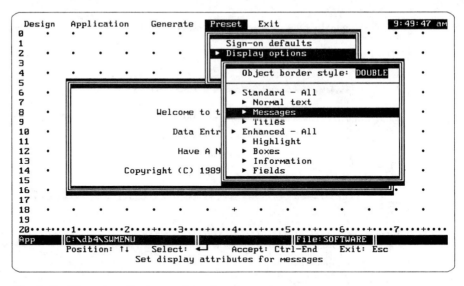

Fig. 9.13. Choosing display options for text or borders.

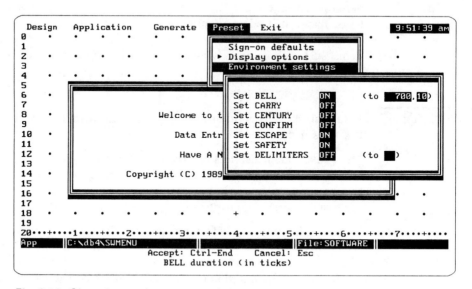

Fig. 9.14. Changing environment settings.

Using the Quick Application Option

9.34 Tip:

To produce a simple menu program, use the Quick Application option.

If you want to create an application in the minimum amount of time, using the Quick Application option may be the best method. This option creates a program that will allow you to select the following functions from a main menu:

- ❑ Add information (append)
- ❑ Change information (edit)
- ❑ Browse information (browse or edit)
- ❑ Discard marked records (pack)
- ❑ Print reports (report form)
- ❑ Produce mailing labels (label form)
- ❑ Exit from the program

Figure 9.15 shows the main menu of a Quick Application program. The generated code can then be modified. This gives you a head start on producing your program code, saving you hours of coding.

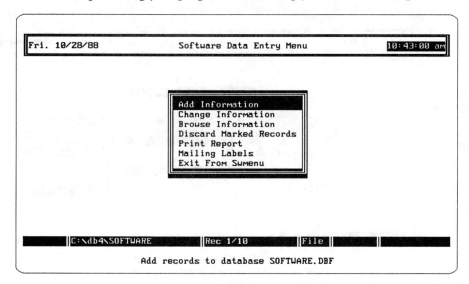

Fig. 9.15. *The SWMENU Quick Application menu.*

When you use the Quick Application option to print reports or labels, the application responds with pop-up windows. In these windows, you can position the record pointer to the record that is to be printed first (see fig. 9.16) and specify the output options before printing begins (see fig. 9.17).

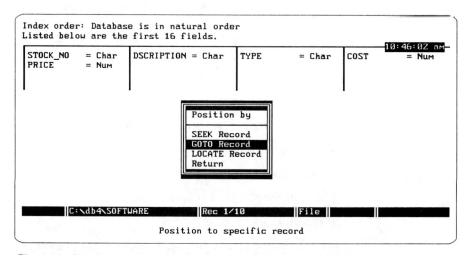

Fig. 9.16. *Positioning the record pointer before printing reports.*

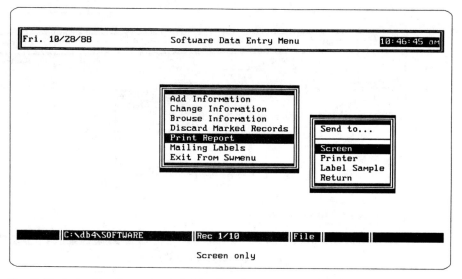

Fig. 9.17. *Selecting the output destination for reports or labels.*

To generate a Quick Application, pull down the **Application** menu (Alt-A), select **Generate quick application**, and press Enter. A window appears, asking you to enter information about the application:

❑ Database file to be used

❑ Screen format, report format, and label format files to use

❑ Index files and index order

❑ The program's author (your name or company, for identification)

❑ The menu heading message

After you enter this information, press Ctrl-End to accept your entries (see fig. 9.18)

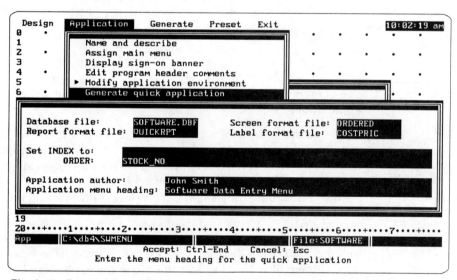

Fig. 9.18. *Entering specifications for a Quick Application.*

You are given a chance to change your mind. If all is correct, highlight Yes and press Enter to proceed with the operation, or select No or press Esc to cancel it (see fig. 9.19).

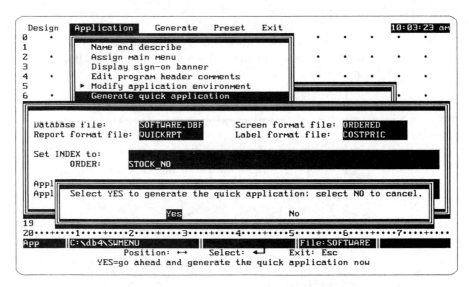

Fig. 9.19. *Generating the application.*

9.35 Tip: **Use screen, label, and report format files with your Quick Applications.**

If you have been working with a database, chances are that you already have created label format and report format files. You also may have created custom screen-input forms. You do not have to "reinvent the wheel" each time you create a Quick Application. Rather, by using existing format files, you can produce a professional-looking program in a matter of minutes.

For example, figure 9.20 shows a screen-format file created for use with the SOFTWARE database. (See Chapter 4 for details on creating a screen-format file). If you specify this file in the Application Definition screen, your custom input form will be used when you access the Append or Edit modes with the **Add Information** or **Change Information** options on the Quick Application's main menu (see fig. 9.21).

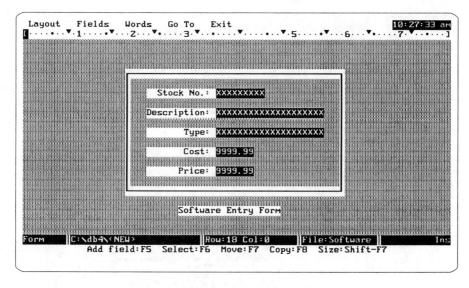

Fig. 9.20. *The data-entry screen form for the SOFTWARE database.*

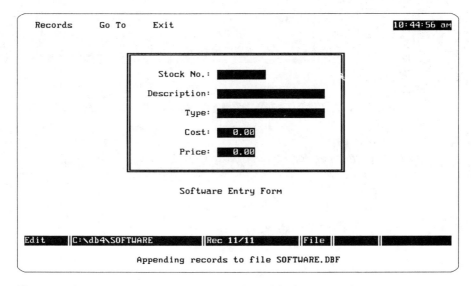

Fig. 9.21. *Using the Add Information option with the screen form.*

9.36 Trick: **Watch your program being created.**

You can watch the program code for your application being created. Before generating your application, select **Display during generation** from the **Generate** menu (see fig. 9.22). The program code will scroll in a window on the screen as it is being created (see fig. 9.23).

After the program (.PRG) file is generated, you can use the **DOS utilities Operations** menu to view its contents. Select **View** to display the code one screen at a time (see fig. 9.24). Or, you can use the TYPE command from the dot prompt to display the file continuously.

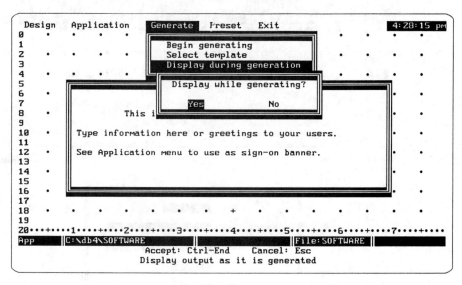

Fig. 9.22. *Choosing the option to display code as it is generated.*

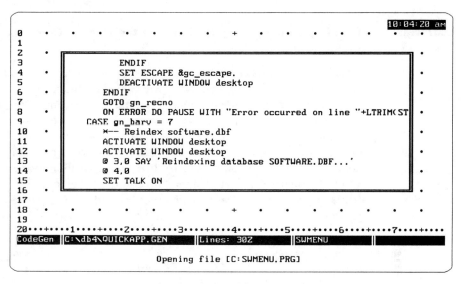

```
                                                        10:04:20 am
0    ·      ·      ·     ·      ·      ·     +     ·      ·      ·     ·      ·
1
2    ·
3                      ENDIF
4    ·                 SET ESCAPE &gc_escape.
5                      DEACTIVATE WINDOW desktop
6    ·             ENDIF
7                  GOTO gn_recno
8    ·             ON ERROR DO PAUSE WITH "Error occurred on line "+LTRIM(ST ·
9         CASE gn_barv = 7
10   ·             *-- Reindex software.dbf
11                 ACTIVATE WINDOW desktop
12   ·             ACTIVATE WINDOW desktop
13                 @ 3,0 SAY 'Reindexing database SOFTWARE.DBF...'
14   ·             @ 4,0
15                 SET TALK ON
16   ·
17
18   ·      ·      ·     ·      ·      ·     +     ·      ·      ·     ·      ·
19
20···+····1····+····2····+····3····+····4····+····5····+····6····+····7····+····
CodeGen ║C:\db4\QUICKAPP.GEN     ║║Lines: 302    ║║SWMENU          ║║
              Opening file [C:SWMENU.PRG]
```

Fig. 9.23. *The program code generated for the application.*

```
                                                        10:36:50 am
****************************************************************************
*
* Program......: C:SWMENU
* Author.......: John Smith
* Date.........: 10-28-88
* Notice.......: Type information here or greetings to your users.
* dBASE Ver....: See Application menu to use as sign-on banner.
* Generated by.: APGEN version 0.96
* Description..: Main menu for Software program

* Notes........:
****************************************************************************
*

SET CONSOLE OFF
IF TYPE("gn_apgen") = "U"   && We were not called from another APGEN program
   CLEAR ALL
   CLEAR WINDOW
   CLOSE ALL
  gn_apgen = 1

                          --  4%  --
      Display control: SPACEBAR:Next screenful,   RETURN:Start/stop scroll.
```

Fig. 9.24. *Viewing the applications program file.*

9.37 Tip:

Modify or run your application from the Control Center or from the dot prompt.

After your application has been generated, you can run it as you would any other dBASE IV program. From the Control Center, highlight the program name in the Applications column and press Enter. You then are asked whether you want to run the application or modify it. If you select **Modify**, the Applications Generator is invoked. You can make changes to the application and save it under the same name or under another file name. If you choose to **Run** the application, you are asked whether you are sure that you want to run the program (see fig. 9.25). If you respond Yes, the screen clears and the program is executed.

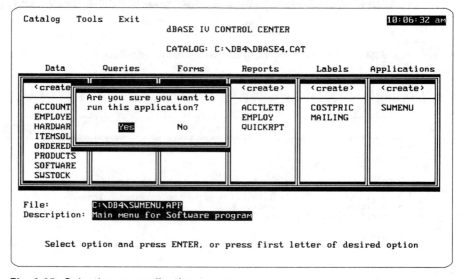

Fig. 9.25. *Selecting an application to run.*

To run the application from the dot prompt, use the DO command, as in the following example:

    . DO SWMENU

To modify the application from the dot prompt, you can edit the program code (.PRG file) using MODIFY COMMAND, or you can invoke the

Applications Generator with `MODIFY APPLICATION`, as in the following example:

. `MODIFY APPLICATION` < *file name of application*>

This command looks for the application file, which has an extension of .APP, and loads it into the Applications Generator. When you make changes to the application, the changes are saved in the new .APP file, and a new .PRG file is generated.

10

Using Advanced Programming Techniques

Using the dBASE IV command language to design the programs you need can help you speed and simplify your work. This chapter presents tips and tricks to help you make the most of dBASE IV command language programming.

Specifically, you learn techniques for using conditional branching, program loops, and subprograms and procedures. In addition, you learn to create basic graphs with the dBASE IV programming language and ASCII characters, as well as to create more sophisticated graphics with Ashton-Tate's CHART-MASTER® program. You also learn how to debug your programs.

Using Conditional Branching

One of the most important programming tools is a conditional branching operation—using the value of a variable to determine the next processing step. In computing weekly wages, for example, the formula you use depends on whether overtime pay is involved:

Wage = Hours worked * Wage rate

or

Wage = 40 Hours * Wage rate
+ Overtime hours * Wage rate * 1.5

The overtime wage rate in this case is assumed to be one and one-half times the regular rate.

Two-Branch Operations

10.1 Tip: **Use the IF . . . ELSE . . . ENDIF command for a two-branch decision operation.**

To direct the program to use one of the two formulas, you need a decision-branching statement. IF...ENDIF is one such statement. The format of the IF...ENDIF command is as follows:

```
IF < a condition>
    The program segment to be executed if the condition
    is true
    .  .  .  .  .
    .  .  .  .
ENDIF
```

You can use either of two approaches to compute wages with IF...ENDIF commands. First, you can compute the wage for all cases and then revise the wage if you encounter an overtime case. In the following examples, the number of hours worked in a week and the normal wage rate are saved in the memory variables mHours and mWageRate. The variable mWage is used to store the computed total weekly wage.

The program segment for computing wages can be written as follows:

```
mWage=mHours * mWageRate
IF mHours>40
    mWage=(mWageRate*40)+(mHours-40) * mWageRate * 1.5
ENDIF
```

Although this program segment produces the correct results, it is not an efficient approach. The program always computes the wage using the first formula (mHours * mWageRate).

The program would be more efficient if the first formula were used only when no overtime is involved. Using a second approach, you can modify the program to direct the processing by adding an ELSE clause to the IF...ENDIF statement in the following format:

```
IF  < a condition>
    The program segment to be executed if the condition
    is true
    .  .  .  .  .
    .  .  .  .
ELSE
    The program segment to be executed if the condition
    is not true
    .  .  .  .  .
    .  .  .  .
ENDIF
```

For example, the program shown earlier can be rewritten as follows:

```
IF mHours>4Ø
    mWage=(mWageRate * 4Ø)+(mHours-4Ø) * mWageRate * 1.5
ELSE
    mWage=mHours * mWageRate
ENDIF
```

This program is a more efficient approach to computing wages because the wage is always computed only once.

10.2 Trick: **To speed processing, use the IIF( ) function to handle a two-branch decision operation.**

If you are using the IF...ELSE...ENDIF command to process a two-branch decision, you can speed the processing by replacing the command with an IIF() function. The format of the IIF() statement is as follows:

IIF(< *condition*>,
    < *expression for cases when condition is true*>,
    < *expression for cases when condition is not true*>)

When the IIF() statement is executed, the condition specified in the argument is evaluated. If the condition is true, the first expression defined in the function is executed. Otherwise, the second expression is processed.

As you have seen, the program segment for computing wages by using the IF...ELSE...ENDIF command can be written as follows:

```
IF mHours>40
    mWage=(mWageRate * 40)+(mHours-40) * mWageRate * 1.5
ELSE
    mWage=mHours * mWageRate
ENDIF
```

The wage is computed by multiplying the number of hours (mHours) by the wage rate (mWageRate) if the number of hours is 40 or less. Otherwise, overtime pay is calculated by using 150 percent of the normal wage rate for the hours over 40.

To simplify the program segment, use the IIF( ) function:

```
mWage=IIF(mHours < =40,mHours * mWageRate,(mWageRate * 40)
    +(mHours-40) * mWageRate * 1.5)
```

10.3 Trick: **Use parentheses to group compound conditions.**

The conditions you can specify in IF, CASE, or other statements that involve logical decisions can use one or more logical operators (.OR. and .AND.) to define a compound condition. For example, specifying each of the following conditions in an IF statement is acceptable:

```
IF AREA_CODE="206"

IF AREA_CODE="206" .OR. AREA_CODE="503"

IF AREA_CODE="206" .OR. AREA_CODE="503" .OR. AREA_CODE="212"

IF AREA_CODE="206" .AND. FIRST_NAME="John" .AND. MALE

IF AREA_CODE="206" .OR. AREA_CODE="503" .AND. FIRST_NAME="John"
IF mVarA=mVarB .AND. mVarC=mVarD .OR. mVarE>mVarF .AND. mVarG
```

Logical operators (.OR. and .AND.) are used to define a compound condition in a decision statement. They are powerful programming tools and should be used with great care. For example, when you use only one logical operator (the second IF statement in the last example) or multiple operators of the same type (the third and fourth IF statements), the meaning of the compound condition is clear.

When you use more than two logical operators of mixed types, however, the compound condition may be confusing and difficult to interpret. The compound conditions in the fifth and sixth IF statements, for example, use a series of .OR. and .AND. logical operators. These statements are interpreted based on the priority rules used for evaluating the conditions. To make sure that the conditions are interpreted correctly, group the conditions with pairs of parentheses.

For example, the sixth IF statement in the last example can be clarified by rewriting it in the following form, using two pairs of parentheses:

```
IF (mVarA=mVarB .AND. mVarC=mVarD) .OR.
   (mVarE>mVarF .AND .mVarG)
```

You must place the parentheses carefully and correctly. Misplaced parentheses will produce quite a different result.

Multiple-Branching Operations

10.4 Tip: **Use DO CASE . . . ENDCASE commands to handle multi-decision branching operations.**

An IF...ELSE...ENDIF command is an efficient way to select one of two courses of action depending on a specified condition being met. If more than two courses of action are to be selected from a set of alternatives, however, use the DO CASE and ENDCASE commands. Between the DO CASE and ENDCASE commands, you specify a course of action for each of the alternative conditions defined in several CASE statements:

```
DO CASE
   CASE < condition 1>
      Course of action for condition 1
   CASE < condition 2>
      Course of action for condition 2
   CASE < condition 3>
      Course of action for condition 3

   .  .  .  .
   .  .  .  .
ENDCASE
```

For example, your program can compute a quantity discount that is a function of quantity sold. Use the DO CASE...ENDCASE command and CASE statements to specify a discount rate for each level of quantity sold:

```
DO CASE
    CASE mQtySold <1ØØ
         mDiscRate=.Ø5                    && 5% discount
    CASE mQtySold>=1ØØ .AND. mQtySold <3ØØ
         mDiscRate=.1Ø                    && 1Ø% discount
    CASE mQtySold>=3ØØ
         mDiscRate=.15                    && 15% discount
ENDCASE
mNetSale=mGrossSale*(1-mDiscRate)
```

Notice that the discount rate (mDiscRate) is set to 0.05, 0.10, and 0.15, respectively, for each case of quantity sold (mQtySold). The net sales figure (mNetSale) is then computed by discounting the gross sales (mGrossSale) by the appropriate discount rate.

The DO CASE...ENDCASE command can be used also for designing a menu-driven program. Different program modules are executed for each case specified, depending on the menu option selected. (A discussion of such a menu design is given in a separate programming tip in Chapter 9.)

10.5 Tip: Use an OTHERWISE statement to handle open-ended cases in decision-branching operations.

When you use the DO CASE...ENDCASE command to direct execution in a multiple-branching operation, add an OTHERWISE statement to handle the open-ended cases. Here is an example:

```
DO CASE
    CASE mChoice="A"
         . . . . .

         . . . . .
    CASE mChoice="B"
         . . . . .

         . . . . .
    OTHERWISE
         . . . . .

         . . . . .
ENDCASE
```

The program segment specified after the OTHERWISE statement is executed only when the conditions defined in all the other CASE statements are not met.

Using Program Loops

This section gives you tips, tricks, and traps regarding the basic structure of program loops as well as some applications for using them.

Understanding the Structure of a Program Loop

10.6 Tip: **Understand the basic structure of a program loop.**

Use a program loop to instruct the computer to perform a repetitive set of tasks. The set of tasks can be specified as a program segment that is carried out over and over, as long as a specified condition is met.

To define a program loop, you can use the DO WHILE...ENDDO statements, specifying between these commands the set of instructions to be carried out repeatedly:

```
DO WHILE  < condition>
   The program segment to be repeated
   .  .  .  .
   .  .  .  .
ENDDO
```

The condition defined in the DO WHILE statement instructs the computer to execute the program segment specified in the loop as long as the condition is true. Otherwise, the computer skips the program segment and exits the program loop.

10.7 Tip: **Use the LOOP command to skip a program loop.**

The LOOP command directs the program to go to the beginning of the loop. When the command is encountered within a program segment in the loop, control is transferred to the beginning of the loop, and the rest of the commands in the segment are ignored:

```
DO WHILE . . . .
      . . . . .
      . . . . .
   LOOP
      . . . . .
      . . . . .
ENDDO
```

To skip a segment of instructions in the program loop, use the LOOP command with a conditional transfer statement:

```
DO WHILE . . .
      . . . . .
      . . . . .
   DO CASE
      CASE . . . . .
         . . . .
         LOOP
      CASE . . . . .
         . . . .
         . . . .
      OTHERWISE
         . . . .
         . . . .
   ENDCASE
      . . . . .
      . . . . .
ENDDO
```

This program segment instructs the program to go back to the beginning of the loop after executing the instructions when the first case condition is true.

10.8 Tip: **Use the EXIT command to interrupt a program loop.**

In the normal course of processing, a program loop is terminated when the condition specified in the DO WHILE statement is no longer true. But you can interrupt processing and terminate the program loop at any time by using the EXIT command in the program segment within the loop:

```
DO WHILE . . .
    .  .  .  .  .
    .  .  .  .  .
    EXIT
    .  .  .  .
ENDDO
```

Whenever the EXIT statement is encountered in the loop, the normal processing sequence is interrupted and program control is transferred to the command immediately following the ENDDO command.

10.9 Trick: **To set up an infinite program loop, use .T. as a condition.**

If you need to process a program segment repeatedly in an infinite loop, specify the logical value of .T. as the condition:

```
DO WHILE .T.
    The program segment to be repeatedly processed
    .  .  .  .
    .  .  .  .
ENDDO
```

Because the condition is always true (.T.), the program segment within the loop is executed over and over.

Infinite loops play an important role in data processing. They are discussed in later sections of this chapter.

10.10 Trick: **Use the Esc key to exit from an infinite loop.**

The program segment defined within the program loop in the preceding trick executes in a continuous cycle. If you want to terminate processing, press the Esc key while the program loop is being executed. If SET ESCAPE OFF is not in effect, the program will stop, and you will see a message similar to the following:

```
*** INTERRUPTED ***
```

< *command line* >

```
Cancel      Ignore      Suspend
```

Press C to terminate program execution. Press I to continue. Press S to halt processing temporarily. Resume processing by issuing the RESUME command at the dot prompt.

_____
10.11 Trap: **You can lose data when using SET ESCAPE OFF.**

Because you are unable to stop program execution using the Esc key when SET ESCAPE OFF is in effect, your program may appear to "lock up" in an infinite loop. If you have to reboot your computer to get out of the loop or halt the program, you may lose data from any open files. Therefore, you should use infinite loops and SET ESCAPE OFF cautiously and only on tested programs.

Using Program Loops in Applications

_____
10.12 Tip: **Use a program loop to access records sequentially in a database file.**

To access each record in a database file, use a DO WHILE...ENDDO program loop. Use the EOF( ) function to terminate the loop when it reaches the end-of-file mark.

The following program segment allows you to display sequentially the contents of each record in EMPLOYEE.DBF:

```
*** LISTNAME.PRG
* List FIRST_NAME and LAST_NAME in EMPLOYEE.DBF
SET TALK OFF
SET ECHO OFF
CLEAR
USE EMPLOYEE
? "Name of Employee"
?
* Set up program loop to scan record
DO WHILE .NOT. EOF()
   ? TRIM(FIRST_NAME)+" "+LAST_NAME
   SKIP                && go to next record
ENDDO
RETURN
```

The LISTNAME.PRG program scans each data record in EMPLOYEE.DBF and displays the values of the LAST_NAME and FIRST_NAME data fields.

Remember to use the SKIP command to move the record pointer to the next record to be accessed. Otherwise, the end-of-file mark never will be reached, and you will display the same record and remain in an infinite loop.

10.13 Tip: **Use a program to total values in a numeric field.**

Using the DO WHILE...ENDDO command, you can set up a program loop to total the values in a database file's numeric field. Such a loop examines sequentially the data-field value in each database record and then adds it to an accumulator variable.

You can total the values in INVENTRY.DBF's ON_HAND data field, for example. To do so, you can set up a program loop to access each data record in the file and add the value of the data field to the accumulator variable mTotal:

```
*** SUMVALUE.PRG
* Sum ON_HAND field values in INVENTRY.DBF
SET TALK OFF
SET ECHO OFF
CLEAR
USE ACCOUNTS
USE INVENTRY
* Clear the accumulator
STORE Ø to mTotal
* List values in ON_HAND
? "ON_HAND Quantity"
?
* Set up program loop to scan data records
DO WHILE .NOT. EOF()
    ? ON_HAND                     && display field value
    mTotal=mTotal+ON_HAND         && add value to total
    SKIP                          && go to next record
ENDDO
* Show total
@1Ø,1Ø SAY "Total ON_HAND quantity. . . .";
    GET mTotal PICTURE "###"
RETURN
```

Figure 10.1 shows the output of SUMVALUE.PRG. The program gives you not only a computed total but also a listing of the values in the ON_HAND data field. (See Trick 10.18 for a shortcut method of averaging, totaling, counting, or finding maximum or minimum values in a database without using a program loop.)

```
ON_HAND Quantity

 3
 5
 4
 2
10
 5
 2
 4          Total ON_HAND quantity ....  82
10
 6
 4
 3
 2
 2
 5
 3
 2
 3
 4
 3
```

Fig. 10.1. The total value in the ON_HAND data field.

Remember to include the SKIP command, which moves the record pointer to the next record to be accessed. Otherwise, you will access the same record over and over.

10.14 Tip: **Use a program loop to count data records in a database file.**

You can set up a program to count data records that meet certain conditions. If you want to count the phone numbers in different area codes in ACCOUNTS.DBF, for example, set up a program loop to scan the AREA_CODE data field and count the phone numbers selectively:

```
*** AREACODE.PRG
* Count phone numbers in area codes 206 and 503
SET TALK OFF
SET ECHO OFF
CLEAR
USE ACCOUNTS
* Clear counter variables
STORE 0 TO mCount206
STORE 0 TO mCount503
? "Area Code Scanned"
?
```

```
* Set up program loop to scan area codes
DO WHILE .NOT. EOF()
    * Display the area code scanned
    ? AREA_CODE
    * Count area codes
    DO CASE
        CASE AREA_CODE="206"
            mCount206=mCount206+1        && count one "206"
        CASE AREA_CODE="503"
            mCount503=mCount503+1        && count one "503"
    ENDCASE
    SKIP
ENDDO
    Display counts
@5,10 SAY "Number of 206 area codes. . . .";
    GET mCount206 PICTURE "###"
@7,10 SAY "Number of 503 area codes. . . .";
    GET mCount503 PICTURE "###"
RETURN
```

The output produced by AREACODE.PRG is shown in figure 10.2. A list of area codes that have been scanned by the program loop is displayed with the computed totals.

```
Area Code Scanned

503
503
503        Number of 206 area codes ....  ▮3
503
503        Number of 503 area codes ....  ▮6
206
206
206
415
503
```

Fig. 10.2. *Counting area codes in ACCOUNTS.DBF.*

10.15 Tip: **Use a program loop to find the maximum or minimum field value in a database file.**

If you want to find a data field's maximum or minimum value, use the DO CASE...ENDCASE command to set up a program loop to scan the field values. To find a maximum field value, choose as the initial maximum either a very small value or the value of the first record.

As you scan the field value of each record, replace the maximum value with any field value that is greater than the current maximum value. If the record does not have a field value greater than the current maximum value, scan the next record. The maximum value is always the largest value in the records scanned. When the end of the file is reached, the maximum value is the largest field value in the database file.

The following sample program segment will find the hardware item with the highest value in HARDWARE.DBF's COST field:

```
*** FINDMAX.PRG
* Find the maximum value in the COST field
SET TALK OFF
SET ECHO OFF
CLEAR
USE HARDWARE
* Use a very small value as an arbitrary maximum value
STORE Ø TO mMaxCost
? "Values of COST scanned"
?
* Set up the program loop to scan records in HARDWARE.DBF
DO WHILE .NOT. EOF()
    ? COST
    IF COST>mMaxCost          && a new maximum is found
        mMaxCost=COST         && update the maximum
    ENDIF
    SKIP                      && scan the next record
ENDDO
* Display the maximum value
@7,1Ø SAY "The maximum value in COST field. . . .";
    GET mMaxCost PICTURE "#,###.##"
RETURN
```

Figure 10.3 shows the highest value in the COST field and a list of the data field's values.

```
Values of COST scanned

1359.00
1695.00
3790.00
  89.00
 560.00    The maximum value in COST field ....  3,790.00
 269.00
 390.00
2190.00
 279.00
 199.00
```

Fig. 10.3. Finding the maximum value in the COST data field.

To find the minimum cost in the HARDWARE.DBF file, you can begin the search process by arbitrarily choosing the value of the first record (or a very large value) as the minimum value. As you scan a record, replace the minimum value with a field value only if that field value is less than the current minimum.

```
*** FINDMIN.PRG
* Find the minimum value in the COST field
SET TALK OFF
SET ECHO OFF
CLEAR
USE HARDWARE
* Use COST in the first record as an arbitrary minimum value
STORE COST TO mMinCost
? "Values of COST scanned"
?
* Set up the program loop to scan records in HARDWARE.DBF
DO WHILE .NOT. EOF()
    ? COST
    IF COST < mMinCost      && a new minimum is found
        mMinCost=COST       && update the minimum
    ENDIF
```

```
    SKIP                           && scan the next record
ENDDO
* Display the minimum value
@ 7,1Ø SAY "The minimum value in COST field. . . .";
    GET mMinCost PICTURE "#,###.##"
RETURN
```

The program's output shows the smallest value in the COST field as well as a list of the COST values scanned by the loop (see fig. 10.4).

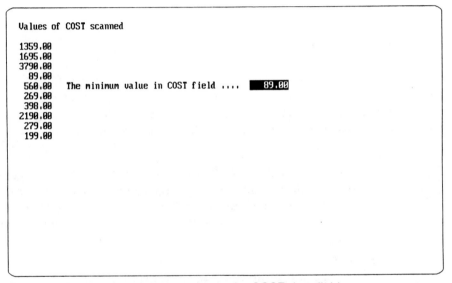

Fig. 10.4. *Finding the minimum value in the COST data field.*

10.16 Tip:

Use a program loop to compute statistics based on the values in a specific data field.

A program loop allows you to scan the values in a specific data field and compute such descriptive statistics as the mean (average) and standard deviation.

To compute the mean value of a set of field values, divide the sum of these values (denoted as x's) by the number of values (N):

$$\bar{x} = \Sigma \, x_i/N \qquad \text{for } i = 1,2,3,. \ldots ., N$$

The symbol x_i is used to denote the field value of the ith data record where i is an index that takes on a value from 1 to N (number of records in the file). The Σ symbol is used to represent the sum of all the field values.

Several formulas can be used to compute the standard deviation of a set of values (x's). The following is a definitional formula for computing a sample standard deviation:

$$ s = \Sigma \sqrt{(x_i - \bar{x})^2 / (N-1)} \qquad \text{for } i = 1, 2, 3, \ldots, N $$

The numerator in the formula is the sum of the squared differences between the field values and the mean value.

The following sample program segment computes the mean and standard deviation of the values in HARDWARE.DBF's COST data field. The variables mSum and mSSD are used to store the sum of the field values and the sum of the squared differences. The variable mNOBS (number of observations) is used to keep track of the number of records in the file. And a program loop is set up to scan the value of the COST data field in each record.

```
*** STATISTS.PRG
* Compute descriptive statistics of COST in HARDWARE.DBF
  SET TALK OFF
  SET ECHO OFF
  CLEAR
  USE HARDWARE
* Clear accumulator variables
  STORE Ø TO mSum
  STORE Ø TO mSSD
  STORE Ø TO mNOBS
* Display the list of raw data
  ? "              >> Raw Data  << "
  ?
  ? SPACE(3)+"Obs.#      Cost"
  ? SPACE(3)+"-----      -------"
* Sum values in the COST field
  DO WHILE .NOT. EOF()       && set up loop to scan records
     mNOBS=mNOBS+1           && count a record
     * Display COST as raw data
     ? SPACE(3)+STR(mNOBS,2,Ø)+STR(COST,12,2)
     mSum=mSum+COST          && add COST to sum
     SKIP
```

```
    ENDDO
*  Compute mean COST value
    mMean=mSum/mNOBS
*  Compute the sum of squared differences
    GO TOP
    DO WHILE .NOT. EOF()
        mSSD=mSSD+(COST-mMean)*(COST-mMean)
        SKIP
    ENDDO
*  Compute the standard deviation
    mStdDev=SQRT(mSSD/(mNOBS-1))
*  Display computed results
    @ 7,30 SAY ">> Descriptive Statistics  <<"
    @ 9,27 SAY "Mean. . . . . . . . . . . . . . . . . .";
    GET mMean PICTURE "#,###.##"
    @11,27 SAY "Standard Deviation. . . .";
    GET mStdDev PICTURE "#,###.##"
    RETURN
```

Figure 10.5 shows the results of executing STATISTS.PRG. Notice that the descriptive statistics and the values in the COST field are displayed.

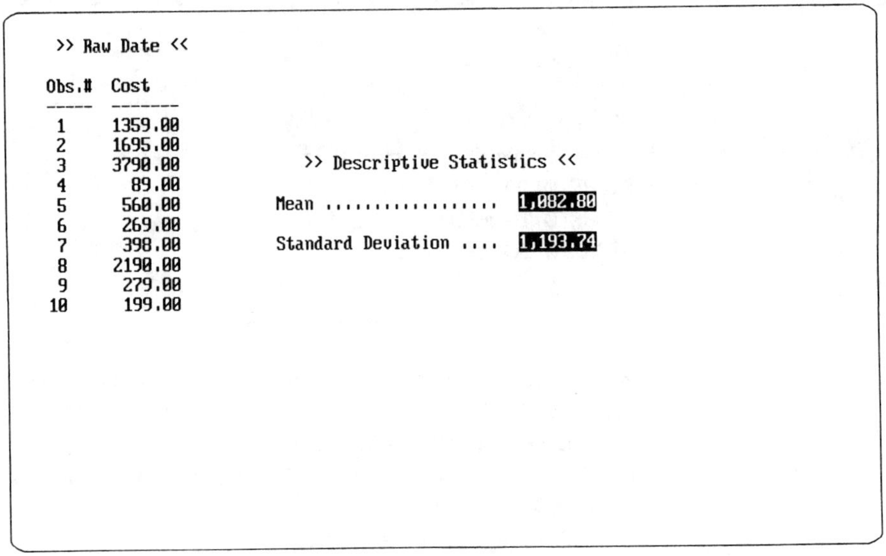

```
>> Raw Date <<

Obs.#  Cost
-----  -------
  1    1359.00
  2    1695.00
  3    3790.00           >> Descriptive Statistics <<
  4      89.00
  5     560.00       Mean ................    1,082.80
  6     269.00
  7     398.00       Standard Deviation ....  1,193.74
  8    2190.00
  9     279.00
 10     199.00
```

Fig. 10.5. Computing descriptive statistics for the COST data field.

10.17 Tip:	**Use a program loop to compute regression coefficients.**

The dBASE IV command language can be used to compute many complex, sophisticated statistics. For example, you can save the values of two economic variables as two data fields, and then write a program using these two variables to compute a regression equation.

The general form of a simple linear regression can be defined as follows:

$$Y_i = a + b\,X_i \qquad \text{for } i = 1, 2, 3, \ldots\ldots, N$$

Y and X are the dependent and independent variables. N denotes the number of observations to be used in the regression. The *a* and *b* are the regression coefficients that can be computed with the following formulas:

$$b = (N \sum X_i \bullet Y_i - \sum X_i \sum Y_i)/(N \sum X_i^2 - (\sum X_i)^2)$$

$$a = (\sum Y_i/N) - b \bullet (\sum X_i/N)$$

For example, you can regress the values in HARDWARE.DBF's COST data field (the dependent variable) on the value of the PRICE data field (the independent variable) by using the following program:

```
*** REGRESS.PRG
* Regressing COST (the dependent variable, Y) on PRICE
* (the independent variable, X) in HARDWARE.DBF
SET TALK OFF
SET ECHO OFF
CLEAR
* Initialize accumulator variables
STORE Ø TO mSumX
STORE Ø TO mSumY
STORE Ø TO mSumXY
STORE Ø TO mSumXSq
STORE Ø TO mNOBS
* Select the database containing the COST and PRICE fields
USE HARDWARE
? SPACE(1Ø)+">> Raw Data  <<"
?
? "The dependent variable . . . . COST"
? "The independent variable . . . PRICE"
?
```

```
? SPACE(3)+"Obs.#    Cost            Price"
? SPACE(3)+"-----    ------          -------"
* Summing up X's, Y's, products of X by Y, X-squares
DO WHILE .NOT. EOF()
    mNOBS=mNOBS+1              && count a record
    ? SPACE(3)+STR(mNOBS,2,0)+STR(COST,12,2)+STR(PRICE,12,2)
    mSumX=mSumX+PRICE
    mSumY=mSumY+COST
    mSumXY=mSumXY+PRICE*COST
    mSumXSq=mSumXSq+PRICE*PRICE
    SKIP                      && scan the next record
ENDDO
* Compute regression coefficients, a and b
mB=(mNOBS*mSumXY-mSumX*mSumY)/(mNOBS*mSumXSq-mSumX*mSumX)
mA=(mSumY/mNOBS) - mB*(mSumX/mNOBS)
* Display results
?
? "  >> Estimated Regression Coefficients << "
?
? "    The intercept, a. . . ." + STR(mA,12,4)
? "    The slope, b. . . . . ." + STR(mB,12,4)
RETURN
```

Figure 10.6 shows the results of REGRESS.PRG's regression analysis. The figure shows the estimated regression coefficients and the listing of raw data that represent the values of HARDWARE.DBF's COST and PRICE data fields.

10.18 Trick: Use the CALCULATE command to perform certain calculations on database records in one pass.

Normally, to perform a financial or statistical calculation on all the records in a database, or on a large number of them, you would need to process the records for each function. For example, suppose that you wanted to calculate the average and sum of numeric values in the SALES field of all records of a database named FINANCE, to count the records in the database, and to store these values in the variables mAvg, mSum, and mCnt. You could use these commands:

```
. USE FINANCE
. AVERAGE Sales TO mAvg
. SUM Sales TO mSum
. COUNT TO mCnt
```

```
        >> Raw Data <<

The dependent variable ..... COST
The independent variable ... PRICE

  Obs.#  Cost      Price
  -----  -------   -------
    1    1359.00   1095.00
    2    1695.00   2399.00
    3    3790.00   4490.00
    4      89.00    159.00
    5     560.00    820.00
    6     269.00    389.00
    7     398.00    495.00
    8    2190.00   2790.00
    9     279.00    389.00
   10     199.00    239.00

 >> Estimated Regression Coefficients <<

    The intercept, a ....   -73.9497
    The slope, b ........     0.8224
```

Fig. 10.6. Displaying the estimated regression results.

If your database has several thousand records, this takes considerable time because the file has to be processed sequentially three times. dBASE IV has a shortcut: the CALCULATE command. It includes several functions to perform multiple calculations in one pass through the database. The format of the command is as follows:

CALCULATE *<scope> <option list>* FOR *<condition>*
WHILE *<condition>* TO *<memory variable>*

The FOR, WHILE, and TO clauses are optional. The option list can contain one or more of these special functions:

AVG(*expression*)	Average of values
CNT( )	Count records
MAX(*expression*)	Maximum value
MIN(*expression*)	Minimum value
NPV(*rate, cash flow value, initial period*)	Net Present Value
STD(*expression*)	Standard deviation
SUM(*expression*)	Sum of values
VAR(*expression*)	Variance of values

In the previous example, both the code and the processing time could be shortened by using the CALCULATE command:

```
. USE FINANCE
. CALCULATE AVG(Sales), SUM(Sales), CNT( ) TO mAvg, mSum, mCnt
```

Using Subprograms and Procedures

If you organize your database management system around small individual program modules, you can use two basic techniques to make these modules work together in a unified system. The tips, tricks, and traps in this section show you how to call another program module and how to define a program module as a procedure.

10.19 Tip: **Design your database system around small program modules.**

When you design and develop a database management system, consider organizing the system in several small program modules. A small program module is easy to create and maintain.

During the system's development stage, individual program modules can be tested separately to eliminate all syntax and logic errors before the modules are linked as a complete system. These program modules can be reorganized as the function of the database management system changes.

Calling Another Program

10.20 Tip: **Use a program module to perform a specific data management function.**

A program module consists of a set of instructions for performing a specific task. One program module can call another whenever it is needed. As you design your database management system, you may want to design a number of program modules, each of which will be used to carry out a specific data-maintenance function.

For example, you can write a program module that appends a new record to a specific database file:

```
*** ADDRECRD.PRG
* A program module for adding a new record to EMPLOYEE.DBF
SET STATUS ON
USE EMPLOYEE
STORE "Y" TO mContinue
DO WHILE UPPER(mContinue)="Y"
   CLEAR
   APPEND BLANK
   @ 4,27 SAY "EMPLOYEE DATA ENTRY FORM"
   @ 8,8  SAY "Employee's Social Security # : ";
      GET ID_NO PICTURE "999-99-9999"
   @ 8,56 SAY          "Sex* : " GET MALE
   @10,22 SAY "Employee's Name: " GET FIRST_NAME
   @10,56 GET LAST_NAME PICTURE "!AAAAAAAAAAAAA"
   @12,29 SAY          "Position: " GET POSITION
   @14,24 SAY   "Date Employed: " GET EMPLY_DATE
   @17,18 SAY " << * Note: Enter T for male, F for female >>"
   @ 1,0  TO 19,79 DOUBLE      && draw a double-line frame
   @ 3,24 TO  5,53             && draw a single-line box
   READ
   @20,20 SAY "Do you want to add another record [Y/N] ?";
      GET mContinue
   READ
ENDDO
RETURN
```

Whenever this ADDRECRD.PRG program module is executed, it appends a data record to EMPLOYEE.DBF. Although the module can be executed as an independent program, you probably will prefer to invoke it from another program whenever you need to add a record to the database file.

The program module that calls ADDRECRD.PRG can be written as follows:

```
*** ADDDATA.PRG
* Adding data to a database file
SET TALK OFF
SET ECHO OFF
STORE " " TO mChoice
DO WHILE .T.
```

```
CLEAR
SET STATUS OFF
@10,10 SAY "Enter [A] to Add a new record, [E] to Exit";
   GETmChoice
READ
DO CASE
   CASE UPPER(mChoice)="A"
      DO ADDRECRD              && call the program module
      LOOP
   CASE UPPER(mChoice)="E"
      EXIT
   ENDCASE
ENDDO
* End of ADDDATA.PRG
```

When the ADDDATA.PRG module is executed, a prompt is displayed requesting that you press either A to add a record or E to exit the program. Press A to call the ADDRECRD.PRG program module (DO ADDRECRD) and transfer control to that module. Then use the custom data-entry screen defined in the ADDRECRD.PRG module to append a record to EMPLOYEE.DBF.

After you enter values in the data fields of the custom data-entry form, you are asked whether you want to add another record to the file. If you press Y, a blank data-entry form is displayed. Press N to exit the program module (see fig. 10.7).

When you press N at the prompt, the character string is assigned to the memory variable mContinue. As a result, the DO WHILE UPPER (mContinue)="Y"...ENDDO program loop terminates, and the program executes the RETURN command immediately after the loop. At this point, control is transferred back to the ADDDATA.PRG calling program.

As you can see, program modules are powerful. They allow you to process instructions repeatedly by simply calling a module whenever you need it.

Using Procedures

When you are developing a database management system, you probably will use certain key modules repeatedly. There are two ways to use these program modules.

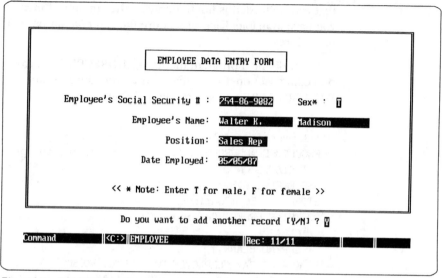

Fig. 10.7. *Data entered in the custom data-entry form.*

In the first method, discussed in the preceding section, you call one program module from another program. When a program module is used in this manner, the disk file containing the module is opened and loaded into memory whenever the module is called. When you exit the called module, the module is erased from memory. Because the file is opened and loaded into memory each time you call the module, processing time can be slowed down slightly if the module is large.

10.21 Trick: **To save processing time, use a procedure to process a key program module repeatedly.**

A better method is to define a frequently used module as a procedure. A procedure works like a regular module but is identified with the keyword PROCEDURE followed by an assigned name at the beginning of each procedure section. When a procedure is called up, it is loaded into memory and remains in memory until you close the procedure. After a procedure has been loaded into memory, you can use it repeatedly to perform a specified task by calling the procedure with a DO command.

You can include a procedure in your program file, or you can store procedures in a separate procedure file. The number of procedures that can be loaded is limited only by the amount of memory (RAM) you have available. Each procedure file can contain up to 1,170 procedures.

You can define a program module (ADDRECRD.PRG, from the preceding section, for example) as a procedure in the DATAPROC.PRG procedure file as follows:

```
*** DATAPROC.PRG
* A procedure file
PROCEDURE ADDRECRD                    && define the procedure name
SET STATUS ON
USE EMPLOYEE
STORE "Y" TO mContinue
DO WHILE UPPER(mContinue)="Y"
   CLEAR
   APPEND BLANK
   @ 4,27 SAY "EMPLOYEE DATA ENTRY FORM"
   @ 8,8  SAY "Employee's Social Security # : ";
      GET ID_NO PICTURE "999-99-9999"
   @ 8,56 SAY            "Sex*: " GET MALE
   @10,22 SAY "Employee's Name: " GET FIRST_NAME
   @10,56 GET LAST_NAME PICTURE "!AAAAAAAAAAAAAA"
   @12,29 SAY         "Position: " GET POSITION
   @14,24 SAY    "Date Employed: " GET EMPLY_DATE
   @17,18 SAY " < < * Note: Enter T for male, F for female >>"
   @ 1,0  TO 19,79 DOUBLE      && draw a double-line frame
   @ 3,24 TO  5,53             && draw a single-line box
   READ
   @20,20 SAY "Do you want to add another record [Y/N] ?";
      GET mContinue
   READ
ENDDO
RETURN
* End of the ADDRECRD procedure
```

In this example, only one procedure is defined in the DATAPROC.PRG procedure file. To add other procedures to the file, specify each of them in a section that begins with the keyword PROCEDURE and an assigned name.

10.22 Tip: **Call the procedure file with the DO command.**

After a procedure has been defined and saved in a procedure file, you can call it (as you would a program module) by using a DO command. By issuing the DO ADDRECRD command, for example, you can call the ADDRECD procedure from the ADDDATA.PRG program module.

Before calling the procedure, however, you must select the procedure file by using the SET PROCEDURE TO command at the beginning of the calling program:

```
*** ADDDATA.PRG
* Data maintenance menu
SET PROCEDURE TO DATAPROC        && select the procedure file
SET TALK OFF
SET ECHO OFF
STORE " " TO mChoice
DO WHILE .T.
   CLEAR
   SET STATUS OFF
   @10,10 SAY "Enter [A] to Add a new record, [E] to Exit ";
      GETmChoice
   READ
   DO CASE
      CASE UPPER(mChoice)="A"
         DO ADDRECRD                && call the program module
         LOOP
      CASE UPPER(mChoice)="E"
         EXIT
   ENDCASE
ENDDO
```

The results of executing the procedure are the same as they would be if the procedure were in the form of an independent program module. But, in most cases, using a procedure reduces the amount of disk accessing time. This is especially true if the procedure contains a large set of instructions. Whenever feasible, use a procedure rather than a program module.

10.23 Tip: **For quickest program execution, place procedures in your program.**

Unless the procedures will be repeatedly used by many program modules, or unless you have a large number of procedures, your program will operate most efficiently if you place the procedures in your program file. This way, dBASE IV does not have to load them from a separate file.

10.24 Tip: **Release memory space by closing a procedure file when you no longer need it.**

Because loaded procedure files compete with other operations for memory space, you should release memory space whenever a procedure file is no longer needed. To remove the contents of a procedure from memory, use the CLOSE PROCEDURE command (see the following trap).

10.25 Trap: **To avoid losing data, close a procedure file only in the calling program.**

You can remove the contents of an active procedure file from memory by issuing the CLOSE PROCEDURE command. However, be sure to close a procedure file only in the calling program. The system may behave unpredictably if you close a procedure when you are in it, and you may have to reboot the computer. As a result, you risk losing valuable data.

10.26 Trap: **Be sure that you have enough memory available before using a procedure file.**

The contents of a procedure file are loaded into memory whenever the file is selected with the SET PROCEDURE TO command and remain in memory until you close the file. Memory space allocated to dBASE IV is thereby diminished. Because dBASE IV uses most of the memory available on a 640K system, do not load too many procedures at one time. Otherwise, you will not be able to continue processing and may run the risk of losing some of the immediate results.

10.27 Tip: **Design a general-purpose program module or procedure to perform a key operation.**

A program module or procedure is an efficient way to process a frequently needed operation in database management. You may want to include in your database management system, for example, a program module or procedure for finding data records in a database file. You can design the module to find a record in a database file by searching a specific data field for a specified key value.

For example, if EMPLOYEE.DBF has been indexed on the LAST_NAME field, you can use the following FINDLAST.PRG program module to find the record for a given key value in the indexed field:

```
*** FINDLAST.PRG
* Find a given last name in the LAST_NAME of EMPLOYEE.DBF
CLEAR
USE EMPLOYEE INDEX BYLAST
SEEK mKeyValue
IF FOUND()
   @15,1Ø SAY "The record found:"
   ?
   DISPLAY
ELSE
   @15,3Ø SAY "No such record!"
ENDIF
@22,1
WAIT
RETURN
```

This program can be called from another program module. The FINDLAST.PRG module selects and indexes EMPLOYEE.DBF with the information saved in BYLAST.NDX (which was created by using the INDEX ON LAST_NAME TO BYLAST command). Then the SEEK command finds a specific record in the database file. The key value for the index field is stored in the memory variable mKeyValue. If the SEEK operation finds a record, the contents of that record are displayed. Otherwise, a No such record! message is returned.

Before invoking the module, the calling program must supply the information contained in the memory variable mKeyValue because the FINDLAST.PRG module needs the information for the SEEK operation. In the calling program LOCATE.PRG, for example, the character string

"Taylor" is assigned to the memory variable before the DO FINDLAST command is issued:

```
*** LOCATE.PRG
SET TALK OFF
SET ECHO OFF
CLEAR
* Find record for "Taylor" in LAST_NAME field of EMPLOYEE.DBF
STORE "Taylor" TO mKeyValue
* Call the program module
   DO FINDLAST
RETURN
```

When you execute LOCATE.PRG, the key value for the index field ("Taylor") is passed to the FINDLAST.PRG module, and the record found by the SEEK operation (SEEK "Taylor") is displayed (see fig. 10.8).

```
      The record found:

Record#  ID_NO        FIRST_NAME    LAST_NAME     POSITION    EMPLY_DATE  MALE
    4    732-08-4589  Doris Y.      Taylor        Sales Rep   08/14/83    .F.




Press any key to continue...
```

Fig. 10.8. *The record found by LOCATE.PRG.*

FINDLAST.PRG is useful for finding a specific record based on the value in the LAST_NAME field of EMPLOYEE.DBF, but the program lacks the flexibility to be used as a general-purpose module. Because the names of the defined database and index files (EMPLOYEE.DBF and BYLAST.NDX) are specified in the program module, FINDLAST.PRG cannot be used to find a record in other database files with key values in other data fields.

However, you can use the names of the database and index files in the modules as parameters. Then different values can be passed to the module from the calling program, and you can use the program module to find a record in any database file.

The following FINDRECD.PRG module, for example, results from modifying FINDLAST.PRG:

```
*** FINDRECD.PRG
* Find and display a data record in a given database file
PARAMETERS mDBF,mNDX,mKeyValue
* Display parameters passed from the calling program
CLEAR
@ 5,20 SAY ">> Search parameters specified   <<"
@ 7,10 SAY "Name of the database file (.dbf): " GETmDBF
@ 9,10 SAY "  Name of the index file (.ndx): " GETmNDX
@11,10 SAY "          Value for the key field: " GETmKeyValue
USE &mDBFINDEX &mNDX
SEEK mKeyValue
IF FOUND()
   @15,10 SAY "The record found:"
   ?
   DISPLAY
ELSE
   @15,30 SAY "No such record!"
ENDIF
@22,1
WAIT
RETURN
```

In FINDRECD.PRG, you can see the names of the database and index files to be passed as parameters (mDBF and mNDX). And the value of the key field is supplied (as mKeyValue) by the calling program. The variables mDBF and mNDX are used with the macro functions to select and index the database file:

```
USE &mDBF INDEX &mNDX
```

The character string in mKeyValue is used in the SEEK operation:

```
SEEK mKeyValue
```

If these parameters are to be passed from the calling program, they must be defined with the PARAMETERS command at the beginning of the program modules. The order of the parameters determines the order in which they are passed from the calling program. They must be passed in the following order: database file name, index file name, and key value for the index field.

The following program calls the FINDRECD.PRG module:

```
*** FINDDATA.PRG
SET TALK OFF
SET ECHO OFF
CLEAR
* Find record for Taylor in LAST_NAME field of EMPLOYEE.DBF
* Call the program module
  DO FINDRECD WITH "EMPLOYEE","BYLAST","Taylor"
* Find record for ASH-DB3ØØ in STOCK_NO field of SOFTWARE.DBF
  DO FINDRECD WITH "SOFTWARE","SWSTCKNO","ASH-DB3ØØ"
RETURN
```

When the FINDRECD program module is called, the WITH operator passes the values of the parameters in the DO command.

For example, to find the record with "Taylor" in the LAST_NAME data field in EMPLOYEE.DBF (which has been indexed with BYLAST.NDX), call FINDRECD.PRG by issuing the following command:

```
DO FINDRECD WITH "EMPLOYEE","BYLAST","Taylor"
```

In this command, the three items defined after the WITH operator are values for the three parameters (mDBF, mNDX, and mKeyValue) specified in the FINDRECD.PRG module. These values are used for the values of the memory variables in the macro functions. As a result, the following commands will be executed:

```
USE EMPLOYEE INDEX BYLAST
SEEK "Taylor"
```

Figure 10.9 shows the output for the record search.

Similarly, you can use the FINDRECD.PRG program module to find a record in another database file based on another key field.

For example, when you issue the following command from FINDDATA.PRG, a record in SOFTWARE.DBF (which has been

```
              >> Search parameters specified <<
        Name of the database file (.dbf) :  EMPLOYEE
          Name of the index file (.ndx) :  BYLAST
          Value for the key field Key :  Taylor



        The record found:

Record#   ID_NO      FIRST_NAME      LAST_NAME      POSITION   EMPLY_DATE MALE
      4   732-88-4589 Doris Y.        Taylor         Sales Rep  08/14/83    .F.



Press any key to continue...
```

Fig. 10.9. *The record found by the FINDRECD.PRG program module.*

indexed on the STOCK_NO field in SWSTCKNO.NDX) will be found by using "ASH-DB300" as the key value:

DO FINDRECD WITH "SOFTWARE","SWSTCKNO","ASH-DB300"

10.28 Trick: **Use a SCAN . . . ENDSCAN loop to process database records.**

Instead of using LOCATE with DO WHILE loops to process records, use the dBASE IV SCAN...ENDSCAN commands. The SCAN loop, as it implies, will scan all records or selected records in a database file and perform the specified operation on them.

For example, if you wanted to execute a procedure named MAILOUT for all records in a database where the state is Texas, you could use this series of commands:

```
USE CUSTOMER
LOCATE FOR STATE = "TX"
DO WHILE .NOT. EOF()
   DO MAILOUT WITH NAME, ADDRESS, STATE, ZIP
   CONTINUE
ENDDO
```

You can get the same results using a SCAN loop with these commands:

```
USE CUSTOMER
SCAN FOR STATE = "TX"
    DO MAILOUT WITH NAME, ADDRESS, STATE, ZIP
ENDSCAN
```

By eliminating the LOCATE, CONTINUE, and DO WHILE statements, you save two lines of code, which can save time in programming and possibly make your program run slightly faster.

10.29 Trick: **Share common variables by declaring them PUBLIC.**

There are two types of memory variables: public and private. A public variable is used to store values that are accessible by any program module at any level. Public variables can be declared in any program module.

For example, you can let all program modules gain access to the values of the mAcct_No and mAcct_Name memory variables. Declare them as public variables in the program module in which they are initialized:

```
PUBLIC mAcct_No, mAcct_name
```

10.30 Trick: **Hide a public variable by declaring it PRIVATE.**

After a variable has been declared public, it is considered a global variable. Its values can be shared by all program modules. However, you can use the same variable name as a local variable in a given module, storing a value relevant only to that module. To do so, declare the variable in the program module as PRIVATE. For example, the variable mSubTotal (which has been declared PUBLIC) may be declared in a program module as PRIVATE:

```
PRIVATE mSubTotal
```

As a result, while you are in that program module, the value of mSubTotal is meaningful to that module only. When you are outside that module, the value stored in the public variable is used when mSubTotal is referenced. In other words, a variable created by PRIVATE is not the same variable as the public one with the same name, but rather the private variable acts as a separate variable belonging to a different procedure.

10.31 Trick: Declare all common variables in the main program.

If you need to share a set of common variables among all program modules, initialize them in the main program instead of declaring them as PUBLIC variables. The values of variables created in a program can be accessed by any lower-level program module that is called from that program.

As an example, the variables mAcctName, mInvDate, and mInvAmount are initialized in MAIN.PRG:

```
*** MAIN.PRG
* The main program that calls PROGA.PRG
SET TALK OFF
SET ECHO OFF
* Initialize common variables
STORE "The Evergreen Lumber Store" TO mAcctName
STORE {5/14/87} TO mInvDate
STORE 799.97 TO mInvAmount
CLEAR
@2,15 SAY ">> Values of memory variables in MAIN.prg <<"
@4,15 SAY " mAcctName : " GET mAcctName
@5,15 SAY "  mInvDate : " GET mInvDate
@6,15 SAY "mInvAmount : " GET mInvAmount PICTURE "$###.##"
* Calling PROGA.PRG program module
DO PROGA
RETURN
```

Notice that the values of these variables are assigned in MAIN.PRG by using the STORE commands. To show that these variables can be shared by the subprograms, MAIN.PRG calls the subprogram PROGA.PRG, which, in turn, calls another subprogram (PROGB.PRG):

```
*** PROGA.PRG
* Program module sharing common variables with MAIN.PRG
@9,15 SAY ">> Values of memory variables in PROGA.PRG <<"
@11,15 SAY " mAcctName : " GET mAcctName
@12,15 SAY "  mInvDate : " GET mInvDate
@13,15 SAY "mInvAmount : " GET mInvAmount PICTURE "$###.##"
* Calling PROGB.PRG
DO PROGB
* Return to MAIN.PRG
RETURN
```

```
*** PROGB.PRG
* Program module sharing common variables with MAIN.PRG
@16,15 SAY ">> Values of memory variables in PROGB.PRG <<"
@18,15 SAY " mAcctName : " GET mAcctName
@19,15 SAY "  mInvDate : " GET mInvDate
@20,15 SAY "mInvAmount : " GET mInvAmount PICTURE "$###.##"
* Return to PROGA.PRG
RETURN
```

The output produced by executing MAIN.PRG (DO MAIN) is shown in figure 10.10. You can see that the values of the common variables assigned in the main program are passed correctly among the program modules.

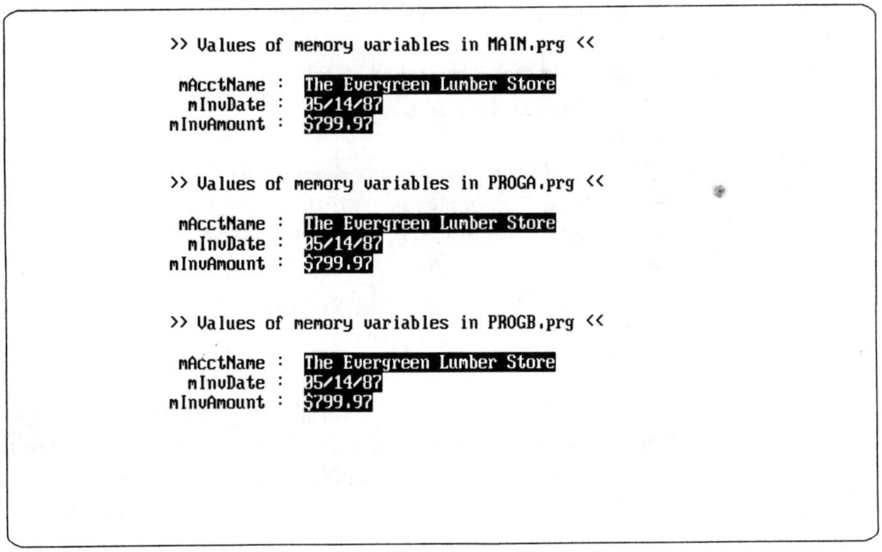

Fig. 10.10. *Values of the variables in all the program modules.*

Creating Graphs

You can use dBASE IV's programming language along with ASCII characters to produce certain types of basic graphs. If your needs for graphics are more sophisticated, you might consider using a program such as CHART-MASTER.

Writing a Graphing Program

10.32 Trick: **Use a text character to produce a bar graph.**

Although dBASE IV's programming language offers a limited capability for producing a wide range of business graphs, you can use it (and a few tricks) to design basic graphs. For example, you can use a series of text graphic characters to form a histogram or bar graph (see fig. 10.11).

```
                    >> SALE DISTRIBUTION BY REGION<<
    !XXXXXXXXXXXXXXXXXXXXXXXXXXXXXXX
    !XXXXXXXXXXXXXXXXXXXXXXXXXXXXXXX     NORTH (30)
    !XXXXXXXXXXXXXXXXXXXXXXXXXXXXXXX
    !
    !XXXXXXXXXXXXXXXXXXXXXXXXXX
    !XXXXXXXXXXXXXXXXXXXXXXXXXX         SOUTH (25)
    !XXXXXXXXXXXXXXXXXXXXXXXXXX
    !
    !XXXXXXXXXXXXXXXXXXXXXXXXXXXXXXXXXXXXXXXXXXXXXXXXXXXXXXXXX
    !XXXXXXXXXXXXXXXXXXXXXXXXXXXXXXXXXXXXXXXXXXXXXXXXXXXXXXXXX     EAST (55)
    !XXXXXXXXXXXXXXXXXXXXXXXXXXXXXXXXXXXXXXXXXXXXXXXXXXXXXXXXX
    !
    !XXXXXXXXXXXXXXXXXXXXXXXXXXXXXXXXXXXXXXXXXXXXXXX
    !XXXXXXXXXXXXXXXXXXXXXXXXXXXXXXXXXXXXXXXXXXXXXXX      WEST (45)
    !XXXXXXXXXXXXXXXXXXXXXXXXXXXXXXXXXXXXXXXXXXXXXXX
    !
    !XXXXXXXXXXXXXXXXXXX
    !XXXXXXXXXXXXXXXXXXX         CENTRAL (20)
    !XXXXXXXXXXXXXXXXXXX

Press any key to continue...
```

Fig. 10.11. *Using text characters to display a bar graph.*

The data used to generate the bar graph in figure 10.11 includes the values in the two BARDATA.DBF data fields. The file structure and contents of BARDATA.DBF are shown in figure 10.12.

CLASSCOUNT represents the sales in a given region (identified by a label in the CLASSLABEL field). In figure 10.11, each bar is displayed as three lines. The length of each bar represents the value in the CLASSCOUNT data field. The following program was used to produce the bar graph:

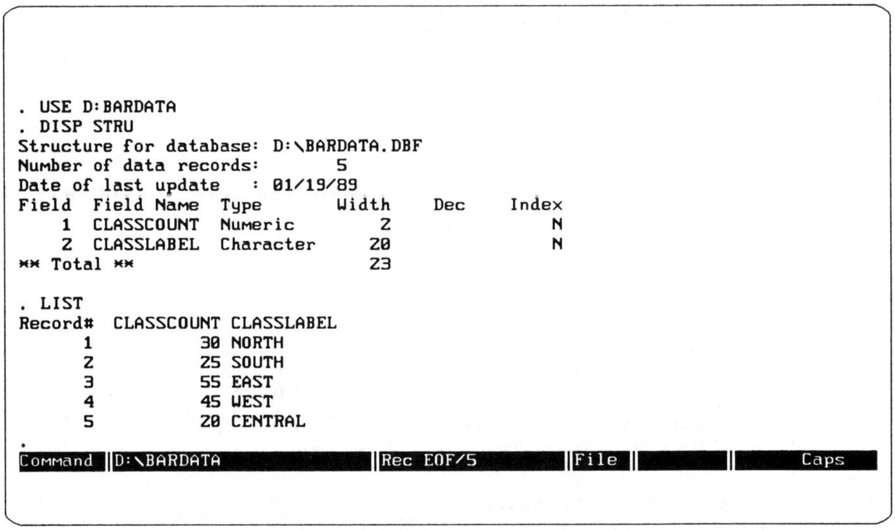

```
. USE D:BARDATA
. DISP STRU
Structure for database: D:\BARDATA.DBF
Number of data records:      5
Date of last update   : 01/19/89
Field  Field Name  Type        Width    Dec    Index
    1  CLASSCOUNT  Numeric        2             N
    2  CLASSLABEL  Character     20             N
** Total **                     23

. LIST
Record#  CLASSCOUNT CLASSLABEL
    1          30 NORTH
    2          25 SOUTH
    3          55 EAST
    4          45 WEST
    5          20 CENTRAL
.
Command ||D:\BARDATA              ||Rec EOF/5       ||File ||      ||    Caps
```

Fig. 10.12. The file structure and contents of BARDATA.DBF.

```
*** BARGRAF.PRG
* A bar graph by using records in BARDATA.DBF
SET TALK OFF
SET ECHO OFF
CLEAR
* Display graph title
@2,24 SAY ">> SALE DISTRIBUTION BY REGION <<"
?
* Define the graphic symbol
STORE "X" TO mSymbol
* Select database file
USE BARDATA
* Process one record at a time
DO WHILE .NOT. .EOF()
    * Display the bar
    ? SPACE(5) +"|"+REPLICATE(mSymbol,CLASSCOUNT)
    ? SPACE(5) +"|"+REPLICATE(mSymbol,CLASSCOUNT) +SPACE(3);
        +TRIM(CLASSLABEL) +" (" +STR(CLASSCOUNT,2,0) +")"
    ? SPACE(5) +"|"+REPLICATE(mSymbol,CLASSCOUNT)
    ? SPACE(5) +"|"
    SKIP              && go to next data record
```

```
ENDDO
@23,1
WAIT
RETURN
```

The text symbol X is stored in the memory variable mSymbol. The horizontal bar is formed by using the REPLICATE() function to display the symbol in mSymbol the number of times stored in CLASSCOUNT.

10.33 Trick: **Use a series of ASCII graphics characters to produce a bar graph.**

You can use a series of ASCII graphics characters as well as text characters to form a bar in a bar graph. In the preceding section, the program BARGRAF.PRG uses a series of text characters (X) to produce the bar graph shown in figure 10.11. The text character is stored in the memory variable named mSymbol.

If you replace the character in the memory variable with an ASCII graphics character, you can produce a bar graph with solid bars (see fig. 10.13). To form a solid bar, use ASCII character 219—a solid square symbol (see the ASCII table in Appendix A at the end of this book).

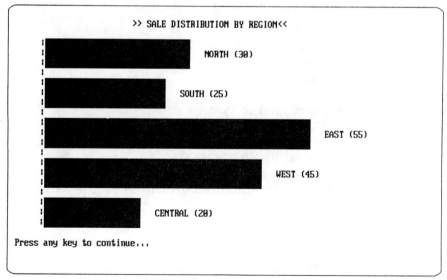

Fig. 10.13. Using ASCII graphics characters to display a bar graph.

The bar graph shown in figure 10.13 was produced by using BARGRAF.PRG (as described in Trick 10.32) after modifying one of the commands in the program as follows:

```
STORE CHR(219) TO mSymbol
```

Experiment with other ASCII characters to determine which you prefer to use for your graphs.

10.34 Trick: **Add colors to a bar graph.**

If you have a color monitor connected to the appropriate adapter card, you can display a bar graph in color. To produce a color bar graph, you use a program with the same logic as that in BARGRAF.PRG (refer to Tricks 10.32 and 10.33) and the data in BARDATA.DBF (see fig. 10.12).

The additional instructions that produce the color bars include a series of SET COLOR TO commands. A different set of colors is defined for each record's text and background. A memory variable (mColorCode) is set up to keep track of which data record is being processed, which in turn determines which set of color combinations should be used to display the variable's value. The memory variable mColor is used to store the color letter codes (R/B, W/B, and so on) for the text and its background colors.

```
*** COLORBAR.PRG
* A color bar graph using records in BARDATA.DBF
SET TALK OFF
SET ECHO OFF
CLEAR
* Select graphic symbol
STORE CHR(219) TO mSymbol
* Set initial screen colors
SET COLOR TO W/B,R/W,B
* Display graph title
@3,24 SAY ">> SALE DISTRIBUTION BY REGION  <<"
?
?
STORE Ø TO mColorCode
* Select database file
USE BARDATA
* Process one record at a time
```

```
DO WHILE .NOT. EOF()
   mColorCode=mColorCode+1
   DO CASE        && determine the color combinations
      CASE mColorCode=1
           mColor="R/B"
      CASE mColorCode=2
           mColor="G/B"
      CASE mColorCode=3
           mColor="R +/B"
      CASE mColorCode=4
           mColor="W/B"
      CASE mColorCode=5
           mColor="RB/B"
   ENDCASE
   SET COLOR TO &mColor
   * Display the bar
   ? SPACE(5)+"|"+REPLICATE(mSymbol,CLASSCOUNT)
   ? SPACE(5)+"|"+REPLICATE(mSymbol,CLASSCOUNT)+SPACE(3);
      +TRIM(CLASSLABEL)+" ("+STR(CLASSCOUNT,2,Ø)+")"
   ? SPACE(5)+"|"+REPLICATE(mSymbol,CLASSCOUNT)
   SKIP                      && go to next data record
ENDDO
SET COLOR TO W/B             && set frame color
@ 1,1 TO 22,79 DOUBLE        && frame the bar graph
@23,1
WAIT
RETURN
```

This program can accommodate up to five classes, each displayed in a separate color. Each bar is formed by three lines of graphics symbols (ASCII character 219). If you need to display more horizontal bars, modify the program by using additional CASE statements to select the color combinations and use a shorter bar length to fit the graph on the screen.

Using CHART-MASTER Bridge

A program called CHART-MASTER, which is published by Ashton-Tate, can be used to create considerably more complex and professional charts and graphs. dBASE IV has a utility program called CHART-

MASTER Bridge that will convert your dBASE IV database files to a format that can be used by CHART-MASTER to graph your data.

To use the CHART-MASTER Bridge utility, add it to your current catalog. From the Control Center, move the cursor to the Applications column. Pull down the **Catalog** menu (Alt-C) and select **Add file to catalog**. A picklist appears, from which you can select the file to be added. Find the CHART-MASTER Bridge application (CHRTMSTR.DBO), highlight it, and press Enter (see fig. 10.14).

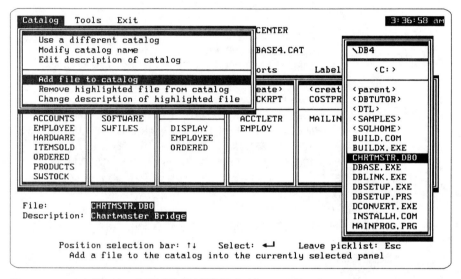

Fig. 10.14. *Adding the CHART-MASTER Bridge application to the catalog.*

After the application is added to the catalog, run the application from the Control Center by highlighting it in the Applications column and pressing Enter (see fig. 10.15). Or, from the dot prompt, you can type DO CHRTMSTR.

When the CHART-MASTER Bridge screen appears, use the **Database** menu to choose the database file to convert to CHART-MASTER format (see fig. 10.16). Use the **Chart** menu to generate your graph. The **Help** menu contains instructions for using CHART-MASTER Bridge.

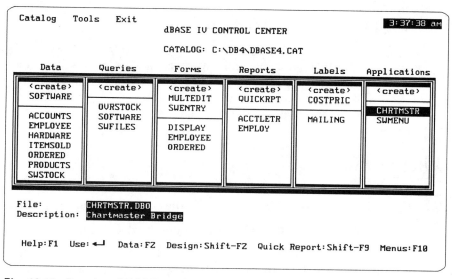

Fig. 10.15. *Running CHART-MASTER Bridge from the Control Center.*

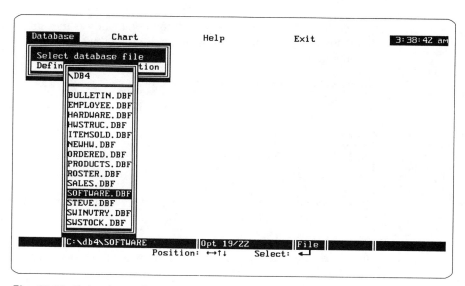

Fig. 10.16. *Selecting a database file for CHART-MASTER Bridge.*

Debugging Your Programs

Test each program module and correct errors in syntax and logic (or "bugs") before linking the modules as a complete system. If a program module has errors, you need to find and correct them. The process of finding and correcting problems is called *debugging*. dBASE IV includes an advanced full-screen debugger called Debug.

Using Debug

10.35 Tip: **Use the dBASE IV DEBUG command to debug your programs.**

The DEBUG command is issued from the dot prompt instead of using the DO command. The format is as follows:

. DEBUG *< program file name or procedure name>*

For example, to debug a program called MAINPROG, issue the following command:

. DEBUG MAINPROG.PRG

Using the debugger, you can check the commands as they are being executed, stop or edit the program, and display the results of expressions.

The Debug screen contains four windows:

❑ The DEBUGGER window

❑ The Edit window

❑ The Breakpoint window

❑ The DISPLAY window

In addition, a Help window appears (headed Debug Commands), listing available commands (see fig. 10.17).

The DEBUGGER window (bottom of screen) shows the current database file, work area, program file, procedure, record number, master index, and line number. The ACTION: prompt is where you enter a Debug command to tell the debugger which action to take next. To reach this prompt, you can press Esc or Ctrl-End.

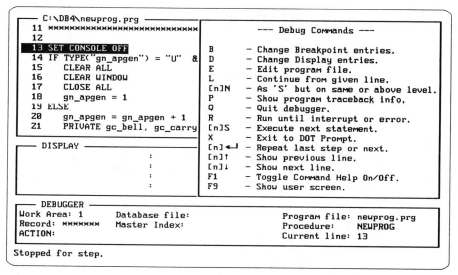

```
┌─ C:\DB4\neuprog.prg ──────────┐
│  11 ×××××××××××××××××××××××××││        --- Debug Commands ---
│  12                           ││
│ 13 SET CONSOLE OFF            ││ B    - Change Breakpoint entries.
│  14 IF TYPE("gn_apgen") = "U" &│ D    - Change Display entries.
│  15    CLEAR ALL              ││ E    - Edit program file.
│  16    CLEAR WINDOW           ││ L    - Continue from given line.
│  17    CLOSE ALL              ││ [n]N - As 'S' but on same or above level.
│  18    gn_apgen = 1           ││ P    - Show program traceback info.
│  19 ELSE                      ││ Q    - Quit debugger.
│  20    gn_apgen = gn_apgen + 1││ R    - Run until interrupt or error.
│  21    PRIVATE gc_bell, gc_carry│[n]S - Execute next statement.
│                               ││ X    - Exit to DOT Prompt.
├─ DISPLAY ─────────────────────┤│ [n]↵ - Repeat last step or next.
│                          :    ││ [n]↑ - Show previous line.
│                          :    ││ [n]↓ - Show next line.
│                          :    ││ F1   - Toggle Command Help On/Off.
│                          :    ││ F9   - Show user screen.
├─ DEBUGGER ────────────────────┴┴──────────────────────────────┤
│ Work Area: 1      Database file:        Program file: newprog.prg │
│ Record: ×××××××   Master Index:         Procedure:    NEWPROG     │
│ ACTION:                                 Current line: 13          │
├───────────────────────────────────────────────────────────────┤
│ Stopped for step.                                              │
└───────────────────────────────────────────────────────────────┘
```

Fig. 10.17. *Using the debugger with the NEWPROG.PRG file.*

10.36 Tip: **Use the Help window to learn the Debug commands.**

As in many other parts of dBASE IV, pressing F1 in the debugger brings up the Help window, which contains a list of available commands. To turn off the Help window and expose the windows underneath, press F1 again.

10.37 Tip: **Use the Debug commands to activate the various windows.**

From the ACTION: prompt in the DEBUGGER window, you can activate the other windows by entering a one-letter command:

E   Edit window
B   Breakpoint window
D   DISPLAY window

To go back to the ACTION: prompt from one of these windows, press Esc or Ctrl-End.

10.38 Tip: **Use the dBASE IV editor to make changes to your program code.**

If you notice any syntax errors or if you want to add or delete commands from your program, use the Edit window to make changes to your program file. Press E at the ACTION: prompt to enter the Edit window (see fig. 10.18).

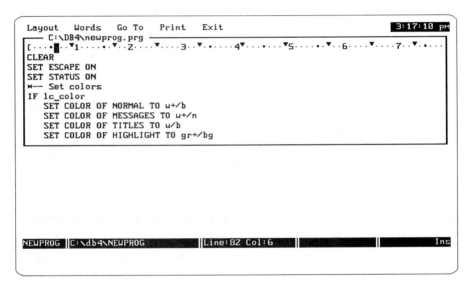

```
 Layout   Words   Go To   Print   Exit                         3:17:10 pm
 ┌─ C:\DB4\newprog.prg ──────────────────────────────────────────────
 [····█··▼1····•·▼··2····▼····3··▼·•····4▼··•···▼5····•·▼··6····▼····7··▼·•··
 CLEAR
 SET ESCAPE ON
 SET STATUS ON
 *── Set colors
 IF lc_color
    SET COLOR OF NORMAL TO w+/b
    SET COLOR OF MESSAGES TO w+/n
    SET COLOR OF TITLES TO w/b
    SET COLOR OF HIGHLIGHT TO gr+/bg




 NEWPROG  C:\db4\NEWPROG           Line:82 Col:6                        Ins
```

Fig. 10.18. *Using the Edit option to make changes in the program.*

Be sure to save the file to keep your changes. The debugger will continue to execute the file using the new file.

10.39 Trap: **Making changes in your file during execution can cause unwanted results.**

Because commands are executed sequentially, one at a time, if you make changes in your program using Debug, be aware of how the changes may effect the execution of subsequent command lines. Be particularly careful when you make any alterations in a program that is in a command loop. If in doubt, you can exit the debugger with the X or Q commands and issue the DEBUG command again using the new file.

10.40 Trick: **Use the Breakpoint option to test for any logical condition.**

If your program is causing unwanted results, but you are not sure where the problem occurs within the program, you may want to set a breakpoint when a certain condition is met.

Press B at the ACTION: prompt to open the Breakpoint window. You can enter as many as 10 conditions, 1 per line. After each program line is executed, the conditions are tested. If one of the conditions is met (evaluated as true [.T.]), then the program is halted and you are returned to the ACTION: prompt. You then may want to clear the breakpoints or edit the program file.

10.41 Trick: **Use the DISPLAY window to monitor the value of expressions.**

To keep track of the current value of any dBASE IV expression at any point during program execution, enter the expressions in the left column of the DISPLAY window. At the ACTION: prompt, press D to access this window. After each program line is executed in Debug, the current value of the expressions in the DISPLAY window are displayed in the right column of that window.

Monitoring Program Execution

10.42 Tip: **To monitor program execution, use SET ECHO ON during the program development stage.**

Even if you choose not to use the dBASE IV debugger, you may want to monitor the program execution as each command in the program is being processed. To monitor execution, issue the SET ECHO ON command at the beginning of the program so that the command being processed and its intermediate results will be displayed.

10.43 Tip: **Use SET DEBUG ON to send echoed commands to the printer.**

You can use the SET ECHO ON command to display instructions on your screen as they are being executed. But the instructions and the results of the program are displayed on the same screen, which can be confusing.

Use the SET DEBUG ON command in the program to separate the echoed commands from the output. The echoed commands will be directed to the printer while the results of the program are shown on the screen. You can monitor program execution by looking at the screen and the printer.

10.44 Tip: **Use SET STEP ON to step through a section of the program during execution.**

A powerful command you can use to trace program execution is the SET STEP ON command. When you issue the SET STEP ON command, you can execute the program line-by-line (in steps).

For example, if you want to trace the execution process while you are executing FINDMAX.PRG, issue the following commands:

```
. SET STEP ON
. DO FINDMAX
```

Before each command line in FINDMAX.PRG is executed, you are prompted for directions:

```
Press SPACE to step, S to suspend, or Esc to cancel...
```

By pressing the space bar to execute each program step, you can observe the intermediate results between steps. (This process is equivalent to using the S command in the dBASE IV debugger.) To suspend or terminate the execution process, press S or the Esc key. To return to normal processing mode after the SET STEP ON operation, issue the SET STEP OFF command.

11

Exploring Advanced Topics

This chapter covers topics for advanced users. Here you find how to exchange data between dBASE IV and other computer programs (including spreadsheet programs such as 1-2-3®, VisiCalc®, and Multiplan®); how to use a non-dBASE program to access data in a dBASE IV database file; and how to import data created in other programs (written in such programming languages as BASIC, Pascal, and FORTRAN). This chapter also covers other powerful features of dBASE IV: the built-in compiler, the RunTime module, and the Structured Query Language (SQL).

Converting dBASE IV Files

You can convert dBASE IV files to a number of different formats so that you can use the data with other programs. The tips, tricks, and traps in this section show you how to convert dBASE IV files to ASCII text files (SDF format), VisiCalc (DIF® format), 1-2-3 (WKS format), Multiplan (SYLK format), and other programs.

11.1 Tip:

You may have to alter file formats to exchange data with other programs.

When you create a database file in dBASE IV, the contents of each record in that file are saved sequentially to a disk file in a unique format. This format may be quite different from that of a file created by another database program. Similarly, the format of data in disk files created by a word processor or by a spreadsheet program (such as 1-2-3) will be different.

Before you attempt to import a data file created by another computer program, you must determine its data format so that you can retrieve the information from the file. And if you need to use another program to process data files created by dBASE IV, you must convert those files into a format that the other program can understand.

The tips, tricks, and traps that follow use the EMPLOYEE.DBF file to illustrate different formats for text files that can be created from a dBASE IV database file. The file structure and its contents are shown in figures 11.1 and 11.2, respectively.

```
. USE EMPLOYEE
. DISPLAY STRUCTURE
Structure for database: C:EMPLOYEE.DBF
Number of data records:       10
Date of last update    : 04/20/88
Field  Field Name Type        Width    Dec    Index
1  ID_NO       Character      11               N
2  FIRST_NAME  Character      15               N
3  LAST_NAME   Character      15               N
4  POSITION    Character      10               N
5  EMPLY_DATE  Date            8               N
6  MALE        Logical         1               N
** Total **                   61
.
```

Fig. 11.1. *The file structure of EMPLOYEE.DBF.*

```
. LIST
Record#  ID_NO         FIRST_NAME  LAST_NAME    POSITION    EMPLY_DATE MALE
      1  123-45-6789 Thomas T.   Smith        President   03/01/81   .T.
      2  254-63-5691 Tina Y.     Thompson     VP          09/22/82   .F.
      3  467-34-6789 Peter F.    Watson       Manager     10/12/82   .T.
      4  732-08-4589 Doris Y.    Taylor       Sales Rep   08/14/83   .F.
      5  563-55-8900 Tyrone T.   Thorsen      Engineer    06/20/82   .T.
      6  823-46-6213 Cathy J.    Faust        Secretary   04/15/83   .F.
      7  554-34-7893 Vincent M.  Corso        Sales Rep   07/20/84   .T.
      8  321-65-9087 Jane W.     Kaiser       Accountant 11/22/82   .F.
      9  560-56-9321 Tina K.     Davidson     Trainee     05/16/86   .F.
     10  435-54-9876 James J.    Smith        Trainee     01/23/86   .T.
.
```

Fig. 11.2. *The contents of EMPLOYEE.DBF.*

Converting Data to ASCII

11.2 Tip:

To exchange data with other programs, use the SDF format.

When you convert a database file to System Data Format (SDF), all data is coded in ASCII format. SDF is considered a universal data format because most computer programs can retrieve data from an ASCII file. If you convert the contents of a database file created in dBASE IV to a text file in SDF format, for example, that file can be read by a word processor or by an application program written in BASIC.

11.3 Tip:

Use the COPY TO command to convert a database file to a text file in SDF format.

To convert an active database file to a text file in SDF format, use the COPY TO command and specify SDF as the file format at the end of the command:

. COPY TO < *name of text file*> SDF

Each record in the file you have converted is now written as a text line in ASCII format. A carriage return and line feed are added at the end of each record. (The carriage return positions the data pointer at the beginning of the text line. The line feed moves the data pointer to the next text line to be processed. The combination of a line feed and a carriage return is equivalent to pressing the Enter key.) Each text line ends with Enter (or Return). This information is important if you need to use other programs to access data in an SDF format file.

11.4 Tip:

Export the contents of a database file to a text file in SDF format with the COPY TO command.

To export the contents of EMPLOYEE.DBF to a text file (in SDF format) named EMPLOYEE.TXT, for example, use the following commands:

. USE EMPLOYEE
. COPY TO EMPLOYEE.TXT SDF

After the COPY operation, the EMPLOYEE.TXT contains the data records of the EMPLOYEE.DBT in SDF format.

You can display the text file created by the COPY TO command by using the TYPE command:

. TYPE < *name of text file*>

Use the TYPE EMPLOYEE.TXT command, for example, to display the contents of the EMPLOYEE.TXT file. You can stop the screen display temporarily by pressing Ctrl-S. Press any key to resume the screen listing after you have viewed a segment of text.

As you can see from figure 11.3, the contents of each EMPLOYEE.DBF data record have been converted into a text line. Information in the data fields is saved as continuous character strings (no separators divide the strings).

```
. TYPE EMPLOYEE.TXT
123-45-6789Thomas T.        Smith          President 19810301T
254-63-5691Tina Y.          Thompson       VP        19820922F
467-34-6789Peter F.         Watson         Manager   19821012T
732-00-4589Doris Y.         Taylor         Sales Rep 19830814F
563-55-8900Tyrone T.        Thorsen        Engineer  19820620T
823-46-6213Cathy J.         Faust          Secretary 19830415F
554-34-7893Vincent M.       Corso          Sales Rep 19840720T
321-65-9087Jane W.          Kaiser         Accountant19821122F
560-56-9321Tina K.          Davidson       Trainee   19860516F
435-54-9876James J.         Smith          Trainee   19860123T
```

Fig. 11.3. *The contents of the EMPLOYEE.TXT text file.*

Characters in a character field are saved as a fixed-length string. (The length of the string is determined by the field length specified in the database file's structure.) Dates are converted to a different format, and the value of the logical field is represented as T or F (without the familiar enclosing periods).

11.5 Tip: **To list the contents of a file to the printer, add the phrase TO PRINT at the end of the TYPE command.**

The format for the command that lists the contents of a file to the printer is as follows:

. TYPE < *name of text file*> TO PRINT

For example, the following command lists the contents of the EMPLOYEE.TXT file to the printer:

. TYPE EMPLOYEE.TXT TO PRINT

11.6 Tip: **Use delimiters to separate character strings in the text file.**

In SDF format, the contents of each record in the database file are saved as a continuous text line, and the contents of the record's data fields are saved as consecutive character strings, without separators. Data items saved in this continuous format may not be suitable for access by other application programs. For example, if you want to write a BASIC program to read the contents of data fields in a text line, these data-field values must be separated by a specific character (such as a comma).

To insert separators between the character strings in a text line, use the DELIMITED operator in the COPY TO command when you create a text file:

. COPY TO < *name of text file*> DELIMITED

The DELIMITED operator encloses the contents of a character field in a pair of double quotation marks and uses commas to separate the contents of data fields. For example, if you want to separate the character strings in a text file named EMPLOYEE.DAT (which is to be converted from EMPLOYEE.DBF), use the DELIMITED operator in the COPY TO command:

. USE EMPLOYEE
. COPY TO EMPLOYEE.DAT DELIMITED

Figure 11.4 shows the results of using delimiters for separating the character strings in the EMPLOYEE.DAT text file. In the figure, each line of the EMPLOYEE.DAT text file represents the contents of a data record in the EMPLOYEE.DBF database file. Values in the data fields are separated by commas. The character string in a character field is "trimmed" to exclude trailing spaces and enclosed in a pair of double quotation marks. Dates are saved as a string of digits representing the year, month, and day (as in 19810301 for March 1, 1981). The logical values .T. and .F. are stored as single letters, T and F, without periods. Values in numeric fields are saved in their original form.

```
. TYPE EMPLOYEE.DAT
"123-45-6789","Thomas T.","Smith","President",19810301,T
"254-63-5691","Tina Y.","Thompson","UP",19820922,F
"467-34-6789","Peter F.","Watson","Manager",19821012,T
"732-08-4589","Doris Y.","Taylor","Sales Rep",19830814,F
"563-55-8900","Tyrone T.","Thorsen","Engineer",19820620,T
"823-46-6213","Cathy J.","Faust","Secretary",19830415,F
"554-34-7893","Vincent M.","Corso","Sales Rep",19840720,T
"321-65-9087","Jane W.","Kaiser","Accountant",19821122,F
"560-56-9321","Tina K.","Davidson","Trainee",19860516,F
"435-54-9876","James J.","Smith","Trainee",19860123,T
```

Fig. 11.4. *The contents of the text file delimited with quotation marks.*

11.7 Tip: Use the DELIMITED WITH operator to define your own delimiters.

You can use the DELIMITED operator in a COPY TO command to convert the contents of a dBASE IV database file to a text file. The character strings in the text file's character fields are delimited by default with a pair of double quotation marks. If you want to use another symbol as the delimiter, specify it by using the DELIMITED WITH operator in the COPY TO command:

. COPY TO < *name of text file*> DELIMITED WITH < *delimiter symbol*>

For example, you can use a backslash in the text file as a delimiter for enclosing the contents of a character field in the database file. Figure 11.5 shows the text file created with the following commands:

```
. USE EMPLOYEE
. COPY TO STAFF.DAT DELIMITED WITH \
```

```
, USE EMPLOYEE
, COPY TO STAFF.DAT DELIMITED WITH \
       10 records copied
, TYPE STAFF.DAT
\123-45-6789\,\Thomas T.\,\Smith\,\President\,19810301,T
\254-63-5691\,\Tina Y.\,\Thompson\,\VP\,19820922,F
\467-34-6789\,\Peter F.\,\Watson\,\Manager\,19821012,T
\732-08-4589\,\Doris Y.\,\Taylor\,\Sales Rep\,19830814,F
\563-55-8900\,\Tyrone T.\,\Thorsen\,\Engineer\,19820628,T
\823-46-6213\,\Cathy J.\,\Faust\,\Secretary\,19830415,F
\554-34-7893\,\Vincent M.\,\Corso\,\Sales Rep\,19840720,T
\321-65-9087\,\Jane W.\,\Kaiser\,\Accountant\,19821122,F
\560-56-9321\,\Tina K.\,\Davidson\,\Trainee\,19860516,F
\435-54-9876\,\James J.\,\Smith\,\Trainee\,19860123,T
```

Fig. 11.5. *The contents of the text file delimited with backslashes.*

Note: As shown in figure 11.5, the character strings in the character fields are "trimmed" when the DELIMITED WITH operator is used in the COPY TO command.

11.8 Tip: **Use DELIMITED WITH BLANK to insert a blank space between two character strings in the text file.**

A common way to separate field values in the text file created from a database file with the COPY TO command is to use a blank space as a delimiter. To do this, use the DELIMITED WITH BLANK clause in the COPY TO command while you are converting the database file.

The field values in each EMPLOYEE.DBF record are separated with a single space when the record is converted to a text line in the STAFF1.DAT text file (see fig. 11.6). In the figure, all the field values, regardless of their types, are separated by single spaces. The character strings in the original character fields are "trimmed."

```
. USE EMPLOYEE
. COPY TO STAFF1.DAT DELIMITED WITH BLANK
    10 records copied
. TYPE STAFF1.DAT
123-45-6789 Thomas T. Smith President 19810301 T
254-63-5691 Tina Y. Thompson VP 19820922 F
467-34-6789 Peter F. Watson Manager 19821012 T
732-08-4589 Doris Y. Taylor Sales Rep 19830814 F
563-55-8900 Tyrone T. Thorsen Engineer 19820620 T
823-46-6213 Cathy J. Faust Secretary 19830415 F
554-34-7893 Vincent M. Corso Sales Rep 19840720 T
321-65-9087 Jane W. Kaiser Accountant 19821122 F
560-56-9321 Tina K. Davidson Trainee 19860516 F
435-54-9876 James J. Smith Trainee 19860123 T
```

Fig. 11.6. *The contents of the text file delimited with blank spaces.*

11.9 Trick: **Use the FIELDS operator to copy the contents of selected data fields to a text file.**

When you create a text file in SDF format from an existing database file, you can select a specific data field or fields from the database file by using the FIELDS operator in the COPY TO command:

. COPY FIELDS < *field list* > TO < *name of text file* > SDF

For example, to create the ROSTER.TXT file shown in figure 11.7, which contains only the first and last names from EMPLOYEE.DBF, issue the following commands:

. USE EMPLOYEE
. COPY FIELDS FIRST _ NAME, LAST _ NAME TO ROSTER.TXT SDF

In figure 11.7, notice that the character strings in the character fields (FIRST_ NAME and LAST_ NAME) are not "trimmed" to save text in SDF format when you use the COPY FIELDS TO command. If you want to "trim" the character strings and delimit them with the default delimiter symbols (double quotation marks) or a custom delimiter symbol, use the DELIMITED WITH operator in the COPY FIELDS command. For example, after you issue the USE EMPLOYEE command, enter any of the following commands:

```
. USE EMPLOYEE
. COPY FIELDS FIRST_NAME, LAST_NAME TO ROSTER.TXT SDF
     10 records copied
. TYPE ROSTER.TXT
Thomas T.     Smith
Tina Y.       Thompson
Peter F.      Watson
Doris Y.      Taylor
Tyrone T.     Thorsen
Cathy J.      Faust
Vincent M.    Corso
Jane W.       Kaiser
Tina K.       Davidson
James J.      Smith
```

Fig. 11.7. ROSTER.TXT created with the COPY TO operation.

. COPY FIELDS FIRST _ NAME, LAST _ NAME TO ROSTER.TXT DELIMITED

. COPY FIELDS FIRST _ NAME, LAST _ NAME TO ROSTER.TXT
DELIMITED WITH \

. COPY FIELDS FIRST _ NAME, LAST _ NAME TO ROSTER.TXT
DELIMITED WITH BLANK

11.10 Tip: **Use the delimited format for merge applications.**

Several popular word processing programs, such as Microsoft Word
and WordStar, use the delimited format for merged data files. When
you embed field names in your form letter documents, the information
from your data file is substituted at print time.

Some programs, such as Microsoft Word, require that a "header" line
be added to the data file to define the field names. For example,
suppose that you have fields for Name, Address, City, State, and ZIP
that you want to use in your document. You can use this command to
copy records to a file in delimited format:

. COPY FIELDS NAME, ADDRESS, CITY, STATE, ZIP TO NAMES.DOC
DELIMITED

Then load the NAMES.DOC file into the word processor and add the header line to the top of the file:

    name, address, city, state, ZIP

Your file might look like this:

    name, address, city, state, ZIP
    "John Smith","1234 Main St.","Ardmore","OK","79876"
    "Mary Jones","3456 Center Rd.","Tulsa","OK","78965"

In your document, you include the same field names. Microsoft Word requires you to surround the names with the double angle-bracket character, as shown in figure 11.8.

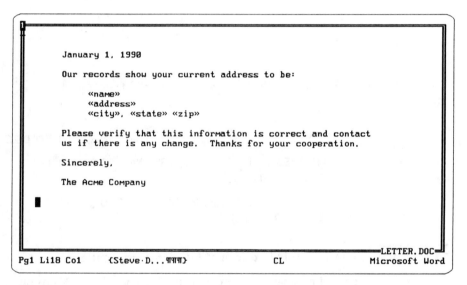

Fig. 11.8. *The double angle-bracket character used to delimit field names.*

11.11 Trick: **Use SET FILTER TO to copy selected records from a database file to a text file.**

If you use the SET FILTER TO command to filter the data records in a database file before issuing the COPY TO command, you can copy selected records from the database file to a text file. The SET FILTER TO command allows you to set a filter condition so that only those data records that meet the condition are subjected to the COPY TO operation.

If you want to copy the EMPLOYEE.DBF records that belong to female employees, for example, specify the filter condition before copying the records to a text file named FEMALES.TXT. Use the following commands:

```
. USE EMPLOYEE
. SET FILTER TO .NOT. MALE
. COPY TO FEMALES.TXT SDF
```

The SET FILTER command specifies that only records whose values in the logical field MALE that are .F. are to be selected for the COPY TO operation that follows. The text file (FEMALES.TXT) created by the COPY TO operation contains only records belonging to female employees in EMPLOYEE.DBF (see fig. 11.9).

```
. USE EMPLOYEE
. SET FILTER TO .NOT. MALE
. LIST
Record#  ID_NO        FIRST_NAME   LAST_NAME    POSITION    EMPLY_DATE MALE
      2  254-63-5691 Tina Y.      Thompson     VP          09/22/82  .F.
      4  732-88-4589 Doris Y.     Taylor       Sales Rep   08/14/83  .F.
      6  823-46-6213 Cathy J.     Faust        Secretary   04/15/83  .F.
      8  321-65-9087 Jane W.      Kaiser       Accountant  11/22/82  .F.
      9  560-56-9321 Tina K.      Davidson     Trainee     05/16/86  .F.

. COPY TO FEMALES.TXT SDF
      5 records copied
. TYPE FEMALES.TXT
254-63-5691Tina Y.      Thompson     VP        19820922F
732-88-4589Doris Y.     Taylor       Sales Rep 19830814F
823-46-6213Cathy J.     Faust        Secretary 19830415F
321-65-9087Jane W.      Kaiser       Accountant19821122F
560-56-9321Tina K.      Davidson     Trainee   19860516F
```

Fig. 11.9. *Setting filter conditions for the COPY TO operation.*

Other examples of filter conditions are the following:

. SET FILTER TO POSITION="Trainee"

. SET FILTER TO POSITION="Trainee" .OR. MALE

. SET FILTER TO POSITION="Trainee" .AND.
EMPLY_DATE>{1/1/85}

11.12 Trick: **To copy a block of records from a database file to a text file, set the record range in a scope condition.**

If you want to copy a block of data records from a dBASE IV database file to a text file, specify the record range as a scope condition in the COPY TO command. To select the set of records to be copied, use the RECNO( ) function to define the record range. For example, if you want to copy the first five records of EMPLOYEE.DBF to a text file named PARTONE.TXT, specify the record range as follows:

. COPY TO PARTONE.TXT SDF FOR RECNO( ) <=5

You can copy one or more sections of the records in EMPLOYEE.DBF to a text file with the following commands:

. COPY TO TEXTFILE SDF FOR RECNO( ) >=5 .AND. RECONO( )<=8

. COPY TO TEXTFILE DELIMITED FOR (RECNO( ) >=2 .AND.
RECNO( ) <=4) .OR. (RECNO( ) >=6 .AND. RECNO( ) <=8)

The first of these COPY TO operations copies records 5 through 8 from EMPLOYEE.DBF to a text file; the second COPY TO statement copies records 2 through 4 and 6 through 8 to another text file.

Converting Data to VisiCalc

11.13 Tip: **Use DIF format to share dBASE IV database files with VisiCalc.**

You can use the VisiCalc spreadsheet program to process data you have saved in a dBASE IV database file. First, use the COPY TO command to convert the contents of the file to a disk file in DIF format (Data Interchange Format). To do this, specify DIF as the file type to be converted with the COPY TO command:

. COPY TO < *name of DIF file*> DIF

When you convert a database file to a DIF file, each record in the database file is converted as a row in the VisiCalc spreadsheet. Each data field of the database file is saved as a spreadsheet column in DIF format.

For example, you can convert the data in EMPLOYEE.DBF to a disk file in DIF format by using the following commands:

```
. USE EMPLOYEE
. COPY TO EMPLOYEE DIF
```

The COPY TO operation creates a disk file in DIF format and automatically attaches a .DIF file extension if you do not specify a file extension.

If you want to view the DIF file in spreadsheet format, you must use the VisiCalc program to display the file. (You cannot use the TYPE command to display the contents of the disk file in a meaningful format.)

Converting Data to 1-2-3

11.14 Tip: **Use WKS format to share dBASE IV database files with 1-2-3.**

To use the 1-2-3 spreadsheet program to access data you have saved in a dBASE IV database file, use the COPY TO command. COPY TO converts the contents of the database file to a disk file in WKS format. Specify WKS as the file type to be converted with the COPY TO command:

```
. COPY TO < name of WKS file> WKS
```

When you convert a database file to a WKS file, each record in the database file is converted to a row in the 1-2-3 spreadsheet. Each data field is saved as a spreadsheet column in WKS format.

To convert the data in EMPLOYEE.DBF to a disk file in WKS format, for example, use the following commands:

```
. USE EMPLOYEE
. COPY TO EMPLOYEE WKS
```

The COPY TO operation creates a disk file in WKS format and automatically attaches the file extension .WKS if you do not specify a file extension.

If you want to view the WKS file in spreadsheet format, you must use 1-2-3 to display it. (You cannot use the TYPE command to display the contents of the disk file in a meaningful format.) A WKS file created with the COPY TO command is shown in figure 11.10. The field names are saved as the first row of the spreadsheet table.

```
A1: [W11] 'ID_NO                                              READY

         A           B            C           D         E     F      G
 1  ID_NO       FIRST_NAME   LAST_NAME    POSITION  EMPLY_DAMALE
 2  123-45-6789Thomas T.     Smith        President 19810301T
 3  254-63-5691Tina Y.       Thompson     VP        19820922F
 4  467-34-6789Peter F.      Watson       Manager   19821012T
 5  732-08-4589Doris Y.      Taylor       Sales Rep 19830814F
 6  563-55-8900Tyrone T.     Thorsen      Engineer  19820620T
 7  823-46-6213Cathy J.      Faust        Secretary 19830415F
 8  554-34-7893Vincent M.    Corso        Sales Rep 19840720T
 9  321-65-9087Jane W.       Kaiser       Accountant19821122F
10  560-56-9321Tina K.       Davidson     Trainee   19860516F
11  435-54-9876James J.      Smith        Trainee   19860123T
12
13
14
15
16
17
18
19
20
26-Apr-87  01:12 PM    HAL
```

Fig. 11.10. The 1-2-3 spreadsheet file converted from EMPLOYEE.DBF.

11.15 Trick: **Use WKS format to exchange data between dBASE IV and Release 2.01 of 1-2-3.**

When you are using Release 1A of 1-2-3, spreadsheet files are saved in WKS format. Although Release 2.01 of the program stores its spreadsheet files in WK1 format, spreadsheets saved in WKS format can be read by Release 2.01.

If you need to use Release 2.01 of 1-2-3 to access the data in a dBASE IV database file, convert the database file to a disk file in WKS format by using the COPY TO command:

. COPY TO < *name of WKS file*> WKS

11.16 Trap: **When you use the COPY TO operation to convert a database file to a spreadsheet for Release 2.01 of 1-2-3, do not specify WK1 as the file type.**

If you specify WK1 as the file type when you use the COPY TO operation to convert a database file to a spreadsheet for Release 2.01 of 1-2-3, the error message Unrecognized phrase/keyword in command is displayed, and the COPY operation is ignored.

Converting Data to Multiplan

11.17 Tip: **Use SYLK format to share dBASE IV database files with the Multiplan spreadsheet program.**

You can use the Multiplan spreadsheet program to access data you have saved in a dBASE IV database file. Use the COPY TO command to convert the contents of the database file to a disk file in SYLK (Symbolic Link) format. To do this, specify SYLK as the file type to be converted with the COPY command:

. COPY TO < *name of SYLK file*> SYLK

When you convert a database file to a SYLK file, each record in the database file is converted to a row in the spreadsheet used by Multiplan. Each data field of the database file is saved as a spreadsheet column in SYLK format.

For example, you can convert the data in EMPLOYEE.DBF to a disk file in SYLK format with the following commands:

. USE EMPLOYEE
. COPY TO PERSONAL SYLK

The disk file created by the COPY TO command is in SYLK format. No file extension is added to the disk file unless you specify one in the COPY TO command.

To view the SYLK file in spreadsheet format, you must use the Multiplan spreadsheet program to display it. (You cannot use the TYPE command to display the contents of the disk file in a meaningful format.)

Converting Data for Use with Other Programs

11.18 Tip:

Use the EXPORT TO command to convert a database file to a PFS®:File, RapidFile™, Framework II™, or dBASE II file.

In dBASE IV, you can use the EXPORT TO command to convert files to formats usable by PFS:File, RapidFile, Framework II, or dBASE II. Specify the type of file after the command and target file name. For example, to convert a database file created by dBASE IV to a disk file in PFS format, use the following sequence:

. EXPORT TO < *name of PFS file*> PFS

In the following example, the EXPORT TO command creates a disk file in PFS format:

. EXPORT TO APFSFILE PFS

Because a PFS file normally has no file extension, the command does not add a file extension to the PFS file unless you specify an extension.

The EXPORT TO command performs a function similar to that of a COPY TO command when it is used to convert a database file to a disk file in a particular data format. But the EXPORT TO command does more than the COPY TO command: it allows you to format the data fields in the database file with a format (.FMT) file before exporting the data to a PFS file.

For example, you can export to a PFS file the contents of EMPLOYEE.DBF, whose data fields are defined with the format file EMPLOYEE.FMT, by using the following commands:

. USE EMPLOYEE
. SET FORMAT TO EMPLOYEE
. EXPORT TO EMPLOYEE.PFS

For exporting to other programs, use the appropriate file type designator:

Program	Type
PFS:File	PFS
dBASE II	DBASEII
FrameWork II	FW2
RapidFile	RPD

As with the COPY TO command, you can specify the fields to be copied with the FIELDS operator, and you can specify a scope or condition to copy selected records.

11.19 Trap: **You can lose data if your field lengths are incompatible.**

dBASE IV allows you to have fields up to 254 characters in length, and you can have up to 255 fields. Some programs do not allow fields of this length or will not allow as many fields. If you try to export records with more fields or longer fields than the target program will support, data may be truncated, and some data may be lost as a result. Before exporting data, be sure that the target program can accept the length and number of fields used.

11.20 Tip: **Use the Control Center Tools menu to convert files to another format.**

You can easily export files from dBASE IV to other formats using the Control Center. Pull down the **Tools** menu (Alt-T), select **Export**, and then choose the format to which you want to convert:

Program/Format name	File extension of output file
RapidFile	.RPD
dBASE II	.DB2
Framework II	.FW2
1-2-3	.WKS
VisiCalc	.DIF
PFS:File	
SYLK-Multiplan	
Text fixed-length (SDF)	.TXT
Blank delimited	.TXT
Character delimited (")	.TXT

Note that if you select **Character delimited**, you can specify the character to use as the delimiter.

Choose the source file from the picklist (see fig. 11.11), and then press Enter. The records are then copied to the new file.

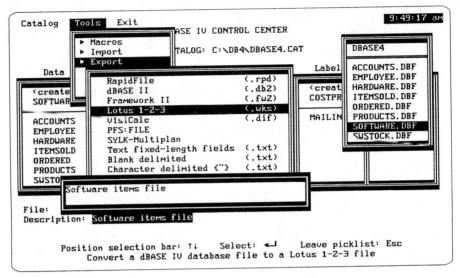

Fig. 11.11. *Using the Tools Export menu to convert database files.*

11.21 Trap: **Do not use an existing file name for the converted disk file unless SET SAFETY ON is in effect.**

When you use the COPY TO or EXPORT TO commands, or when you use the Control Center **Export** option, to convert a database file created by dBASE IV to a disk file of another format, do not use an existing file name. If you do, the converted disk file may replace the original database file.

For example, the following command usage is not recommended:

```
. USE EMPLOYEE
. COPY TO EMPLOYEE.DBF SYLK
```

If the default setting SET SAFETY ON is in effect when the COPY TO command is executed, you are informed that the file already exists and you are prompted to indicate whether you want to overwrite it. However, if you have set SET SAFETY to OFF in previous operations, the original database file is overwritten automatically without warning. To protect your data during the file conversion operation, issue the SET SAFETY ON command so that you will be warned if you try to overwrite an existing file.

Processing Data

Using external programming languages, you can use your dBASE IV data to produce charts and graphs. This section offers tips, tricks, and traps that show you one way to accomplish this kind of task.

Using External Programs To Process Data

11.22 Trick: **Use an external program to process data created by dBASE IV.**

Although the dBASE IV command language is one of the most powerful programming languages offered as part of a database program, the mathematical or graphics capabilities provided by such programming languages as FORTRAN, Pascal, or BASIC offer additional flexibility. These mathematical tools are helpful in developing programs that involve complex computations.

You can process data created within dBASE IV by executing a program written in another language (such as BASIC) at the dot prompt. To do so, convert the contents of a database file to a text file in the format that the external program can read. Then execute the external program at the dot prompt.

11.23 Trap: **Be sure that you have enough memory to run an external program.**

As mentioned in previous chapters, because dBASE IV uses most of the system memory on a 640K system, you should be sure that enough memory is available before running an external program from within dBASE IV. If not enough memory is available, you may need to exit dBASE IV before running the external application.

Producing a Pie Graph

11.24 Trick: **Use a BASIC program to produce a pie graph based on the data in a database file.**

dBASE IV does not provide commands for drawing the lines and circles needed for many business graphs (such as line and pie graphs).

A solution to this problem is to write an external program in a conventional language (such as BASIC). In this way, you can produce the graphs you need, based on the data stored in your dBASE IV database file.

Convert the contents of the database file to a text file format that the external program can recognize. For example, you can write a program in BASIC to create a pie graph based on the values in SWSALES.DBF. The file structure and contents of SWSALES.DBF are shown in figure 11.12.

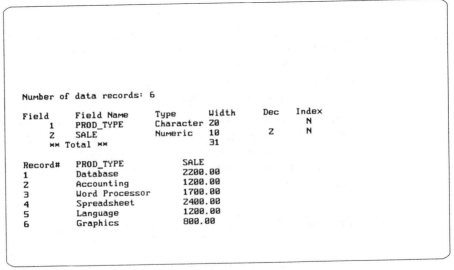

```
Number of data records: 6

Field    Field Name    Type       Width   Dec   Index
   1     PROD_TYPE     Character  20            N
   2     SALE          Numeric    10      2     N
         ** Total **              31

Record#  PROD_TYPE          SALE
1        Database           2200.00
2        Accounting         1200.00
3        Word Processor     1700.00
4        Spreadsheet        2400.00
5        Language           1200.00
6        Graphics           800.00
```

Fig. 11.12. The file structure and contents of SWSALES.DBF.

Before processing the data in the SWSALES.DBF database file, convert its contents to a text file (named PIEDATA.DAT) in the format BASIC can read. To do this, issue the following commands:

```
. USE SWSALES
. COPY TO PIEDATA.DAT DELIMITED
```

The text file (PIEDATA.DAT) created by the COPY TO command contains the labels and values needed to display a pie graph. After the converted data has been stored in the format BASIC can read, execute the program. The following BASIC program (PIEGRAPH.BAS) displays the data in the PIEDATA.DAT file as a pie graph (shown in fig. 11.13):

```
10 '*** PIEGRAPH.BAS
20 'L$(I), V(I) are arrays for storing the labels and values
30 'for the Ith record of PIEDATA.DBF
40 'N=number of data records
50 KEY OFF:SCREEN 1:WIDTH 80:CLS
60 DIM L$(10),V(10)
70 '*** Initialize variables
80 PI=3.14159                    'Value of pi
90 XC=330: YC=95                 'Set center of the pie graph
100 RADIUS=150                   'Set radius of the circle
110 '*** Reading data from the data file PIEDATA.DAT
120 OPEN "PIEDATA.DAT" FOR INPUT AS #1
130 K=0
140 IF EOF(1) THEN 180
150 K=K+1
160 INPUT #1,L$(K),V(K)
170 GOTO 140
180 N=K                          'number of records or divisions
190 '*** Summing up the values in the V-array
200 SUM=0
210 FOR I=1 TO N
220 SUM=SUM+V(I)
230 NEXT
240 '*** Assign the graph title
250 TITLE$="SOFTWARE SALES BY PRODUCT TYPE"
260 CLS
270 '*** Draw a double-line box
280 LINE(0,0) - (639,180),,B
290 LINE(3,2) - (636,178),,B
300 '*** Display the graph title
310 LOCATE 2,(80-LEN(TITLE$))/2:PRINT TITLE$
320 '*** Draw the circle center at (XC,YC)
330 CIRCLE(XC,YC),RADIUS,,,,5/11
340 '*** Draw division lines
350 A0=0                         'The beginning angle
360 FOR I=1 TO N
370 A=A0+2*3.14156*(V(I)/SUM)    'The angle of the arc
380 X=XC+RADIUS*COS(A)
390 Y=YC+RADIUS*SIN(A)*5/11
400 LINE (XC,YC) - (X,Y)
410 '*** Position a label at (R,C)
```

```
420 MIDPOINT=AØ +(A-AØ)/2
430 YL=YC +(RADIUS +4)*SIN(MIDPOINT)*5/11
440 XL=XC +(RADIUS +4)*COS(MIDPOINT)
450 IF XL>(XC +1Ø) THEN 5ØØ
460 IF XL <(XC-1Ø) THEN 49Ø
470 XL=XL-LEN(L$(I))/16
480 GOTO 5ØØ
490 XL=XL-LEN(L$(I))*8
500 R=INT(YL/8) +1
510 C=INT(XL/8) +1
520 LOCATE R,C:PRINT L$(I)
530 AØ=A
540 NEXT I
550 LOCATE 24,18:INPUT AKEY
560 SYSTEM
570 END
```

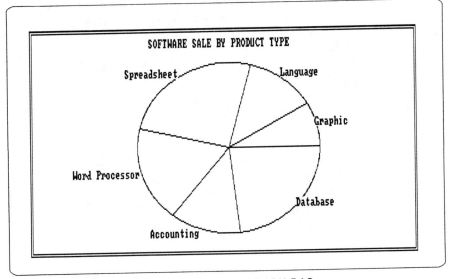

Fig.11.13. *The pie graph produced by PIEGRAPH.BAS.*

The pie graph shown in figure 11.13 was produced by executing the BASIC program at the dot prompt:

. RUN BASICA PIEGRAPH

When the RUN command is processed, the program is executed and control is transferred to the BASIC program. After the BASIC program has been processed, issue the SYSTEM command within the BASIC program to pass control back to dBASE IV.

Any system programs needed to process an external program with the RUN command must be present in the current directory or have been defined in the DOS PATH command. (See Chapter 1 for a discussion of how to execute an external program by using the RUN command in dBASE IV.)

Importing Data

You easily can import data to dBASE IV from other programs, including PFS:File, dBASE II, FrameWork II, RapidFile, and 1-2-3. This section discusses ways to accomplish this task from both the dot prompt and the Control Center.

Importing Data from ASCII Files

11.25 Tip: **Use the APPEND command to import data from a text file.**

Data created by other applications programs and saved in an ASCII text file can be read into a dBASE IV file. Depending on the way in which data elements in the file are delimited, you can append the contents of the text file to a database file with a defined file structure. The format of the APPEND command is as follows:

. APPEND FROM $<$ *name of text file* $>$ DELIMITED WITH $<$ *delimiter* $>$

For example, to read the data in the STAFF.DAT text file into the database file named PERSONAL.DBF, issue the following commands:

. USE PERSONAL
. APPEND FROM STAFF.DAT DELIMITED WITH \

The backslash is defined as the delimiter in the APPEND command. To see what the contents of the text file look like, refer to figure 11.14. All the character strings are delimited with backslashes, and all the data elements are separated by commas.

```
. TYPE STAFF.DAT
\123-45-6789\,\Thomas T.\,\Smith\,\President\,19810301,T
\254-63-5691\,\Tina Y.\,\Thompson\,\VP\,19820922,F
\467-34-6789\,\Peter F.\,\Watson\,\Manager\,19821012,T
\732-08-4589\,\Doris Y.\,\Taylor\,\Sales Rep\,19830814,F
\563-55-0900\,\Tyrone T.\,\Thorsen\,\Engineer\,19820620,T
\823-46-6213\,\Cathy J.\,\Faust\,\Secretary\,19830415,F
\554-34-7893\,\Vincent M.\,\Corso\,\Sales Rep\,19810720,T
\321-65-9087\,\Jane W.\,\Kaiser\,\Accountant\,19821122,F
\560-56-9321\,\Tina K.\,\Davidson\,\Trainee\,19860516,F
\435-54-9876\,\James J.\,\Smith\,\Trainee\,19860123,T
```

Fig. 11.14. *The contents of the STAFF.DAT text file.*

The data elements of the text file's fields are determined by the file structure of the active database file. For example, the letter T or F at the end of each line in the STAFF.DAT text file can be interpreted as the value of either a character field or a logical field, depending on the file structure of PERSONAL.DBF. Similarly, the string of numeric digits in a text line (such as 19810301) can be treated as a date (3/1/81) or a numeric value, based on the type of data field to which it is to be appended. The file structure of PERSONAL.DBF, which is used to store the data imported from STAFF.DAT, is shown in figure 11.15.

When you convert the contents of a text file to a database file with the APPEND command, each line of the text file is saved as a data record. Data elements in a text line are saved in the data fields, whose types and lengths are defined by the file structure of the database file. For example, the contents of PERSONAL.DBF, whose records are appended by importing the contents of the STAFF.DAT text file, are shown in figure 11.16.

```
Number of data records: 0

Field     Field Name    Type         Width    Dec   Index
    1     ID_NO         Character      11            N
    2     FIRST_NAME    Character      15            N
    3     LAST_NAME     Character      15            N
    4     POSITION      Character      10            N
    5     EMPLY_DATE    Date            8            N
    6     MALE          Logical         1            N
** Total **                           61
```

Fig. 11.15. *The file structure of PERSONAL.DBF.*

```
. USE PERSONAL
. APPEND FROM STAFF.DAT DELIMITED WITH \
     10 records added
. LIST
Record#  ID_NO        FIRST_NAME    LAST_NAME     POSITION    EMPLY_DATE  MALE
     1   123-45-6789  Thomas T.     Smith         President   03/01/81    .T.
     2   254-63-5691  Tina Y.       Thompson      VP          09/22/82    .F.
     3   467-34-6789  Peter F.      Watson        Manager     10/12/82    .T.
     4   732-08-4589  Doris Y.      Taylor        Sales Rep   08/14/83    .F.
     5   563-55-8900  Tyrone T.     Thorsen       Engineer    06/20/82    .T.
     6   823-46-6213  Cathy J.      Faust         Secretary   04/15/83    .F.
     7   554-34-7893  Vincent M.    Corso         Sales Rep   07/20/84    .T.
     8   321-65-9087  Jane W.       Kaiser        Accountant  11/22/82    .F.
     9   560-56-9321  Tina K.       Davidson      Trainee     05/16/86    .F.
    10   435-54-9876  James J.      Smith         Trainee     01/23/86    .T.
```

Fig. 11.16. *The database file converted from the STAFF.DAT text file.*

11.26 Tip: **Use a delimiter to identify a character string in an imported text file.**

Although you can import an ASCII text file in SDF format (System Data Format) without using a delimiter to identify the character strings, doing so is not recommended. If you do not delimit character strings with a delimiter symbol (quotation marks or backslashes, for example), all the character strings must be defined in a fixed length. And each string occupies the same number of characters regardless of the actual length of the string.

For example, you can read the first data element in a line of a file in SDF format into the character field LAST_NAME, whose field length is defined as 10 characters. The first 10 characters of the text line are used for the field contents. As a result, every character string in the beginning of the text line must be 10 characters long. If the actual string is shorter than 10 characters, you must fill the string with blank spaces:

```
JOHN       SMITH
JONATHAN   DAVIDSON
JO         LEE
```

These blank spaces waste disk space.

A better approach is to enclose the character strings with delimiters (such as quotation marks) so that only the actual string of characters is saved in the text file:

```
"JOHN","SMITH"
"JONATHAN","DAVIDSON"
"JO","LEE"
```

Importing Data from Other Programs

11.27 Tip: **Use the TYPE operator to import data from disk files created by another program.**

You can convert data files created by spreadsheet programs and other filing programs to dBASE IV database files by using the TYPE operator in the APPEND command:

```
. APPEND FROM < name of disk file> TYPE < file type>
```

The file types supported for importing into dBASE IV are listed here:

Name of Program	File Type
1-2-3 (release 1A)	WKS
1-2-3 (release 2)	WK1
VisiCalc	DIF
Multiplan	SYLK
RapidFile	RPD
FrameWork II	FW2

Here are three examples of how the file types are used:

```
. USE SALEDATA
. APPEND FROM SALES.WKS TYPE WKS

. USE PRODUCTS
. APPEND FROM SALEITEM.DIF TYPE DIF

. USE PERSONAL
. APPEND FROM STAFF TYPE SYLK
```

11.28 Tip:

Use the IMPORT command to convert a PFS:File, RapidFile, Framework II, or dBASE II file to dBASE IV format.

In dBASE IV, you can use the IMPORT FROM command to convert files from PFS:File, RapidFile, Framework II, or dBASE II. Specify the type of file after the command and source file name. For example, to convert a database file created in PFS format, use the following sequence:

```
. IMPORT FROM < name of PFS file> PFS
```

For importing from other programs, use the appropriate file type designator:

Program	Type
PFS:File	PFS
dBASE II	DBASEII
FrameWork II	FW2
RapidFile	RPD
1-2-3	WK1

Using the Control Center To Import Files

11.29 Tip: **Use the Control Center to import files.**

You can easily import files using the Control Center. Pull down the **Tools** menu (Alt-T), select **Import**, and then select the format of the source file (see fig. 11.17).

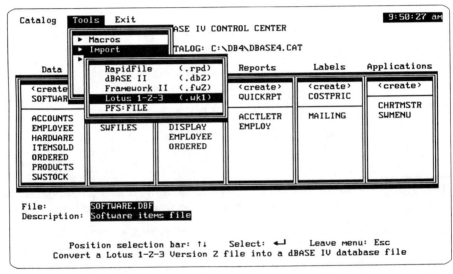

Fig. 11.17. *Using the Tools Import menu to convert database files.*

Choose the source file name from the picklist presented. If the file is not in the current directory, select the appropriate directory from the picklist. After you find the source file, highlight it and press Enter. The records are then copied to a dBASE IV file.

11.30 Trap: **The import function cannot directly convert 1-2-3 Release 1A (.WKS) files.**

Notice that the only 1-2-3 format supported by the **Import** operation is the WK1 format. If you need to import .WKS files, use the APPEND FROM command. Or you can use the database design screen, select the **Append** menu, and then select the **Copy records from non-dBASE file** option. This will allow you to specify a WKS file format.

Using the dBASE IV Compiler

Previous versions of dBASE used a command interpreter to execute program files. This means that each command line is interpreted by the dBASE system each time it is encountered in a program. The disadvantage to languages that use an interpreter is that the interpretation process can slow program execution speed.

dBASE IV compiles programs before executing them. This means that the entire program is converted to a machine-language program (object code) before the program is executed for the first time. Compiled programs can run much faster because the interpretation process is eliminated.

The disadvantage to compiling is that when the program file is first run, it can take several seconds for the compilation process to be completed. When you have created and executed program files and report, screen, and label format files with dBASE IV, you probably have noticed the Compiling... message and the delay before execution begins. The longer the program or the more complex the format file, the more time it takes to compile. When you make changes to the program or format file, it must be recompiled before execution.

11.31 Trap: **Compiled files cannot be used with earlier versions of dBASE.**

Previous versions of dBASE did not compile program files. Therefore, after you have compiled a dBASE IV file, the resulting object code can be run only using dBASE IV. dBASE IV program object-code files can be recognized by the file extension .DBO.

If you need to run a program under dBASE III or dBASE III Plus, you can use the source-code (.PRG) program file. You must be sure, however, that no new dBASE IV commands or functions are included in the program, because these will not be recognized by earlier versions of dBASE.

Using the RunTime Module

11.32 Tip: **Use the RunTime module if you plan to distribute dBASE IV program applications.**

If you will be developing programs for distribution to others, you may want to use the dBASE IV Developer's Edition. The Developer's Edition contains a RunTime distribution module, which allows your dBASE IV program files to be run by persons who do not have a copy of dBASE IV.

The RunTime system uses two utility programs to convert your applications for distribution: BUILD and DBLINK. The BUILD program compiles your dBASE IV programs into a format that cannot be modified by other users. The program thereby protects your code from being altered by unauthorized persons. DBLINK can take several related dBASE IV object files and link them into a single executable file. This feature allows you to have fewer files on your distribution disk.

11.33 Trap: **Compiled code cannot be modified.**

Because code cannot be modified after it is compiled, do not use RunTime until your application has been thoroughly tested. Use the dBASE IV debugger to help find problems in your programs (see Chapter 10). If any errors are found, you can modify your source code (.PRG) file, and then recompile the program. Because using the RunTime utilities creates an extra step in the process of preparing your programs for distribution, be sure that your program is as nearly perfect as you can make it before using RunTime.

Using Source Code from Other Compilers

11.34 Tip: **Use Step IVWard™ to convert programs created for other dBASE compilers.**

A number of compilers for dBASE III Plus and dBASE IV code are available from third-party software vendors. The most popular of these are Clipper™, FoxBase, and QuickSilver™. Although these programs support an extended set of dBASE commands, the programs may limit the dBASE commands that you can use in compiled applications.

Ashton-Tate publishes a program called Step IVWard that will convert source code created for these compilers to dBASE IV program code. If you have previously created applications for use with one of these compilers, you may want to purchase Step IVWard to facilitate the process of converting your code to dBASE IV.

Using SQL

Just as dBASE has become a standard relational database language for microcomputers, SQL (Structured Query Language) has become a standard language for accessing relational databases in the mainframe and minicomputer world. By offering a version of SQL with dBASE IV, Ashton-Tate hopes to bridge the microcomputer, minicomputer, and mainframe computer environments, making database files available to users at various levels.

An advantage of SQL is that data can be accessed using a minimum number of commands. Although SQL may appear to be simple, that impression is deceptive. The language actually is quite complex and cannot be covered within the scope of this book. However, a brief introduction to SQL can give you some idea of the alternative ways of accessing data that are available to you with dBASE IV SQL. Also refer to Appendix D for a summary of the SQL commands.

Learning SQL Basics

11.35 Tip: **Learn the basic concepts of SQL.**

In dBASE, you are accustomed to thinking of data in terms of records and fields. A record can contain many fields, and a database file can contain many records. In SQL, a database file is called a *table*. A table contains rows and columns. This concept is similar to the way data is handled in spreadsheets, such as Multiplan or 1-2-3. In dBASE terms, a row is equivalent to a record, and a column is equivalent to a field. (You can understand tables easily by visualizing how data is displayed in dBASE IV's Browse mode: each record is on a row, each field is in a column.) All SQL commands refer to the rows and columns of a table.

11.36 Tip: **Access SQL mode from the dot prompt or within your program files.**

Because some of the SQL and dBASE IV commands are similar, to use SQL commands, you must be in SQL mode. Once in SQL mode, you can use SQL commands plus many of the dBASE IV commands and functions.

From the dBASE IV dot prompt, you can enter SQL mode using the following command:

```
. SET SQL ON
```

You can tell when you are in SQL mode because the dot prompt becomes an SQL dot prompt:

```
SQL.
```

To leave SQL mode and return to the dBASE IV dot prompt, use the following command:

```
SQL. SET SQL OFF
```

You also can use the SET SQL ON/OFF commands within your dBASE IV programs. These commands allow you to switch between dBASE IV and SQL operations.

11.37 Trick: **Have dBASE IV run in SQL mode automatically.**

If you want to start dBASE IV in SQL mode, you can place one of these statements in your CONFIG.DB file:

```
SQL = ON
```

or

```
COMMAND = SET SQL ON
```

See Chapter 2 for more information on using the CONFIG.DB file to set up your programming environment.

11.38 Trap: **If you forget to end an SQL command with a semicolon, you will get an error message.**

In dBASE IV programming, a semicolon usually means continuation. The semicolon is used to show that a command line continues on the next line. This convention can cause confusion because the semicolon means the opposite in SQL mode; in SQL mode, the semicolon is used to indicate the end of a command. SQL commands may be spread out over several lines to make them more readable. The program interprets a semicolon as the termination of the command.

When you leave off the semicolon from the end of an SQL command, you get an error message (see fig. 11.18). To add the semicolon, select **Edit** from the error box. The cursor is then placed at the end of the command line so that you can complete the statement.

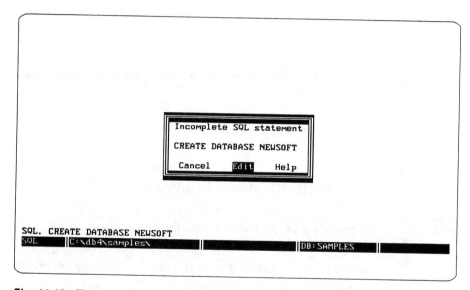

Fig. 11.18. The error box displayed when an SQL statement is incomplete.

11.39 Trick: Use the editing window to enter multi-line commands.

SQL allows you to enter statements on multiple lines for easier reading. As mentioned earlier, the semicolon indicates the end of the command in SQL. To type statements on separate lines before ending the command, use the Ctrl-Home key to pop up the editing window. The dBASE IV text editor is invoked. Enter the statements required using as many lines as needed. End the command sequence with a semicolon, and then press Ctrl-End to execute the command (see fig. 11.19)

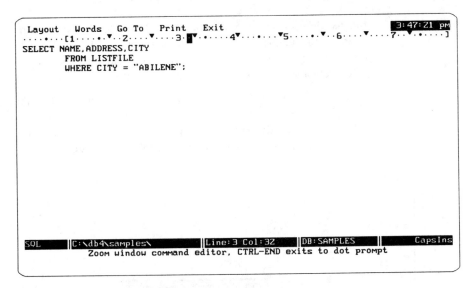

Fig. 11.19. Using the editing window to enter multi-line commands.

Creating and Using an SQL Database

11.40 Tip: **Create an SQL database to hold your tables.**

You must create an SQL database before you can create a table to hold information. A database can contain several tables and all the files related to the tables, including views, indexes, and catalogs.

To create an SQL database, type a command using the following syntax:

SQL. CREATE DATABASE < *database name*>;

For example, you can use the following command to create a database called NEWSOFT:

SQL. CREATE DATABASE NEWSOFT;

The program creates a subdirectory with the same name as the database. For example, if you are currently working in a directory named \DBASE, a subdirectory named \DBASE\NEWSOFT is created to hold the NEWSOFT database.

11.41 Tip: **Use the START command to access an SQL database.**

To use an SQL database, you must enter a command using the following syntax:

> SQL. START DATABASE < *database name*>;

Only one database can be used at a time. When you use the START command to open another database, the current database is closed.

11.42 Tip: **Use the STOP command before trying to delete a database.**

You can use the STOP command to close the current database. The format is as follows:

> SQL. STOP DATABASE;

Because you cannot delete an open database, you must use the STOP command to close an open database before you try to delete it. After a database is closed, you can use the DROP command to delete it:

> SQL. DROP DATABASE < *database name*>;

11.43 Trap: **Deleting a database erases all tables and other files related to it.**

Using the DROP command to delete a database deletes any tables you have created in that database. The data contained in those tables can no longer be used. Be sure that you will have no need for such data before attempting to delete a database.

11.44 Tip: **Use the CREATE TABLE command to design tables to store your data.**

The CREATE TABLE command lets you specify the columns (fields) and the data types for each column. Whereas dBASE IV gives you a screen form to enter information when creating a dBASE IV database file, SQL requires you to specify the information in the CREATE TABLE command itself. The format is as follows:

> SQL. CREATE TABLE < *table name*>
>   (< *column name*> < *data type*>
>   < *column name*> < *data type*>) ;

Of course, you can use as many column names and data types as needed. The preceding example creates a table with two columns.

Notice that the column names and data types are surrounded by parentheses. As with all SQL commands, the sequence is terminated with a semicolon.

11.45 Tip: **Understand the data types available for use with SQL tables.**

Before you can create a table, you must understand the eight data types available to you:

- ☐ SMALLINT: an integer up to six digits in length, either negative or positive

- ☐ INTEGER: an integer up to 11 digits in length, either negative or positive

- ☐ DECIMAL(*digits,decimals*): a number with a fixed number of decimal places. Example: DECIMAL(9,3) would indicate a number having up to nine digits, including a sign (–) and three decimal places.

- ☐ NUMERIC(*digits,decimals*): like DECIMAL except the number of digits specified includes a decimal point

- ☐ FLOAT(*digits,decimals*): a floating point number, which may be specified with exponential notation, such as –7.77 +125

- ☐ CHAR(*length*): a character string up to the length specified. The maximum length allowed is 254.

- ☐ DATE: a date field

- ☐ LOGICAL: a true or false value

Here is an example of a CREATE TABLE command sequence used to create a table called ITEMS:

```
SQL. CREATE TABLE Items
     ( Stock_no    CHAR(9) ,
       Price       NUMERIC(7,2) );
```

dBASE IV creates a dBASE IV database file corresponding to the specifications you give in the CREATE TABLE command.

Modifying Data in an SQL Table

11.46 Tip: **Use the INSERT command to add data to a table.**

To add new rows (records) to a table, use the INSERT command. If you are entering data in the same order as the columns in the table, you use this format:

SQL. INSERT INTO < *table name*>
        VALUES (< *values list*>) ;

For example, to add a row to the ITEMS table, you use the following sequence:

SQL. INSERT INTO Items
        VALUES ("ASH-DB4ØØ",795.ØØ) ;

However, if the data you are adding is in a different order, or if the number of data items added is less than the total number of columns in the table, you can specify the columns to which the data is to be assigned. The format is as follows:

SQL. INSERT INTO < *table name*>
        (< *column list*>)
        VALUES (< *values list*>) ;

For example, to add a row containing just the Price information, you use the following sequence:

SQL. INSERT INTO Items
        (Price)
        VALUES (795.ØØ) ;

11.47 Tip: **Use the UPDATE command to alter data in an existing table.**

If you need to change the data in rows that meet a certain condition, use the UPDATE command. Here is the format:

SQL. UPDATE < *table name*>
        SET < *column name*> = < *expression*>
        WHERE < *condition*>;

For example, to discount prices by $10.00 for products selling for more than $200.00 in the ITEMS table, you use this command:

```
SQL. UPDATE Items
       SET Price = (Price - 10.00)
       WHERE Price > 200.00;
```

This sequence is similar to using the REPLACE command and the FOR clause in the dBASE IV command language.

11.48 Trap: **When removing selected rows, always use a WHERE clause with the DELETE command to avoid losing data.**

The DELETE command removes any number of rows from a table, meeting the condition you specify. The format is as follows:

```
SQL. DELETE FROM < table name>
       WHERE < condition>;
```

For example, to remove rows for products in the ITEMS table that have a price of less than $100.00, use the following sequence:

```
SQL. DELETE FROM Items
       WHERE Price < 100.00;
```

The WHERE clause is optional. If you do not specify a condition, however, all rows are deleted from the table. Before the deletion, a warning message appears, and you can press Esc to abort the DELETE operation.

Displaying Data in SQL

11.49 Tip: **Use the SELECT command to examine data in your tables.**

The SELECT command is used to display the data that is stored in your tables. The basic format of the SELECT command is as follows:

```
SQL. SELECT < columns>
       FROM < tables>;
```

For example, to display the STOCK_ NO and PRICE columns from all rows in the ITEMS table, use the following sequence:

```
SQL. SELECT Stock_no, Price
       FROM Items;
```

A shortcut to use when displaying all the columns in a table is the asterisk (*) wild card. The following sequence is equivalent to the preceding one because the ITEMS table has only two columns:

```
SQL. SELECT *
       FROM Items;
```

In either case, the columns and rows you choose are displayed on-screen (see fig. 11.20).

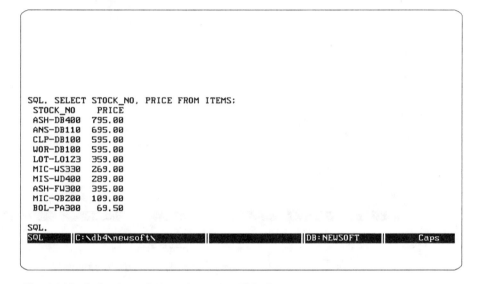

```
SQL. SELECT STOCK_NO, PRICE FROM ITEMS;
  STOCK_NO     PRICE
  ASH-DB400   795.00
  ANS-DB110   695.00
  CLP-DB100   595.00
  WOR-DB100   595.00
  LOT-L0123   359.00
  MIC-WS330   269.00
  MIS-WD400   289.00
  ASH-FW300   395.00
  MIC-QB200   109.00
  BOL-PA300    69.50

SQL.
SQL        C:\db4\newsoft\                        DB:NEWSOFT        Caps
```

Fig. 11.20. *Selecting all rows from the ITEMS table.*

11.50 Tip: **Use the WHERE clause to display selected data.**

As with the dBASE IV DISPLAY and LIST commands, the SELECT command offers a number of options that allow you to examine specific records (rows) or fields (columns). The WHERE clause is similar to the FOR clause used in dBASE IV. The format for using the WHERE clause in SELECT commands is as follows:

```
SQL. SELECT < columns>
       FROM < tables>
       WHERE <condition>;
```

For example, to display only items that have prices over $350.00 from the ITEMS table, use the following sequence:

```
SQL. SELECT *
     FROM Items
     WHERE Price > 350.00;
```

The resulting display is shown in figure 11.21.

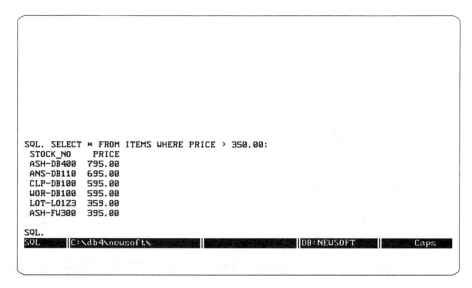

```
SQL. SELECT * FROM ITEMS WHERE PRICE > 350.00;
  STOCK_NO    PRICE
  ASH-DB400   795.00
  ANS-DB110   695.00
  CLP-DB100   595.00
  WOR-DB100   595.00
  LOT-L0123   359.00
  ASH-FW300   395.00

SQL.
SQL        C:\db4\newsoft\                              DB:NEWSOFT        Caps
```

Fig. 11.21. *Using the WHERE clause to specify records to select.*

11.51 Tip: **Use dBASE IV functions to select data.**

Many dBASE IV functions and commands can be used while in SQL mode. This option offers great flexibility when selecting or manipulating data. For example, if you want to display all items with stock numbers beginning with the letter A, you can use the dBASE IV LEFT( ) function. The LEFT( ) function returns the number of characters specified starting at the left side of a string. In the next example, LEFT(Stock_no,1) is used to return one character from the left side of STOCK_ NO:

```
SQL. SELECT *
     FROM Items
     WHERE LEFT(Stock_no,1) = "A";
```

Figure 11.22 shows the resulting display from this SELECT query.

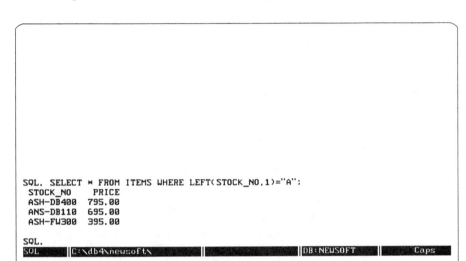

```
SQL. SELECT × FROM ITEMS WHERE LEFT(STOCK_NO,1)="A";
  STOCK_NO    PRICE
  ASH-DB400   795.00
  ANS-DB110   695.00
  ASH-FW300   395.00

SQL.
SQL      C:\db4\newsoft\                              DB:NEWSOFT              Caps
```

Fig. 11.22. Using the LEFT( ) function to select rows.

Knowing Some Restrictions of SQL

11.52 Trap: **Some dBASE IV commands and functions cannot be used when SQL is set to ON.**

Because of possible interference between dBASE IV language commands and SQL commands, some dBASE IV commands and functions cannot be used in SQL mode. Pay close attention to the commands you use when in SQL mode, because using an invalid command can cause unpredictable results or even lock up your system.

The following dBASE IV commands are *not* allowed in SQL mode:

APPEND
APPEND FROM
APPEND MEMO
ASSIST
AVERAGE
BROWSE

CALCULATE
CHANGE
CONTINUE
CONVERT TO
COPY INDEXES/TAG
COPY MEMO
COPY STRUCTURE
COPY TO ARRAY
COUNT
CREATE FROM
CREATE/MODIFY
CREATE/MODIFY APPLICATION
CREATE/MODIFY LABEL/?
CREATE/MODIFY QUERY/?
CREATE/MODIFY REPORT/?
CREATE/MODIFY SCREEN/?
CREATE/MODIFY VIEW/?
DELETE/DELETE TAG
DISPLAY
DISPLAY STRUCTURE
EDIT
EXPORT TO
FIND
GO/GOTO
IMPORT FROM
INDEX
INSERT
JOIN
LABEL FORM
LIST
LIST STRUCTURE
LOCATE
MODIFY STRUCTURE
PACK
RECALL
REINDEX
REPLACE
REPORT FORM
RESET
ROLLBACK
SCAN

```
SEEK
SELECT
SET
SET BLOCKSIZE
SET CARRY
SET CATALOG
SET DESIGN
SET FIELDS
SET FILTER
SET INDEX
SET INSTRUCT
SET MEMOWIDTH
SET NEAR
SET ORDER
SET RELATION
SET SKIP
SET TITLE
SET UNIQUE
SET VIEW
SET WINDOW OF MEMO
SKIP
SORT
SUM
TOTAL ON
UNLOCK
UPDATE
USE
ZAP
```

The following dBASE IV functions are *not* allowed in SQL statements:

```
&
ACCESS( )
ALIAS( )
BAR( )
BOF( )
CALL( )
CHANGE( )
COL( )
COMMAND( )
COMPLETED( )
DBF( )
DELETED( )
```

```
DISKSPACE()
EOF
ERROR()
FIELD()
FILE()
FKLABEL()
FKMAX()
FLOCK()
FOUND()
GETENV()
IFF()
INKEY()
ISALPHA()
ISCOLOR()
ISLOWER()
ISMARKED()
ISUPPER()
LASTKEY()
LIKE()
LINENO()
LKSYS()
LOOKUP()
LUPDATE()
MAX()
MDX()
MEMLINES()
MEMORY()
MENU()
MESSAGE()
MIN()
MLINE()
NDX()
NETWORK()
ORDER()
OS()
PAD()
PCOL()
POPUP()
PRINSTATUS()
PROGRAM()
PROMPT()
```

```
PROW()
READKEY()
RECCOUNT()
RECNO()
RECSIZE()
RLOCK()
ROLLBACK()
ROW()
SEEK()
SET()
TAG()
TYPE()
VARREAD()
VERSION()
```

Refer to Appendix D for a list of SQL commands that can be used in dBASE IV SQL mode.

A

ASCII Character Set

The table lists the ASCII characters and their codes in decimal notation. Characters can be displayed with

? CHR(n)

where *n* is the decimal ASCII value. You can enter characters that do not appear on the keyboard by holding down the Alt key while you enter the ASCII value, using the numeric keypad. The standard interpretations of ASCII codes 0 to 31 are presented in the Ctrl column.

Hex	Dec	Screen	Ctrl	Key	Hex	Dec	Screen	Ctrl	Key
00h	0		NUL	^@	1Ah	26	→	SUB	^Z
01h	1	☺	SOH	^A	1Bh	27	←	ESC	^[
02h	2	●	STX	^B	1Ch	28	∟	FS	^\
03h	3	♥	ETX	^C	1Dh	29	↔	GS	^]
04h	4	◆	EOT	^D	1Eh	30	▲	RS	^^
05h	5	♣	ENQ	^E	1Fh	31	▼	US	^_
06h	6	♠	ACK	^F	20h	32			
07h	7	●	BEL	^G	21h	33	!		
08h	8	◘	BS	^H	22h	34	"		
09h	9	○	HT	^I	23h	35	#		
0Ah	10	◙	LF	^J	24h	36	$		
0Bh	11	♂	VT	^K	25h	37	%		
0Ch	12	♀	FF	^L	26h	38	&		
0Dh	13	♪	CR	^M	27h	39	'		
0Eh	14	♫	SO	^N	28h	40	(		
0Fh	15	☼	SI	^O	29h	41	)		
10h	16	►	DLE	^P	2Ah	42	*		
11h	17	◄	DC1	^Q	2Bh	43	+		
12h	18	↕	DC2	^R	2Ch	44	,		
13h	19	‼	DC3	^S	2Dh	45	-		
14h	20	¶	DC4	^T	2Eh	46	.		
15h	21	§	NAK	^U	2Fh	47	/		
16h	22	▬	SYN	^V	30h	48	0		
17h	23	↨	ETB	^W	31h	49	1		
18h	24	↑	CAN	^X	32h	50	2		
19h	25	↓	EM	^Y	33h	51	3		

Hex	Dec	Screen	Hex	Dec	Screen	Hex	Dec	Screen
34h	52	4	62h	98	b	90h	144	É
35h	53	5	63h	99	c	91h	145	æ
36h	54	6	64h	100	d	92h	146	Æ
37h	55	7	65h	101	e	93h	147	ô
38h	56	8	66h	102	f	94h	148	ö
39h	57	9	67h	103	g	95h	149	ò
3Ah	58	:	68h	104	h	96h	150	û
3Bh	59	;	69h	105	i	97h	151	ù
3Ch	60	<	6Ah	106	j	98h	152	ÿ
3Dh	61	=	6Bh	107	k	99h	153	Ö
3Eh	62	>	6Ch	108	l	9Ah	154	Ü
3Fh	63	?	6Dh	109	m	9Bh	155	¢
40h	64	@	6Eh	110	n	9Ch	156	£
41h	65	A	6Fh	111	o	9Dh	157	¥
42h	66	B	70h	112	p	9Eh	158	₧
43h	67	C	71h	113	q	9Fh	159	ƒ
44h	68	D	72h	114	r	A0h	160	á
45h	69	E	73h	115	s	A1h	161	í
46h	70	F	74h	116	t	A2h	162	ó
47h	71	G	75h	117	u	A3h	163	ú
48h	72	H	76h	118	v	A4h	164	ñ
49h	73	I	77h	119	w	A5h	165	Ñ
4Ah	74	J	78h	120	x	A6h	166	ª
4Bh	75	K	79h	121	y	A7h	167	º
4Ch	76	L	7Ah	122	z	A8h	168	¿
4Dh	77	M	7Bh	123	{	A9h	169	⌐
4Eh	78	N	7Ch	124	|	AAh	170	¬
4Fh	79	O	7Dh	125	}	ABh	171	½
50h	80	P	7Eh	126	~	ACh	172	¼
51h	81	Q	7Fh	127	⌂	ADh	173	¡
52h	82	R	80h	128	Ç	AEh	174	«
53h	83	S	81h	129	ü	AFh	175	»
54h	84	T	82h	130	é	B0h	176	░
55h	85	U	83h	131	â	B1h	177	▒
56h	86	V	84h	132	ä	B2h	178	▓
57h	87	W	85h	133	à	B3h	179	│
58h	88	X	86h	134	å	B4h	180	┤
59h	89	Y	87h	135	ç	B5h	181	╡
5Ah	90	Z	88h	136	ê	B6h	182	╢
5Bh	91	[	89h	137	ë	B7h	183	╖
5Ch	92	\	8Ah	138	è	B8h	184	╕
5Dh	93	]	8Bh	139	ï	B9h	185	╣
5Eh	94	^	8Ch	140	î	BAh	186	║
5Fh	95	_	8Dh	141	ì	BBh	187	╗
60h	96	`	8Eh	142	Ä	BCh	188	╝
61h	97	a	8Fh	143	Å	BDh	189	╜

Hex	Dec	Screen	Hex	Dec	Screen	Hex	Dec	Screen
BEh	190	╛	D4h	212	╘	EAh	234	Ω
BFh	191	╗	D5h	213	╒	EBh	235	δ
C0h	192	╚	D6h	214	╓	ECh	236	∞
C1h	193	╧	D7h	215	╫	EDh	237	φ
C2h	194	╤	D8h	216	╪	EEh	238	∈
C3h	195	╟	D9h	217	╛	EFh	239	∩
C4h	196	─	DAh	218	┌	F0h	240	≡
C5h	197	┼	DBh	219	█	F1h	241	±
C6h	198	╞	DCh	220	▄	F2h	242	≥
C7h	199	╟	DDh	221	▌	F3h	243	≤
C8h	200	╚	DEh	222	▐	F4h	244	⌠
C9h	201	╔	DFh	223	▀	F5h	245	⌡
CAh	202	╩	E0h	224	α	F6h	246	÷
CBh	203	╦	E1h	225	β	F7h	247	≈
CCh	204	╠	E2h	226	Γ	F8h	248	°
CDh	205	═	E3h	227	π	F9h	249	•
CEh	206	╬	E4h	228	Σ	FAh	250	·
CFh	207	╧	E5h	229	σ	FBh	251	√
D0h	208	╨	E6h	230	μ	FCh	252	n
D1h	209	╤	E7h	231	τ	FDh	253	²
D2h	210	╥	E8h	232	Φ	FEh	254	■
D3h	211	╙	E9h	233	θ	FFh	255	

B

Summary of Function and Control Keys

Default Settings for the Function Keys

From the Control Center:

Key	Function
F1 (Help)	Show Help screen
F2 (Data)	Browse or Edit data
F3 (Previous)	Move to previous field, object, or page
F4 (Next)	Move to next field, object, or page
F5 (Field)	Add field to layout
F6 (Select)	Select fields or text
F7 (Move)	Move selected fields or text
F8 (Copy)	Copy selected fields or text
F9 (Zoom)	Enlarge or shrink data input area or memo field
F10 (Menus)	Pull down menus
Shift-F1 (Pick)	Display picklist
Shift-F2 (Design)	Invoke design screen
Shift-F3 (Find Previous)	Search for previous occurrence of string

Key	*Function*
Shift-F4 (Find Next)	Search for next occurrence of string
Shift-F5 (Find)	Search for specified string
Shift-F6 (Replace)	Replace search string with another string
Shift-F7 (Size)	Change size of field or object
Shift-F8 (Ditto)	Copy data from previous record into field in current record
Shift-F9 (Quick Report)	Print a report
Shift-F10 (Macros)	Access macros prompt box

From the dot prompt:

Key	*Equivalent dBASE IV Command*
F1	HELP;
F2	ASSIST; (access Control Center)
F3	LIST;
F4	DIR;
F5	DISPLAY STRUCTURE;
F6	DISPLAY STATUS;
F7	DISPLAY MEMORY;
F8	DISPLAY;
F9	APPEND;
F10	EDIT;

Note: You can reprogram function keys F2 through F10, Shift-F1 through Shift-F9, and Ctrl-F1 through Ctrl-F10 with the SET FUNCTION command. The F1 key always is reserved for Help; and the Shift-F10 key is reserved for the **Macro** menu.

Cursor Navigation and Editing Keys

Certain keys have different uses depending on the mode you are in: Edit, Browse, Word Wrap, Layout, Queries, or Memo.

Key(s)	Action
Right arrow (→)	Move right one positiom
Left arrow (←)	Move left one position
Down arrow (↓)	Move down one row
Up arrow (↑)	Move up one row
PgDn	Move to next screen
PgUp	Move to previous screen
End	Move to end of field, last field in record, end of line, or last column
Home	Move to beginning of field, beginning of record, left margin, or first column
Backspace	Delete previous character
Ctrl-Backspace	Delete previous word
Tab	Move to next field, next tab stop, or next column; insert tab character
Shift-Tab	Move to previous field, previous tab stop, or previous column
Enter	Move to next field or next line; break line
Esc	Exit without saving changes, cancel selection
Del	Delete selected item
Ins	Toggle Insert mode on or off
Ctrl-right arrow (→)	Scroll to next word or next field
Ctrl-left arrow (←)	Scroll to previous word or previous field
Ctrl-PgDn	Scroll to end of text or document, or last record

Key(s)	Action
Ctrl-PgUp	Scroll to beginning of text or document, or first record
Ctrl-Home	Open memo field
Ctrl-End	Exit and save changes; exit memo field
Ctrl-Enter	Save work without exiting
Ctrl-KR	Read file into current file
Ctrl-KW	Write selection or file to another file
Ctrl-N	Insert a new line
Ctrl-T	Delete to next word
Ctrl-Y	Delete line; delete to end of line
Ctrl-U	Delete item; mark record for deletion

Summary of dBASE IV Commands and Functions

Definition of Terms

The following special terms are used in this appendix. When you enter the commands, enter only the file name or other element; do not enter the angle brackets ($<\ >$).

<file name>

A string of up to eight characters, including the underscore, with a file extension (for example, .DBF, .DBT, .FMT, .FRM, .LBL, .MEM, .NDX, .PRG, and .TXT). A sample file name is EMPLOYEE.DBF.

<data field name>

A string of up to 10 characters, including the underscore.

LAST_NAME

<data field list>

A series of data field names separated by commas.

LAST_NAME, FIRST_NAME, AREA_CODE, PHONE_NO

<variable name>

A string of up to 10 characters, including underscores.

TOTALPRICE

<variable list>

A series of variable names separated by commas.

HOURS, PAYRATE, GROSSWAGE, TOTALSALE

<expression>

An alphanumeric or numeric expression.

<character expression>

A collection of alphanumeric data joined with plus signs.

"Employee's Name: " + TRIM(LAST_NAME) + FIRST_NAME + MIDDLENAME

<numeric expression>

A collection of numeric data joined with arithmetic operators (+, −, *, /, ^).

40*PAYRATE + (HOURS−40)*PAYRATE*1.5

<expression list>

A series of expressions separated by commas.

expression 1, expression 2, expression 3, ...

<qualifier>

A clause that begins with FOR, followed by one or more conditions.

FOR AREA_CODE="206" FOR ANNUAL_PAY <=25000 FOR
LAST_NAME="Smith" .AND. FIRST_NAME="James C."

Summary of Commands

?

Displays the contents of an expression on a new display line.

```
? "Employee's name..."+FIRST_NAME+LAST_NAME
? HOURS*PAYRATE
? "Gross Pay..."+STR(GROSSPAY,7,2)
```

??

Displays output on the same display line.

```
?? "Invoice number: "+INVNO
```

???

Directs characters directly to the printer.

```
??? CHR(27) + "X"
```

@<*row,column*> GET

Displays user-formatted data at the screen location specified by <*row,column*>.

```
@5,10 GET LAST_NAME
@8,10 GET SC_NO PICTURE "###-##-####"
```

@<*row,column*> SAY

Displays user-formatted data on the screen or printer at the location specified by <*row,column*>.

```
@5,10 SAY LAST_NAME
@5,10 SAY "Last name..." LAST_NAME
@10,5 SAY "Annual salary:" ANNUAL_PAY PICTURE "$##,###.##"
```

@<*row,column*> SAY . . . GET

Displays user-formatted data on the screen or printer at the location specified by <*row,column*>; used for appending or editing a data field.

```
@5,1Ø SAY "Last name : " GET LAST_NAME
```

@<*row,column*> CLEAR TO <*row,column*>

Clears a portion of the screen.

```
@3,1Ø CLEAR TO 12,2Ø
```

@<*row,column*> FILL TO <*row,column*> COLOR

Changes the color of an area of the screen.

```
@4,5 FILL TO 1Ø,18 COLOR G/N
```

@<*row,column*> TO <*row,column*>

Displays a box on-screen. DOUBLE specifies a double-line box, PANEL shows a solid border in inverse video, and COLOR attributes may be specified.

```
@4,6 TO 8,1Ø DOUBLE COLOR G/N
@4,6 TO 8,1Ø PANEL
```

ACCEPT

Assigns an alphanumeric string to a memory variable, with or without a prompt.

```
ACCEPT "Enter your last name..." TO LASTNAME
ACCEPT TO LASTNAME
```

ACTIVATE MENU

After a bar menu has been defined, this command makes it active. Optionally, the cursor may be set at the menu pad specified.

```
ACTIVATE MENU Empmenu PAD Search
```

ACTIVATE POPUP

After a pop-up menu has been defined, this command makes it active.

```
ACTIVATE POPUP Empmenu
```

ACTIVATE SCREEN

After a window is active, this command restores output to the entire screen.

ACTIVATE WINDOW

Directs screen output to a defined window. Use the ALL option to activate all defined windows.

```
ACTIVATE WINDOW Empwind
ACTIVATE WINDOW ALL
```

APPEND

Adds a data record to the end of the active database file. The data fields are the field labels on the entry form.

```
USE EMPLOYEE
APPEND
```

APPEND BLANK

Same as APPEND but does not display an entry form.

```
USE EMPLOYEE
APPEND BLANK
```

APPEND FROM

Adds data records from one database file (FILE1.DBF) to another
database file (FILE2.DBF), with or without a qualifier. The optional
TYPE qualifier specifies the format of the imported file.

```
USE FILE2
APPEND FROM FILE1

USE FILE2
APPEND FROM FILE1 TYPE SDF FOR ACCT_NO="10123"
```

APPEND FROM ARRAY

Appends records to the database from values stored in an array.

```
APPEND FROM ARRAY Empdata FOR LASTNAME = "Jones"
```

APPEND FROM MEMO

Places a text file into a specified memo field of the current record.
The OVERWRITE option replaces the existing contents of the memo
field with the new text.

```
APPEND FROM MEMO Remarks FROM Letter.txt OVERWRITE
```

ASSIST

Activates the Control Center menu.

AVERAGE

Computes the average of a numeric expression and assigns the value
to a memory variable or array, with or without a condition.

```
AVERAGE ANNUAL_PAY TO AVERAGEPAY
AVERAGE QTY_SOLD TO AVG_SALE FOR MODEL_NO="XYZ"
AVERAGE HOURS*PAYRATE TO ARRAY AVERAGEPAY FOR .NOT. MALE
```

BEGIN TRANSACTION

Indicates the beginning of transactions processing, which logs all changes made to data so that data can be restored to its original state with the ROLLBACK command.

BROWSE

Displays for review or modification records from the active database file in tabular format.

```
USE EMPLOYEE
GO TOP
BROWSE
```

BROWSE FIELDS

Browses selected data fields in the current database file.

```
USE EMPLOYEE
GO TOP
BROWSE FIELDS FIRST_NAME, LAST_NAME, PHONE_NO
```

CALCULATE

Calculates one or more statistical and financial functions on the entire database or on selected records and optionally stores the results in a memory variable or an array.

```
CALCULATE AVG(Salary),MAX(Salary) FOR OFFICE="Chicago"
TO Avsal,Mxsal
```

CALL

Calls a binary program file module that previously has been put in memory with the LOAD command.

```
CALL Progmod
```

CANCEL

Terminates the processing of a program file and returns the program to the dot prompt.

```
IF EOF( )
CANCEL
ENDIF
```

CHANGE

Displays the data records in an active database file sequentially, with or without a qualifier.

```
USE EMPLOYEE
CHANGE
```

```
USE EMPLOYEE
CHANGE FOR AREA_CODE="206"
```

CHANGE FIELDS

Displays selected data fields sequentially, with or without a qualifier.

```
USE EMPLOYEE
CHANGE FIELDS ANNUAL_PAY
```

```
USE EMPLOYEE
CHANGE FIELDS AREA_CODE,PHONE_NO FOR AREA_CODE="206"
```

CLEAR

Clears the screen.

CLEAR ALL

Closes all open database files (including .DBF, .NDX, .FMT, and .DBT files) and releases all memory variables.

CLEAR FIELDS

Releases the data fields that have been created by the SET FIELDS TO command.

CLEAR GETS

Causes the subsequent READ command to be ignored for the @...SAY...GET commands issued before the command.

```
@5,1Ø SAY "Account number : " GET ACCT_NO
CLEAR GETS
@7,1Ø SAY "Account name : " GET ACCT_NAME
READ
```

CLEAR MEMORY

Releases or erases all memory variables.

CLEAR MENUS

Clears all user menus from the screen and from memory.

CLEAR POPUPS

Clears all pop-up menus from the screen and from memory.

CLEAR TYPEAHEAD

Empties the typeahead buffer.

CLEAR WINDOWS

Clears all windows from the screen and from memory.

CLOSE

Closes various types of files.

```
CLOSE ALL
CLOSE ALTERNATE
CLOSE DATABASES
CLOSE FORMAT
CLOSE INDEX
CLOSE PROCEDURE
```

COMPILE

Compiles a dBASE IV source code program file into an executable object code file.

CONTINUE

Resumes the search started with the LOCATE command.

```
USE EMPLOYEE
LOCATE FOR AREA_CODE="206"
DISPLAY
CONTINUE
DISPLAY
```

CONVERT

In multi-user applications, adds a field to the database structure for record locking.

COPY TO

Copies selected fields of a source database file to a new file, with or without a qualifier. The TYPE clause specifies the format of the output file.

```
USE EMPLOYEE
COPY TO ROSTER.DBF FIELDS FIRST_NAME, LAST_NAME
COPY TO SALARY.DBF FIELDS LAST_NAME, ANNUAL_PAY
FOR MALE TYPE SDF
```

COPY FILE

Duplicates an existing dBASE IV file of any type.

```
COPY FILE MAINPROG.PRG TO MAIN.PRG
COPY FILE COST.FMT TO NEWCOST.FMT
COPY FILE ROSTER.FRM TO NAMELIST.FRM
```

COPY INDEXES

Used to convert indexing (.NDX) files to tags in a multiple indexing (.MDX) file. The default .MDX file is the production indexing file.

```
COPY INDEXES NAME.NDX,STATE.NDX TO PERSONS.MDX
```

COPY MEMO

Copies the information in a memo field to a file. The ADDITIVE option appends the information to the output file.

```
COPY MEMO REMARKS TO INFO.TXT ADDITIVE
```

COPY STRUCTURE

Copies the data structure to another database file.

```
USE COST COPY STRUCTURE TO NEWCOST.DBF
```

COPY STRUCTURE EXTENDED

Creates a database of records that contains the structure of the current database.

```
COPY TO NEWFILE.DBF STRUCTURE EXTENDED
```

COPY TAG

Converts tags from a multiple indexing (.MDX) file to indexing (.NDX) files. The default .MDX file is the production indexing file.

```
COPY TAG NAME OF NAMES.MDX TO NAME.NDX
```

COPY TO ARRAY

Places the values of records into an array. The array must have been previously declared.

```
DECLARE PEOPLE[9]
COPY TO ARRAY PEOPLE NAME FOR NAME="Jones"
```

COUNT

Counts the number of records in the active database file and assigns the number to a memory variable.

```
USE EMPLOYEE
COUNT TO NRECORDS
COUNT FOR ANNUAL_PAY>="50000" .AND. MALE TO RICHMEN
```

CREATE

Sets up a new file structure and adds data records, if desired.

```
CREATE EMPLOYEE
```

CREATE APPLICATION

Runs the Applications Generator; used to create a dBASE IV application.

```
CREATE APPLICATION NEWPROG
```

CREATE FROM

Creates a database from the structure stored in a file created with COPY STRUCTURE EXTENDED.

```
CREATE PEOPLE.DBF FROM NEWFILE.DBF
```

CREATE LABEL

Displays a design form to set up a label file (.LBL).

```
CREATE LABEL MAILLIST
```

CREATE QUERY

Displays the query design screen, which allows the user to create a new query file (.QBE).

```
USE EMPLOYEE
CREATE QUERY FINDEMPL
```

CREATE REPORT

Displays a design form to set up a report-form file (.FRM).

```
CREATE REPORT WEEKLY
```

CREATE SCREEN

Creates a new screen file (.SCR) and format file (.FMT).

```
USE EMPLOYEE
CREATE SCREEN SHOWEMPL
```

CREATE VIEW

Creates a new view query file.

```
USE EMPLOYEE
CREATE VIEW SAMPLE
```

CREATE VIEW FROM ENVIRONMENT

Creates a view (.VUE) file that can be used with dBASE III Plus.

DEACTIVATE MENU

Erases an active menu bar from the screen, making it inactive.

DEACTIVATE POPUP

Erases an active pop-up menu from the screen, making it inactive.

DEACTIVATE WINDOW

Erases an active window from the screen, making it inactive.

DEBUG

Executes a dBASE IV program using the full-screen debugger.

    DEBUG EMPLOY.PRG

DECLARE

Declares a one- or two-dimensional array of memory variables.

    DECLARE PEOPLE[9]

DEFINE BAR

Defines a bar for a pop-up menu. The optional MESSAGE line is displayed at the bottom of the screen, and the SKIP option specifies when a bar is accessible.

    DEFINE BAR 3 OF NAMEMENU PROMPT "Choose name"
    MESSAGE "Please make a selection" SKIP FOR MALE

DEFINE BOX

Defines a box to be printed in a report.

    DEFINE BOX FROM < column> TO < column> HEIGHT < lines>
    SINGLE/DOUBLE

DEFINE MENU

Assigns a name and optional message to a menu.

    DEFINE MENU NAMES MESSAGE "Please make a selection"

DEFINE PAD

Defines a pad for a bar menu.

```
DEFINE PAD UPDATE OF MENU1 PROMPT "Update" AT 1,15
MESSAGE "Make a selection"
```

DEFINE POPUP

Defines a pop-up window menu.

```
DEFINE POPUP UPDATE FROM 2,4 TO 6,10 PROMPT FIELD NAME
```

DEFINE WINDOW

Defines a screen window.

```
DEFINE WINDOW UPDATE FROM 4,6 TO 8,12 DOUBLE COLOR W,G
```

DELETE

Marks the records in the active database file with a deletion symbol.

```
USE EMPLOYEE
DELETE
DELETE RECORD 5
DELETE NEXT 3
DELETE FOR AREA_CODE="503"
```

DELETE TAG

Removes an index tag from a multiple indexing (.MDX) file.

```
DELETE TAG NAME OF PEOPLE.MDX
```

DIR

Displays the file directory.

DIR	Displays .DBF files
DIR *.* .PA	Displays all files
DIR *.PRG	Displays program files
DIR *.NDX	Displays index files
DIR X*.DBF	Displays .DBF file names beginning with X
DIR ??X???.PRG	Displays .PRG file names that have six letters and X as the third character
DIR ???.*	Displays all file names that are three characters long

DISPLAY

Shows the contents of the data records one screen at a time.

```
USE EMPLOYEE
DISPLAY
DISPLAY RECORD 3
DISPLAY NEXT 2
DISPLAY LAST_NAME,FIRST_NAME
DISPLAY AREA_CODE,PHONE_NO FOR AREA_CODE="206"
```

DISPLAY FILES

Shows a directory of files.

DISPLAY MEMORY

Shows the contents of active memory variables.

DISPLAY STATUS

Shows the current processing situation, including the names of active files, the work area number, and so forth.

DISPLAY STRUCTURE

Shows the data structure of an active database file.

```
USE EMPLOYEE
DISPLAY STRUCTURE
```

DISPLAY USERS

Shows users logged into a network using dBASE IV.

DO

Executes a program file.

```
DO MAINPROG
```

DO CASE . . . ENDCASE

A multiple-avenue branching command.

```
DO CASE
   CASE ANSWER="Y"
      . . .
   CASE ANSWER="N"
      . . .
OTHERWISE
RETURN
ENDCASE
```

DO WHILE . . . ENDDO

A program loop command.

```
DO WHILE .NOT. EOF( )
. . .
. . .
ENDDO
```

EDIT

Displays a data record for editing.

```
USE EMPLOYEE
GOTO 5
EDIT

USE EMPLOYEE
EDIT RECORD 5
```

EJECT

Advances the printer paper to the top of the next page.

END TRANSACTION

Indicates the end of transactions processing. This command stops logging changes made to data so that the data no longer can be restored to its original state with the ROLLBACK command.

ERASE

Removes a file from the directory. The file to be erased must be closed.

```
ERASE SALE.DBF
ERASE SAMPLE.PRG
```

EXIT

Exits from a program loop, as in the following one created with DO WHILE...ENDDO.

```
DO WHILE .T.
   ...
   IF EOF( )
      EXIT
   ENDIF
   ...
ENDDO
```

EXPORT TO

Converts a dBASE IV file to another file format, specified in the TYPE clause: PFS, dBASEII, FW2 (Framework II), or RPD (RapidFile).

```
EXPORT TO NEWNAMES TYPE PFS
```

FIND

Searches for the first data record in an indexed file with a specified search key.

```
USE EMPLOYEE
INDEX ON AREA_CODE TO AREAS
FIND "206"
DISPLAY
```

FUNCTION

Indicates a procedure as a user-defined function.

```
FUNCTION SALARY
   PARAMETERS PAY, BONUS
   TOTALPAY = PAY + BONUS
RETURN (TOTALPAY)

? SALARY(1000,75)
   1075
```

GO BOTTOM

Positions the record pointer at the last record in the database file.

```
USE EMPLOYEE
GO BOTTOM
```

GO TOP

Positions the record pointer at the first record in the database file.

```
USE EMPLOYEE
GO TOP
```

GOTO

Positions the record pointer at a specified record.

```
USE EMPLOYEE
GOTO 4
```

HELP

Calls up the help screens. Can be used with a keyword to specify the subject.

```
HELP
HELP CREATE
HELP JOIN
```

IF

A conditional branching command.

```
WAIT "Enter your choice ([Q] to quit) " TO CHOICE
IF CHOICE="Q"
RETURN
ELSE
 . . .
 . . .
ENDIF
```

IMPORT FROM

Converts another file format to a dBASE IV file (see EXPORT TO).

```
IMPORT FROM OLDFILE TYPE PFS
```

INDEX

Creates a key file in which all records are ordered according to the contents of the specified key field. The records can be arranged in alphabetical, chronological, or numerical order. If specifying a tag of a multiple indexing (.MDX) file instead of an indexing (.NDX) file, the descending order option can be used.

```
INDEX ON AREA _CODE TO AREACODE
INDEX ON AREA _CODE + PHONE _ NO TO PHONES
INDEX ON NAME TO TAG NAME OF PEOPLE.MDX DESCENDING
```

INPUT

Assigns a data element to a memory variable using information entered from the keyboard.

```
INPUT PAYRATE
INPUT "Enter units sold :" TO UNITSSOLD
```

INSERT

Adds a new record to the database file at the current record location.

```
USE EMPLOYEE
GOTO 4
INSERT
GOTO 6
INSERT BEFORE
GOTO 5
INSERT BLANK
```

JOIN

Creates a new database file by merging specified data records from two open database files.

```
SELECT A
USE NEWSTOCKS
SELECT B
USE STOCKS
JOIN WITH NEWSTOCKS TO ALLSTOCK FOR STOCK_NO=A->STOCK_NO

JOIN WITH NEWSTOCKS TO ALLSTOCK FOR STOCK_NO=A->STOCK_NO;
FIELDS MODEL_NO, ON_HAND, ON_ORDER
```

LABEL FORM

Displays data records with labels specified in a label file.

```
USE EMPLOYEE
LABEL FORM ROSTER
LABEL FORM ROSTER TO PRINT
LABEL FORM ROSTER TO AFILE.TXT
LABEL FORM ROSTER FOR AREA_CODE="206" .AND. MALE
```

LIST

Shows the contents of selected data records in the active database file.

```
USE EMPLOYEE
LIST
LIST RECORD 5
LIST LAST_NAME,FIRST_NAME
LIST LAST_NAME,FIRST_NAME FOR AREA_CODE="206" .OR. MALE
```

LIST FILES

Shows a directory of files.

LIST HISTORY

Shows a list of commands stored in the HISTORY buffer.

LIST MEMORY

Shows the name, type, and size of each active memory variable. Also shows the amount of memory allocated to and used by dBASE IV.

LIST STATUS

Lists the current processing situation, including the names of active files, the work area number, and so forth.

```
LIST STATUS
LIST STATUS TO PRINT
```

LIST STRUCTURE

Displays the data structure of the active database file.

```
USE EMPLOYEE
LIST STRUCTURE
LIST STRUCTURE TO PRINT
```

The IN clause specifies an unselected work area.

```
LIST STRUCTURE IN NAMES TO FILE STRUC.TXT
```

LIST USERS

Shows the users logged into a dBASE IV network.

LOAD

Loads a binary program file into memory.

LOCATE

Sequentially searches data records of the active database file for a record that satisfies a specified condition.

```
USE EMPLOYEE
LOCATE FOR LAST_NAME="Smith"
LOCATE FOR UPPER(FIRST_NAME)="JAMES"
LOCATE FOR FIRST_NAME="J" .AND. LAST_NAME="S"
```

LOGOUT

In a network, logs a user out of the program.

LOOP

Transfers execution from the middle of a program loop to the beginning of the loop.

```
DO WHILE .T.
...
...
IF...
LOOP
ENDIF
...
ENDDO
```

MODIFY COMMAND/FILE

Invokes the text editor to create or edit a program file (.PRG), a format file (.FMT), or a text file (.TXT). The default file extension is .PRG. With the command MODIFY FILE, no default file extension is provided.

```
MODIFY COMMAND MAINPROG
MODIFY COMMAND BILLING.PRG
MODIFY COMMAND EMPLOYEE.FMT
MODIFY COMMAND TEXTFILE.TXT
```

MODIFY APPLICATION

Uses the Applications Generator to change an existing application.

MODIFY LABEL

Creates or edits a label file (.LBL) for the active database file.

```
USE EMPLOYEE
MODIFY LABEL MAILLIST
```

MODIFY QUERY/VIEW

Creates or edits a query file.

```
USE EMPLOYEE
MODIFY QUERY FINDEMPL
```

MODIFY REPORT

Creates or edits a report file (.FRM) for the active database file.

```
USE QTYSOLD
MODIFY REPORT WEEKLY
```

MODIFY SCREEN

Creates or edits a screen file (.SCR).

```
USE EMPLOYEE
MODIFY SCREEN SHOWEMPL.SCR
```

MODIFY STRUCTURE

Displays for modification the structure of the active database file.

```
USE EMPLOYEE
MODIFY STRUCTURE
```

MOVE WINDOW

Relocates a window on the screen. The BY clause specifies movement relative to the current position.

```
MOVE WINDOW UPDATE TO 5,8
MOVE WINDOW UPDATE BY 6,1
```

NOTE

Marks the beginning of a remark line in a program.

```
SET TALK OFF
SET ECHO OFF
NOTE Enter hours worked and payrate from the keyboard
INPUT "Enter hours worked... " TO HOURS
INPUT "       hourly rate... " TO PAYRATE
. . .
. . .
```

ON ERROR/ESCAPE/KEY

Specifies a command to execute if an error is detected or if the Escape key or any key is pressed.

```
ON ERROR DO FIX
ON ESCAPE DO PREVIOUS
ON KEY DO LEAVE
```

ON PAD

Specifies a pop-up menu to be activated when a pad is selected.

```
ON PAD LOCATE OF MENU1 ACTIVATE POPUP FINDMENU
```

ON PAGE

Performs a certain command when a specified line is reached on the current page.

```
ON PAGE AT LINE 24 DO FOOTERS
```

ON READERROR

Performs a command when an error is encountered during a full-screen operation.

```
ON READERROR DO WARNING
```

ON SELECTION PAD

Specifies a command to execute when a certain bar menu pad is selected.

```
ON SELECTION PAD SEARCH OF MENU1 DO GOFIND
```

ON SELECTION POPUP

Specifies a command to execute when a selection is made from a pop-up menu. The ALL option performs the command for all pop-up menus.

```
ON SELECTION POPUP NAMES DO GOFIND
ON SELECTION POPUP ALL DO GOFIND
```

PACK

Removes data records marked for deletion by the DELETE command.

```
USE EMPLOYEE
DELETE RECORD 5
PACK
```

PARAMETERS

Assigns local variable names to data items that are to be passed from a calling program module.

```
***** Program: MULTIPLY.PRG *****
* A program to multiply variable A by variable B
PARAMETERS A,B,C
C=A*B
RETURN
```

The preceding program is called from the main program.

```
* The main program
HOURS=38
PAYRATE=8.5
DO MULTIPLY WITH HOURS,PAYRATE,GROSSPAY
? "Gross Wage =",GROSSPAY
RETURN
```

PLAY MACRO

If a keyboard macro has been created, this command executes the specified macro.

PRINTJOB/ENDPRINTJOB

These two commands indicate the beginning and end of a print job.

PRIVATE

Declares private variables in a program module.

```
PRIVATE VARIABLEA, VARIABLEB, VARIABLEC
```

PROCEDURE

Identifies the beginning of each procedure in a procedure file.

PROTECT

In a network, used for data security by allowing for password protection and data encryption.

PUBLIC

Declares public variables or arrays to be shared by all program modules.

```
PUBLIC VARIABLEA, VARIABLEB, VARIABLEC
PUBLIC ARRAY <elements>
```

QUIT

Closes all open files, terminates dBASE IV processing, and exits to DOS.

READ

Activates all the @...SAY...GET commands issued since the last CLEAR, CLEAR ALL, CLEAR GETS, or READ was issued.

```
USE EMPLOYEE
@5,1Ø SAY "Last name  : " GET LAST_NAME
@6,1Ø SAY "First name : " GET FIRST_NAME
READ
```

RECALL

Recovers all data records marked for deletion.

```
RECALL
RECALL ALL
RECALL RECORD 5
```

REINDEX

Rebuilds all active indexing (.NDX) and multiple indexing (.MDX) files.

```
USE EMPLOYEE
SET INDEX TO AREACODE
REINDEX
```

RELEASE

Deletes all or selected memory variables.

```
RELEASE ALL
RELEASE ALL LIKE NET*
RELEASE ALL EXCEPT ???COST
```

Also used to release assembly language program modules, menus, pop-up menus, and windows from memory.

```
RELEASE MODULE ASMPROG
RELEASE MENUS NEWNAME
```

RENAME

Changes the name of a disk file.

```
RENAME XYZ.DBF TO ABC.DBF
RENAME MAINPROG.PRG TO MAIN.PRG
RENAME MAILIST.LBL TO MAILLIST.LBL
```

REPLACE

Changes the contents of specified data fields in an active database file.

```
USE EMPLOYEE
REPLACE ALL ANNUAL_PAY WITH ANNUAL_PAY*1.Ø5
REPLACE FIRST_NAME WITH "James K." FOR FIRST_NAME="James C."
REPLACE ALL AREA_CODE WITH "2Ø6" FOR AREA_CODE="216"
```

The ADDITIVE option applies only to memo fields. It appends data to the contents of a memo field.

```
REPLACE NOTES WITH "This is the last notation." ADDITIVE
```

REPORT FORM

Displays information from the active database file with the custom form specified in the report form (.FRM) file.

```
USE QTYSOLD                              Sends output to screen
REPORT FORM WEEKLY

REPORT FORM WEEKLY TO PRINT              Sends output to printer

REPORT FORM WEEKLY TO                    Sends output to text file
TEXTFILE.TXT
```

RESET

Used with the transaction processing commands BEGIN/END TRANSACTION and ROLLBACK, this command resets the integrity flag for a file the user does not want to ROLLBACK.

RESTORE FROM

Retrieves memory variables from a memory (.MEM) file.

```
RESTORE FROM MEMLIST.MEM
RESTORE FROM MEMLIST ADDITIVE
```

RESTORE MACROS FROM

Retrieves macros stored in the current macro library.

RESTORE WINDOW

Retrieves window definitions from a file.

RESUME

Resumes execution of a program or procedure after it has been stopped by the SUSPEND command.

RETRY

Reexecutes a command that caused an error.

RETURN

Terminates a program and either returns to the dot prompt or transfers execution to the calling program module.

ROLLBACK

Restores the contents of a database during transaction processing (see BEGIN/END TRANSACTION).

RUN

Executes an .EXE, .COM or .BAT DOS disk file from within dBASE IV.

```
RUN B:XYZ
```

XYZ.EXE, XYZ.COM, or XYZ.BAT is an executable disk file in a DOS directory.

SAVE TO

Stores all or selected memory variables to a memory (.MEM) file.

```
SAVE TO ALLVARS
SAVE TO VARLIST ALL EXCEPT NET*
SAVE TO VARLIST ALL LIKE COST????
```

SAVE MACROS

Stores macros to a disk file.

```
SAVE MACROS TO MACFILE.KEY
```

SAVE WINDOW

Stores window definitions to a file.

```
SAVE WINDOW UPDATE,SEARCH TO WINDO.WIN
```

SCAN

Searches a file and performs a command on records meeting a
specified condition.

```
SCAN NEXT 100 FOR NAME = "Jones" WHILE STATE = "MN"
REPLACE MAILED WITH "Y"
ENDSCAN
```

SEEK

Searches an indexed database file for the first data record containing
the specified key expression.

```
USE EMPLOYEE
INDEX ON AREA_CODE TO AREACODE
SEEK "206"
```

SELECT

Places a database file in a specified work area.

```
SELECT 1
USE EMPLOYEE
SELECT A
USE COSTS
```

SET

Sets control parameters for processing. The default settings (indicated by uppercase letters) are appropriate for most purposes.

SET ALTERNATE on/OFF

Creates a text file, as designated by the SET ALTERNATE TO command, to record the processing activities.

SET AUTOSAVE on/OFF

Saves each record to disk as it is entered when ON. When OFF, records are saved when the record buffer is filled.

SET BELL ON/off

Turns on/off the warning bell.

SET BELL TO *<frequency,duration>*

Specifies how the bell will sound.

SET BLOCKSIZE TO

Specifies the default block size of memo files. Up to 32 blocks of 512 bytes may be used.

SET BORDER TO

Specifies the default border for menus and windows.

SET CARRY on/OFF

Carries the contents of the previous record into an appended record.

SET CARRY TO *< field list>*

Specifies fields to carry forward when SET CARRY ON is in effect.

SET CATALOG ON/off

Adds files to an open catalog.

SET CATALOG TO

Creates, opens, and closes a catalog file.

SET CENTURY on/OFF

Shows the century in date displays.

SET CLOCK on/OFF

Turns the clock display on and off.

SET CLOCK TO *< row,column>*

Specifies the location of the clock display.

SET COLOR ON/OFF

Sets the output display to a color or monochrome monitor. The default is the mode from which dBASE IV is started.

SET COLOR TO

Sets the color screen attributes. Following is the syntax of the SET COLOR TO command:

SET COLOR TO < *standard,enhanced,border,background* >

Following is a list of available colors and their letter codes.

Color	Letter
Black	N
Blue	B
Green	G
Cyan	BG
Blank	X
Red	R
Magenta	RB
Brown	GR
White	W

An asterisk (˙) indicates blinking characters; a plus sign (+) indicates high intensity.

For example, to set standard video to yellow characters on a red background, and enhanced video to white letters on a red background, with a yellow screen border, use the following command:

SET COLOR TO GR +/R,W/R,GR

SET CONFIRM on/OFF

When OFF, the cursor automatically moves to the next entry field when the current field is filled.

SET CONSOLE ON/off

Turns the video display on/off.

SET CURRENCY TO

Specifies the symbol for the currency unit used.

SET CURRENCY LEFT/right

Specifies the location of the currency symbol.

SET DATE

Specifies the format for date expressions.

SET DATE AMERICAN	(mm/dd/yy)
SET DATE ANSI	(yy.mm.dd)
SET DATE BRITISH	(dd/mm/yy)
SET DATE ITALIAN	(dd-mm-yy)
SET DATE FRENCH	(dd/mm/yy)
SET DATE GERMAN	(dd.mm.yy)
SET DATE USA	(mm-dd-yy)
SET DATE DMY	(dd/mm/yy)
SET DATE YMD	(yy/mm/dd)

SET DEBUG on/OFF

Traces the command errors during processing. When DEBUG is ON, messages from SET ECHO ON are routed to the printer.

SET DECIMALS TO

Sets the number of decimal places for values.

SET DECIMALS TO 4

SET DEFAULT TO

Designates the default disk drive.

SET DEFAULT TO B:

SET DELETED on/OFF

Determines whether data records marked for deletion are to be ignored.

SET DELIMITERS on/OFF

Marks field widths with the delimiter defined by means of the SET DELIMITERS TO command.

SET DELIMITERS TO

Specifies the characters for marking a field.

```
SET DELIMITERS TO '[]'
SET DELIMITERS ON
```

SET DESIGN ON/off

When OFF, prevents a user from entering design mode.

SET DEVELOPMENT ON/off

Compares the date and time stamp on .PRG and .OBJ files and recompiles .PRG files if the date has changed. When OFF, the date and time are not checked.

SET DEVICE TO SCREEN/PRINTER/FILE <*filename*>

Directs output from @...SAY commands to the device specified.

SET DISPLAY TO

Specifies the monitor and number of display lines used: MONO, COLOR, EGA25, EGA43, MONO43.

SET ECHO on/OFF

Displays instructions during execution.

SET ENCRYPTION on/OFF

When ON, allows for encryption of a new database file when PROTECT is used.

SET ESCAPE ON/off

Controls the capability of aborting execution with the Esc key. When ESCAPE is ON, pressing Esc aborts execution of a program.

SET EXACT on/OFF

Determines how two alphanumeric strings are compared.

SET FIELDS on/OFF

Activates the selection of data fields named with the SET FIELDS TO command.

SET FIELDS TO

Selects a set of data fields to be used in one or more files.

```
USE EMPLOYEE
SET FIELDS TO LAST_NAME, FIRST_NAME
SET FIELDS ON
```

SET FILTER TO

Defines the filter conditions.

```
USE EMPLOYEE
SET FILTER TO AREA_CODE="216"
```

SET FIXED on/OFF

Sets all numeric output to the fixed number of decimal places defined by SET DECIMALS TO.

SET FORMAT

Selects a custom format defined in a format (.FMT) file.

SET FULLPATH on/OFF

Returns a full file and path name in functions returning file names, as in MDX( ), NDX( ), and DBF( ).

SET FUNCTION

Redefines a function key for a specific command.

```
SET FUNCTION F10 TO "QUIT;"
```

SET HEADING ON/off

Uses field names as column titles for the display of data records with the DISPLAY, LIST, SUM, and AVERAGE commands.

SET HELP ON/off

Determines whether the Help screen is displayed.

SET HISTORY ON/off

Turns the HISTORY feature on and off.

SET HISTORY TO

Specifies the number of executed commands to be saved in the HISTORY buffer.

```
SET HISTORY TO 10
```

SET HOURS TO 12/24

Selects the time display format.

SET INDEX TO

Opens the specified index files, or sets the index order using tags in multiple indexing files.

```
SET INDEX TO NAME.NDX
```

```
SET INDEX TO NAME.NDX ORDER TAG NAMES OF LIST.MDX
```

SET INSTRUCT ON/off

Determines whether instruction boxes will appear during full-screen operations.

SET INTENSITY ON/off

Displays data fields in reverse video with the EDIT and APPEND commands.

SET LOCK ON/off

Determines whether records are locked in a multi-user system.

SET MARGIN TO

Adjusts the left margin for all printed output.

```
SET MARGIN TO 1Ø
```

SET MEMOWIDTH TO

Defines the width of memo field output. The default width is 50.

```
SET MEMOWIDTH TO 3Ø
```

SET MESSAGE TO

Displays an alphanumeric string in the message window.

```
SET MESSAGE TO "Hello!"
```

SET NEAR on/OFF

When a search is unsuccessful, setting NEAR to ON positions the record pointer at the expression nearest to the one sought instead of at the end of the file.

SET ODOMETER TO

Specifies how often the record counter display is updated. May be set from 1 (the default) to 200.

SET ORDER TO

Sets up an open indexing file as the controlling indexing file, or specifies a tag in a multiple indexing file.

```
SET ORDER TO 2
SET ORDER TO TAG NAME OF LIST.MDX
```

SET PATH TO

Defines the search directory path.

```
SET PATH TO C:\DBDATE\SALES
```

SET PAUSE on/OFF

Displays the result of SQL SELECT commands one screen at a time.

SET POINT TO

Changes the character used for the decimal point.

SET PRECISION TO

Sets the range, from 10 to 20, for the number of digits used for precision in numeric operations. The default is 16.

SET PRINTER on/OFF

When ON, directs output not generated with @...SAY commands to the printer or a file.

SET PRINTER TO

Specifies the printer device name.

SET PROCEDURE TO

Opens a specified procedure file.

SET REFRESH TO

On a network, determines how often the screen is refreshed.

SET RELATION TO

Links two open database files according to a common key expression.

SET REPROCESS TO

On a network, sets the number of times a file is retried.

SET SAFETY ON/off

Displays a warning message when overwriting an existing file.

SET SCOREBOARD ON/off

Displays or hides dBASE messages on the top line.

SET SEPARATOR TO

Changes the symbol for separating numbers. The default is the comma.

SET SKIP TO

When used with SET RELATION, allows the record pointer in a related database to be updated before the active database record pointer is changed.

SET SPACE ON/off

Determines whether a space is printed between expressions when the ? and ?? commands are used.

SET SQL on/OFF

Accesses SQL mode.

SET STATUS ON/off

Displays or hides the status bar at the bottom of the screen.

SET STEP on/OFF

Causes execution to pause after each command.

SET TALK ON/off

Displays interactive messages during processing.

SET TITLE ON/off

Displays the catalog file title prompt.

SET TRAP on/OFF

Activates debugger when an error occurs or Esc is pressed.

SET TYPEAHEAD TO

Specifies the size of the typeahead buffer. Possible values are 0 to 32,000 characters; the default is 20 characters.

```
SET TYPEAHEAD TO 30
```

SET UNIQUE on/OFF

When on, prepares an ordered list with the INDEX command, allowing only the first record with identical keys to be displayed.

SET VIEW TO

Selects the view file.

```
SET VIEW TO EMPLOY
```

SHOW MENU

Displays a bar menu, but does not make it active.

```
SHOW MENU SEARCH PAD NAMES
```

SHOW POPUP

Displays a pop-up menu, but does not make it active.

SKIP

Moves the record pointer forward or backward through the records in the database file.

```
USE EMPLOYEE
GOTO 3
DISPLAY
SKIP 3
DISPLAY
SKIP -1
DISPLAY
```

SORT

Rearranges data records on one or more key fields in ascending or descending order. The default setting is ascending order.

```
USE EMPLOYEE
SORT ON AREA_CODE TO AREACODE
SORT ON ANNUAL_PAY/D TO RANKED
SORT ON AREA_CODE, LAST_NAME /C TO PHONLIST
   FOR AREA_CODE="206"
```

STORE

Assigns a data element to a memory variable.

```
STORE 1 TO COUNTER
STORE "James" TO FIRSTNAME
```

SUM

Totals the value of a numeric expression and stores the total in a memory variable.

```
USE EMPLOYEE
SUM ANNUAL_PAY TO TOTALPAY
SUM ANNUAL_PAY*0.1 TO DEDUCTIONS
```

SUSPEND

Suspends the execution of a program or procedure.

TEXT

Displays a block of text on the screen or printer; used in a program.

```
***** Program: BULLETIN.PRG *****
SET PRINT ON
TEXT
This is a sample message to be displayed on the printer
when this program is executed.
ENDTEXT
```

TOTAL

Totals the numeric values of the active database file on a key field and stores the results to another file.

```
USE STOCKS
TOTAL ON MODEL_NO TO BYMODEL
TOTAL ON STOCK_NO TO BYSTOCNO FOR ON_HAND>="2"
```

TYPE

Displays the contents of a disk file to the screen or printer. The NUMBER option prints line numbers.

```
TYPE MAINPROG.PRG NUMBER
TYPE EMPLOYEE.FMT TO PRINT
```

UNLOCK

Makes records available to other users.

UPDATE

Uses records in one database file to update records in another file.

```
SELECT A
USE RECEIVED
SELECT B
USE STOCKS
UPDATE ON STOCK_NO FROM RECEIVED REPLACE ON_HAND
    WITH ON_HAND +A->ON_HAND
```

USE

Opens an existing database file. The indexing file or indexing order can be specified, and the NOUPDATE option makes the file read-only.

```
USE EMPLOYEE
USE EMPLOYEE ORDER TAG NAME NOUPDATE
```

WAIT

Causes execution to pause until a key is pressed.

```
WAIT
WAIT TO CHOICE
WAIT "Enter your answer (Y/N)? " TO ANSWER
```

ZAP

Removes all data records from the database file without deleting the data structure.

```
USE EMPLOYEE
ZAP
```

dBASE IV Functions

Functions normally return a value, either a logical (.T. or .F.), a numeric, or a character value. Most end in parentheses. Some may require that one or more arguments (values) be included within the parentheses, while some require no argument or have a default argument. For example, to print the integer 45.678, the following function can be used:

```
. ? INT(45.678)
     45
```

However, the end-of-file function returns a true or false value, and unless an alias is specified within the parentheses, the current database file in use is assumed.

```
. TEST = EOF( )
.? TEST
   .F.
```

&

Macro substitution.

$

String is within another string.

ABS( )

Absolute value.

ACCESS( )

Access level of current user.

ACOS( )

Angle in radians of a cosine.

ALIAS( )

Alias name of specified work area.

ASC( )

ASCII code of first character of a string.

ASIN( )

Arcsine, angle in radians for a sine.

AT( )

Starting position of a string within another string.

ATAN( )

Arctangent, angle in radians for a tangent.

ATN2( )

Arctangent, when the cosine and sine of a point are specified.

BAR( )

Most recently selected bar number from a pop-up menu.

BOF( )

Beginning of file.

CALL( )

Binary program module.

CDOW( )

Day of week from a date.

CEILING( )

Smallest integer greater than or equal to value.

CHANGE( )

Record change.

CHR( )

Character value of a number.

CMONTH( )

Month name from date.

COL( )

Cursor column position.

COMPLETED( )

Transaction completion.

COS( )

Cosine for angle in radians.

CTOD( )

Converts string to date.

DATE( )

System date.

DAY( )

Number of day of month.

DBF( )

Database in use.

DELETED( )

Record marked for deletion.

DIFFERENCE( )

Difference between two strings.

DISKSPACE( )

Bytes available on default drive.

DMY( )

Converts to dd/mm/yy format from date expression.

DOW( )

Number of day of week from date.

DTOC( )

Converts date to string.

DTOR( )

Converts degrees to radians.

DTOS( )

Converts date to string in format CCYYMMDD.

EOF( )

End of file.

ERROR( )

Error message number.

EXP( )

Exponent.

FIELD( )

Field name from specified field number.

FILE( )

File exists.

FIXED( )

Converts floating point numbers to numeric decimals.

FKLABEL( )

Function key label.

FKMAX( )

Number of function keys.

FLOAT( )

Converts numeric values to floating point.

FLOCK( )

File locking.

FLOOR( )

Largest integer less than or equal to value.

FOUND( )

LOCATE, SEEK, or CONTINUE successful.

FV( )

Future value.

GETENV( )

DOS environment setting.

IIF( )

Immediate IF. If condition is true, uses first value. Otherwise, uses second value.

INKEY( )

Key code of last key pressed.

INT( )

Integer.

ISALPHA( )

Character is alphabetic.

ISCOLOR( )

System will display color.

ISLOWER( )

Character lowercase.

ISMARKED( )

Database header marked for change.

ISUPPER( )

Character uppercase.

KEY( )

Key expression for index.

LASTKEY( )

ASCII value of last key pressed.

LEFT( )

Leftmost characters of a string.

LEN( )

Length of a string.

LIKE( )

Compares similarity of strings.

LINENO( )

Line number of command.

LKSYS( )

Log in name of user, date, and time of record/file lock.

LOCK( )

Lock multiple records.

LOG( )

Natural logarithm.

LOG10( )

Common log to base 10.

LOOKUP( )

Search for record and return value from a field.

LOWER( )

Convert to lowercase.

LTRIM( )

Remove leading blanks.

LUPDATE( )

Date of last update.

MAX( )

Larger of two expressions.

MDX( )

Multiple index file name.

MDY( )

Converts date to Month Day, Year format (such as April 16, 1989).

MEMLINES( )

Number of lines in a memo field.

MEMORY( )

Available RAM in kilobytes.

MENU( )

Active menu name.

MESSAGE( )

Error message.

MIN( )

Smaller of two values.

MLINE( )

Extracts text line from memo.

MOD( )

Remainder from division of two numbers.

MONTH( )

Month number from date.

NDX( )

Index file name.

NETWORK( )

System running on network.

ORDER( )

Index order file or tag.

OS( )

Operating system name.

PAD( )

Name of last pad selected.

PAYMENT( )

Payment for amortized loan.

PCOL( )

Printer column position.

PI( )

Pi, 3.14159.

POPUP( )

Name of active pop-up menu.

PRINTSTATUS( )

Printer ready (.T. if ready; .F. if not).

PROGRAM( )

Program or procedure executing when error occurred.

PROMPT( )

Prompt of last pop-up or menu option selected.

PROW( )

Printer row position.

PV( )

Present value.

RAND( )

Random number.

READKEY( )

Number for key pressed to exit a full-screen command.

RECCOUNT( )

Number of records in database.

RECNO( )

Current record number.

RECSIZE( )

Record size.

REPLICATE( )

Repeats character.

RIGHT( )

Rightmost characters of string.

RLOCK( )

Locks multiple records.

ROLLBACK( )

Rollback successful.

ROUND( )

Round number.

ROW( )

Cursor row position.

RTOD( )

Converts radians to degrees.

RTRIM( )

Removes trailing blanks.

SEEK( )

Finds expression in indexed database.

SELECT( )

Highest unused work area.

SET( )

Status of SET commands.

SIGN( )

Positive or negative sign of number.

SIN( )

Sine of an angle.

SOUNDEX( )

Phonetic match.

SPACE( )

String of blanks.

SQRT( )

Square root.

STR( )

Converts number to string.

STUFF( )

Replaces a portion of a string with another string.

SUBSTR( )

Extracts characters from a string.

TAG( )

Indexes tag name.

TAN( )

Tangent of an angle.

TIME( )

System time.

TRANSFORM( )

PICTURE formatting of data.

TYPE( )

Data type.

UPPER( )

Converts to uppercase.

USER( )

Log in name of user.

VAL( )

Converts character numbers to numeric values.

VARREAD( )

Name of field or variable being edited.

VERSION( )

dBASE IV version number.

YEAR( )

Numeric value of year from date.

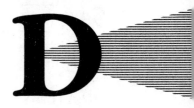

SQL Command Summary

ALTER TABLE

Adds columns to an existing table.

```
ALTER TABLE Employee
ADD (Dept_no CHAR(3), Division CHAR(3));
```

CLOSE

Closes an open cursor previously defined with DECLARE CURSOR.

```
CLOSE Employ;
```

CREATE DATABASE

Creates a new directory and database to contain tables and related files.

```
CREATE DATABASE Employ;
```

CREATE INDEX

Creates an index for a table. The DESC option specifies a descending table. The UNIQUE option will not index if column values are not unique.

```
CREATE UNIQUE INDEX Lname
ON Employee
Last_name DESC;
```

CREATE SYNONYM

Defines an alternate name for a table or view.

```
CREATE SYNONYM Emp FOR Employee;
```

CREATE TABLE

Defines a new table in the current database.

```
CREATE TABLE Employee
(First _name CHAR(12), Last _name CHAR(15),
Ss _no INTEGER);
```

CREATE VIEW

Creates a virtual table, or view, from columns in one or more existing tables. WITH CHECK OPTION permits updating of values that meet conditions set with WHERE in SELECT. A SELECT statement follows the AS clause.

```
CREATE VIEW Norecord
AS SELECT *
FROM Employee
WHERE Ss _no = Ø
WITH CHECK OPTION;
```

DBCHECK

Checks the structure of .DBF and .MDX files against the SQL catalog tables.

```
DBCHECK Employee;
```

DBDEFINE

Creates a catalog table entry for a dBASE database file.

```
DBDEFINE Employee;
```

DECLARE CURSOR

Defines a cursor with a SELECT statement to process rows from a result table.

```
DECLARE Snum CURSOR FOR
SELECT Last_name, Ss_no
FROM Employee
WHERE Last_name > "Jones";
```

DELETE

Removes specified rows from a table.

```
DELETE FROM Employee
WHERE SS_no < 1;
```

DROP DATABASE

Deletes a database and all .DBF and .MDX files in the associated directory.

```
DROP DATABASE Employ;
```

DROP INDEX

Deletes an index.

```
DROP INDEX Lname;
```

DROP SYNONYM

Deletes a synonym previously defined with CREATE SYNONYM.

```
DROP SYNONYM Emp;
```

DROP TABLE

Deletes a table.

```
DROP TABLE Employee;
```

DROP VIEW

Deletes a view definition.

```
DROP VIEW Norecord;
```

FETCH

Moves a cursor (previously defined with DECLARE CURSOR) to the next row of a result table; assigns values to dBASE memory variables.

```
FETCH Snum INTO Name1, Socno;
```

GRANT

Allows access to tables and views. User IDs must have been assigned with the PROTECT command.

```
GRANT ALL
ON Employee
TO David;
```

The following privileges may be specified: ALTER, DELETE, INDEX, INSERT, SELECT, and UPDATE (*<columns>*).

```
GRANT INSERT, SELECT
ON Employee
TO David;
```

INSERT

Inserts rows into a table or view. Either a VALUES clause or a SELECT statement can be included.

```
INSERT INTO Employee
VALUES ("Smith","Bert",467899989);
```

```
INSERT INTO Employee
SELECT *
FROM Persons
WHERE Last_name = "Smith";
```

LOAD DATA

Imports data from an external, non-SQL file and adds it to an existing table. File types include SDF, DIF, WKS, SYLK, FW2 (FrameWorkII), RPD (RapidFile), dBASEII, and DELIMITED.

```
LOAD DATA FROM C:\Dbase\Emprec
INTO TABLE Employee
TYPE SDF;
```

OPEN

Opens a cursor and executes the SELECT statement specified in a DECLARE CURSOR command.

```
OPEN Snum;
```

REVOKE

Reverse of the GRANT command; revokes access privileges.

```
REVOKE INSERT,SELECT
ON Employee
FROM David;
```

ROLLBACK

Restores a table to its contents before commands executed within a BEGIN/END TRANSACTION block (see dBASE IV commands in Appendix C).

```
ROLLBACK;
```

RUNSTATS

Updates database statistics in the SQL system catalog tables.

```
RUNSTATS Employee;
```

SELECT

Selects rows and columns from tables to produce a result table for display. The FROM statement identifies the tables or views to use. Several optional clauses are available:

INTO	Transfers values from a row into a list of dBASE memory variables
WHERE	Specifies search conditions
GROUP BY	Groups rows having columns with the same value
HAVING	Specifies search conditions to restrict groups
UNION	Combines result tables
ORDER BY	Specifies the order in which rows will appear
DESC	Specifies a descending order
FOR UPDATE OF	Indicates columns that may be updated
SAVE TO TEMP	Saves the result table to a temporary table

The basic syntax for the preceding clauses is as follows:

```
SELECT < columns or * for all >
INTO < variables>
FROM < tables or views>
WHERE < condition>
GROUP BY < columns>
HAVING < condition>
UNION < subselect>
ORDER BY < column> DESC
SAVE TO TEMP < table> (< columns>);
```

Following are examples of the SELECT command:

```
SELECT *
FROM Employee;

SELECT First_name, Last_name
FROM Employee
WHERE Last_name = "Jones"
ORDER BY First_name;
```

SHOW DATABASE

Lists available SQL databases.

```
SHOW DATABASE;
```

START DATABASE

Activates a database, making all tables and views in that database available for use with SQL commands.

```
START DATABASE Employ;
```

STOP DATABASE

Closes the current database.

```
STOP DATABASE;
```

UNLOAD DATA

Exports data from an SQL table to an external non-SQL file. See LOAD DATA for file types.

```
UNLOAD DATA TO C:\Dbase\Emprec
FROM TABLE Employee
TYPE SDF;
```

UPDATE

Alters the values in columns of specified rows of a table or view.

```
UPDATE Employee
SET First _name = "David"
SET Last _name = "Jones"
WHERE Ss _no = 456876959;
```

The WHERE CURRENT OF clause specifies a cursor that has been defined with DECLARE CURSOR.

```
UPDATE Employee
SET First _name = "David"
SET Last _name = "Jones"
WHERE CURRENT OF Snum;
```

Index

551

More Computer Knowledge from Que

LOTUS SOFTWARE TITLES

1-2-3 QueCards.............................. 21.95
1-2-3 QuickStart............................. 21.95
1-2-3 Quick Reference....................... 6.95
1-2-3 for Business, 2nd Edition 22.95
1-2-3 Business Formula Handbook.......... 19.95
1-2-3 Command Language 21.95
1-2-3 Macro Library, 2nd Edition........... 21.95
1-2-3 Tips, Tricks, and Traps, 2nd Edition 21.95
Using 1-2-3, Special Edition 24.95
Using 1-2-3 Workbook and Disk,
  2nd Edition 29.95
Using Lotus HAL............................ 19.95
Using Symphony, 2nd Edition 26.95

DATABASE TITLES

dBASE III Plus Handbook, 2nd Edition 22.95
dBASE IV Handbook, 3rd Edition 23.95
dBASE IV Tips, Tricks, and Traps, 2nd Edition 21.95
dBASE IV QueCards 21.95
dBASE IV Quick Reference.................. 6.95
dBASE IV QuickStart........................ 21.95
dBXL and Quicksilver Programming:
  Beyond dBASE 24.95
R:BASE Solutions: Applications
  and Resources............................ 19.95
R:BASE System V Techniques
  and Applications 21.95
R:BASE User's Guide, 3rd Edition........... 19.95
Using Clipper............................... 24.95
Using Reflex................................ 19.95
Using Paradox, 2nd Edition................. 22.95
Using Q & A, 2nd Edition................... 21.95

MACINTOSH AND APPLE II TITLES

HyperCard QuickStart: A Graphics Approach 21.95
Using AppleWorks, 2nd Edition 21.95
Using dBASE Mac 19.95
Using Dollars and Sense 19.95
Using Excel................................. 21.95
Using HyperCard: From Home to HyperTalk.. 24.95
Using Microsoft Word: Macintosh Version 21.95
Using Microsoft Works 19.95
Using WordPerfect: Macintosh Version 19.95

APPLICATIONS SOFTWARE TITLES

CAD and Desktop Publishing Guide 24.95
Smart Tips, Tricks, and Traps............... 23.95
Using AutoCAD............................. 29.95
Using DacEasy 21.95
Using Dollars and Sense: IBM Version,
  2nd Edition 19.95
Using Enable/OA 23.95
Using Excel: IBM Version.................... 24.05
Using Managing Your Money 19.95
Using Quattro 21.95
Using Smart 22.95
Using SuperCalc4.......................... 21.95

WORD-PROCESSING AND DESKTOP PUBLISHING TITLES

Microsoft Word Techniques and Applications 19.95
Microsoft Word Tips, Tricks, and Traps 19.95
Using DisplayWrite 4 .... 19.95
Using Microsoft Word, 2nd Edition.......... 21.95
Using MultiMate Advantage, 2nd Edition 19.95
Using PageMaker on the IBM............... 24.95
Using PFS: First Publisher.................. 22.95
Using Sprint 21.95
Using Ventura Publisher.................... 24.95
Using WordPerfect, 3rd Edition 21.95
Using WordPerfect 5 .... 24.95
Using WordPerfect Workbook and Disk 29.95
Using WordStar, 2nd Edition................ 21.95
WordPerfect Advanced Techniques 19.95
WordPerfect Macro Library 21.95
WordPerfect QueCards...................... 21.95
WordPerfect Quick Reference............... 6.95
WordPerfect QuickStart 21.95
WordPerfect Tips, Tricks, and Traps,
  2nd Edition 21.95
WordPerfect 5 Workbook and Disk.......... 29.95

HARDWARE AND SYSTEMS TITLES

DOS Programmer's Reference 24.95
DOS QueCards 21.95
DOS Tips, Tricks, and Traps................ 22.95
DOS Workbook and Disk.................... 29.95
IBM PS/2 Handbook 21.95
Managing Your Hard Disk, 2nd Edition....... 22.95
MS-DOS Quick Reference.................. 0.95
MS-DOS QuickStart........................ 21.95
MS-DOS User's Guide, 3rd Edition.......... 22.95
Networking IBM PCs, 2nd Edition........... 19.95
Programming with Windows................. 22.95
Understanding UNIX: A Conceptual Guide,
  2nd Edition............................... 21.95
Upgrading and Repairing PCs 24.95
Using Microsoft Windows 19.95
Using OS/2 .... 22.95
Using PC DOS, 2nd Edition 22.95

PROGRAMMING AND TECHNICAL TITLES

Advanced C: Techniques and Applications ... 21.95
Assembly Language Quick Reference 6.95
C Programmer's Library 21.95
C Programming Guide, 3rd Edition.......... 24.95
C Quick Reference......................... 6.95
C Standard Library......................... 21.95
Debugging C 19.95
DOS and BIOS Functions Quick Reference... 6.95
QuickBASIC Quick Reference 6.95
Turbo Pascal for BASIC Programmers 18.95
Turbo Pascal Program Library.............. 19.95
Turbo Pascal Quick Reference............. 6.95
Turbo Pascal Tips, Tricks, and Traps........ 19.95
Using Assembly Language 24.95
Using QuickBASIC 4....................... 19.95
Using Turbo Pascal 21.95
Using Turbo Prolog 19.95

Que Order Line: **1-800-428-5331**

SELECT QUE BOOKS TO INCREASE YOUR PERSONAL COMPUTER PRODUCTIVITY

dBASE IV Handbook, 3rd Edition

by George T. Chou, Ph.D.

Learn dBASE IV quickly with Que's new *dBASE IV Handbook*, 3rd Edition! dBASE expert George Chou leads you step-by-step from basic database concepts to advanced dBASE features, using a series of Quick Start tutorials. Experienced dBASE users will appreciate the extensive information on the new features of dBASE IV, including the new user interface, the query-by-example mode, and the SQL module. Complete with comprehensive command and function reference sections, *dBASE IV Handbook*, 3rd Edition, is an exhaustive guide to dBASE IV!

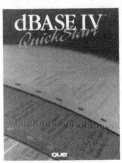

dBASE IV QuickStart

Developed by Que Corporation

The fast way to dBASE IV proficiency! More than 100 two-page illustrations show how to create common dBASE applications, including address lists and mailing labels. You are led step-by-step through dBASE IV basics, including many essential procedures and techniques. Simplify the complexity of dBASE IV with this visually oriented book—*dBASE IV QuickStart!*

dBASE IV QueCards

Developed by Que Corporation

dBASE IV QueCards—the easy-to-use reference to dBASE IV! QueCards are 5″ × 8″ cards, housed in a sturdy 3-ring binder. Convenient tabs help organize the cards into sections on functions, commands, and dBASE applications, with each card explaining proper command usage and offering helpful hints that improve your dBASE efficiency. The cards can be used with the built-in easel or removed and placed next to your computer keyboard. When you have difficulty remembering important commands or steps for developing and using dBASE applications, use *dBASE IV QueCards*—the fast and comprehensive dBASE IV reference!

dBASE IV Quick Reference

Developed by Que Corporation

Put dBASE IV commands and functions at your fingertips with Que's *dBASE IV Quick Reference*. Whether you use a laptop or a desktop computer, this portable reference provides immediate access to information often buried in traditional text. This compact guide is an instant reference to often-used dBASE IV commands and functions!

ORDER FROM QUE TODAY

Item	Title	Price	Quantity	Extension
852	dBASE IV Handbook, 3rd Edition	$23.95		
873	dBASE IV QuickStart	21.95		
75	dBASE IV QueCards	21.95		
867	dBASE IV Quick Reference	6.95		

Book Subtotal _____

Shipping & Handling ($2.50 per item) _____

Indiana Residents Add 5% Sales Tax _____

GRAND TOTAL _____

Method of Payment

☐ Check   ☐ VISA   ☐ MasterCard   ☐ American Express

Card Number _____ Exp. Date _____

Cardholder's Name _____

Ship to _____

Address _____

City _____ State _____ ZIP _____

If you can't wait, call **1-800-428-5331** and order TODAY.

All prices subject to change without notice.

FOLD HERE

_____

_____

_____

_____

Que Corporation
P.O. Box 90
Carmel, IN 46032

REGISTRATION CARD

Register your copy of *dBASE IV Tips, Tricks, and Traps*, 2nd Edition, and receive information about Que's newest products. Complete this registration card and return it to Que Corporation, P.O. Box 90, Carmel, IN 46032.

Name _____ Phone _____

Company _____ Title _____

Address _____

City _____ State _____ ZIP _____

Please check the appropriate answers:

Where did you buy *dBASE IV Tips, Tricks, and Traps*, 2nd Edition?
- ☐ Bookstore (name: _____)
- ☐ Computer store (name: _____)
- ☐ Catalog (name: _____)
- ☐ Direct from Que _____
- ☐ Other: _____

How many computer books do you buy a year?
- ☐ 1 or less
- ☐ 6–10
- ☐ 2–5
- ☐ More than 10

How many Que books do you own?
- ☐ 1
- ☐ 6–10
- ☐ 2–5
- ☐ More than 10

How long have you been using dBASE software?
- ☐ Less than 6 months
- ☐ 6 months to 1 year
- ☐ 1–3 years
- ☐ More than 3 years

What influenced your purchase of *dBASE IV Tips, Tricks, and Traps*, 2nd Edition?
- ☐ Personal recommendation
- ☐ Advertisement   ☐ Que catalog
- ☐ In-store display   ☐ Que mailing
- ☐ Price   ☐ Que's reputation
- ☐ Other: _____

How would you rate the overall content of *dBASE IV Tips, Tricks, and Traps*, 2nd Edition?
- ☐ Very good   ☐ Satisfactory
- ☐ Good   ☐ Poor

How would you rate the chapter on *configuring dBASE IV*?
- ☐ Very good   ☐ Satisfactory
- ☐ Good   ☐ Poor

How would you rate the chapter on *creating reports and mailing lists*?
- ☐ Very good   ☐ Satisfactory
- ☐ Good   ☐ Poor

What do you like best about *dBASE IV Tips, Tricks, and Traps*, 2nd Edition?

What do you like least about *dBASE IV Tips, Tricks, and Traps*, 2nd Edition?

How do you use *dBASE IV Tips, Tricks, and Traps*, 2nd Edition?

What other Que products do you own?

For what other programs would a Que book be helpful?

Please feel free to list any other comments you may have about *dBASE IV Tips, Tricks, and Traps*, 2nd Edition.

_____

_____

_____

_____

_____

_____

FOLD HERE

_____

_____

_____

_____

Que Corporation
P.O. Box 90
Carmel, IN 46032